Modelling High-Level Cognitive Processes

Modelling High-Level Cognitive Processes

Richard P. Cooper

With contributions from
Peter Yule, John Fox, and David W. Glasspool

Psychology Press
Taylor & Francis Group
NEW YORK AND HOVE

Camera ready copy for this book was provided by the author.

First published by
Lawrence Erlbaum Associates, Inc., Publishers
10 Industrial Avenue
Mahwah, NJ 07430

This edition published 2013 by Psychology Press

Psychology Press
Taylor & Francis Group
711 Third Avenue
New York, NY 10017

Psychology Press
Taylor & Francis Group
27 Church Road, Hove
East Sussex BN3 2FA

Psychology Press is an imprint of the Taylor & Francis Group, an informa business

First issued in paperback 2013

Cover design by Kathryn Houghtaling Lacey

Library of Congress Cataloging-in-Publication Data

Cooper, Richard P.
Modelling high-level cognitive processes / Richard P. Cooper ; with contributions from Peter Yule, John Fox, and David W. Glasspool.
p. cm.
Includes bibliographical references and index.
ISBN 0-8058-3883-X (cloth : alk. paper)
1. Cognition—Computer simulation. 2. Cognition—Mathematical models. I. Title.
QP395 .C66 2002
612.8'2'0113—dc21 2002018862
CIP

ISBN13: 978-0-415-65023-6 (paperback)

Contents

Preface

What this Book is About

This book is a practical guide to building computational models of high-level cognitive processes and systems. High-level processes are those central cognitive processes involved in thinking, reasoning, planning, and so on. These processes appear to share representational and processing requirements, and it is for this reason that they are considered together in this text.

Cognitive modelling developed from work on Artificial Intelligence in the 1960s, when researchers became interested in computational aspects of natural, as opposed to artificial, intelligence. Work in the late 1960s and 1970s focussed on topics such as game playing, mathematical reasoning, language understanding, and problem solving. This work treated natural intelligence as *symbol manipulation*, and computational models from this era were concerned with how symbol manipulation could give rise to intelligent behaviour.

A relatively small band of specialists continued developing models until the 1980s when new techniques of *connectionist* modelling combined with greater access to computers inspired something of a boom. Work using the older-style symbolic approach continued, and significant advances were made (e.g., Newell, 1990; Anderson & Lebiere, 1998), but symbolic modelling benefitted little from the connectionist boom.

Connectionist techniques have now been fashionable for nearly twenty years. They have led to substantial advances in our understanding of many lower-level cognitive processes (such as object and word recognition), but their contribution to progress on the sorts of questions concerning natural intelligence raised by early modellers has been less spectacular. This book returns to those questions, and in particular to issues raised when attempting to model high-level cognitive processes. The approach is by example: the purpose and methods of modelling higher cognitive processes are demonstrated through a series of example models in a range of domains. The aim is not to present a novel theory of cognition, but to present a set of tools and techniques for developing such theories.

As noted above, many higher cognitive processes appear to share representational and processing requirements. These requirements involve the representation and use of knowledge or information. They are strongly suggestive of a symbolic approach to modelling. The approach adopted throughout this text is therefore primarily symbolic in orientation. It is important to understand, however, that this approach does not necessarily entail a strong view on the mental manipulation of symbols. Rather, symbolic models may be interpreted in more abstract terms as indicating information states through which the cognitive system passes as information is processed and behaviour is generated.

One might reasonably ask why a symbolic approach might lead to progress on understanding higher cognitive processes now when it hasn't led to such progress over the last twenty years. The answer is that it *has* led to progress over the last twenty years, and it continues to do so. In addition, new insights and better understanding are likely, given more powerful computers, powerful new tools and techniques such as those presented here, and greater awareness of the methodological issues involved in modelling higher cognitive processes.

The COGENT Cognitive Modelling Environment

In order to gain a working knowledge of cognitive modelling it is essential to go through the process of building computational models of cognitive processes. This can't be done without a programming language or environment in which to build the models. Several general purpose programming languages, including Prolog, Lisp, and C, have been used to successfully build cognitive models, and any of these languages could have been chosen for the "base" language for this book. However, none of these languages is designed specifically for cognitive modelling, and considerable programming expertise is required to use any of them. Hence, this book adopts COGENT, a modelling environment designed specifically to support cognitive modelling.

All models discussed in this book are developed within the COGENT environment. COGENT provides a graphical interface in which models may be sketched as "box and arrow" diagrams. Such diagrams are common in psychological theorising, and COGENT builds on concepts such as functional modularity associated with them. Boxes within box and arrow diagrams may be fleshed-out with rules or configured through properties to obtain appropriate behaviours. COGENT also provides support for specifying experimental tasks consisting of blocks of trials analogous to those carried out within standard experimental psychology. Models may then be evaluated by running them on such tasks and comparing their behaviour with that of human participants.

Getting COGENT

In order to get the most out of this book, readers should download and install the COGENT software. They may then work through the examples and projects provided. COGENT is available for most Windows™ and UNIX systems. It may be downloaded from the COGENT website at:

`http : //cogent.psyc.bbk.ac.uk`

Instructions for downloading are provided on the website.

The website also includes complete user documentation, full licencing information, downloadable versions of all models described in this book, and a model archive. Users are encouraged to explore the archive and submit their own COGENT models to be added to the archive. The website will also be updated with further documentation and teaching material as it becomes available.

How To Use This Book

COGENT is both a useful teaching tool and a productive research tool, and this book is designed to be of use to both students of cognitive modelling and active researchers. For students, the book provides essential background material plus an extensive set of example models, exercises, and project material. Researchers of both symbolic and connectionist persuasions will find the book of interest for its approach to cognitive modelling, which emphasises methodological issues. They will also find that the COGENT environment itself has much to offer.

The book is divided into three parts (see Figure 0). Part 1 considers foundational and background issues. Part 2 provides a series of case studies spanning a range of cognitive domains. Part 3 reflects upon issues raised by the case studies. Teachers of cognitive modelling may use material from Part 1 to structure lectures and practical sessions, with chapters in Part 2 forming the basis of in-depth student projects.

The principal inter-relations between chapters are shown in Figure 0. Chapter 1 is foundational. It introduces the aims of cognitive modelling and presents various general approaches. Strengths and limitations of cognitive modelling are also discussed. The chapter concludes with a brief presentation of the rationale for COGENT. This is followed up in Chapter 2, which provides a tutorial-style introduction to the environment. The tutorial introduces many features of COGENT through the development of a model of human memory.

Chapters 3 to 8 consider different domains of cognitive processing. Each of these chapters begins with some background material on relevant psychological findings. This is followed by a detailed description of several models that capture aspects of those findings. The chapters then conclude with discussion of some of the modelling issues raised. Project work and pointers to further reading are also given in each of these chapters.

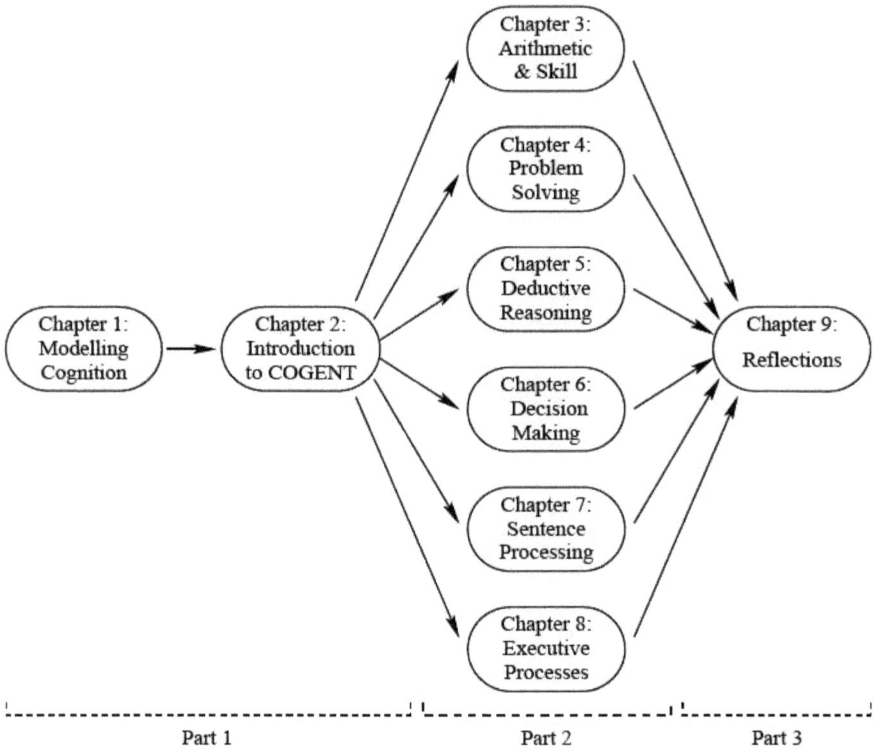

Figure 0: The basic structure of this text

Chapters 3 to 8 are all reasonably self-contained, so after working through Chapters 1 and 2 the interested reader should be able to jump to any of these chapters. In some cases additional knowledge of COGENT beyond that introduced in Chapter 2 may be required. For this readers are directed to the COGENT user-manual available from the website.

The closing chapter, Chapter 9, reviews the issues raised in other chapters and suggests some directions for future research.

Acknowledgements

This book has been a collaborative effort and I am pleased to acknowledge the contributions of Peter Yule, John Fox, and David Glasspool, who co-authored various chapters. They also provided useful comments on structure, content, and presentation throughout the text. In this respect John's comments were particularly valuable.

The book brings together three strands of research: work on the COGENT modelling environment, work on modelling with COGENT, and work on modelling methodology. The intellectual history of each is heavily influenced by John Fox and Tim Shallice, with whom I had the good fortune to work as a postdoctoral research fellow at University College London from 1990 to 1995. I would like to thank them both for their continuing support, guidance and friendship.

Initial work on COGENT was carried out with support from the UK's Joint Council Initiative in Cognitive Science and Human-Computer Interaction (grant G9212530 "A Specification Language for Cognitive Modelling" awarded to John Fox and Tim Shallice). The project aimed to develop an existing specification language, Sceptic (Hajnal, Fox, & Krause, 1989; Cooper & Farringdon, 1993), for cognitive modelling. The result was a prototype of the COGENT system. Further development work was funded by the UK's Engineering and Physical Sciences Research Council (grant GR/L03637 "A Development Environment for Cognitive Science and Cognitive Neuroscience"). This allowed the prototype system to be developed into a viable cognitive modelling environment. I am grateful to the UK Research Councils for this financial support, without which COGENT would not have been possible.

I implemented the COGENT prototype in 1994/95, using the UNIX operating system and Sun's XView toolkit. The first Windows™ version of COGENT was produced by David Sutton in 1997/98, and the current system, which uses the GTK+ toolkit to unify the Windows™ and UNIX versions, retains several features introduced in that version. The experiment scripting functionality, which allows extended computational experiments to be performed under COGENT, was developed by Peter Yule.

Early work on COGENT was performed in close collaboration with John Fox and John Morton. Additional input was provided by Jonathan Farringdon, David Glasspool, and Tim Shallice. I am grateful for the early encouragement provided by these colleagues. COGENT has developed steadily since 1995, with input from a variety of early users, programmers, and other interested parties. With regard to early users, I wish to thank Sofka Barreau, Philip Beaman, Fergus Bolger, Mark Ennis, Grant Miller, Mike Ramscar, and Richard Young for their remarkable patience during COGENT's early days, and for their constructive suggestions which helped to transform the system into a useful, and usable, tool. I am also grateful to Richard Young for his collaborative efforts in developing the model of multi-column subtraction presented in Chapter 3.

A number of reviewers commented on drafts of one or more chapters. The constructive criticism provided by Aiden Feeney, Tom Ormerod, Rolf Plötzner, Frank Ritter, Tim Shallice, Lon Shapiro, Gerhard Strube, Peter Wiemer-Hastings, and particularly Richard Young was most helpful in making this a better text. I am also grateful to the people at LEA, and particularly Emily Wilkinson, for showing such enthusiasm and support for the book project, and for guiding it from start to finish.

Finally, I would like to thank Rikke for putting up with me during what she predicted would be a neverending project. I am pleased that time proved her pessimism to be unfounded. Thanks also to my parents for accepting my decision to pursue my academic career half a world away from home, and especially to my mother, who did not live to see the end of this project. This book is dedicated to her.

Richard P. Cooper
London

Part I

Background

Chapter 1

Modelling Cognition

Richard P. Cooper and John Fox

Overview: This chapter introduces the basic concepts of cognitive modelling. The historical context is briefly reviewed and some ways that cognitive modelling may be used in theory development are described. Pros and cons of the enterprise are then discussed. This is followed by a detailed description of several major approaches to modelling (symbolic, connectionist, hybrid, and architectural). The chapter concludes with some remarks on our own view of the field, and on the role of COGENT, the modelling environment used throughout the rest of this book.

1.1 What is Cognitive Modelling?

This book is about understanding human cognition — the mental processes involved in thought, reasoning, language, and so on. The basic premise on which it is founded is that the development of computer models of cognitive processes can further our understanding of those processes by allowing us to evaluate computational mechanisms that might underlie behaviour.

A model in any field, whether it be engineering, architecture, molecular biology, or cognitive science, is a representation of something that may be used in place of the real thing. Traditionally the representation might be made out of wax, clay, metal, or wood. Thus an architect may produce a wooden model of a building in order to demonstrate or evaluate the building's appearance. Similarly an engineer may produce models of bridges to evaluate the relative strengths of competing designs.

A computer model has the same function as a traditional model, but rather than being made out of clay or wood, it consists of a representation in some precisely-specified computer language. Like the traditional wood or clay model, the representation abstracts away unimportant features or characteristics of the thing being modelled, but it retains all that is essential. Thus, a computer model of an aeroplane wing for use in testing aerodynamics might abstract the colour and weight of the wing, but would retain the important features of size, shape, and curvature, for these features are critical to the aerodynamic behaviour of the wing.

A computer model in cognitive science is much the same kind of thing — it is an abstract representation that may be used in place of the real thing. The difference in cognitive science is that the thing being modelled is a cognitive process. So, cognitive modelling is the development of computer models of cognitive processes, and the use of such models to simulate or predict human behaviour.

1.2 A Sample Model

It is perhaps useful to begin by considering, for illustration purposes, what a cognitive model might look like. Consider the task confronting a doctor when attempting to make a diagnosis. This is a typical example of the kind of high-level cognitive process which we are concerned with in this text. The doctor's task is roughly as follows: a patient arrives at the doctor's office complaining of some symptom (the presenting symptom). The doctor then reviews the patient's medical history, takes some measurements, and asks the patient for more information about his/her symptoms. On the basis of the information collected, the doctor may ask yet more questions or carry out further tests. Finally, the doctor decides what he/she thinks is causing the patient's symptoms, and makes a diagnosis.

A cognitive model of this task might consist of a computer program that could take as input some representation of the stimulus (e.g., the patient's medical history and presenting symptom) and produce as output a representation of the doctor's response (whether to seek further information by querying another symptom or performing a test, or whether to make a diagnosis). A simple model might consist of a series of stages, whereby the medical history and presenting symptom initially lead the doctor to propose several competing hypotheses (e.g., either the patient has asthma or bronchitis). A second stage might then involve selecting the hypothesis corresponding to the disease that is most frequent in people who share the patient's medical history (e.g., that the patient has asthma). The symptom profile of this common disease might then be recalled. The next stage may involve querying the patient about further symptoms associated with the hypothesised disease, or about the precise nature of the presenting symptom.

In a fully fledged computational model each of the above processes would form part of the computer program, and the doctor's expected behaviour could be simulated by running or executing the computer program. If the doctor's actual behaviour differs from that which was predicted by the model, we know that the model is inadequate, and we can examine ways of addressing the model's shortcomings. If the model is accurate, and especially if it is accurate across a range of situations, then we may have some confidence that we understand the cognitive processes underlying performance in the diagnosis task.

This sample model is an abstract representation of the hypothesised cognitive processes of the doctor. The model is a representation of the processes because elements in the model correspond to elements of the hypothesised processes. It is abstract because it leaves out much of the detail of the actual cognitive processing (e.g., the cognitive processing is carried out by neural tissue rather than a computer chip). It is hoped that this detail is not important to the overall behaviour of the doctor. Lastly, if the model is accurate it may be used in place of a doctor, to predict how a doctor's diagnostic behaviour might change over time for example, or to evaluate strategies to lessen the chances of mis-diagnosis.

1.3 What Makes a Good Model?

A good model has two critical properties:

1. It is *complete*, to the extent that the model does not abstract out aspects of the original that have an important influence on the properties or behaviour of the original (e.g., a model of fluid flow in a pipe should not ignore friction between the pipe wall and the fluid); and
2. It is *faithful*, to the extent that the abstraction process does not introduce component properties or relationships that are not features of the original (e.g., a model building made out of children's clay might suggest that a real building is malleable).

These properties have their origin in the way a model abstracts from the thing being modelled. Completeness is about not abstracting details that are important. Faithfulness is about not introducing confounding details during the abstraction process.

It is important to realise that neither of the above properties is absolute, in the sense that a model is always a model for a specific purpose. The colour scheme of a model aeroplane, for example, is more relevant than the minutiae of its aerodynamics if the model is intended to help identify planes from different countries. On the other hand the reverse is true if the model is intended to allow exploration of aerodynamic design changes. For a model to be useful for a specific purpose it must be sufficiently complete and faithful that the model builder can correctly derive or deduce from the model properties of the real object which were previously unknown (e.g., whether a building will be functional or aesthetically pleasing).

1.4 The Rise of Cognitive Modelling

The modern era of empirical/cognitive psychology is often dated to the work of Ebbinghaus (1885), who set himself tasks such as learning lists of nonsense words in order to study the processes underlying memory. Since that time, the study of cognitive processes has gone through several shifts in emphasis and approach.

Early researchers used introspection as their primary empirical technique. At the beginning of the twentieth century introspection was criticised as being subjective and hence non-scientific. The rejection of introspection was accompanied by the rise of the Behaviourist School, which dominated psychology in the English speaking world for much of the first half of the twentieth century. Behaviourists believed that internal mental states could not be studied in an objective manner. They avoided all talk of mental states, and attempted to account for all behaviour in terms of simple stimulus-response links.

Around the middle of the twentieth century it was demonstrated conclusively that, at least for some higher mental processes such as language and skilled behaviour, simple stimulus-response links could not explain the full range of behaviours of which most humans are capable. It was shown that stimulus-response links were necessarily mediated by internal mental states, and hence that internal mental states were essential for causal explanations of these cognitive processes. Behaviourism was thus supplanted by a new psychology. The picture of cognition that arose in this new psychology was one in which the mind was an "information processor" and cognition was "information processing".

Within information processing psychology, sensory processes (such as vision and hearing) act as input devices, converting information from the surrounding environment into some internal form or representation. Mental processes manipulate and transform these representations, often triggering responses via output processes. This view of cognition has received support from fifty years of careful empirical work and remains current. The last half of the twentieth century, however, witnessed two major changes in approach. First, computer simulation techniques were adopted in order to explore and develop complex theories of cognitive processing and to evaluate competing theoretical accounts of empirical phenomena. The use of these techniques is one of the distinguishing features of the discipline of cognitive science. Second, brain imaging techniques were developed in order to localise cognitive processing and relate the functioning of the mind to the functioning of the brain. This relation is the primary focus of the newly emerged discipline of cognitive neuroscience.

Computer simulation techniques have allowed cognitive models such as that described in the previous section to be developed. To illustrate further consider the list-learning experiments of Ebbinghaus (1885). A cognitive model of list-learning would detail the mechanisms or processes by which the stimuli (the elements of the list) are stored and recalled, and any possible intervening mechanisms or processes involved in information consolidation (e.g., rehearsing the list) or information loss (e.g., through forgetting elements of the list). Such a model is considered in Chapter 2.

1.5 Modelling and Simulation

In many scientific domains modelling provides a way of investigating the rules or laws that govern complex systems that are only partly understood. This is normally achieved through building a model that we think will have similar characteristics to the real system and studying the characteristics of the model. Modelling within cognitive science follows this basic approach, with *simulation* being the principal method of studying a model's characteristics.

A common example of simulation is seen in modern weather forecasting. This involves determining relevant characteristics of the atmosphere, such as temperature, air pressure, and wind speed, across a grid of points, and then using mathematical equations that describe how the characteristics change with time to predict the values for the characteristics a short time later. By applying the mathematical equations over and over, meteorologists simulate the weather and are able to predict characteristics of the atmosphere at some later time. The simulation does not involve real wind currents or real temperatures. Instead, elements of the model (e.g., arrays of numbers) correspond to characteristics of the object of simulation.

The use of simulation in cognitive modelling parallels that in meteorology. A cognitive model specifies a number of processes, the initial characteristics of those processes, and the way in which those characteristics change through interactions with other processes within the model. Simulation involves repeatedly working through all of the interactions to determine how the characteristics of the system change over an extended time period.

Simulation is particularly useful when it is difficult to understand the behaviour of the system being modelled. Any system that is made up of many interacting components can be difficult to understand. If, in addition, some or all of those components have properties which make them individually difficult to understand, then understanding of the complete system is likely to be compromised further. This can happen when the components are:

- heterogeneous (i.e., there are many qualitatively different kinds of component within the system, each of which is idiosyncratic so their behaviour cannot be summarised with some uniform function);
- non-linear, stochastic and/or asynchronous in their response functions (i.e., components produce outputs that cannot be simply extrapolated from previous outputs, and they produce such outputs at times determined by the components themselves, rather than by some external clock);

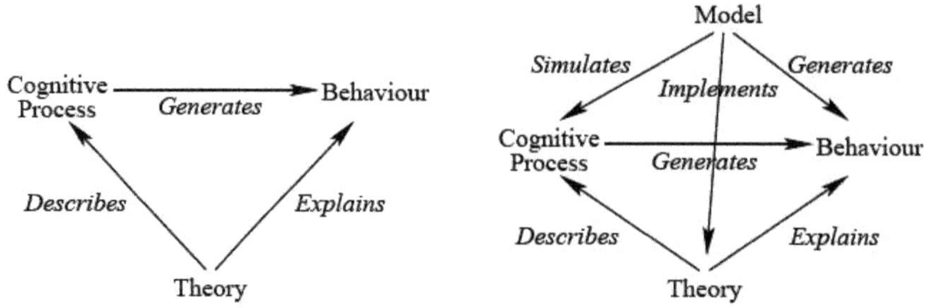

Figure 1.1: Some relations between behaviour, a cognitive process underlying that behaviour, a theory of the process, and a model of the process. The left panel shows the classical relations. The right panel shows the added dimension provided by modelling.

- densely connected to other components (i.e., there are many interactions between components); and
- recursively defined (i.e., components are themselves defined in terms of sub-components with these properties).

Unfortunately many psychological theories posit interacting processes or components that share many or all of these properties. Psychological theories are thus often highly complex. Simulation provides an effective means of determining the consequences or predictions of such interacting processing systems.

Indeed, most aspects of cognitive processing have formed the target of one or more cognitive models. Thus there are cognitive models of perceptual processes (such as those involved in analysing a visual image), attentional processes, motor and action control processes, memory, problem solving, reasoning, categorisation, and so on. In most cases, the techniques of simulation have led to greater understanding of the underlying cognitive processes.

1.6 The Role of Cognitive Modelling

Standard theorising in cognitive psychology is concerned with three types of entity: behaviours, cognitive processes underlying behaviours, and theories of those cognitive processes. Figure 1.1 (left) illustrates some of the relations between these three types of entity. The "classical" view (without modelling) is that a theory explains a behaviour by describing the cognitive processes that generate that behaviour. Modelling adds an extra dimension to this picture. A model generates behaviour, implements a theory, and simulates a cognitive process (as shown in the right panel).

Each object and relation in Figure 1.1 could form the focus of substantial discussion. For present purposes we will focus on just one triangle from the figure: that involving theory, behaviour (or empirical phenomena), and a model that implements the theory and generates the behaviour.

A theory in cognitive psychology typically takes the form of a series of related statements or assumptions, perhaps supplemented with a diagram. As in most sciences a theory is generally intended to "explain" some known empirical phenomena, and make predictions about other phenomena. The explanation consists of an argument demonstrating that the known empirical phenomena are consequences of the assumptions, and the predictions are additional assertions that may be tested through experiment. If the predictions are met then the theory gains further support. If the predictions are not met the theory is falsified and must be modified or abandoned. This is not a bad thing, for it means that we have learnt something: that one or more of the theory's assumptions is false.

This simplified picture is somewhat idealised. In most cases theories within cognitive psychology are under-specified in that the assumptions are incomplete or imprecise. Correspondingly, the relation between assumptions and data (including both prior data and predicted data) is generally qualitative rather than quantitative. Cognitive modelling helps to address these issues, and hence serves an important role in cognitive scientific explanation.

Few theories within cognitive psychology are stated in precise and unambiguous terms. Modelling forces theoretical precision by requiring that a theory be computationally complete. That is, in order to construct a model it is necessary to specify all aspects of a theory in the kind of detail required by a computer program. This means that no details can be left out, and that no aspects of a model may be vague, ambiguous, or open to alternative interpretations. Thus, although a model may abstract away some details of cognitive processing, it must still be "computationally complete".

As discussed below, the requirement for computational completeness is not without a cost, but it also has a subsidiary benefit — that of supporting clear, precise communication. A computational model can be an effective way of expressing and communicating a theory in objective terms. Verbal or diagrammatic theory specifications are generally open to interpretation. Models presented in clear publicly-specified theoretically-neutral computer languages do not suffer from this difficulty. In certain cases they also lend themselves to formal analysis of their properties, allowing theoreticians to derive logically necessary consequences from the theoretical assumptions without even running the computer model.

1.7 Further Benefits of Cognitive Modelling

Theories of cognitive processing are frequently complex. As noted above, it can therefore be difficult to accurately determine the behaviour of a theory by reasoning directly from its assumptions. This is especially true for theories that posit multiple heterogeneous sub-processes and when the explanations of empirical phenomena depend upon interactions between these sub-processes. A significant advantage of cognitive modelling is that it allows detailed evaluation of such theoretical proposals. Furthermore, once a model has been developed it is possible to investigate the impact of changes in theoretical assumptions on the model's behaviour. Modelling thus allows both evaluation and exploration of theories and their consequences.

A further benefit of cognitive modelling arises from its use as a supplement to cognitive neuropsychology. Cognitive neuropsychology is concerned with different patterns of behaviour that follow neurological damage, and the use of such patterns to inform theories of normal cognitive functioning. The relevance of cognitive modelling to cognitive neuropsychology lies in the fact that once one has developed (and evaluated) a model of normal cognitive functioning in some domain (e.g., language production), one can "damage" or lesion the model in some principled way and then compare the behaviour of the lesioned model with that of relevant neurological patients (e.g., patients with language production deficits). A successful model will be able to account for both normal and impaired performance.

The relation between modelling and cognitive neuropsychology goes both ways. While modelling can further our understanding of cognitive functioning and its breakdown, the breakdown of cognitive functioning can also provide a source of data against which models may be tested.

1.8 Some Objections to Cognitive Modelling

Much cognitive modelling is motivated by the benefits described above, but cognitive modelling is not without its difficulties. These difficulties primarily arise from the need to make detailed assumptions about representation and processing that are necessary for execution of the model. The detail of these assumptions means that they may be very difficult to justify empirically. Two arguments — that of the behaviourist and that of the cautious scientist — require special consideration.

As we have seen, the behaviourist approach to psychology held that psychological theories should deal only with observables of behaviour. They should not theorise about processes that intervene between the input (stimulus) and the output (response), because such processes cannot be observed. While behaviourism is no longer popular, the need to specify intervening processes in the kind of detail required by cognitive modelling may leave some with an uneasy feeling.

At present there are few cognitive scientists who dispute the existence of intervening processes. It is possible that neuroimaging techniques will one day provide direct evidence for the detail of these processes, but until that day cognitive scientists must adopt other means to provide support for their theorising about intervening processes. These means may include appeals to principles such as simplicity and parsimony. For example, given two theories that claim to account for the same behaviour, one may favour the theory with fewer assumptions or simpler intervening processes. Stronger support may be obtained, however, by using modelling to ensure that the theories are complete and fully consistent with behaviour. In other words, the response to the behaviourist's objection is that intervening processes have proven to be necessary in accounting for the complexity of cognitive functioning. Given that such processes are necessary, cognitive modelling allows us to examine the nature and consequences of hypothesised intervening processes in detail.

The cautious scientist is less sceptical about intervening processes than the behaviourist, but is still uncomfortable about making assumptions that are not fully justified on empirical grounds. To illustrate, a scientist studying memory for lists of words may be happy to postulate a process of memory decay, whereby words of the list gradually become unavailable for recollection. If this process is to be incorporated into a model, however, one must specify details of the process. Is decay a probabilistic process whereby words may spontaneously disappear from memory, or can memory representations vary in their strength, with decay affecting strength? In the former case, what function governs the probability of a word decaying at any specific moment? In the latter case, how does strength change with time, and is there some strength threshold below which words are inaccessible? The cautious scientist may argue that he or she has insufficient evidence to answer these questions, and hence prefer to settle for a less detailed description of the decay process. As a result, he or she will be inclined to balk at models that include specification that goes beyond that which can be justified on purely empirical (or even theoretical) grounds.

The cautious scientist's objection is a less extreme form of the behaviourist's objection. It is an objection to the computational completeness that modelling requires. Whether this is a limitation or disadvantage of cognitive modelling is unclear. It could be argued, for example, that computational completeness is a significant advantage, for it makes clear that the stance of the cautious scientist is incomplete. An additional benefit of cognitive modelling is therefore that it can make clear to us the limitations of our knowledge. Knowing what we don't know is an important stage in understanding.

Of course the counters to these objections do not absolve the modeller from a basic responsibility: to relate models to both theory and data. One of the great strengths of cognitive modelling is the way that it may complement the approaches of empirical and theoretical psychology.

1.9 Approaches to Cognitive Modelling

While those who practice cognitive modelling generally agree on the benefits of the enterprise, they often disagree about how the enterprise should be approached. There are several schools of cognitive modelling, and advocates of one are frequently critics of another. The schools differ in their assumptions about mental representation and their view on the relation between a cognitive model and the brain.

The connectionist school argues that properties of the neural tissues that implement the information processing mechanisms of the mind are critical to the way the mind works. As such, they build models that consist of many simple interacting units functioning in parallel. The units are typically understood as analogues of neurons or neural cell assemblies. Symbolic cognitive models, in contrast, generally make the assumption that information processing can be described in terms of the manipulation of symbolic representations (as defined below). Within the symbolic approach the neural substrate is viewed as an implementation medium that is of secondary importance.

The symbolic and connectionist approaches to modelling share little beyond the basic idea that the functioning of the mind is computational in nature and so can be simulated by a machine. The two approaches are frequently presented as disjoint and even in opposition to each other. However, both approaches have strengths and weaknesses. This has led to attempts to develop hybrid symbolic/connectionist systems that combine the strengths and circumvent the weaknesses of the individual approaches.

Two further approaches to modelling are the architectural approach and the dynamical approach. The former involves adopting a hypothesised organisation of the complete set of information processing structures that comprise the mind/brain, and using this to guide the development of models. The latter is more mathematical in emphasis. In its most extreme form it argues against the use of internal mental representations of the form used by any of the other approaches. The claim of the dynamical approach is that mental processing may be described by differential equations in much the same way as the trajectory of a comet may be described by differential equations, but, as in the case of the comet, mental processing does not involve solving equations. Rather, it involves responding to the mental equivalents of forces. The dynamical approach, with its rejection of mental representation, is not well suited to modelling high-level cognitive processes, and will not be discussed further in this book.

1.9.1 Symbolic Models

The symbolic approach to cognitive modelling developed from early work by Newell and colleagues (e.g., Newell, Shaw, & Simon, 1958; Ernst & Newell, 1969) on logical inference and human problem solving. After developing an explicit theory of problem solving, they specified the theory as a sequence of steps that could be performed by a computer program.

Symbolic Propositional Representations

An essential element of the early computational work of Newell and colleagues was the representation of information relevant to a problem in a symbolic, propositional form, and the manipulation by the program of this representation. Consider a simple descriptive statement such as:

the red pyramid is on the blue cube

This may be analysed as a conjunction of *propositions* concerning the objects (a pyramid and a cube), their properties (red and blue, respectively), and the relation between the two (that the pyramid is on the cube). The information may be represented formally as follows:

`pyramid(p) & red(p) & cube(c) & blue(c) & on(p, c)`

Each conjunct of this representation is a symbolic proposition: a statement that consists of symbols (e.g., `p` or `red`) which refer to objects, properties, or relations, and that may be either true or false, depending on the state of the objects to which the proposition applies.

Symbolic propositional representations have two desirable properties: systematicity and compositionality (see Fodor & Pylyshyn, 1988). A representation is systematic if it consists of a number of parts and the result of replacing some of the parts with other parts of the same kind is also a meaningful representation. Thus, if `on(p, c1)` is a meaningful representation and `c1` and `c2` both refer to objects, then `on(p, c2)` will be a meaningful representation. It may not be true, but it will be meaningful. A representation is compositional if it consists of parts and the meaning of the whole is a function of the meaning of the parts. The representation `on(p, c1)` is compositional because it consists of parts (`on`, `p` and `c1`) and its meaning is a function of the meaning of those parts. Representations that are compositional and systematic may be manipulated by rules that are dependent only on the form of the representation and not on the meaning of the representation. It is this manipulation that is central to many symbolic cognitive models.

Symbolic representations may also be embedded to represent information of arbitrary complexity. Thus, the statement that:

Joe believes that the pyramid is green

may be represented by the compound proposition:

`pyramid(p) & believes(joe, green(p))`

Similarly the statement that:

Joe believes the blue pyramid to be green

may be represented by the compound proposition:

`pyramid(p) & blue(p) & believes(joe, green(p))`

Note that the proposition `believes(joe, green(p))` may be true even if the embedded proposition `green(p)` is false.

Symbolic propositional representations provide a general means of representing information. Symbolic models adopt this general representational device, and supplement it with symbol manipulation rules that operate on representations to transform them or build new representations. A symbolic cognitive model is therefore a model of the mechanisms by which symbolic propositional representations are manipulated and transformed from one form to another.

A Simple Symbolic Model

To illustrate symbolic modelling consider the task of transitive inference (as investigated by, for example, DeSotto, London, & Handel, 1965; Clark, 1969). Subjects performing the task are given two statements concerning individuals and relations between them (such as *Anna is shorter than Beth* and *Caroline is taller than Beth*) and asked to either judge the truth of a third statement (e.g., *Is Anna shorter than Caroline*?) or to generate a true statement concerning the two unrelated individuals (if such a statement exists).

How might a symbolic model perform the transitive inference task? Such a model might first convert the given statements into propositional form. It could then apply rules of inference to the propositions in order to test or derive a conclusion. In the simplest case of deriving a conclusion, this might proceed as follows:

Given statements:
Anna is taller than Beth
Beth is taller than Caroline
Propositional encoding:
`taller(anna, beth)`
`taller(beth, caroline)`
Inference rule 1 (part of long-term knowledge):
`taller(X, Y) & taller(Y, Z)` $\Rightarrow$ `taller(X, Z)`
Result of applying rule 1:
`taller(anna, caroline)`

Verbal decoding:

Anna is taller than Caroline

In this, and all examples throughout this book, symbols beginning with a capital letter (e.g., `X`, `Y`, `Z`) denote variables, which may be mapped onto other symbols (e.g., the individuals `anna`, `beth` and `caroline`) in the application of an inference rule.

Only one inference rule is required for the above simple case. Suppose however that we are dealing with a more complex case, in which the given information involves both *taller* and *shorter*. For example:

Given statements:

Anna is shorter than Beth
Caroline is taller than Beth

Propositional encoding:

`shorter(anna, beth)`
`taller(caroline, beth)`

Inference rule 2 (long-term knowledge):

`shorter(X, Y)` ⇒ `taller(Y, X)`

Result of applying rule 2:

`taller(beth, anna)`

Inference rule 1 (long-term knowledge):

`taller(X, Y)` & `taller(Y, Z)` ⇒ `taller(X, Z)`

Result of applying rule 1:

`taller(caroline, anna)`

Verbal decoding:

Caroline is taller than Anna

This case requires one extra step: use of a second inference rule to transform the *shorter* relation into a *taller* relation. One might therefore predict from this simplest of models that the second case will take subjects longer than the first case. Indeed, this has been found to be the case (DeSotto *et al.*, 1965; Clark, 1969). The account therefore receives some empirical support. Furthermore, empirical evidence points to faster solution times when information is stated in terms of *taller* as opposed to *shorter*, supporting the transformation of *shorter* to *taller*, rather than the reverse.

Symbolic Programming Languages

Several symbolic computer programming languages have been created to simplify the development of systems that use symbolic representations. The two most popular such languages are Lisp (e.g., Winston & Horn, 1981; Wilensky, 1984) and Prolog (e.g., Bratko, 1986; Sterling, 1986; Clocksin & Mellish, 1987). Lisp was developed in the early 1960s by John McCarthy and colleagues at MIT (based in part on work by Newell, Shaw and Simon at CMU). Prolog was developed by Alain Colmeraur and colleagues in France in the early 1970s. There are significant differences between the languages, but both provide ways of representing symbolic and propositional information, as well as variables and mechanisms for binding symbols or propositions to those variables. A great many symbolic models have been developed in Lisp and/or Prolog, and the languages continue to be popular for symbolic cognitive modelling.

Production Systems

Lisp and Prolog are general purpose symbolic programming languages. This means that while each supports the symbolic representation of information, each also employs a generic, flexible, control mechanism that is motivated by mathematical and logical concerns. Consequently the languages impose minimal constraints on models developed within them. This may be appropriate, however it has been argued that general purpose programming languages fail to capture important aspects of the nature or character of mental processing: specifically that mental processing can be understood in terms of the cyclic application of rules to a representation of one's current beliefs. This view has led to the development of production systems, which are general frameworks within which symbolic models may be expressed.

A production system consists of two fundamental components: a propositional database or store (in which current propositions, such as `taller(beth,anna)`, are stored) and a rule database (in which inference rules are held). Production systems function in a cyclic manner, with each cycle consisting of two phases. In the *recognise phase*, an inference rule is selected from the rule database according to a set of standard principles. In the *act phase* the selected rule is applied. The result is typically an alteration to the propositional store. The cycle may then repeat, with a different rule being selected and applied. Processing terminates either when the recognise phase fails to select a rule or when the selected rule explicitly signals the end of processing.

A production system's propositional store is generally referred to as its working memory, and the propositions contained in the store are referred to as working memory elements, or WMEs. The rule database (which may include many thousands of rules) is referred to as production memory, and the rules within the database are referred to as productions. Productions correspond to long-term knowledge, including both general knowledge and task-specific knowledge, and, like the inference rules in the previous section, typically contain variables that allow them to apply to many different WMEs.

More formally, a production consists of a set of conditions and a set of actions. For example, a variant on inference rule 2 (from the previous section) might consist of one condition and two actions:

IF:	`shorter(X, Y)`
THEN:	delete `shorter(X, Y)`
	add `taller(Y, X)`

This particular rule employs two kinds of actions (working memory addition and deletion), but other actions are possible (e.g., issuing motor commands, or terminating processing).

The variables contained within the rule (`X` and `Y`) mean that the rule may apply to any instance of the *shorter* relation. An *instantiated production* or *production instance* results from *mapping* or *binding* the variables. Thus, in the previous production rule `X` and `Y` might be bound to `anna` and `beth` respectively, yielding the following production instance:

IF:	`shorter(anna, beth)`
THEN:	delete `shorter(anna, beth)`
	add `taller(beth, anna)`

The result is an instruction to transform a specific instance of the *shorter* relation into the equivalent *taller* relation.

This example demonstrates that productions may add or delete specific propositions to or from working memory. WMEs, in contrast to productions, are generally specific and transient. As processing proceeds working memory evolves through the addition and deletion of individual WMEs as each production is applied. Productions, in contrast to WMEs, are non-specific and long-term. They are non-specific because they contain variables (and hence may apply in a range of situations). They are long-term because once entered in production memory they are generally not deleted.

One of the key elements of a standard production system is its conflict resolution procedure: the process within the recognise phase that governs the selection of one instance of a rule from all possible rule instances. Often, during the recognise phase, the contents of working memory will be such that the conditions of many different rules are met, and even a single rule may have its conditions met by many different WMEs (leading to many different instances of the rule). Different production systems employ different principles for selecting one rule instance from the set of applicable rule instances. Example mechanisms include: avoiding rule instances that have been selected previously, favouring rules with many conditions (and hence which are specific to the current situation) over rules with few conditions (which are more general and may be seen as specifying default or fall-back behaviours), favouring rules whose conditions match recently created WMEs over rules whose conditions match WMEs that have been present in working memory for some time, associating activation values with rule instances and selecting the most active rule instance, and (if all else fails) selecting one rule instance at random from those that have not been ruled out by other principles.

A production system model therefore consists of three components: a conflict resolution strategy (normally viewed as a fixed processing mechanism); a specification of the initial contents of working memory (i.e., the information on which the subject is able to act); and a set of productions (specifying both task-specific knowledge and general knowledge relevant to the task). Detailed examples of specific production systems applied to simple arithmetic are discussed in Chapter 3.

Analogies may be drawn between elements of the production system approach and the possible structure of the mind. In particular, the production system concept of working memory is an analogue of the psychological concept of working memory, and the production system concept of production memory is an analogue of the psychological concept of long-term memory. While these analogies are intriguing, they should not be taken literally. For example, the production system concept of working memory is generally not limited in capacity or subject to decay. The psychological concept is. Similarly, production memory is not normally divided into different types of long-term memory. In contrast, many psychologists distinguish between several forms of long-term knowledge, including procedural and declarative, and within declarative between episodic and semantic.

Production systems date back to the work of Post (1943), with the first implementations developed in the 1950s. However, it is of some interest to note that many production system concepts (such as rule-based processing and condition-action associations) were preempted over 20 years earlier by Selz (1913, 1922), an Austrian psychologist from the Gestalt school (see Chapter 4). Selz argued, at a time when British and American psychology was strongly behaviouristic, that problem solving involved the mental application of condition/action rules, and that associations between stimuli and responses were a function of the properties of and relations between stimuli in a given situation. Both notions are clearly visible in current conceptions of production systems.

1.9.2 Connectionist Models

One fundamental assumption of symbolic modelling is that cognitive functioning is largely independent of the implementation medium (i.e., neural tissue). This allows the development of abstract models that are based on high-level symbol manipulation. The connectionist approach rejects this assumption. Advocates of connectionism argue that properties of neural tissue (such as massively parallel computation through the interaction of many simple processing units) are of critical importance in modelling cognitive processes, and that cognition emerges from the interactions between processing units. From this perspective, they argue, it is a mistake to try to understand cognition purely in terms of the manipulation of symbols.

Table 1.1: Featural representations of some animals

		Animals				
		is mammal	can fly	has fur	has long tail	is vegetarian
Features	Person	1	0	0	0	0
	Cat	1	0	1	1	0
	Dog	1	0	1	1	0
	Bat	1	1	0	0	0
	Bird	0	1	0	1	0
	Mouse	1	0	1	1	1

Parallel Distributed Processing

Neurophysiology tells us that the brain consists of many billions of neurons. Each neuron may be analysed as a simple computing device which receives electrical impulses from other neurons. If the sum of impulses received in quick succession is sufficiently great, the neuron generates its own impulse, and transmits this to other neurons. Individual neurons operate in parallel, and computation is distributed across many interconnected neurons. The connectionist school of cognitive modelling has adopted an abstraction based on this parallel distributed approach to computation, and developed models of cognitive processes in terms of interacting networks of simple computing units.

Feature-Based Representations

The rejection of symbol manipulation by connectionism entails the rejection of symbolic propositional representations. It does not, however, entail the rejection of mental representation. Rather, it calls for a different approach. Standard connectionist networks consist of sets of nodes, with nodes having activation values (which may be thought of as corresponding to the firing rates of neurons). A representation in a connectionist network is thus a configuration of activation values across a set of nodes.

To illustrate, consider the highly artificial case of a network consisting of five nodes, with each node representing one of the following five features: *is mammal*, *can fly*, *has fur*, *has long tail*, and *is vegetarian*. A pattern of activation in which the first node is highly active and all other nodes are inactive might represent (or characterise) a person (or the category of people). Different patterns of activity across the nodes may represent different animals (or categories). Thus, Table 1.1, in which active nodes are indicated by the digit 1 and inactive nodes by the digit 0, illustrates the activities of nodes corresponding to a range of animals.

If we adopt a fixed order of features, we may represent the various types of animals by feature vectors. A person would correspond to the vector $\langle 1, 0, 0, 0, 0 \rangle$, and a cat would correspond to the vector $\langle 1, 0, 1, 1, 0 \rangle$. Note that this representation is unable to distinguish between cats and dogs: both have the same featural representation. In practice, many more features are typically needed to discriminate between possible represented objects.

Feature-based representations are well able to represent instances of objects or classes of objects (depending on the interpretation of the representation), but they lack the expressive power of symbolic propositional representations. Thus, the representation of relations between objects is only possible through indirect means (e.g., by using separate units to represent the relation and each object that lies in the relation) and those means generalise poorly to the representation of embedded propositions. While these limitations are not insurmountable (see Pollack, 1990), connectionist models nevertheless tend to focus on aspects of cognition that do not require the representation of relational information.

An Illustrative Model

To illustrate a simple connectionist-style model consider the task of category learning (e.g., Kendler & D'Amato, 1955; Kendler & Kendler, 1975). Subjects performing this task are presented with a set of objects or exemplars that differ along several dimensions (e.g., colour, shape, size), and required to learn which objects belong in which categories. After being shown an object, the subject may nominate a possible category. If the subject is incorrect he or she will be told the correct category. Most subjects are able to learn this task after a few tens of trials (assuming the number of dimensions is not too great and the categories share some underlying structure).

Consider the near trivial case in which objects differ along two dimensions (size and colour), with large objects belonging in category A and small objects belonging in category B. A connectionist model of performance on the task might consist of two sets of nodes, with four nodes in one set – the "input" nodes, corresponding to the features *large*, *small*, *black* and *white* — and two nodes in the other set — the "output" nodes, corresponding to the categories A and B. Each node in the input set would have a connection to each node in the output set, as in Figure 1.2.

Connections within connectionist networks are weighted, and activation may "flow" along a connection in proportion to the connection's weight. If the weights of the connections in Figure 1.2 from *large* to A and from *small* to B are near to one, and all other weights are near to zero, presentation of the feature vector $\langle 1, 0, 1, 0 \rangle$ (representing a large black object) to the input nodes will cause the output node for category A to become active. In contrast, presentation of the feature vector $\langle 0, 1, 0, 1 \rangle$ (representing a small white object) will cause the node

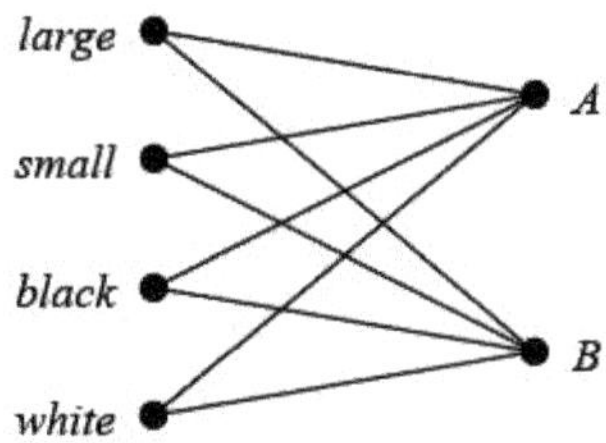

Figure 1.2: A simple network for the categorisation task

for category *B* to become active.

Learning, Generalisation and Graceful Degradation

Connectionist networks often exhibit several properties that make them particularly appropriate for modelling cognitive phenomena: learning from examples, generalisation to new examples, and graceful degradation in the face of ill-formed input or damage to the network.

Learning Suppose the connection weights in Figure 1.2 are initially set to random values. When an input vector is presented to the network, the output nodes will become active. For each input vector there is a unique target output vector (either $\langle 1, 0 \rangle$ or $\langle 0, 1 \rangle$). If the output generated by a given input fails to match the correct output (which is available to the subject, because the subject is given feedback on his or her categorisations), then the connection weights may be adjusted to improve the input/output mapping. For example, if the activation of an output node is greater than in the target pattern, then the weights on all connections feeding positive activation to the node should be decreased by a small amount (and the weights on all connections feeding negative activation to the node should be increased by a small amount). The opposite adjustment may be made if the activation of an output node is less than in the target pattern. Such weight adjustments will result in the network generating a more accurate categorisation when the input pattern is repeated at a later time. This is the basis of delta-rule learning, a simple but effective learning algorithm for one class of connectionist network.

When applied to the categorisation task described in the previous section, delta-rule learning results in strong weights between input features and output categories that co-occur. If, however, a feature is sometimes present and sometimes absent in a category (e.g., black or white, when categorisation is based on size), then the weight from the node representing that feature to the target category will be increased on some trials and decreased on other trials. If the feature is entirely independent of the category, the increases and decreases will average out and the resultant weight will be close to zero.

Generalisation One variant of the concept learning task involves presenting subjects with one set of exemplars in a training phase, and allowing subjects to learn the categories of all exemplars through feedback. Subjects are then presented with new exemplars, which share some but not all features with items from the training set. The subject's task is to generalise from previous experience and categorise these new exemplars. Connectionist networks provide a natural approach to such generalisation tasks, and for many tasks networks can be demonstrated that exhibit generalisation performance similar to that of human subjects.

Modelling Degraded Input Connectionist networks also lend themselves to modelling tasks in which input representations are partially degraded (corresponding, for example, to visual input under suboptimal viewing conditions, or auditory input with high levels of background noise). Feature-based input representations may be corrupted by random perturbations to one or more features with minimal effects on the network's behaviour. This allows the development of networks that show effects of input degradation similar to those obtained in experiments involving human subjects.

Graceful Degradation Large scale connectionist models, coupled with now standard learning techniques, typically develop some redundancy in their functioning. Consequently, such networks are relatively unaffected by minor damage (such as removing some nodes or some connections, or adding noise to activation values). This graceful degradation has been argued to provide a realistic reflection of the behaviour of the brain after natural cell death or even after minor brain damage. Several studies have also shown that larger scale damage to normally functioning connectionist networks can yield behaviours similar to those exhibited by patients with significant neural damage (e.g., Plaut & Shallice, 1993).

Types of Connectionist Network

Many different types of connectionist network have been developed. The network in Figure 1.2 is a simple feed-forward network (also known as a perceptron) consisting of two layers of nodes mediated by one layer of connections. Such networks are limited in their computational power: it can be shown mathematically that there are certain stimulus/response mappings that they cannot perform (Minsky & Papert, 1988). This limitation is not present in multi-layer perceptrons — feed-forward networks consisting of additional layers of units that mediate the stimulus/response relation — but such networks require more complex approaches to learning, and such approaches are generally considered to be biologically and psychologically implausible (Crick, 1989).

The layered structure of feed-forward networks also imposes limits on the sequential behaviour of such networks. Thus, feed-forward networks can only perform stimulus/response mappings in which a single response is associated with a single stimulus. They cannot perform mappings in which different responses are associated with different sequences of stimuli. Recurrent networks (see Jordon, 1986; Elman, 1990) overcome this limitation by including feedback connections between layers. These connections feed a representation of the state of processing at one point in time back into earlier layers of the network. Such connections allow, for example, the pattern of activation of an internal layer of nodes produced while processing one stimulus to affect the processing of the next stimulus. Recurrent networks have been used to model some of the sequential aspects of language.

Networks with feedback connections may also be used for non-sequential tasks by fixing the input vector and allowing repeated cycles of processing until the output vector stabilises. Networks of this form, which are known as attractor networks, have been used to model recognition processes, where a degraded representation of a stimulus may be refined through successive processing cycles (see, for example, Plaut & Shallice, 1993).

Networks need not have a layered structure. Associative networks (Hopfield, 1982; Hertz, Krogh, & Palmer, 1991) do not distinguish between input and output nodes. Any node within an associative network may be connected to any other node and functioning of the network corresponds to fixing or clamping the activation values of some nodes and allowing activation to flow along connections until the activations of unclamped nodes stabilise. Associative networks effectively act as pattern completion devices. They may be trained (again using standard learning algorithms) to store a number of activation patterns. After training the presentation of a partial pattern results in reconstruction of the original pattern. Interference between stored patterns may occur, giving associative networks some properties similar to human memory (Hopfield, 1982).

A different style of processing is evident in interactive activation networks. Nodes within these networks generally represent relatively high level concepts (e.g., letters or words: McClelland & Rumelhart, 1981), and "compete" for activation through processes of self excitation and mutual inhibition (see McClelland, 1992). Thus within McClelland and Rumelhart's interactive activation model of word recognition (McClelland & Rumelhart, 1981), nodes representing words receive excitation from nodes representing letters (which in turn receive activation from nodes representing features of the visual input), but word nodes mutually inhibit each other. Mutual inhibition ensures that only one word node may be active at a time. Similar inhibitory processes operate at the letter level to ensure that only one letter at each position of the word is active at a time. Interactive activation networks are appropriate for modelling tasks in which multiple sources of information interact to yield a single discrete outcome.

1.9.3 Hybrid Symbolic/Connectionist Models

Symbolic and connectionist approaches to modelling have both strengths and weaknesses. Arguably, the strengths of one approach are the weaknesses of the other, and *vice versa*. There is therefore the possibility that more adequate cognitive models may be developed by adopting a hybrid approach, in which both symbolic and connectionist aspects are incorporated. Cooper and Franks (1993) distinguish two types of hybrid model, corresponding to two ways in which symbolic and connectionist approaches have been combined. Physically hybrid models consist of separate symbolic and connectionist subsystems. These subsystems typically perform different functions and interact to yield the behaviour of the system as a whole. Non-physically hybrid systems, in contrast, consist of a single system (which is fully symbolic or fully connectionist), but that system can be described as functioning in both symbolic and connectionist terms.

The rationale for the physically hybrid approach is as follows. Symbolic models have achieved their greatest successes in relative high-level cognitive domains, such as reasoning and problem solving. Low-level domains, such as perception, are better modelled by connectionist approaches. This view is supported by the fact that there are relatively few tasks or domains for which both symbolic and connectionist models exist. It also suggests that tasks that can be decomposed into a mixture of high-level sub-processes and low-level sub-processes might be best modelled by hybrid systems in which separate subsystems perform the separate sub-functions.

One system that employs the physically hybrid approach is Sun's model of common-sense reasoning (Sun, 1994). The model uses two subsystems: a symbolic system for representing reasoning rules (such as *all men are mortal*) and a connectionist system for representing the "sub-conceptual content" of the elements involved in those rules (e.g., the concept of *Socrates* and the category of *men*). Sub-conceptual content is represented using fine-grained feature-based representations. Links between the subsystems allow the simulation of flexible rule-based reasoning.

The non-physically hybrid approach is well illustrated by the connectionist production system of Touretzky and Hinton (1988). Touretzky and Hinton showed how connectionist techniques could be used to implement the structures and processes of a typical symbolic production system (including working memory, production memory, and symbolic rules containing variables). In principle, a symbolic production system model of a specific task could be simulated by Touretzky and Hinton's system by providing the system with an appropriate, feature-based representation of the symbolic rules. The functioning of such a system could be legitimately described in both connectionist and symbolic terms.

1.9.4 Cognitive Architectures

The last decade has seen the rise of an alternative approach to cognitive modelling that is orthogonal to the symbolic/connectionist distinction. This is the use of cognitive architectures (Newell, 1990). Cognitive architectures are theories of the large-scale structure and organisation of cognitive processing. They are theories of the functional subsystems that make up the mind/brain, and the modes of interaction between those subsystems.

The concept of cognitive architecture derives from an analogy with that of computer architecture. A computer architecture consists of a configuration or structuring of a number of components (a central processing unit, a data bus, RAM, disk drives, input and output devices, etc.). A cognitive architecture similarly consists of such a configuration, where components may include a short-term or working memory, a long-term memory, a language subsystem, perceptual and motor subsystems, one or more learning mechanisms, and so forth.

Cognitive architectures attempt to provide a general framework or set of constraints within which models of specific tasks or domains may be developed. The basic approach was first championed by Newell (1990) (see also Newell, 1973). Examples include Soar (Laird, Newell, & Rosenbloom, 1987; Newell, 1990), ACT-R (Anderson, 1983, 1993; Anderson & Lebiere, 1998), CAP (Schneider & Detweiler, 1987; Schneider & Oliver, 1991), and EPIC (Meyer & Kieras, 1997; Kieras, Meyer, Ballas, & Lauber, 2000). Soar and EPIC are symbolic architectures based on production system concepts. ACT-R, which is described further below, is a hybrid architecture. CAP is a connectionist architecture.

The architectural perspective on cognition views behaviour on any particular task as the product of a general architecture working with task-specific knowledge. Development of a model of a task within an architecture therefore involves supplying the architecture with appropriate task-specific knowledge. For architectures based on production systems, this generally involves supplying an appropriate set of production rules. For other architectures it involves supplying the knowledge in the form of input/output patterns with which the architecture may be trained.

Of the above mentioned architectures, ACT-R is currently the most highly influential. ACT-R is a physically hybrid architecture. At its centre is an activation-based production system. This consists of the standard production system components (as described in Section 1.9.1), augmented with a learning mechanism and perceptual and motor subsystems. What makes ACT-R distinctive is that elements in working memory have activation levels, and these activations may be propagated to production instances. Conflict resolution is then effected by firing the first production instance that becomes sufficiently active. Production firing results in the addition of new working memory elements, the excitation of existing elements, or the execution of motor commands. ACT-R has been used to model a wide range of phenomena, including choice tasks, arithmetic, memory for word lists, analogy, and dual task performance (Anderson & Lebiere, 1998).

1.10 Strategies for the Use of Simulation

There are thus several distinct approaches that may be adopted in developing a cognitive model. There are also several distinct ways in which modelling and simulation may be used to advance our knowledge and understanding. Simulation provides a collection of tools and methods that can be used within different scientific disciplines for different scientific purposes and even at different stages in the development of a field. The following paragraphs consider some of the different strategies for using computer simulation within cognitive modelling. The strategies are discussed in order of increasing scientific power.

The first kind of simulation method might be called a "fishing trip", by analogy with the angler who casts a fishing rod into a pond with little idea of what may be in the pond, or even if there is anything of interest in the pond at all. The angler may be gambling but is probably not wasting his or her time, because after a few casts some useful information may have been found about the pond. Either there are fish in the pond, or there probably aren't, and one should try fishing elsewhere.

The fishing trip method of simulation therefore consists of attempting to develop a model of some task or behaviour in order to learn more about the task. Fishing trips can be useful to cognitive scientists just as they are to anglers, particularly when they are trying to make sense of a new approach or a new scientific area. In trying to build a simulation of some task, for example, we may discover that we are unclear about what we think the problem is, what the possible solutions are, that the kind of theory we were thinking about is too simple, or even that there is some very good reason why it cannot work at all.

The second strategy involves implementing a pre-existing (verbally specified) theory, and determining if the theory behaves as claimed. This form of modelling is particularly useful when the verbal theory is highly complex. This form of modelling is a kind of sufficiency test: it allows one to determine if a set of theoretical assumptions (as outlined in the verbal specification) is sufficient to account for the target behaviour. If they are sufficient, all well and good. If they are not, one may then go on a fishing trip in an attempt to find how they might be altered.

A different approach to simulation involves carrying out an *a priori* analysis of the properties of the kind of theory that is being considered. One may develop a model and determine, for example, how sensitive its behaviour is to the underlying theoretical assumptions. In this way one may identify critical parameters and appropriate values for those parameters. Equally one may identify theoretical assumptions that are secondary — assumptions that have non-significant effects on the behaviour of the model.

Finally, the most powerful use of simulation techniques is in supporting the conventional use of the hypothetico-deductive method that is widely used by scientists across many disciplines. This method involves using a model to simulate behaviour beyond that which was employed in the development of the model, and thereby generating predictions or hypotheses. These hypotheses may then be tested by conducting behavioural experiments with real people. If people behave as the model predicts then the model gains empirical support.

1.11 Closing Remarks

In this chapter we have discussed the nature and roles of cognitive modelling and described the principal modelling techniques that have been adopted by the cognitive science community.

Historically, different sub-communities have taken rather different approaches to modelling. Some have preferred to take a "top-down" approach starting with high level cognitive functions like reasoning or problem solving and trying to understand the kinds of cognitive processes that are needed to implement such functions, and traditionally the methods adopted have emphasised symbol manipulation and representation of knowledge. Other scientists have preferred a "bottom-up" approach, to give a detailed account of observed behaviour in tasks like concept learning or reading; these are often well-explained by connectionist or statistical mechanisms. Arguments between these two communities can be quite vigorous, frequently centering on the question of whether the mechanisms of mind/brain are "really" symbolic or "really" connectionist.

Another dimension along which cognitive models can be compared concerns whether they set out to provide unified accounts of cognitive processes, typically as large-scale information processing architectures, or whether they are "micro-models" of small scale phenomena. Debates are again lively. Advocates of micro-modelling argue that cognitive scientists should put explanation of natural phenomena first, and not build theoretical palaces that cannot be justified empirically. Other scientists emphasise the need to develop unified theories of intelligence and cognition, and the information processing principles that make any kind of intelligence possible. This dimension actually implies a trade-off between broad theoretical generality and detailed empirical adequacy, so examples of models can be found at all points in between the two extremes.

In this book we set out to be inclusive rather than disputatious. To do this we have tried to demonstrate an integrated approach to cognitive modelling which we hope will have something to offer to researchers of all persuasions. In particular we introduce a set of tools and methods, collectively called the COGENT cognitive modelling environment, which we think can be used to support many cognitive modelling styles. We believe that COGENT can offer this for several reasons.

First, we view the set of tools that COGENT offers as merely that, tools; we don't need to take a position on whether the different kinds of representation that the system offers embody some sort of truth about the mind or brain. As we have discussed, computational models are intrinsically abstractions from reality, and modelling always represents some kind of approximation. It is up to the individual COGENT user to decide to what extent his or her model embodies reality.

Second, we observe that different ways of thinking and modelling are productive in different sub-areas of cognitive science, so COGENT supports several standard approaches. COGENT users may build rule-based, activation-based, simple connectionist or even conventional numerical simulations. Indeed they may even build hybrid models that combine different representations.

Third, we have tried to provide sufficient representational and computational power to permit scientists to build simulations at grossly different scales, from micro-models to unified architectures or anywhere in between. Indeed a user can arrange that different parts of the system of interest are modelled at different levels or detail. COGENT supports a highly modular approach to modelling cognitive systems, with any or all modules programmable at a coarse level, or in finer detail by recursively composing modules out of smaller components to whatever level is required.

Finally, we believe that COGENT is equally sympathetic to the theoretician and the empirically minded scientist. We believe that it offers an unprecedented range of formal tools with the expressive power to accommodate many different theoretical frameworks. On the other hand we know that science proceeds through systematic experiment, with careful collection and analysis of data in varied and controlled conditions, and rigorous comparison of predictions and observations. Apart from the modelling tools COGENT provides it also includes facilities for managing computational experiments, automatically running simulations under varying assumptions and storing the data, comparing simulation results with laboratory data, and so on. We hope that subsequent chapters will clearly demonstrate these capabilities, and help to build bridges between the many different sub-communities of cognitive science.

1.12 Further Reading

Dawson (1998) provides an excellent introduction to the computational theory behind cognitive science, including chapters on symbolic modelling, connectionist modelling, and the relation between the two. Dawson also discusses the key issue of levels of description, which is addressed in several places throughout this book. Further background is provided in the opening chapters of Green and Others

(1996).

There are relatively few texts that focus on symbolic modelling. Scott and Nicolson (1991), which provides a set of "cognitive science projects", is one exception. A more advanced text, which focuses on the production system approach, is Klahr, Langley, and Neches (1987). Anderson and Lebiere (1998) is also of considerable interest. This book presents a number of symbolic models spanning several high-level cognitive domains. It uses the ACT-R cognitive architecture to provide a unified framework for the models.

The connectionist approach is better served by texts. Much of the connectionist revival in the 1980s can be traced to the two volumes by McClelland, Rumelhart and the PDP research group (McClelland & Rumelhart, 1986; Rumelhart & McClelland, 1986b), and these remain of significant scientific interest. More recent texts include McLeod, Plunkett, and Rolls (1998) and O'Reilly and Munakata (2000). The second of these is also strong on the rationale of cognitive modelling.

Van Gelder (1998) presents a manifesto for the dynamical approach to modelling. The manifesto is accompanied by a number of critical commentaries. Examples of the dynamical approach can be found in the edited collection of Port and van Gelder (1995).

The case for cognitive architectures is presented by Newell (1990, 1992). Newell's focus is on one specific "candidate" architecture, Soar, but his arguments are phrased in general terms. Some concerns about the architectural approach are expressed in the commentaries accompanying Newell (1992), and by Cooper and Shallice (1995).

Chapter 2

An Introduction to COGENT

Richard P. Cooper and Peter Yule

Overview: The COGENT modelling environment is introduced through an overview of its principal features and a detailed worked example — a model of serial position effects in free recall from verbal short term memory. The example is used to illustrate the process of model building and evaluation within COGENT. Issues covered include: research programme management; representation; creating and editing box and arrow diagrams; COGENT's rule language; facilities for producing graphical output; facilities for separating a cognitive model from its task environment; and facilities for developing simple experiment scripts.

2.1 COGENT: Principal Features

COGENT is a computational modelling environment that provides a system within which information processing models of cognitive processes may be developed and explored. The system provides a range of functions that allow students and researchers alike to explore ideas and theories relating to cognitive processes without commitment to a particular architecture. COGENT has been designed to simplify rigorous development and testing of models, and to aid data analysis and reporting. Among the functions provided by the COGENT environment are:

- A visual programming environment;
- A range of standard functional components, including rule-based processes, memory buffers, simple connectionist networks, input "sources", and output "sinks";
- An expressive, extensible, rule-based modelling language and implementation system;

- Mechanisms for the control of inter-component communication;
- Automated data visualisation tools, including tables, graphs, and animated diagrams;
- A powerful model testing environment, supporting Monte Carlo-style simulations and an "experiment-based" scripting language;
- Research programme management tools, allowing related models to be encapsulated within a research programme and providing a graphical display of the relations between models within such a programme;
- Version control on models; and
- Support for documentation of the research.

2.1.1 The Visual Programming Environment

COGENT simplifies the process of model development by providing a visual programming environment in which models may be created, edited, and tested. The visual programming environment allows users to develop cognitive models using a box and arrow notation that builds upon the concepts of functional modularity (from cognitive psychology) and object-oriented design (from computer science). Functional modularity views a cognitive process as the product of a set of interacting sub-processes, where each sub-process has an identifiable function that contributes to the whole and the interactions between sub-processes are limited in range (see, for example, Fodor, 1983). Object-oriented design analyses complex computational systems in terms of sub-systems of different types, with the behaviour of each sub-system being determined in part by its type and the values of a set of properties that are specific to each type of sub-system (see, for example, Rumbaugh, Blaha, Premerlani, Eddy, & Lorensen, 1991; Graham, 1994).

Models are specified in COGENT by sketching their functional components using COGENT's graphical model editor. Thus, Figure 2.1 shows a box and arrow diagram depicting a classic theory from cognitive psychology — the Modal Model of memory (Atkinson & Shiffrin, 1968, 1971). The diagram shows five functional components, four of which are central to the Modal Model: *I/O Process* (a process that acts as an interface between the memory systems and any task to which they are applied), *STS* (a short-term store in which information is temporarily placed while it it rehearsed), *LTS* (a long-term store in which information is consolidated), and *Rehearsal* (a process that transfers information from *STS* to *LTS*). The one remaining component of the diagram — *Task Environment* — is a compound box (i.e., a box containing further internal structure) that is used to administer a task when testing the model.

Different shaped boxes within a COGENT box and arrow diagram represent different types of component. Hexagonal boxes represent processes that transform information, rounded rectangular boxes represent buffers that store information, and rectangular boxes represent compound systems with internal structure. Simi-

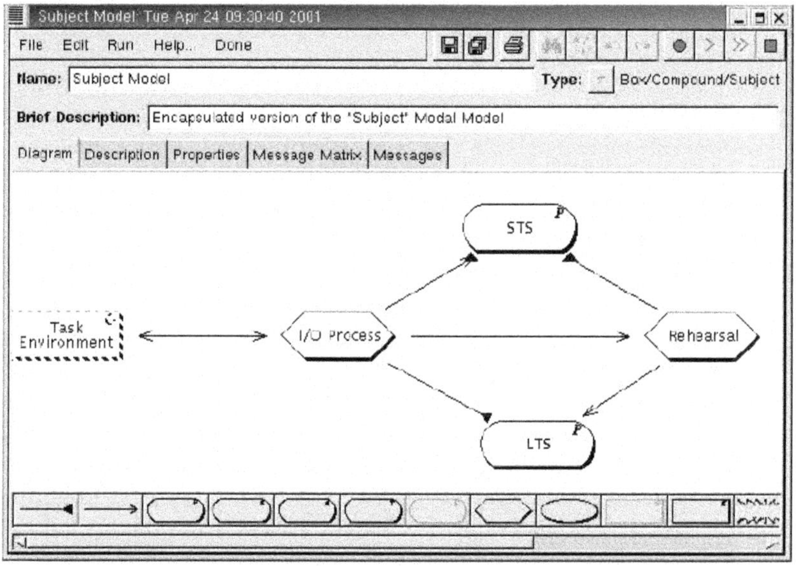

Figure 2.1: A box and arrow diagram of the Modal Model of memory (as developed later in this chapter)

larly, different styles of arrows indicate different types of communication between the components, such as reading information from a buffer or sending messages to a process. The graphical model editor provides facilities for creating models using these and other standard types of component. Components provided in addition to the above include simple feed-forward networks, interactive activation networks and input/output devices.

A number of different types of information may be associated with a model. This information may be viewed or edited by selecting the appropriate tab on the main portion of the model editor window (Figure 2.1). The **Diagram** view is shown in the figure. Other views (**Description**, **Properties**, **Message Matrix**, and **Messages**) provide access to: a text window into which notes or comments on the model may be entered; the set of properties and parameters that control aspects of the model's execution; a two-dimensional map that shows, during model execution, inter-component communication; and a text-based view of messages generated or received by the model's top-level box.

2.1.2 Standard Component Types

COGENT provides a library of standard configurable components (boxes and arrows). Models are constructed by assembling these components into a box and arrow diagram and then configuring them as necessary. The component library includes:

Rule-based processes: Rule-based processes manipulate information according to user-specified symbolic rules. A powerful rule language and rule interpreter allow rule-based processes to perform complex manipulations and transformations of information. Such processing may be contingent upon the contents of other COGENT objects.

Memory buffers: Buffers are general information storage devices. They may be used for both short term and long term storage, and different subtypes of buffer may be used to store information in different formats (e.g., propositional, tabular, and analogue). The detailed behaviour of any instance of a buffer is determined by its properties, which specify such things as capacity limitations, decay parameters, and access restrictions. The use of properties to specify buffer behaviour (and in fact, the behaviour of all COGENT objects) leads to components that are both flexible (i.e., can perform a variety of functions) and well-specified (i.e., the various property values fully define the computational behaviour of the component).

Connectionist networks: COGENT is intended primarily for high-level symbolic modelling. Nevertheless, COGENT's generalised processing engine allows direct interface with some simple connectionist objects (two-layer feed-forward networks and interactive activation networks). This facility makes COGENT suitable for a variety of hybrid modelling applications. As in the case of buffers, precise network behaviour is determined by properties associated with the network. These properties govern learning rate, initialisation, the activation function, etc.

I/O sources and sinks: Specialised data source components allow data to be fed into other components in a controlled manner. Data sinks by contrast allow the collection of data from other components during model execution. Three types of data sink — text-based sinks, tabular sinks, and graphical sinks — allow a range of options for storage and presentation of model output.

Inter-module communication links: Inter-module communication is indicated within a COGENT box and arrow diagram by arrows drawn between the boxes. Two basic types of arrow are provided: read arrows and write/send arrows.

Further details of these component types are given below.

2.1.3 The Rule-Based Modelling Language

COGENT's rule-based modelling language allows complex processes to be specified in terms of production-like rules. Each rule consists of a set of conditions

IF: `operator(Move,possible)` is in *Possible Operators*
`evaluate_operator(Move,Value)`
THEN: delete `operator(Move,possible)` from *Possible Operators*
add `operator(Move,value(Value))` to *Possible Operators*

Box 2.1: A simple rule that updates a buffer

and a set of actions. Conditions include logical operations whose outcome may be true or false, such as testing the equality of data elements, as well as operations that set variables, such as matching some information stored in a buffer. Actions allow messages of various forms to be sent to other boxes. The rule language is highly expressive. While this introduces some complexities, structured rule editors simplify the process of specifying rules and other tools allow the processing of rules during model execution to be monitored.

An example rule is shown in Box 2.1. This rule fires when *Possible Operators* (a buffer) contains an element of the form `operator(Move,possible)`, and the condition `evaluate_operator(Move,Value)` can be satisfied. On firing, the rule deletes one element from *Possible Operators* (`operator(Move,possible)`) and adds another (`operator(Move,value(Value))`).

Rules are contained within processes (the hexagonal boxes within a COGENT box and arrow diagram: see Figure 2.1), and may be supplemented with user-defined conditions. Such conditions may be used to provide additional control over the circumstances in which rules apply. This is illustrated by the rule in Box 2.1: `evaluate_operator(Move,Value)` is a call to a user-defined condition, the definition of which is specified elsewhere. The condition definition language is based on Prolog (see Bratko, 1986; Sterling, 1986; Clocksin & Mellish, 1987), a highly expressive AI programming language which provides COGENT with substantial flexibility.

The rules and condition definitions of a process are listed in a standard format within the process' Rules and Condition Definitions view. This view also provides access to specialised rule editing facilities. Figure 2.2 shows this view for *Select Operators*, a process from a model of problem solving described in Chapter 4.

2.1.4 Automated Data Visualisation Tools

COGENT provides a number of visualisation tools to assist in the monitoring and evaluation of a model. These tools take the form of additional types of box, and allow data to be displayed in standard tabular or graphical forms. More sophisticated visualisations may also be crafted through use of a generalised graphical display box.

Tables Tables allow data to be displayed in a standard two-dimensional format, as in Figure 2.3. Messages sent to a table specify values for the various cells. Tables are updated dynamically during the execution of a model, with details of table layout for any particular table (e.g., row height, column width, row and column labels, etc.) being governed by that table's properties.

Two types of table are provided. Output tables are write-only: data sent to such tables are displayed but cannot be inspected by other components. Buffer tables are read/write: other components connected to the buffer with read access may query the value in any cell. This querying is governed by the buffer's access properties, which allow access to be based on either temporal features of buffer elements (e.g., primacy, recency) or spatial features of the elements (e.g., left/right, right/left).

Graphs Data may be displayed graphically in several standard formats, including line graphs, scatter plots, and bar charts. Figure 2.4 shows a line graph of data generated by a model of the Glanzer and Cunitz (1966) free recall task. A single graph may be used to display multiple data sets in different colours. Messages sent to a graph specify data points or style information relating to a particular data set. As with tables, graphs are updated dynamically during model execution and presentational details are controlled through configurable properties associated with the graph.

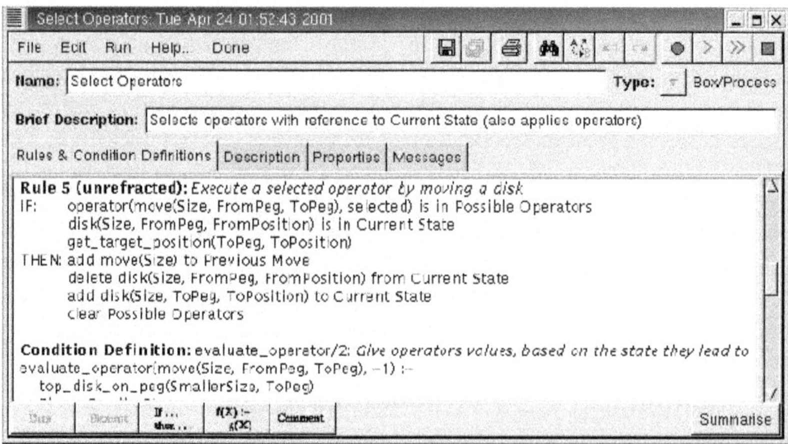

Figure 2.2: Some rules from the *Select Operator* process within a problem solving model (see Chapter 4)

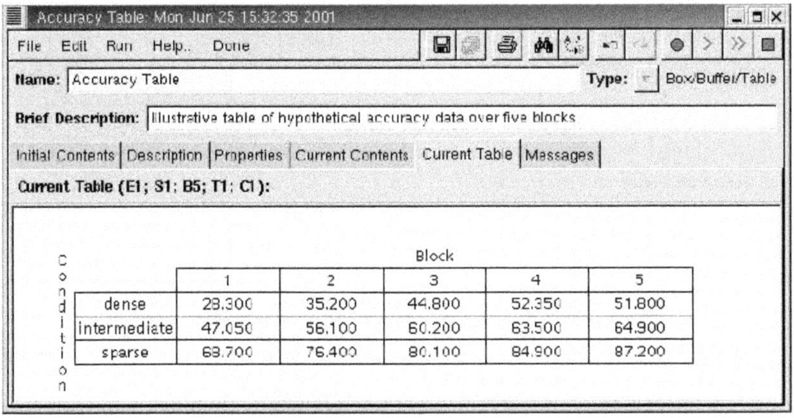

Figure 2.3: A table buffer, displaying data accumulated over five blocks of a task

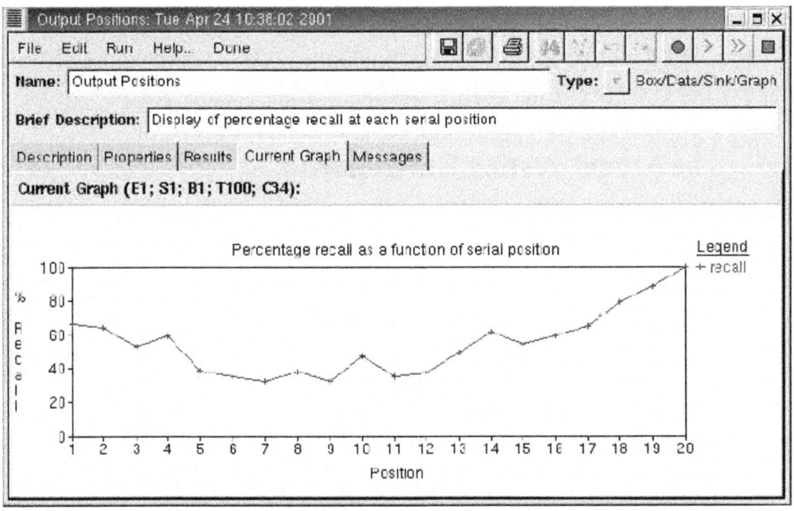

Figure 2.4: A graphical buffer, showing a line graph summarising output from a model of memory applied to a free recall task

Generalised Graphical Output Facilities are also provided for more general graphical output. Propositional buffers may be augmented with visualisation rules which map buffer elements to graphical objects (e.g., lines, shapes, or text at specified coordinate positions), and these graphical objects may be stored and viewed directly within analogue buffers. To illustrate, Figure 2.5 shows a visualisation of the contents of a propositional buffer whose contents represent disks in the

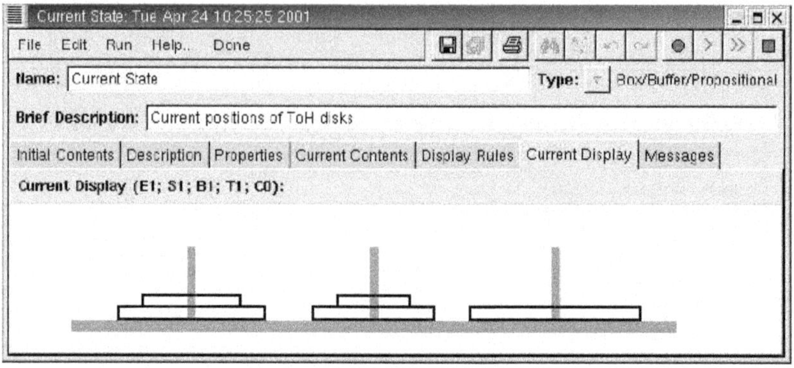

Figure 2.5: A visualisation of a propositional buffer's contents, showing an intermediate state of the Tower of Hanoi problem

Tower of Hanoi problem. (This problem is discussed at length in Chapter 4.) Displays associated with propositional and analogue buffers are dynamically updated whenever the contents of the buffer change.

2.1.5 The Model Testing Environment

All COGENT models share an underlying processing system that supports four levels of execution: trial, block, subject, and experiment. These levels correspond directly to their analogues in experimental psychology. The simplest way of using COGENT is to run a single trial. Normally this involves presenting a single stimulus and gathering a single response. However, it is also possible to specify extended experimental designs, in which, for example, numerous virtual subjects are run in each of several experimental conditions, with each experimental condition involving a number of blocks and each block involving a number of trials. Such designs are constructed through a special purpose experiment script editor.

The model testing environment also provides a range of facilities for monitoring and debugging models. Monitoring is provided through the **Messages** view available on each component's window. This view shows all messages generated or received by a component. Thus, Figure 2.6 shows the messages relating to the *Select Operators* process mentioned above after 7 processing cycles. Each line shows the cycle on which the message was received or generated, the source of the message (e.g., Rule 5 of *Select Operator*), the message's destination (e.g., *Previous Move*), and the message's content (e.g., `add(move(30))`). Other facilities allow the traffic between components within a compound box to be monitored (through the box's **Message Matrix** view), and the execution of specific conditions within rules to be traced.

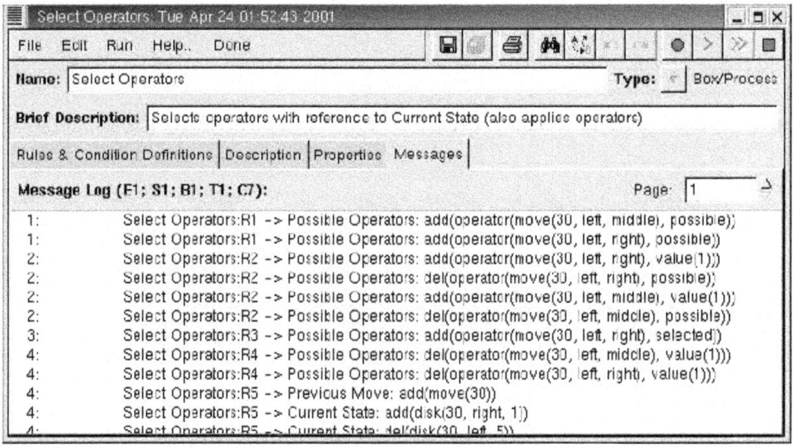

Figure 2.6: The **Messages** view of *Select Operators*

2.1.6 Research Programme Management

The development of a cognitive model typically takes place over an extended period of time. COGENT supports this development through tools for managing sets of models within a *research programme* (see Lakatos, 1970). These tools include a graphical display of the models contained within a research programme (showing ancestral links between models), facilities for version control on models (e.g., copying and archiving), documentation support, and a front-end to the graphical model editor described above.

Access to research programme management tools is through the Research Programme Manager, shown in Figure 2.7. The left side of the window shows all research programmes registered with COGENT. When a research programme is selected its history is displayed in the frame on the right in the form of a tree. Each node in the tree corresponds to a separate model, and double-clicking on a node opens COGENT's model editor on the corresponding model. The progress of time is represented in the history diagram along the horizontal axis, with models to the right being developed after models to the left. Links in the tree show ancestral relations between successive versions of the same model. As can be seen from the figure, several versions of a model may be explored in parallel.

2.2 An Illustrative Task: Free Recall

The remainder of this chapter introduces many of the basic concepts of COGENT through a tutorial-style development of an implementation of a classic cogni-

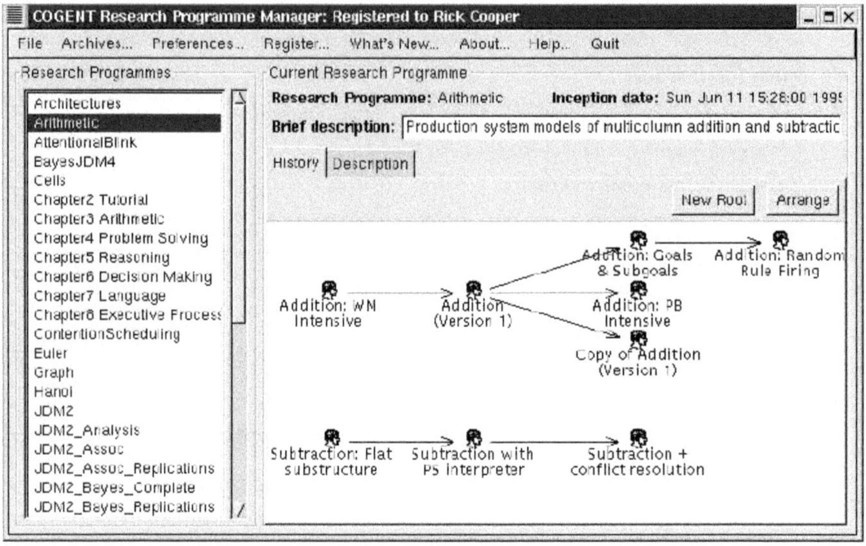

Figure 2.7: The research programme history view

tive model: Atkinson and Shiffrin's so-called "Modal Model" of human memory (Atkinson & Shiffrin, 1968, 1971). The model, called "modal" because most psychologists subscribed to it at one point, is no longer current (though elements of it remain in more recent theories of memory), but it is used here because it serves as a good illustration of how COGENT can be used to implement concepts and models from the psychological literature.

The Modal Model was developed to explain the recency and primacy effects in free recall serial position curves (Glanzer & Cunitz, 1966; Postman & Phillips, 1965). In a free recall paradigm, participants are presented with a list of words, one at a time, and instructed to memorise the words as well as possible so that they may recall as many as possible in a subsequent free recall phase. Because the words are presented serially, it is possible to plot the average accuracy of recall at each point in the series, as in Figure 2.8. The typical finding is that the curve is roughly U-shaped: words at the beginning of the list are recalled relatively well, as are words at the end of the list, but those in the middle are poorly recalled. The peak at the beginning is known as the *primacy effect* and the peak at the end is known as the *recency effect*.

The recency effect can be explained by postulating two distinct memory stores: a limited-capacity but relatively reliable Short-Term Store (STS), and an unlimited capacity but relatively unreliable Long-Term Store (LTS). According to the Modal Model, the items in the recency portion of the free recall curve are recalled well because they are still held in the STS, whereas those earlier in the curve are

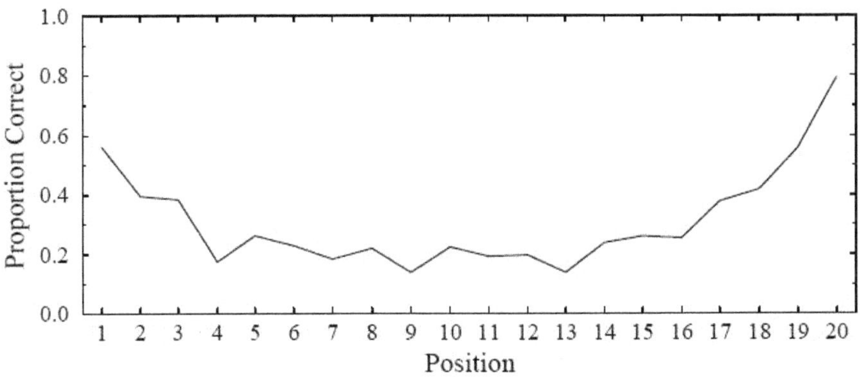

Figure 2.8: Typical recall accuracy as a function of serial position in the free recall task (adapted from Glanzer & Cunitz, 1966)

recalled relatively poorly since they are only held in the decay-prone LTS. If participants can recall from either store, one would expect a peak at the end of the curve, spanning as many items as the postulated capacity limitation of STS will allow (e.g., 7±2 items: Miller, 1956).

The primacy effect requires a different explanation. In the Modal Model it is assumed to result from a limited-capacity process of *Rehearsal*, which is used to transfer information from STS to LTS. The explanation depends on the fact that at the beginning of the list there are relatively few items to rehearse, so these items receive disproportionately more rehearsal than items later in the list. Assuming that more rehearsal implies better recall, they should therefore be remembered better.

2.3 Getting Started

Exercise 2.1: Download the COGENT software from the web site given in the preface and follow the installation instructions given on the web site. Ensure that the installation is successful before continuing. ◇

As noted in Section 2.1.6, COGENT groups models into research programmes which support the development of a model through time. This development process is illustrated by the current tutorial, in which a succession of more sophisticated versions of the Modal Model will be constructed. We therefore begin by creating a new research programme that will contain these models.

Exercise 2.2: Start COGENT and select File → New... from the menu bar at the top of the COGENT window. A dialogue box will appear prompting you for a name for the new research programme. Enter an appropriate name (avoid using slash characters in the name) and click on Create. Your new research programme will be registered in the left panel of the COGENT window. The right panel should be empty. ◇

A number of basic research programme functions are available from the File menu option at the top of the COGENT window. These allow creating, copying, renaming, deleting, and printing. These functions are also available from the popup menu that appears when you right-click on the name of a research programme in the panel on the left of the window.

A further set of research programme management functions is available within COGENT's archive browser, which is accessed through the Archive... button on the top of the main window. These functions allow complete research programmes to be converted to or from a single compacted file, which may then be copied to floppy disk or sent by email.

2.4 Specifying Basic Experimenter Functions

The first consideration that arises in much modelling concerns the context or task in which the model is to be tested. In order to simulate free recall, it will be necessary to present to the model a sequence of stimuli and to collect from the model the set of recalled stimuli. COGENT provides basic facilities for doing this in the form of data sources and data sinks as referred to in Section 2.1.2. Figure 2.9 shows how three COGENT boxes of different types may be arranged to provide the necessary functionality. The box on the left, *Input Words*, is a data source. It will present the list of words to the model. The box on the right, *Output Words*, is a text data sink. It will collect the model's output. The box in the centre, *I/O Process*, is a process that, when the model is complete, will provide an interface between the model and the task environment.

Exercise 2.3: The first step in constructing the Modal Model (as for any COGENT model) is to sketch an appropriate box and arrow diagram. Return to the COGENT Research Programme Manager window, and select the project that you created earlier. Click on the New Root button on the right side of the window. An icon (with the label *Unnamed*) will appear in the history panel. This icon corresponds to a blank model that will be developed in subsequent exercises into a simple version of the Modal Model. ◇

There are two ways to create new models within COGENT. Use of the New Root button as described above creates an empty model. Alternatively, an existing

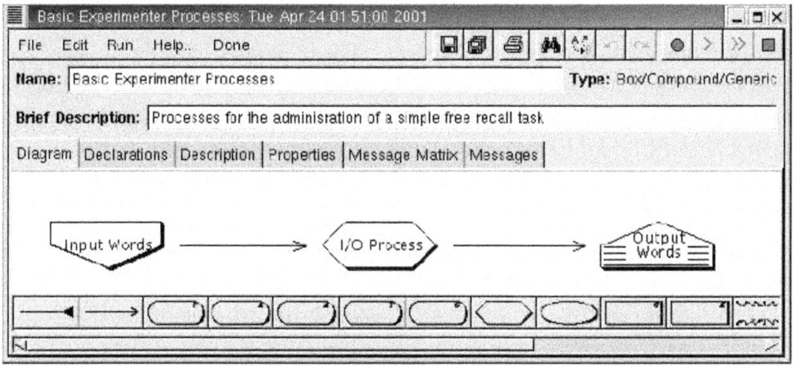

Figure 2.9: An outline system for Modal Model development

model can be copied by right-clicking on its icon and selecting **Create Copy** from the popup menu that appears. This creates an exact copy of the existing model, which may then be modified without affecting the original model.

Exercise 2.4: Double-click on the *Unnamed* icon created in the previous exercise. This will open a new window containing the specification of the model. Because the model is empty most of the data fields in the window will be empty. Give the model a name and a brief description by typing into the appropriate fields. The structure of the diagram that we are building is shown in Figure 2.9. You might copy the name and description from that figure. ◇

Box and arrow diagrams are created and edited by selecting instances of boxes from the palette at the foot of a model's window (see Figure 2.9) and placing them on the **Diagram** canvas. Each button on the palette corresponds to a different type of box (or arrow), and the type of a box is indicated by its shape and annotations. Thus, rectangles with rounded ends correspond to buffers, hexagons correspond to processes, and the five sided figures correspond to data sources and data sinks. Once a box has been placed on the canvas, its position may be adjusted by dragging the box with the mouse. Alternatively it may be deleted by right-clicking on it and selecting **Delete** from the popup menu that appears.

Exercise 2.5: Add the three boxes shown in Figure 2.9 to your blank canvas. Be sure that each box is of the correct type. Do not at this stage worry about drawing the arrows or labelling the boxes. ◇

Every box in a box and arrow diagram may be opened either by double-clicking on it or by right-clicking on it and selecting **Open** → **Edit...** from the popup menu that appears. When a box is opened a new window is created and the details of the box are displayed in that window. These details include the box's name, description, contents, properties, etc. The basic layout follows that of Figure 2.9, but the views available in the main portion of the window are dependent on the box type, because different types of box have different types of information associated with them.

Exercise 2.6: Open each of the boxes in your model and name them by entering an appropriate name in each box's Name field. After naming each box save your edits (by clicking on the "Save to disk" button at the top of the box's window) and close it by using the Done button on the menu-bar at the top of the box's window. ◇

COGENT provides two types of arrow, corresponding to two different types of communication that may occur between boxes. Pointed arrows are referred to as send (or write) arrows. These indicate that information may be sent along the arrow in the indicated direction. Blunt triangular arrows are referred to as read arrows. These indicate that information may be extracted from a box (normally a buffer) by another box. (There are no read arrows in Figure 2.9. See Figure 2.1 for examples.) Arrows with combined standard and blunt triangular heads indicate that the arrow's source box may both send information to and extract information from the arrow's destination box.

Arrows are drawn on the diagram canvas by first selecting the arrow type from the palette, left-clicking on the arrow's source box, dragging the cursor to the arrow's destination box, and releasing the mouse button. Combined read/write arrows may be created by drawing separate read and write arrows between the appropriate boxes. Arrows may be deleted or modified by right-clicking on them and selecting the desired function from the popup menu that appears. Their end-points may also be adjusted by dragging them from one box to another.

Exercise 2.7: Fill in the arrows between the Modal Model components. Refer to Figure 2.9 where necessary. ◇

The next stage in specifying the functions of the experiment environment involves populating the boxes with appropriate information. *Input Words* requires a sequence of words. As a temporary stand-in *I/O Process* may be specified to pass all information that it receives (from *Input Words*) directly to *Output Words*. As the model is developed this specification will be updated such that words are stored in and recalled from a full implementation of the Modal Model.

All COGENT boxes contain things, but different types of box contain different types of thing. Data sources contain input data elements such as:

send `memorise(black)` to *I/O Process*

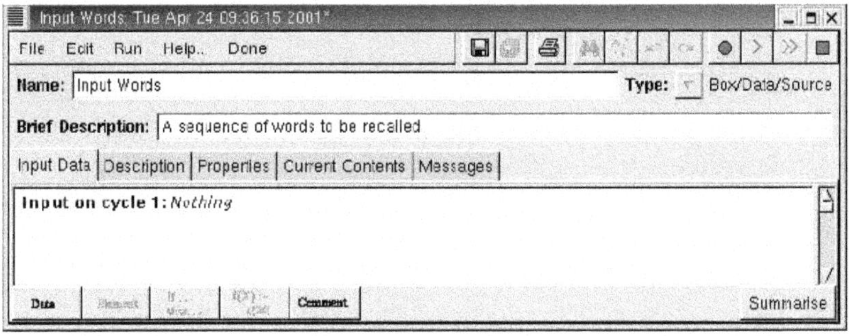

Figure 2.10: The data source with one dummy element

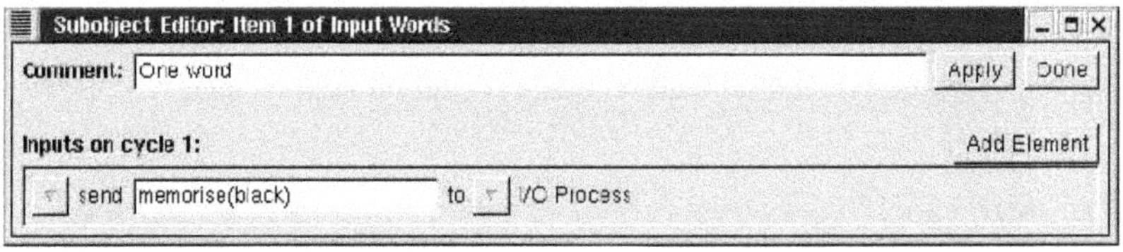

Figure 2.11: The data element editor, showing a complete specification of the first element

This input data element is a COGENT instruction that, when processed, results in a message of the form `memorise(black)` being sent to the box named *I/O Process*.

An input data element may be added to a data source by opening the data source (by double-clicking on it) and clicking on the **Input Data** button on the palette at the bottom of the data source's window and then clicking on the window's central canvas. Doing this will create a new, empty, data input element, as in Figure 2.10. The element may then be edited (to specify its content and its destination) by double-clicking on it and entering the appropriate information in the data element editor that appears.

The data element editor (see Figure 2.11) consists of a space for a comment describing the element, a label indicating the cycle on which the input will be received (as described below), three buttons (**Apply**, **Done** and **Add Element**), and a panel which displays the element's content. When the editor is opened on an empty element this panel will be blank. Content may be added by clicking on the **Add Element** button and selecting a type of element from the menu that appears. In the current case, we are only interested in elements of type **send**, as we wish to send a message to *I/O Process*. Appropriate content can thus be specified by selecting **send** from the menu, and filling in the details of the message content and destination. The message content should be typed in the text field following the word **send**. It should be of the general form `memorise(`*word*`)`, where, as discussed

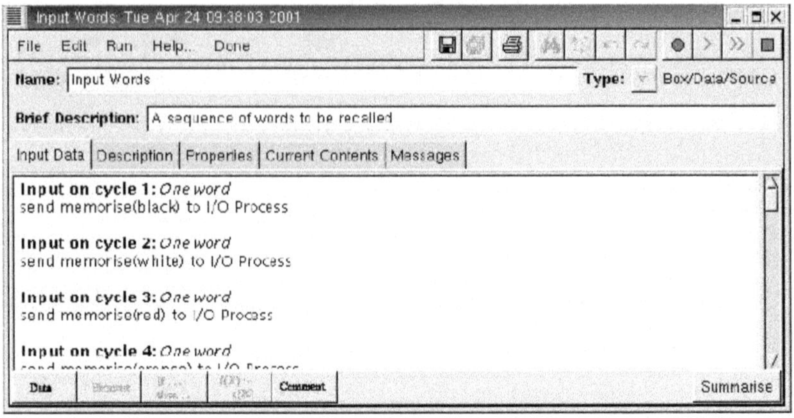

Figure 2.12: A view of the completed data source

below, *word* should consist entirely of letters, without spaces, and should begin with a lower-case letter. The message destination may be selected from the list of box names shown on the popup menu that appears when the button following the word "to" is selected. Once the message has been specified the data element editor may be closed using the Done button. The message should then appear in full on the main canvas of *Input Words*.

Exercise 2.8: Create 20 input data elements in *Input Words*, such that 20 different words are passed to *I/O Process* on successive processing cycles. Once all elements have been entered, save *Input Words* by clicking on its "Save to disk" button. The final contents of the data source should be similar to Figure 2.12. For current purposes the words used do not matter, but in a realistic free recall experiment word frequency, imagibility, and length would be controlled for. That is, the words would be of approximately equal frequency, imagibility and length. They would also be randomised within the list, such that different subjects received different word sequences. Randomisation will be addressed later in the chapter. ◇

When a model is executed, the elements of any data sources within the model are fed into the model at specified times. The time at which an element is fed in is indicated by the cycle number, which is like a clock that ticks as the model runs, with one tick per cycle. Thus, with *Input Words* specified as in Figure 2.12, the message `memorise(black)` will be passed to *I/O Process* on the first tick. On the second tick, the message `memorise(white)` will be passed to *I/O Process*, and so on. Each "tick" is referred to as a single step of the model's execution cycle.

Table 2.1: The run buttons and their meanings

●	Initialise	Initialise all components of the model
>	Step	Step through one processing cycle
»	Run	Run until termination
■	Stop	Halt processing

The four red buttons in the top right corner of a box's window control execution of the model. Their functions are described in brief in Table 2.1. The four buttons are repeated on all windows for convenience only. Each button initialises, steps, runs, or stops the complete model. Initialisation effectively sets the execution clock to zero. Once a model has been initialised, it can be stepped through individual cycles (using the step button), or run until it terminates (using the run button). The stop button allows processing to be interrupted.

Exercise 2.9: Open *I/O Process* and select the **Messages** view from the list of tabs across the top of the window's canvas area. This view displays messages received and sent by the box when the model is run. Click the initialise button and then the step button. The following message should appear in the window's canvas area:

1: Input Words → I/O Process: memorise(black)

This shows that on cycle 1, *I/O Process* received a message from *Input Words*, and the content of that message was `memorise(black)`.

Step through a few more cycles, and try running the fledgling model to termination. All words in *Input Words* should be sent in succession to *I/O Process*. The model should then terminate. ◇

The next stage in developing the model environment involves specifying a rudimentary behaviour for *I/O Process*. So far, this process receives messages but does nothing with them. Processes may contain rules, which may be triggered into acting by the receipt of messages. The rules' actions may then modify buffers or pass messages to other model components. In the absence of any buffers in the present fledgling model, we will create a simple rule that forwards all received messages straight to *Output Words*.

COGENT rules consist of a set of conditions, a set of actions, and, optionally, a trigger. The conditions are statements that may, at any time, be true or false of the model's state. The actions are similar to data source elements: they may involve sending messages to other boxes, or modifying buffers by adding or deleting

Rule 1 (unrefracted): *A very simple rule to send input straight to output*
TRIGGER: `memorise(Word)`
IF: True
THEN: send `Word` to *Output Words*

Box 2.2: A rule that forwards to-be-memorised words to *Output Words*

buffer elements. A trigger is a special device that allows rules to be activated only when the process containing them receives a message that matches the trigger. Rules and their processing are described in more detail below.

The forwarding rule required for the present task is shown in Box 2.2. This rule has a trigger (`memorise(Word)`), no specific conditions (as indicated by "IF: True"), and a single action (to send `Word` to *Output Words*). The use of upper-case letters in the two instances of `Word` is critical. This indicates that `Word` is a variable. Its value is not fixed to any specific word (e.g., `black` or `white`), but may vary depending on the message that is received by the process. Thus, when the process receives the message `memorise(black)`, `Word` will be temporarily mapped (or bound) to `black`, and `black` will be sent to *Output Words*. When the process receives the message `memorise(white)`, however, `Word` will be temporarily mapped (or bound) to `white`, and `white` will be sent to *Output Words*. Variable binding is discussed in more depth in Section 2.6.2.

A rule is created by opening the process which is to contain it (e.g., *I/O Process*), placing a dummy rule on the main canvas (by clicking on the If...Then... button on the palette and then clicking on the canvas, in a way analogous to the creation of data source elements and box and arrow elements), and editing that dummy rule (by double-clicking on the dummy rule, again in a way analogous to the editing of data source elements and box and arrow elements).

The rule editor, which is shown in Figure 2.13, is similar to the data element editor, but it has several additional fields to allow specification of a rule's trigger, conditions, and actions. There are also several checkboxes to allow specification of various attributes of a rule's execution (such as whether the rule is triggered by a message or whether it can fire whenever its conditions hold). Use of the rule editor parallels use of the data element editor. The Add Condition button provides access to a menu that lists a wide range of pre-specified COGENT conditions. The Add Action button gives access to a menu of different action types. If the checkbox for Rule is triggered? is checked, the Trigger: field will be activated, and a trigger term for the rule may be specified.

Exercise 2.10: Use the rule editor to specify the above rule in *I/O Process*. Be sure that variables are used appropriately (i.e., that `Word` begins with an upper-case

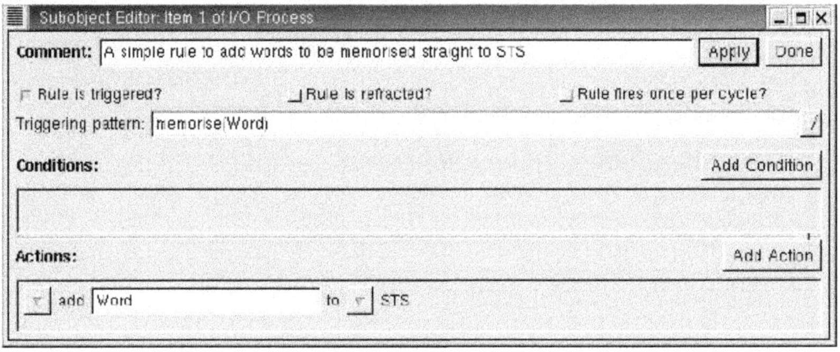

Figure 2.13: The rule editor, showing a rule that sends all input directly to *Output Words*

`W`) and that no space is left between `memorise` and the opening bracket. When finished, run the model and examine the **Messages** view of each box. Notice how the variable in the rule (`Word`) is bound differently on each cycle. Notice also the computational parallelism in the model: while *Input Words* is generating one word, *I/O Process* is processing the previous word, and *Output Words* is recording the word before that. Thus, all boxes may be active at the same time. ◇

2.5 The Modal Model in COGENT

Now that the experimental infrastructure is in place, we may begin to specify the psychological content of the model: the short-term store, the long-term store, the rehearsal process, and a recall mechanism.

2.5.1 Building the Short-Term Store

We begin by adding a short-term store to the *I/O Process*. (Recall that the short-term store was held to be responsible for the recency effects in free recall.) The short-term store may be implemented within COGENT as a propositional buffer. The *I/O Process* must be able to write to this buffer (when it receives messages corresponding to words to be memorised) and read from the buffer (when it needs to recall all memorised words). An appropriate box and arrow representation is shown in Figure 2.14.

Exercise 2.11: We could carry on by augmenting the box and arrow diagram in Figure 2.9 with boxes necessary to implement the Modal Model. However, it is better practice to preserve the initial skeletal model and work on a copy. Therefore, close the version of the model you were working on above by finding the top-level

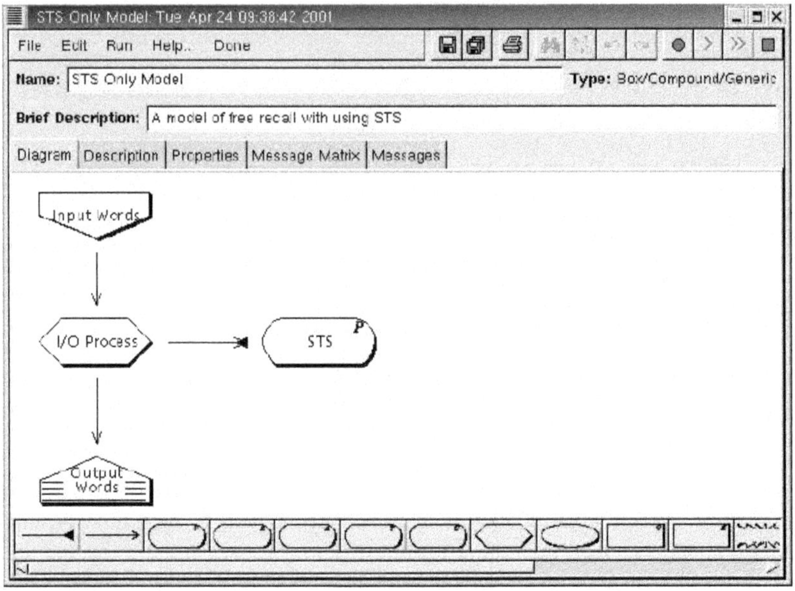

Figure 2.14: The box and arrow diagram with the Short-Term Store

box (i.e., that named **Basic Experimenter Processes** in Figure 2.9) and clicking on its **Done** button. Be sure to save any edits. Go back to the Research Programme Manager window and create a new version of the model based on the initial model by right-clicking on the initial model's node and selecting **Create Copy** from the popup menu that appears. A new node corresponding to a copy of the initial model will appear on the history diagram. Open the copy by double-clicking on this node, and revise its name and description. (Figure 2.14 contains suggestions for possible values for these fields.) Modify the box and arrow diagram to yield something equivalent to that in Figure 2.14. Be sure that the *STS* box is labelled, that it is a propositional buffer, and that it has arrows of both types leading to it from *I/O Process*. ◇

We are now ready to add a rule to *I/O Process* that will transfer incoming words to *STS*. Rule 1 of Box 2.3 is suitable. This rule will replace the temporary rule given in Box 2.2. The only significant difference between this rule and the earlier one is the action. (The use of the variable `X` in place of the variable `Word` is not significant. It simply demonstrates that the name of a variable is not important, so long as the name is used consistently throughout the rule.) The rule may be changed by opening *I/O Process*, double-clicking on the rule (to open the rule editor), using the menu-button to the left of the existing **send** action to change the

Rule 1 (unrefracted): *Add words straight to STS*
TRIGGER: `memorise(X)`
IF: True
THEN: add `X` to *STS*

Rule 2 (unrefracted): *Recall from STS*
TRIGGER: `recall`
IF: `X` is in *STS*
THEN: send `X` to *Output Words*

Box 2.3: Rules for memorisation and recall of words using *STS*

action type to add, and then filling in the variables appropriately.

Exercise 2.12: Create the rule as described above. Be sure that upper-case letters are used for the variables, and that the same letter is used for both variables. Save the edits, open *STS*, and select the Current Contents view from the list of tabs across the top of the canvas area. Run the model and observe how elements are now added to *STS* as the model runs. ◇

A second rule is required for recall. When recall is triggered, this rule should fire once for each element in *STS*, and send a copy of that element to *Output Words*. Rule 2 of Box 2.3 is appropriate. There are two important features of this rule. First, its trigger is `recall`. The rule relies upon a message of this form being sent to *I/O Process* to trigger the rule and hence the process of recalling all memorised words. Second, the rule includes a condition that tests for elements in *STS*. This condition is specified in the rule editor by selecting match from the Add Condition menu.

Below, *Input Words* will be modified such that, once it has sent all the words to be memorised to *I/O Process*, it will send an additional message of the form `recall`. This message will not trigger Rule 1 — the rule for memorising words — as it doesn't match Rule 1's trigger. However, it will trigger the rule for recalling words (Rule 2). Similarly, words sent to the process for memorising will not trigger recall, because they will be sent as messages of the form `memorise(Word)`, which will not match the recall rule's trigger.

Exercise 2.13: Add the above rule to *I/O Process*. The resulting process should have two rules, as shown in Figure 2.15. Also add an input data element to *Input Words* that sends `recall` to *I/O Process* after all the words have been sent. Run the model and note how the words are first added to *STS*, and then recalled from *STS* and sent to *Output Words* on the final processing cycle. Notice in particular that

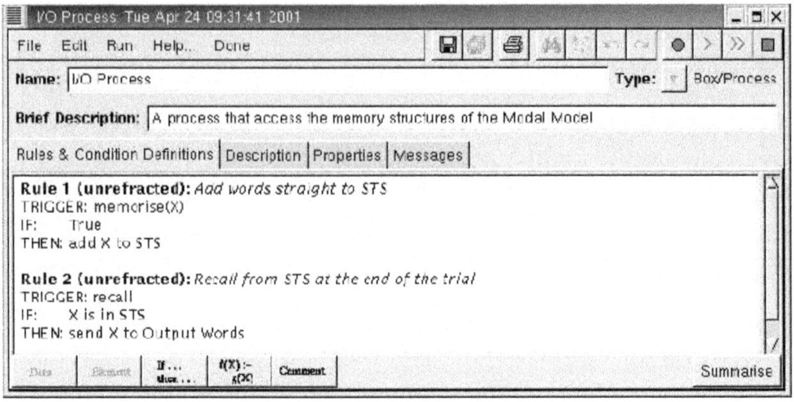

Figure 2.15: Rules in *I/O Process*

all words are recalled at the same time. Unless otherwise specified, COGENT rules are fired with all possible variable bindings. On the final processing cycle, there are 20 different variable bindings for the rule (corresponding to the 20 different words in the input sequence). Each variable binding generates a separate instance of the rule, and each instance fires on the last cycle, effectively in parallel. ◇

Now as was mentioned before, in the Modal Model the short-term store is supposed to be capacity-limited with a span of about 7 items. This limitation may be placed on the buffer by setting a *property* associated with the buffer. Properties control various aspects of the functioning of all boxes. In the case of buffers, they control aspects such as capacity, decay, and access.

Exercise 2.14: Switch to the Properties view of the *STS* box (by selecting Properties from the list of tabs above the canvas of the *STS* box). Find the Limited Capacity property and set it by checking its checkbox. This property works in conjunction with the Capacity property, which should be set to 7. At this point, also find the On Excess property and set it to Oldest. Now return to the Current Contents view, re-initialise the model and step through the trial again. You should see that the number of items in *STS* grows until it reaches 7, after which point new additions to the buffer over-write existing elements — in this case the oldest element is always the one to be replaced. Return to the properties view, change the On Excess property to Random, and again step through the trial, viewing the current contents. This time, when the capacity limit is reached, a randomly selected item should be over-written by each new element. Run the model over the complete input data several times (with On Excess set to Random) and observe the output that appears in *Output Words* on each run. You should notice that words near the end of the list appear in the output more frequently than words near the beginning of the list. Thus, this one-buffer memory model generates a recency effect. Explore other values of the On Excess property. Explain the effects that the various values have on the model's behaviour. ◇

2.5.2 Adding the Long-Term Store

The short-term store alone can generate a respectable recency effect, but to produce a primacy effect as well we need to add two more components: a long-term store (*LTS*) — another propositional buffer — and a rehearsal process (*Rehearsal*). The rehearsal process is meant to be a way of transferring information from the short-term store to the long-term store. *Rehearsal* should therefore be able to read from *STS* and write to *LTS*. In order to recall from *LTS*, *I/O Process* should also be able to read *LTS*. Figure 2.16 shows the box and arrow diagram.

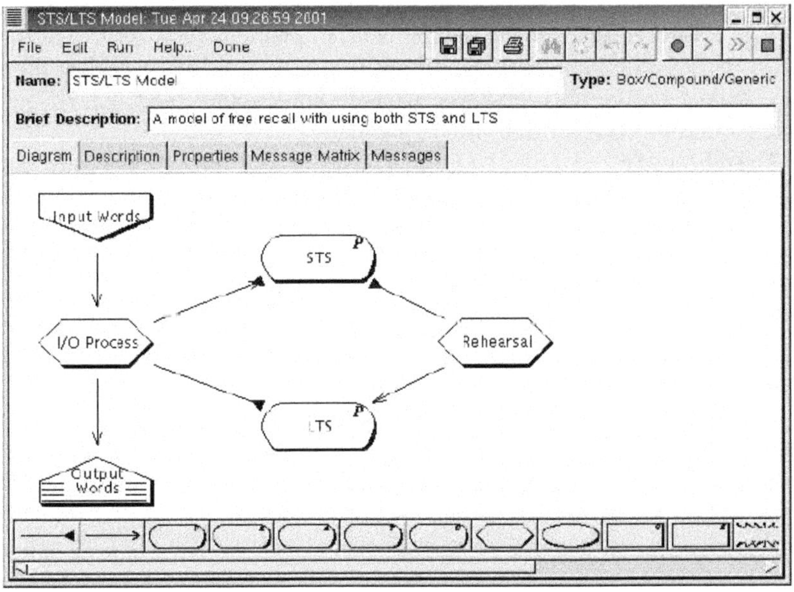

Figure 2.16: Box and arrow diagram of the full Modal Model

Exercise 2.15: Use the Research Programme Manager to create a copy of the model with the short-term store, and modify the box and arrow diagram of the copy to produce something equivalent to Figure 2.16. ◇

Rule 1 (unrefracted): *Rehearse from STS to LTS*
IF: `X` is in *STS*
THEN: add `X` to *LTS*

Box 2.4: A rehearsal rule that rehearses all words simultaneously

Next we need to make *Rehearsal* do something. Recall that its purpose is to take elements from *STS* and transfer them to *LTS*, and that it is capacity-limited. *Rehearsal* therefore requires a different kind of rule from the ones used previously. Firstly, the rehearsal process is not triggered by messages sent to it. Rather, it monitors *STS* and rehearses on the basis of elements found there. A rule such as Rule 1 of Box 2.4 might therefore seem reasonable. This rule has no trigger, and therefore is not restricted to firing only when some triggering message is received by *Rehearsal*. The difficulty with the rule relates to the second difference between this rule's requirements and the requirements of previous rules: the rehearsal process is capacity limited, so it should not rehearse all words in *STS* at the same time. Rule 1 will do this, however, because unless other specified, all possible instantiations of COGENT rules fire in parallel.

The rehearsal process may be limited by using other attributes of rules. Specifically, by limiting Rule 1 to fire at most once per cycle, we can be sure that only one word is ever rehearsed on each cycle. However, in this case a second attribute of the rule is also important. The refracted attribute controls whether a rule can fire multiple times with the same instantiations or values of its variables (possibly on different cycles). Refracted rules are limited such that they fire only once for any given instantiation of their variables. Thus, if a rule is refracted each time it fires it will fire with a different instantiation.

In the case of the rehearsal rule, if it were refracted (and this is the default for non-triggered rules), then it would rehearse a different word on each cycle (until all words had been rehearsed). As words come into *STS* one at a time, the effect of this would be that every word would get rehearsed exactly once. This is not what is required, as it would mean every word would be transferred to *LTS*, and hence every word would be available to recall. Instead, we require the rehearsal rule to be unrefracted, so the same word may be rehearsed again and again. This means some words may not be rehearsed at all. Those words will only be available to recall as long as they remain in *STS*.

Exercise 2.16: Open *Rehearsal* and create a new rule in the Rules and Condition Definitions view. Edit the new rule by double-clicking on it and entering the conditions and actions as given in the previous paragraph. Ensure that the three checkboxes are set appropriately: the rule should not be triggered, it should not

Rule 2 (unrefracted): *Stop rehearsal when recall begins*
TRIGGER: `recall`
IF: True
THEN: send `stop` to *Rehearsal*

Box 2.5: A rule to terminate rehearsal

be refracted, and it should fire (at most) once per cycle. Now if you switch to the **Current Contents** view of *LTS*, initialise and step through the model using the **Step** button, after a few steps you should see words accumulating in *LTS*. ◇

If you run a trial at this point, you will discover that it never stops. (Use the **Stop** button to terminate such runaway execution.) This is because the rehearsal rule is always able to fire, whatever else has happened. Consequently the model will continue rehearsing, even after recall. An *ad hoc* solution to this problem is to draw a send/write arrow from *I/O Process* to *Rehearsal*, and add a new rule to *I/O Process* that forcibly stops rehearsal. The special message `stop` may be sent to any COGENT box. Upon receipt, the box will immediately stop processing until COGENT is re-initialised. An appropriate rule is given in Box 2.5. With this and the previous recall rule (Box 2.3), a single `recall` message to *I/O Process* will both terminate rehearsal and trigger recall.

Exercise 2.17: Draw a send/write arrow from *I/O Process* to *Rehearsal* and create the above rule in *I/O Process*. Try running the model again to check that it terminates at the appropriate time. ◇

The rehearsal process is now complete, but the model requires that recall be possible from both *LTS* and *STS*. One solution to this would be to add another recall rule (similar to that in Figure 2.15) that matches against *LTS* instead of *STS*. An alternative solution is to define a new condition and use this as a condition of a single recall rule. The advantage of this solution is that it allows both recall rules to be condensed into one (and the advantage of this is that it allows the model to be modified to produce serial, rather than parallel, recall, as described later in the chapter).

COGENT provides a range of standard conditions, from simple matching of terms against buffer contents (as illustrated in the above rules) to more elaborate conditions relating to arithmetic, list processing, term comparison, and so on. COGENT also provides a mechanism to define additional conditions, and use these *user-defined* conditions in rules.

A condition consists of three main parts: a functor (which is essentially the condition's name), a set of arguments (which are the variables or terms related by

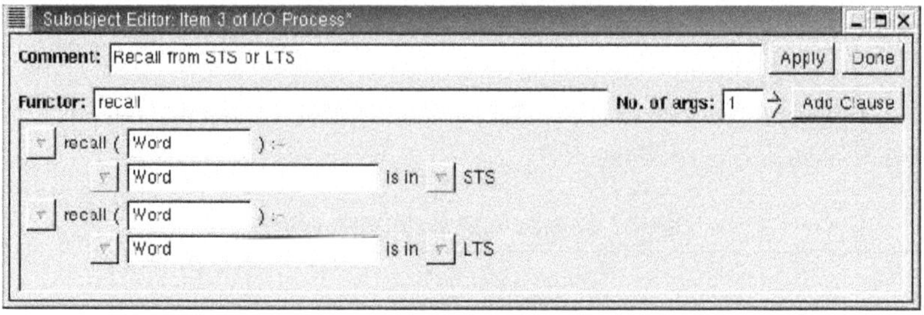

Figure 2.17: The condition editor, showing the recall condition

the condition), and a set of clauses (which define the cases when the condition is true). COGENT's condition editor, which is similar to the data element editor and the rule editor, helps to ensure that each of these parts is specified correctly.

Figure 2.17 shows the condition editor with an appropriate definition for the condition required for recall from either *STS* or *LTS*. The top line of the editor is the same as that for all COGENT editors: it consists of a space for a comment that describes the condition and the **Apply** and **Done** buttons for saving and closing the editor. The second line has a field for the condition's functor, a field for the number of arguments, and a button for adding clauses to the condition's definition. The panel below this contains the actual definition (in a pseudo-Prolog format).

Working through the definition in Figure 2.17, we see that this condition's functor is `recall`, and that it has one argument. As described in Section 2.6 below, arguments are often written in brackets following the functor. The definition therefore defines a condition that could be referred to as `recall(X)` (where `X` is the single argument). Alternatively, when reference is not being made to any specific argument, the number of arguments may be written after the functor as in `recall/1`. Note that this form is not part of the COGENT representation and processing language — it should not occur in a COGENT model — rather, it is a convenient shorthand.

The definition of the `recall/1` condition is shown in the lower half of Box 2.6. It has two cases, corresponding to when `Word` is in *STS* or when `Word` is in *LTS*. The symbol ":–" in the definition means "is true if". The first case therefore defines `recall(Word)` to be true if `Word` is an element of the *STS* buffer. The second case defines `recall(Word)` to be true if `Word` is an element of the *LTS* buffer. The two cases are interpreted as alternative possibilities.

Exercise 2.18: Define the `recall` condition. To do this, open *I/O Process* and ensure that the **Rules and Condition Definitions** view is displayed. Select the insert condition button from the palette at the bottom of the window (i.e., the button marked `f(X) :– g(X)`), and click on the *I/O Process* canvas. This will create a new,

Rule 2 (unrefracted): *Recall from STS or LTS*
TRIGGER: `recall`
IF: `recall(X)`
THEN: send `X` to *Output Words*

Condition Definition: `recall/1`: *Recall may be from STS or LTS*
`recall(Word)` :–
  `Word` is in *STS*
`recall(Word)` :–
  `Word` is in *LTS*

Box 2.6: The rule for recalling words, with the definition of `recall/1`

dummy, condition. Double-click on the dummy condition to open the condition editor, and enter a comment describing the condition's intended function. Also enter the condition's functor (i.e., `recall`) and its number of arguments. Now, click the Add Clause button. A new entry will appear in the lower section of the window. Set the argument of that entry to `Word`. (Be sure to use an upper-case `W`, as in this context `Word` is a variable.) Right-click on the button at the far left, to pull down a menu. Navigate to the Add subcondition menu and select match. A new match subcondition will appear. Set it to match a `Word` from *STS*. Now repeat the process to define the second clause that matches against *LTS*. Check that the final definition looks like that given in Figure 2.17, then apply the changes and close the condition editor. ◇

Once defined, the `recall/1` condition may be used within the conditions of a COGENT rule. Specifically, the conditions of the rule for recalling elements from memory should be modified to use the `recall/1` condition instead of matching against *STS*, as in the top portion of Box 2.6.

Exercise 2.19: Modify the recall rule to use the `recall/1` condition. To do this, again open *I/O Process* and ensure the Rules and Condition Definitions view is displayed. Double-click on the existing recall rule to open the rule editor on that rule. Right-click on the button at the left of the existing condition (`X` is in *STS*) to pull down the menu, and navigate to the Change condition type sub-menu and from there to the Prolog sub-menu. You should see an entry for recall/1. Select this. COGENT should replace the previous match condition with a `recall/1` condition. Specify the condition's argument (the variable `X`) and close the rule editor. The full set of rules and condition definitions for *I/O Process* should now be as shown in Figure 2.18. Try running the model several more times, noting the words recalled in *Output Words*. The model should now recall words from both *STS* and

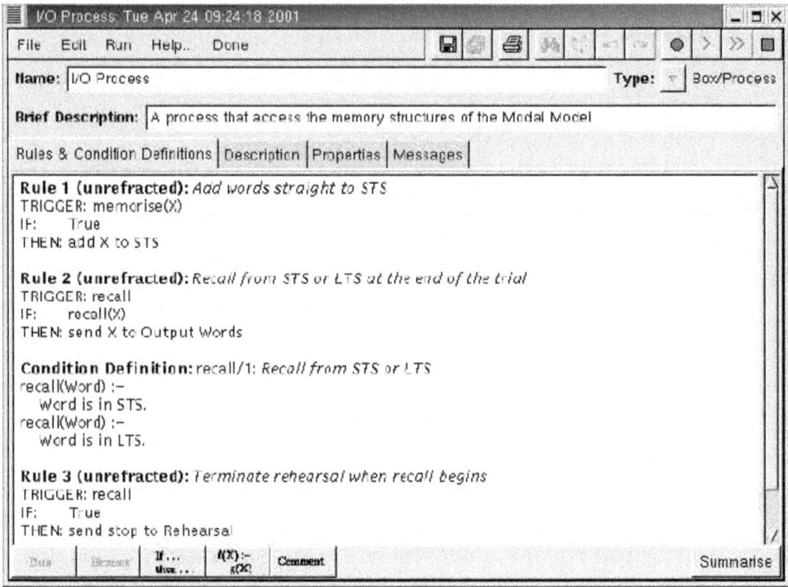

Figure 2.18: The complete rule set for Input/Output

LTS, and biases towards both primacy and recency should be evident. ◇

One last modification to the basic model is required. Close inspection of the recalled words reveals that the model may recall the same word twice on a single run. This is because elements that are in both *STS* and *LTS* will satisfy both clauses of the definition of `recall/1`. Consequently, the recall rule will fire for both occurrences. This can be fixed by setting the refracted attribute of the recall rule. As noted above, if a rule is refracted it will only fire once for each instantiation of its variables. If the recall rule is refracted, it will not recall a word from both *STS* and *LTS*, because that would yield two instantiations of the same variable. The recall rule should therefore be refracted.

Exercise 2.20: Edit the recall rule once more and set its refraction attribute. Close the editor and run the model a few more times. Check that the same word is no longer recalled twice. ◇

2.6 Representation and Variable Binding

The Modal Model as developed thus far has illustrated various concepts related to representation, the use of variables, and the binding of variables within rules. The purpose of this section is to give a more complete description of COGENT's representation language and to provide further detail on the mechanisms of variable binding.

Any information processing model requires that the information to be processed is represented in a consistent way so that the model can apply well-defined mechanisms to process or manipulate the representations. Within COGENT it is necessary to be able to represent, for example, the information contained within buffers and the content of messages that pass between components. COGENT's representation language is borrowed from Prolog, a programming language originally developed for artificial intelligence applications. The following sections give an overview of the language. More information may be obtained from any standard Prolog text (e.g., Bratko, 1986; Clocksin & Mellish, 1987).

2.6.1 Representation in COGENT

The principal representational unit of COGENT (and Prolog) is the *term*. All information that is to be represented must be represented via terms. There are a number of different types of term, allowing the representation of different types of information. Table 2.2 gives a brief description and examples of each type. Any or all of these terms could appear within COGENT as, for example, an element within a buffer or the content of a message.

Numbers

Numbers are represented within COGENT using the standard notation consisting of digits and an optional decimal point. Following Prolog, COGENT treats integers (e.g., `9`) and real numbers (e.g., `3.14159`) slightly differently. Be aware that, for example, `6` and `6.0` are *not* identical.

Atoms

Atoms are generally used to represent atomic things, that is, to represent symbols that have no internal structure (or whose internal structure is not relevant to the current task). Any unbroken sequence of letters or other characters that begins with a lower-case letter (such as `cat`) is interpreted by COGENT to be an atom, provided that the characters following the first letter are upper-case letters, lower-case letters, digits, or the underscore character ("_"). Thus `dog`, `four_legs`, and `a_X3bu` are all atoms. Other combinations of characters can also be made into atoms by enclosing them in single quotation marks. The following are thus also atoms: `'CAT'`, `'four-legs'`, `'A&B'`.

Table 2.2: Types of term within COGENT's representation language

Type	Description	Examples
Number	Represents numeric information	`3` 12.00 `−7.24`
Atom	Represents information with no internal structure	`column` `x23` `cat`
Variable	Represents information that is unknown or that varies	`X` `Time` `Height`
List	Represents sequences of information	`[mouse, cat, dog, horse]` `[london]`
Compound Term	Represents complex information with arbitrary internal structure	`goal(subtract(c2, c1))` `features(X, [legs(4)])`

Variables

Variables allow the representation of information that is either unknown or that may vary. Like atoms, variables are denoted by sequences of letters, digits, and underscore characters, but variables must begin with an upper-case letter or the underscore character. Thus, `CAT`, `Rat_4`, and `_myvar` are all variables. Note that variables must not have quotation marks around them: a character sequence beginning with an upper-case letter that is surrounding by single quotes is understood by COGENT (and Prolog) to be an atom.

Lists

Much of the power of the representation language comes from the possibility of constructing new terms from other elements of the language. Lists are one type of term that employs this construction. Lists are generally used to represent sequences of information. Thus, a list might be an appropriate representation to use when modelling a task involving a sequence of activities, where order in the sequence is important.

Syntactically, a list consists of a left square bracket followed by a comma-separated sequence of terms followed by a right square bracket. Thus, `[cat, elephant, fish, lion, dog, fish]` is a list with six atomic elements. Lists can have any number of elements, but the list with zero elements is special. It is known as the empty list, and represented as [ ].

A second common use of lists is to represent sets of things (or even multi-sets: sets whose elements may occur more than once). This can be done by simply ignoring the sequential ordering information contained in the list representation.

Thus, the list [cat, elephant, fish, lion, dog] may be used to represent a set, rather than a sequence, of animal names, provided that the functions and processes that operate on the representation do not make use of order information contained within the list.

The elements of a list need not be atoms — they may be terms of any type. Hence, variables and lists may occur as elements of a list. Thus, [cat, ANIMAL, fox, [rabbit, rat, mouse]] is a list whose second element is a variable, whose first and third elements are atoms, and whose fourth element is itself a list.

Compound Terms

Compounds terms are, like lists, terms built from other terms. They are frequently used to represent structured information in which the structure is more complex than that which occurs in lists. Compound terms allow, for example, the representation of the meaning of sentences in terms of representations of the sentence parts. Thus, the meaning of "Tigger is miaowing" might be represented by the compound term miaows(tigger).

In general, a compound term consists of an atom (in the above case miaows) immediately followed by a left round bracket followed by a comma-separated sequence of other terms, followed by a right round bracket. The initial atom is referred to as the compound term's *functor*. The sub-terms between a compound term's brackets are known as its arguments, and the number of arguments is the term's *arity*. Note that the comma-separated sequence of terms cannot be empty (i.e., the arity of a compound term cannot be 0), and there must not be any space between the compound term's functor and the opening round bracket. Space may be inserted freely between a compound term's arguments (or between those arguments and the commas that separate them), and should be used consistently to improve the readability of the representation.

The example compound terms given in Table 2.2 illustrate that compound terms may be embedded (i.e., an argument of a compound term may itself be a compound term), or contain lists and variables within their arguments. Highly complex representations may be built by using this structuring of terms.

Operators

In the language as described so far, a compound term representing a simple arithmetic expression (e.g., 3 + 4) must be written using a very clumsy notation: '+'(3, 4). This is a compound term whose functor is '+' and whose arity is 2. The representation language allows some compound terms (especially arithmetic expressions) to be written in a more readable way through the use of operators.

Certain pre-defined functors are understood by COGENT (and Prolog) to be operators. Binary operators — operators with exactly two arguments — may be written between their arguments. Thus, a term of the form '+'(3, 4) can be written in the conventional way, as 3 + 4. Note that the brackets and the single quotes are not required when the alternative notation is used. Operators may be used in all kinds of terms (not just arithmetic expressions). Thus, `has − fur` is the same as '−'(has, fur), and a/b is the same as '/'(a, b).

The set of pre-defined operators includes all of the standard arithmetic operators (+, −, *, /, > and <). These operators can be used in complex expressions, and when used in such expressions they have the usual precedences. Thus, 3 + 4 * 5 is is a compound term with arity 2 and functor "+". The second argument of this term is 4 * 5, itself a compound term. Precedence can be over-ridden by using round brackets. Thus (3 + 4) * 5 is is a compound term with arity 2 and functor "*". The first argument of this term is 3 + 4, again a compound term.

A second common use of operators within COGENT is in specifying positional information for objects within analogue buffers. As described elsewhere, analogue buffers contain terms that represent objects located in one-dimensional or two-dimensional space. A graphical object may be centred (or aligned vertically or horizontally) by using the `aligned` operator in the object's position specification:

```
text("Centred text", (300, 200) aligned (c, c), [colour(green)])
```

2.6.2 Unification: Matching and Variable Binding

The combination of compound terms and variables provides a general, expressive representational system. The representational system also provides a mechanism for matching terms (e.g., in the triggering patterns and conditions of rules) and binding variables. Consider Rule 1 of Box 2.7, which comes from a production system interpreter and which operates on two buffers, *Productions* and *Matches*. Suppose that, at some point in processing, *Productions* contains the term:

```
prod([subtrahend(0)], [do(copy_minuend)])
```

The first condition of Rule 1 may be satisfied if the compound term `prod(C, A)` may be matched with this element. This in turn involves mapping or binding the variable `C` to `[subtrahend(0)]` and the variable `A` to `[do(copy_minuend)]`. The operation in which `prod(C, A)` is matched to a buffer element to produce this binding is known as unification. Table 2.3 shows several examples of unification between terms and the resultant variable bindings. Notice that, in the case of compound terms and lists, unification is a recursive process: two compound terms unify if they have the same functor and arity and each of their arguments unify; two lists unify if they have the same length and each of their arguments unify.

Returning to Rule 1 of Box 2.7, unification of the rule's first condition with the element in *Productions* effectively yields a new instance of the rule, as shown

Rule 1 (unrefracted): *Add matching production instances to match memory*
IF: `prod(C, A)` is in *Productions*
`preconditions_hold(C, M)`
THEN: add `prod(C, A, M)` to *Matches*

Rule 1 with variables partially instantiated:
IF: `prod([subtrahend(0)], [do(copy_minuend)])` is in *Productions*
`preconditions_hold([subtrahend(0)], M)`
THEN: add `prod([subtrahend(0)], [do(copy_minuend)], M)` to *Matches*

Box 2.7: A sample rule from a production system interpreter, and a partially instantiated instance of the rule

Table 2.3: Examples of terms, their unification, and the resultant variable bindings

Terms	Their Unification	Variable Bindings
`X` `word(green)`	`word(green)`	`X` ↦ `word(green)`

`f(alpha, B, gamma)`
`f(A, beta, G)`
	`f(alpha, beta, gamma)`	`A` ↦ `alpha`
		`B` ↦ `beta`
		`G` ↦ `gamma`

`f(X)` `g(X)`	Unification fails	
`f([a, B], [])` `f([B, a], M)`	`f([a, a], [])`	`B` ↦ `a` `M` ↦ `[]`
`f([a, B], [])` `f(L, B)`	`f([a, []], [])`	`B` ↦ `[]` `L` ↦ `[a, []]`
`f([a, B], [])` `f([B, B], B)`	Unification fails	

in the lower half of the box. In this instance the variables `C` and `A` have been instantiated with the terms resulting from the successful match against *Productions*. The rule's second condition inherits the instantiation of the variables, and so is more specific than in the abstract rule. The rule's action also inherits the instantiation of variables, and is similarly more specific. In order for this instance of the rule to fire, however, the second (more specific) condition must also be satisfied. This condition may lead to the variable `M` becoming instantiated before the rule fires. Alternatively, the second condition may fail (i.e., there may be no way in which the variables in the condition may be successfully instantiated, given the instantiation of `C`). In this case the rule will not fire.

The buffer that is being matched (*Productions*) may also contain multiple elements that match the rule's first condition. In such cases each matching element leads to a separate instance of the rule, differing only in the terms to which the variables C and A are instantiated. All instances of all rules are normally considered on each COGENT processing cycle (unless the rule is explicitly marked to fire at most once on any cycle). Thus, a single rule may fire multiple times on the same cycle, each time with a different instantiation. (COGENT rules may therefore be understood as statements of predicate logic, in which the variables are implicitly universally quantified.)

2.7 Augmenting the Experiment Environment

The Modal Model developed in Section 2.5 captures basic primacy and recency effects in free recall, but in order to see this it is necessary to examine by hand the serial position of recalled words over a number of runs of the model. Thus the behaviour of the model is not easily interpreted. A second difficulty with the model as developed is that the order of the input stimuli is fixed. Both of these deficiencies are deficiencies of the experimental context within which the model was developed, rather than deficiencies of the model *per se*. This section addresses these deficiencies by first separating the model from the task environment, and then elaborating the task environment to include randomisation of stimuli and graphical presentation of output.

2.7.1 Encapsulation of Subject and Task Functions

The current model consists of four boxes which implement the Modal Model itself (*I/O Process*, *STS*, *LTS* and *Rehearsal*) and two boxes that relate specifically to the task environment (*Input Words* and *Output Words*). There are sound methodological reasons for wishing to separate the model from its environment. Such a separation improves the clarity of the model specification, and opens up the possibility of developing different task environments in which to evaluate the model. COGENT's compound box type allows this separation to be achieved. Compound boxes are boxes that contain box and arrow diagrams. They are appropriate when a complex model contains functionally separable components which are, themselves, moderately complex. In such cases one or more components may be encapsulated within a compound box, simplifying the model's "top-level" box and arrow diagram. Compound boxes may also be used to separate a cognitive model and its task environment, with separate compound boxes used for each.

Compound boxes are represented within a COGENT box and arrow diagram as rectangles. Like all other boxes, arrows may be drawn to or from them, allowing communication between the compound (and its component boxes) and other boxes in a box and arrow diagram. COGENT supports two kinds of compound box: generic compounds and subject compounds. These are distinguished on box and arrow diagrams by the letters "G" and "S" respectively in the top right corner of their rectangles. Generic compounds have all of the functionality of the top-level box and arrow diagram. Subject compounds are deliberately provided for the development of cognitive models (and not task environments). As such, there are several limits on their functionality. For example, the box and arrow diagram within a subject compound may not contain data sources or data sinks. Those box types may only occur in generic compounds. Similarly various functions (e.g., relating to performing statistical calculations on model outputs) are not accessible within process boxes that reside within a subject compound.

A model in which the cognitive (or subject) model and task environment are not differentiated may be converted into one in which they are by creating two compound boxes on the main box and arrow window (for the subject and the task environment), and then moving the components of the original model into the appropriate compound boxes. This may be achieved by cutting and pasting from the main box and arrow canvas to the box and arrow canvases of the two compounds, or by using special interface functions that allow boxes to be *promoted* or *demoted* between compounds.

Exercise 2.21: Close all versions of your Modal Model and return to the Research Programme Manager window. Create a new copy of the model based on the previous version. This copy is to be transformed into a cleaner version that separates the subject model from the task environment. Open the new copy, rename it (e.g., to *Subject/Environment Model*), and create two new compound boxes. One of those compounds should be a generic compound. Name it *Task Environment*. The other should be a subject compound. Name it *Subject Model*. The box and arrow diagram should now appear as in Figure 2.19. Move each box from the original model into the appropriate compound by right-clicking on each box, selecting Demote from the popup menu that appears, and then selecting from the sub-menu the name of the appropriate compound into which the box should be demoted. *Input Words* and *Output Words* should be demoted to *Task Environment*. The other boxes should be demoted to *Subject Model*. Notice how, when a box is demoted, COGENT automatically updates arrows to and from the compound into which it is demoted. Rearrange the boxes on each box and arrow canvas as necessary. The top-level box and arrow diagram should appear as in Figure 2.20. The *Subject Model* box and arrow diagram should appear as in Figure 2.1. Run the model to check that it still works as intended. Examine the Message Matrix view of each box and arrow diagram as the model is running. This view shows a global view of messages passing between boxes within a compound. It should show stimuli being sent from *Task Environment* to *Subject Model* and responses being sent from *Subject Model* to *Task Environment*. ◇

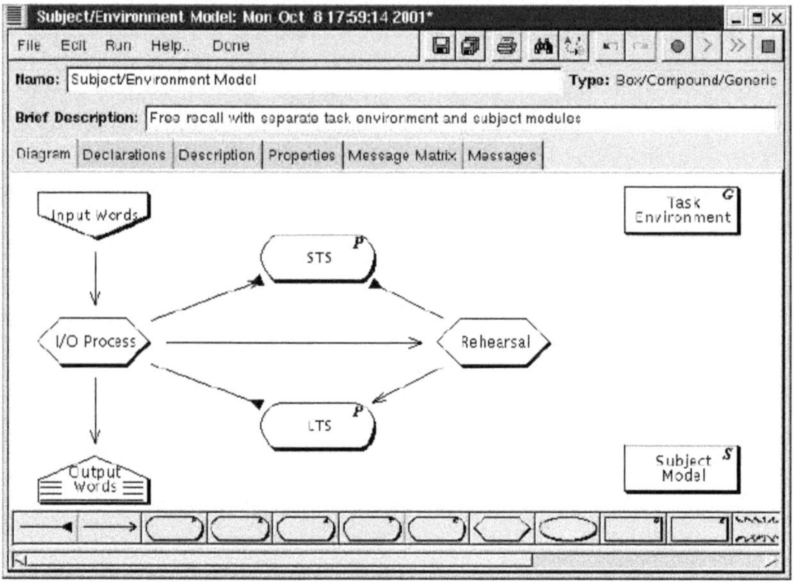

Figure 2.19: The first stage in encapsulating the task environment and subject model functions

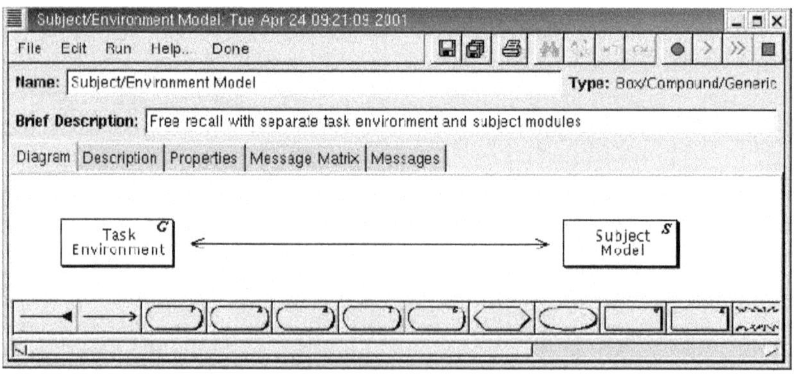

Figure 2.20: The top-level box and arrow diagram of the revised Modal Model

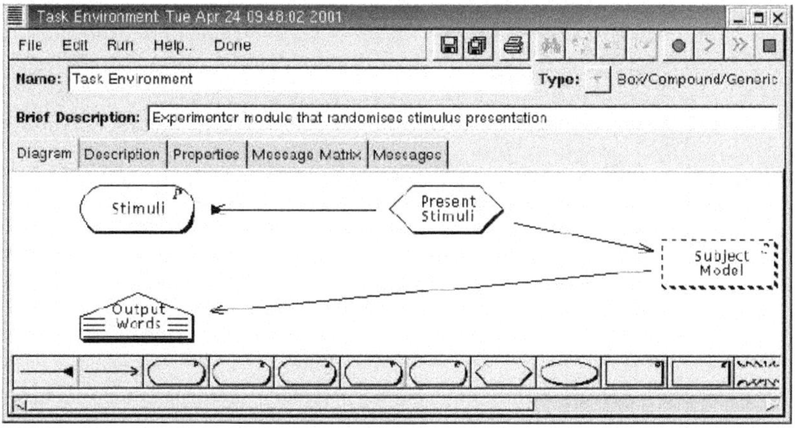

Figure 2.21: The top-level box and arrow diagram of the revised Modal Model

2.7.2 Randomisation of Input Stimuli

Once the task environment and subject model are cleanly separated, it is possible to elaborate the task environment without the risk of confusing aspects of the task environment with aspects of the subject model. As noted above, one deficiency of the task environment was the way stimuli were presented in a fixed order. This property of data sources may be side-stepped by replacing *Input Words* with a random access buffer containing the stimuli and a coupled process that, on each cycle, selects a stimulus from that buffer and presents it to *I/O Process*. Figure 2.21 shows an appropriately revised box and arrow diagram for *Task Environment*. Notice that in this diagram *Present Stimuli* can both read from and write to *Stimuli*. This version of the model requires that the Access property of *Stimuli* is set to Random, and that its initial contents are the 20 words.

Exercise 2.22: Modify the box and arrow diagram of *Task Environment* from the previous model to that shown in Figure 2.21. Specify appropriate initial contents of *Stimuli*. (To do this, open *Stimuli* and use the Add Element button on the palette to add a dummy element, then double-click on the dummy element to edit it. Each element should be of the form `word(`x`)` where x is one of the words from the list of stimuli.) Also make sure the Access property of *Stimuli* is set to Random. (Random access is the default, so the property's value should not need to be changed, but examine the buffer's properties just to be on the safe side and check that the value is correct.) ◇

The next step in upgrading *Task Environment* involves providing appropriate rules for *Present Stimuli*. Two rules are required: one to present the stimuli and a second

Rule 1 (refracted; once): *Present one stimulus word on each cycle*
IF: `word(Word)` is in *Stimuli*
THEN: send `memorise(Word)` to *Subject Model:I/O Process*
delete `word(Word)` from *Stimuli*

Rule 2 (refracted): *Trigger recall when all stimuli have been presented*
IF: not `word(AnyWord)` is in *Stimuli*
THEN: send `recall` to *Subject Model:I/O Process*

Box 2.8: Upgraded rules for *Present Stimuli*

to trigger recall when all stimuli have been presented. The rules in Box 2.8 achieve these functions.

Rule 1 presents one stimulus word to *I/O Process* on each cycle, and simultaneously removes that word from *Stimuli*. This prevents the rule from presenting the same word twice. The fact that the rule is refracted would have the same effect, but Rule 2 uses the fact that words are removed from *Stimuli* as they are presented to trigger recall when *Stimuli* becomes empty. Notice that Rule 1 is marked to fire once per cycle (so only one word is presented at a time) and the condition of Rule 2 includes a negation (i.e., not). This has the effect of testing if all stimuli have been processed: the condition succeeds if and only if there are no terms in *Stimuli* that match `word(AnyWord)`.

Exercise 2.23: Add the above two rules to *Present Stimuli*. Note that to add the negated condition in Rule 2 it is necessary first to specify a standard match condition (of the form "`AnyWord` is in *Stimuli*") and then to add a "qualifier" to this condition by selecting Add qualifier and then selecting not from the pull-down menu immediately to the left of the condition.

Initialise the model and run it a few times. Convince yourself that the model works as intended. (If it does not, check that you have entered the rules correctly.) Notice that the Initialise property of *Stimuli*, which by default is set to Each Trial, is crucial in re-loading the stimuli into the buffer at the beginning of each run. ◇

One side-effect of randomising the input stimuli is that interpretation of output is now more difficult. Since words may be presented at any point during processing, it is necessary to note down the order of presentation to be sure that recency and primacy biases remain. *Task Environment* may be extended to also perform this function, and provide as output a list of the serial positions of recalled words.

This extension requires that the order of presentation of each word is recorded, and that this record is used by a collation process during the recall phase to "score" the model's responses. The first of these requirements may be addressed by mod-

Rule 1 (refracted; once): *Present one stimulus word on each cycle*
IF: `word(Word)` is in *Stimuli*
the current cycle is `Cycle`
THEN: send `memorise(Word)` to *Subject Model:I/O Process*
delete `word(Word)` from *Stimuli*
add `presented(Word, Cycle)` to *Stimuli*

Box 2.9: A modified stimulus presentation rule

Rule 1 (unrefracted): *Send the presentation cycle of recalled words to output*
TRIGGER: `Word`
IF: `presented(Word, Cycle)` is in *Stimuli*
THEN: send `Cycle` to *Output Positions*

Box 2.10: A rule that records the presentation cycle of each word

ifying Rule 1 of Box 2.8 to that shown in Box 2.9. A further process, *Collate Responses*, may then be introduced between *I/O Process* and *Output Words*. *Collate Responses* should receive messages from *I/O Process*, read presentation order information from *Stimuli*, and send that order information to *Output Words* (which could, for current purposes, be renamed *Output Positions*).

Exercise 2.24: Modify the stimulus presentation rule and the box and arrow diagram of *Task Environment* as described above. Note that the second condition of the rule ("the current cycle is `Cycle`") is available under the miscellaneous sub-menu of the Add condition menu. Also modify the recall rule in *I/O Process* to send recalled words to *Collate Responses* rather than *Output Words*. ◇

All that remains is one rule in *Collate Responses* that should, on receipt of a recalled word, check the presentation cycle of that word (by looking up the information in *Stimuli*) and send the presentation cycle (rather than the word itself) to *Output Positions*. This may be achieved by Rule 1 of Box 2.10, which relies upon the presentation cycle of each word being recorded by Rule 1 of Box 2.9.

Exercise 2.25: Insert the above rule in *Collate Responses*. Initialise and run the model a few times. Confirm that primacy and recency effects are evident in the position information that appears in *Output Positions*. ◇

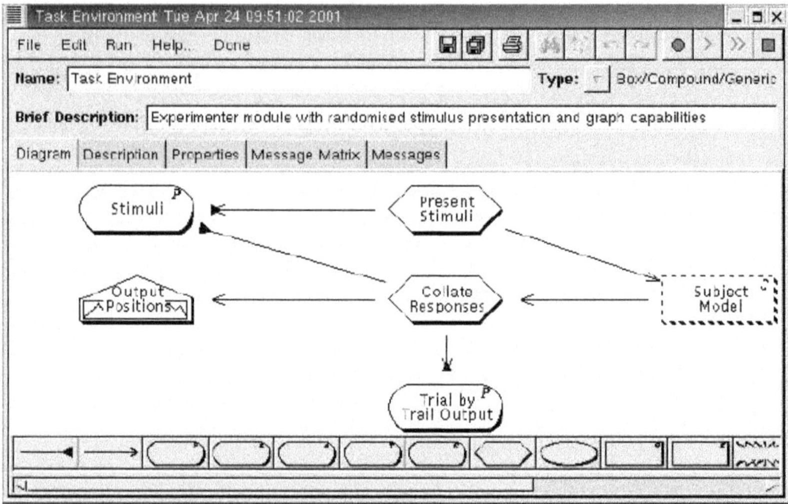

Figure 2.22: *Task Environment*, with graphical output and collating of responses over multiple runs of the model

2.7.3 Graphical Display of Recall Frequency

A further possible improvement to *Task Environment* involves recording serial position data over multiple runs of the model and presenting the results graphically, as in Figure 2.4. This requires an additional propositional buffer in *Task Environment* (to store data over multiple runs) and conversion of *Output Positions* from a text data sink to a graphical data sink. Figure 2.22 shows the complete revised box and arrow diagram.

The propositional buffer (*Trial by Trial Output* in Figure 2.22) should contain counts of how many times a word from each position has been recalled since the model was last initialised. It might therefore contain 20 `recalled/2` elements, in which the first argument of each element is an integer specifying the position and the second argument is an integer specifying the number of times a word from that position has been recalled. Adopting this representation requires that *Trial by Trial Output* initially contains 20 elements of the form `recalled(1,0)`, `recalled(2,0)`, `recalled(3,0)`, ..., `recalled(20,0)`. *Trial by Trial Output* should also re-initialise on each experiment (rather than each trial), so that it may collate information across trials. (The model has been set up such that each "run" corresponds to one COGENT trial. Below it is explained how an experiment consisting of multiple runs may be constructed.)

With *Trial by Trial Output* as specified above, *Collate Responses* requires two rules: one to update the counters in *Trial by Trial Output* whenever a word is

Rule 1 (unrefracted): *Update the recall count for each cycle*
TRIGGER: `Word`
IF: `presented(Word, Cycle)` is in *Stimuli*
`recalled(Cycle, N)` is in *Trial by Trial Output*
`N1` is `N + 1`
THEN: delete `recalled(Cycle, N)` from *Trial by Trial Output*
add `recalled(Cycle, N1)` to *Trial by Trial Output*

Rule 2 (unrefracted): *Update the graph at the end of a trial*
TRIGGER: `system_end(trial)`
IF: `recalled(X, N)` is in *Trial by Trial Output*
the current trial is `T`
`Y` is `100 * (N/T)`
THEN: send `data(recall, X, Y)` to *Output Positions*

Box 2.11: Rules for *Collate Responses*

recalled, and a second to transfer the values of the counters to the *Output Positions* graph at the end of each trial. The rules in Box 2.11 achieve these functions.

Rule 1 of Box 2.11 is triggered by receipt of a word (presumably recalled by *I/O Process*). The cycle on which the recalled word was presented is then determined (by reference to *Stimuli*), and the counter updated. Updating the counter involves two "conditions": one which gets its current value (`N`), and a second which increments this value. Note that within COGENT arithmetic is performed within a rule's conditions. This is because variables may not be bound by a rule's actions, and incrementing the counter requires binding `N1` to `N + 1`. The counter is actually incremented by replacing the relevant buffer element in *Trial by Trial Output*.

Rule 2 of Box 2.11 makes use of `system_end(trial)`. This is a special trigger that COGENT automatically generates at the end of each trial. The trigger allows bookkeeping operations, such as those of *Collate Responses*, to be keyed to the end of each trial (or to the end of other major units of processing). For each serial position (`X`), the rule determines the number of times a word from that position has been recalled (`N`) and converts this into a percentage by dividing by the total number of recall opportunities (i.e., the current trial counter) and multiplying by 100. The resulting value is sent within a `data/3` term to *Output Positions*.

Graphical data sinks (and graphical buffers) interpret their contents as specifications of points on a graph. An element of the form `data(recall, 3, 48.2)`, for example, specifies a data point for `recall` at 3 units in the horizontal and 48.2 units in the vertical. The **Current Graph** view assembles all data points for each data set (where the first argument of the `data/3` term, in this case `recall`, specifies the data set) and presents them as a graph. Graph attributes such as format (line graph, bar chart, or scatter plot) and colour may also be specified by terms sent to the box. Thus, `recall` data may be shown as a red line graph with data points indicated by filled squares by sending the following `type/3` element to the data sink:

```
type(recall, line, [colour(red), fill(true), marker(square)])
```

Aspects of the graphical display that are independent of data set (e.g., the range of the two variables and labels for the axes and the complete graph) are set through the graphical box's properties. In the case of *Output Positions*, the properties should specify that the X label is "Serial Position" and the X units range from 1 to 20, divided into $20 - 1 = 19$ units, and that the Y label is "% Recall" and the Y units range from 0 to 100, divided into 5 units. (The graph may also be set to re-initialise on each experiment, although this is not critical.)

Exercise 2.26: Augment *Task Environment* to provide graphical output as described above. This involves: updating the box and arrow diagram for *Task Environment*; setting the Initialise property of *Trial by Trial Output* to Each Experiment and the initial contents of *Trial by Trial Output* to terms of the form `recalled(`P`, 0)` for each position, P, from 1 to 20; setting the display properties of *Output Positions*; and updating the rules of *Collate Responses* to those given above.

Initialise and run the model with *Output Positions* open in Current Graph view. On the first run the model should generate a ragged graph representing the recall of words on a single run. Run the model again (without initialising). The graph, which now represents data averaged over two trials, should become a little smoother. Continue running the graph until a clear picture of the data emerges. After about 25 runs both primacy and recency effects should be evident. ◇

2.7.4 Specifying a Complete Experiment

The finishing touch to this version of the combined subject model and task environment involves specifying an "experiment" consisting of 25 runs of the task. As noted in Section 2.1.5, COGENT includes a scripting language which may be used to specify complex experimental designs. Scripts are attached to the Run button, such that clicking on that button runs the current script. The default script associated with each model consists of a single COGENT trial, but the scripting language allows specification of complete experiments, consisting of multiple virtual subjects completing a pre-specified number of blocks of trials.

The current script may be viewed or edited by selecting Script... from the Run menu at the top of any box's window. This pops up the execution window (see Figure 2.23), with the current script in view. The default script consists of a simple

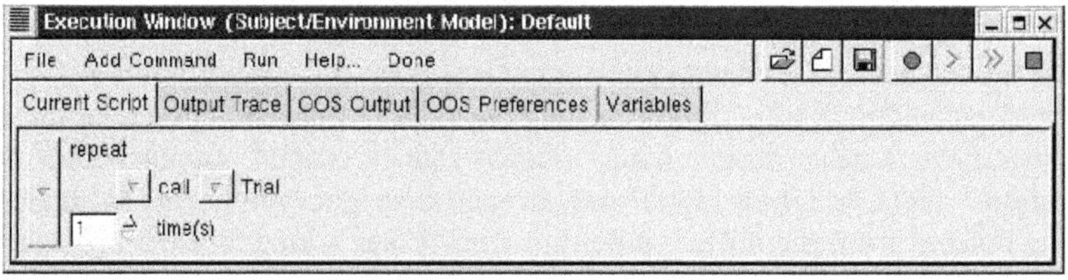

Figure 2.23: The default script associated with the Modal Model

repeat loop:

```
repeat
    call Trial
1 time(s)
```

Trial is another predefined script. It consists of a trial level initialisation, running until the end of the trial, and some standard end of trial processing. The number of trials completed when the Run button is pressed may be altered by altering the number of repetitions of Trial in the default script. Alternatively, more complex scripts may be created by using the pull-down menus at the top of the window to add further script commands, including commands for sequential control (e.g., while ... do ..., if ... then ... else ..., etc.) and commands for setting property values. These script commands may be assembled to specify procedural aspects of arbitrarily complex experiments, allowing direct comparison of model and human behaviour.

Exercise 2.27: Set the number of repetitions of Trial to 25. Save the script (using the "Save to disk" button at the top of the execution window), re-initialise, and run the model. The model should now complete 25 runs of the task before stopping. Run the model again without re-initialising to yield 50 trials worth of data. Notice how the *Output Positions* graph becomes smoother as more data are collected. ◇

2.8 Extending the Modal Model

The serial position curves generated by the the Modal Model in its current state exhibit primacy and recency, but they differ from serial recall curves obtained in laboratory experiments in two ways: recall from the middle of the list is too good (averaging above 50% — well above that of most experimental participants) and the primacy effect is too strong. Both of these aspects of the model's performance may be attributed to the lack of decay from the long-term store, which is supposed to be of less than perfect reliability.

COGENT supports decay of items held in buffers by means of buffer properties. Such properties have already been seen when considering different behaviour of limited capacity buffers. All buffers may have decay imposed upon their elements by specifying a decay function and a decay rate. COGENT supports three decay functions: Half Life, Linear, and Fixed. In each case, decay may lead to an element being deleted from the buffer sometime after it was added to the buffer. (Buffer elements do not normally have activation values associated with them, so decay does not work through some kind of decrease in element activation.) A second property, Decay Constant, specifies the rate of decay, with higher values of the constant corresponding to slower decay.

With Half Life decay, the probability of an element decaying on any cycle is constant, and Decay Constant specifies the half life of elements. Thus, if Decay Constant is 20 the probability of an element surviving 20 cycles after it was added will be 0.5. With Linear decay, the probability of an element decaying on any given cycle increases the longer the element remains in the buffer. If Decay Constant is 20 the probability of an element being deleted within 15 cycles will be 0.75 (i.e., 15/20), and the probability of being deleted within 20 cycles will be 1.0. With Fixed decay and Decay Constant of 20, each element in the buffer will decay exactly 20 cycles after it was added.

Exercise 2.28: Open the *LTS* box of the latest version of the model and switch to its Properties view. Set the Decay property of *LTS* to Half Life, and the Decay Constant to 20, then return to the graph view and run a block of 25 trials. You should see that the primacy effect has been greatly reduced, or even abolished completely. The recency effect should still be strong. Try increasing the *LTS* Decay Constant. This makes items less likely to decay during a trial. The primacy effect should also increase. ◇

Another way that the performance of the model may be altered is to change its rehearsal rate. Recall that *Task Environment* sends one word per cycle during the memorisation phase, and that *Rehearsal* transfers one item per cycle to *LTS*. The model therefore effectively rehearses one item per input item. This may be doubled by creating a copy of the rehearsal rule.

Exercise 2.29: Open *Rehearsal* and create a copy of the rehearsal rule by right-clicking on the rule and selecting Copy. Initialise and run the model. You should see another increase in the size of the primacy effect, as well as a raising of the level of the central portion of the curve. On a related note, check the Duplicates property of *LTS*. This allows multiple copies of the same word in *LTS*, and should improve recall because words that have been rehearsed multiple times will be added to *LTS* multiple times, and hence will be less prone to decay. ◇

Rule 2 (refracted; once): *Serial recall at the end of the trial*
TRIGGER: `recall`
IF: `recall(Word)`
THEN: send `Word` to *Task Environment:Collate Responses*
send `recall` to *I/O Process*

Box 2.12: The rule to ensure serial recall (from *I/O Process*)

The above considerations about time suggest another way in which the model may be improved. Although the experimenter sends words to the subject serially (i.e., one at a time), the subject currently does not recall serially. A more realistic subject model would recall words one at a time, on separate cycles, rather than in one parallel burst on a single cycle. Serial recall may be achieved by setting the Rule fires once per cycle and Rule is Refracted attributes on the recall rule, and changing the rule's actions so that, when the rule fires, it sends a message to trigger itself on the next cycle. Such behaviour, where a process contains a rule that sends a message to the process, requires that the Recurrent property of the process in question be set. The full rule is given in Box 2.12. Note that, since the rule is refracted, it will only recall each word that is in either *STS* or *LTS* once, and when all words have been recalled the rule's condition will fail (even though the rule is triggered by the message it generated on the previous cycle). This will prevent the rule from firing again and allow the trial to terminate.

Exercise 2.30: Open *I/O Process*, set its Recurrent property to Yes, and edit the recall rule as above. Check that the model now performs serial recall. How does this affect the shape of the serial position curve generated by the model? ◇

Exercise 2.31: You have been introduced to a range of properties that can affect the behaviour of the model, including capacity limitations, behaviour when that capacity is exceeded, decay type and rate, and rehearsal rate. Another property of interest is the Access property of buffers, which offers the options FIFO (First-In/First-Out), LIFO (Last-In/First-Out), and Random, and controls the order in which items are read from buffers. Explore how variation in the value of this (and other properties) affects the model's behaviour. ◇

2.9 Further Reading

Space limitations prohibit presentation of further details of COGENT. Users are encouraged to explore the COGENT user documentation. Discussion of the background to COGENT and its capabilities is included in Cooper and Fox (1998). This paper is based on an earlier version of COGENT which lacked many of the features described in this chapter, but much of the discussion remains relevant.

The COGENT representation language is based on Prolog, and any good Prolog text (e.g., Bratko, 1986; Clocksin & Mellish, 1987) will provide a sound description of the language. Prolog also forms the basis of the condition definition language, so a good knowledge of Prolog will help when developing models.

Cooper (1995) gives a semi-formal description of the processing engine used to interpret COGENT models. This paper presents a state transition model of the basic processing cycle, as well as some motivation for the use of object-oriented techniques in cognitive modelling. The relevance of these techniques is discussed further by Mather (2001) and Cooper (2001).

More detailed descriptions of the Modal Model, the free recall task, and subject behaviour on this task can be obtained from the original works (Atkinson & Shiffrin, 1968, 1971) or from any good text on memory (e.g., Baddeley, 1990).

Part II

Modelling in Specific Domains

Overview

The chapters in Part 1 have provided essential background material. Part 2 is concerned with developing and applying that material in domains ranging from sentence processing to executive processes. The purpose of this section is to provide a map of the domains and issues addressed in Part 2.

Two principal topics are addressed in Chapter 3: cognitive skill and production system models. Production systems are argued to provide a good framework for modelling cognitive skill (among other things), and this argument is backed up by production system models of two arithmetic tasks: multicolumn addition and multicolumn subtraction. Of particular interest is the model of multicolumn subtraction, which can account for many of children's subtraction errors in a straightforward way. Perhaps the most important issue that is left unresolved is that no account is given of the acquisition of cognitive skill. In fact, theories and production system models of skill acquisition do exist (e.g., Anderson, 1981, 1982, 1993; Newell, 1990). The lack of any account of skill acquisition in the chapter is due to space limitations, rather than any intrinsic conflict between the production system framework and the computational requirements of skill acquisition.

The primary focus of Chapter 4 is problem solving. The chapter is concerned more with the computational requirements of problem solving — the cyclic proposal, evaluation, selection, and application of operators or moves, and the need in some cases for a goal stack — than with the empirical evaluation of problem solving models. However, later chapters demonstrate that the basic processing cycle introduced when modelling problem solving behaviour has significant generality: it may also be applied in domains such as deductive reasoning (Chapter 5) and sentence processing (Chapter 7).

Chapter 5 presents two models of human deductive competence on syllogistic reasoning tasks. Both models generate similar behaviour on the full set of 64 syllogisms, but they achieve this by very different means: one through the construction and subsequent revision of a "mental model" consisting of tokens representing individuals and the other through the construction of a set-theoretic diagram. In this way the models illustrate two different algorithms for the same set of stimulus/response behaviours, and raise the question of indistinguishability:

can behavioural evidence distinguish between model-based and set-theoretic approaches to deductive reasoning? The "mental model" model also illustrates the requirement of "computational completeness" introduced in Chapter 1. The intended workings of mental model construction and revision are easy to specify in informal terms, but specification at the level required by the computational model raises many difficulties. The result is a large number of rules relating to specific cases for both mental model construction and mental model revision.

Decision making and categorisation are the domains of interest in Chapter 6. The chapter has a subtext, however, comparative modelling. Three competing models of two medical diagnosis tasks are developed (based on Bayesian, associationist, and hypothesis testing approaches). Each of the models contains parameters that allow aspects of their behaviour to be tuned to fit empirical findings. It is suggested that an appropriate methodology for parameter estimation is to consider multiple dependent measures, and set parameters to fit only a subset of these, allowing other dependent measures to be predicted from the models. Although no single diagnosis model is found to yield a perfect account of the observed human behaviour, development of a range of models for the same tasks clarifies the strengths and weaknesses of the various approaches.

The domains considered in Chapters 3 to 6 are covered in most texts on thinking and reasoning. Chapter 7 considers a rather different domain: sentence processing. Sentence processing is different because it is usually automatic and effortless. When given a problem or syllogism it generally requires a deliberate act of will to solve it. When given a sentence it generally requires a deliberate act of will not to process it. Merely attending to a sentence will result in some attempt to process it. Given this qualitative difference, one might argue that sentence processing should not be considered alongside high-level cognitive processes such as problem solving, deductive reasoning, and decision making. Indeed, this is at the heart of the modularity hypothesis (Fodor, 1983). However, there are strong counters to this argument. Sentence processing has been shown to be sensitive to effects of knowledge (e.g., linguistic and visual context). Arguably the automaticity of sentence processing is a consequence of it being a highly practiced cognitive skill. From this perspective there is no qualitative difference between the automaticity with which an average person processes sentences and the way in which a chess Grand Master assesses the layout of pieces during a game of chess.

For the above reasons it is reasonable to at least consider the computational requirements of sentence processing. Such consideration reveals a role for the proposal, evaluation, selection, and application of operators and for stack-like data structures. Each of these is familiar from other high-level cognitive domains. The computational requirements of sentence processing therefore appear to be continuous with those of more standard high-level cognitive processes. This warrants the inclusion of sentence processing in this volume.

A further issue that is raised in Chapter 7 is the distinction between competence and performance. The basic idea is that competence refers to idealised knowledge of a domain. Performance results from the cognitive system's use of this knowledge. It is claimed that this use may be sub-optimal (e.g., because of memory or processing limitations), so there may be a gap between actual performance and the idealised performance that would be predicted from competence.

The competence/performance distinction is also touched upon in Chapter 5 in relation to deductive reasoning. In this case the distinction is between deductive competence and deductive performance. The competence/performance distinction has some important lessons for modelling. It also raises some issues which cognitive modelling is well-placed to address. These lessons and issues are amongst those discussed in Part 3.

Chapter 8 is concerned with executive processes. These processes are distinct from other high-level cognitive processes because they operate on the cognitive system itself rather than on the external environment. Thus, executive processes are concerned with issues such as setting overall goals, resource allocation and control, co-ordination, and integration of sub-processes. As such, the issues raised by attempting to model executive processes differ from those raised by attempting to model behaviour in specific domains. Of particular concern is that a model of executive processes requires models of individual sub-processes on which to operate. Thus, a model of resource allocation cannot be evaluated without associated models that employ resources and whose behaviour is sensitive to resource allocation. In the context of Chapter 8, highly simplified models of sub-processes are employed to allow modelling of the executive process to progress. The extent to which simplifications made in modelling these sub-processes affect overall behaviour of the system is unclear, but the general problem suggests that careful attention to methodology is required when developing models of executive processes.

Chapter 3

Arithmetic: A Cognitive Skill

Richard P. Cooper

Overview: This chapter presents arithmetic as an acquired cognitive skill, and illustrates how aspects of this skill can be modelled within two production systems. The chapter's primary aims are to provide an in-depth illustration of the workings of production systems, and to demonstrate one way in which models may be developed with the support of empirical data. The chapter concludes with a discussion of limitations of the simple production system approach.

3.1 Cognitive Skills

A cognitive skill is an acquired ability to perform some cognitive task with a high degree of fluency. Examples include mental arithmetic, chess playing, and reading mirror writing. Cognitive skills are interesting because anyone of normal intelligence can, with sufficient practice and dedication, become highly proficient in most cognitive skills. This was illustrated in the case of reading mirror writing by Kolers and Perkins (1975), who gave participants extensive training on reading text that was printed upside-down or mirrored. Initially participants were able to perform the task, but they were very slow. As the participants practiced, however, their reading grew faster. After extensive training (reading 200 pages) it was almost as fast as their reading of standard text.

Skill acquisition shows that the cognitive apparatus is highly flexible. It is able to adapt to a variety of complex tasks, although that adaptation can require substantial practice. It is common to assume that that adaptation involves a change to the knowledge or information used by the cognitive apparatus, rather than a fundamental change to the way in which the cognitive apparatus functions.

Consider the case of mental arithmetic. Anyone of normal intelligence can acquire the skills required to perform large addition, subtraction, multiplication, or division problems. These skills take the form of procedures or rules that should be followed in order to solve different types of arithmetic problems. Someone skilled at arithmetic must know how and when to apply these rules, and it is the rules and a facility with their use that constitutes the skill. Cognitive skills therefore engender a division between knowledge and a system that applies that knowledge. This chapter uses the cognitive skills of multicolumn addition and subtraction to illustrate this division.

Production systems (see Chapter 1) are particularly suited to the modelling of cognitive skills because they are general purpose processing systems. A secondary aim of this chapter is therefore to illustrate the production system approach to cognitive modelling by developing production systems for the cognitive skills under consideration. This twin approach is intended to clarify both the nature of the knowledge underlying a cognitive skill and some of the requirements of a system that can apply that knowledge.

3.2 Multicolumn Addition

Multicolumn addition refers to the task of adding two large numbers, using a standard procedure. Consider the following sum:

$$\begin{array}{ccccccc} & 3 & 4 & 5 & 7 & 8 & 2 & + \\ & 8 & {}_1 1 & {}_1 7 & {}_1 4 & 2 & 3 \\ \hline 1 & 1 & 6 & 3 & 2 & 0 & 5 \end{array}$$

The standard procedure for performing multicolumn addition involves working from right to left, treating each column as a separate addition problem. The digits in one column are summed. If the sum exceeds 10, the units digit is written under the column and the tens digit is carried to the next column on the left. Otherwise the sum itself is written under the column. The procedure is relatively simple and easy to learn. However, correct performance requires appropriate control of successive steps. The nature of this control may be elucidated by a production system model of the process.

3.2.1 The Basic Production System

As discussed in Chapter 1, production systems are domain-general processing systems that perform particular tasks by operating with task-specific production rules. Consequently, a production system for multicolumn addition may be decomposed

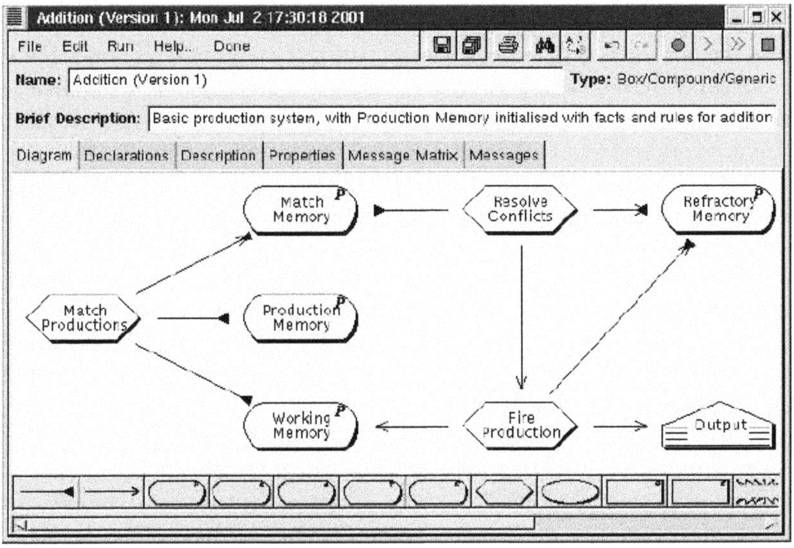

Figure 3.1: The box and arrow structure of a simple production system

into two distinct parts: the production system itself, and the production rules necessary for multicolumn addition. We focus first on the production system.

Components of the System

Production systems consist of two primary memory stores, a working memory that contains transient information and a production memory that contains rules that guide behaviour. Processing operates in two phases. In the *recognise* phase the system selects a rule whose conditions are met by the contents of the working memory. In the *act* phase the system applies the selected rule, modifying the working memory and/or generating external behaviour.

On the basis of the above, one might suspect that the box and arrow structure of a production system would consist of two buffers and a process. In fact, additional components are required. Figure 3.1 shows these components. *Working Memory* and *Production Memory* are the two memory stores referred to above. It is assumed that *Working Memory* will contain a propositional representation of critical features of the task to which the production system is applied, and that *Production Memory* will contain rules that may be applied to change *Working Memory* or effect behaviour. The *Match Productions* process is required to test the conditions of rules contained in *Production Memory* against the contents of *Working Memory*. It copies instances of all production rules whose conditions are satisfied to a third buffer, *Match Memory*. *Match Memory* is required because, at any stage of processing, the conditions of multiple production rules may be satisfied by the contents of *Working Memory*. In such cases only one rule should fire (i.e., be applied). The contents of *Match Memory* are therefore examined by another process, *Resolve Conflicts*, which selects a single production instance from *Match Memory* and passes it to *Fire Production*, which applies the rule (modifying *Working Memory* or generating behaviour in *Output*). Any modifications to *Working Memory* may result in new production instances matching, and hence in the whole process repeating.

The one buffer not described above, *Refractory Memory*, is used by *Resolve Conflicts* to ensure that a single instance of a production rule does not fire multiple times. Many production systems use this refraction method to ensure that instances of rules fire once (when they first become applicable), rather than on every processing cycle. Once an instance of a rule has been selected for firing it is recorded in *Refractory Memory*. It may then be blocked from firing on subsequent processing cycles. *Fire Production* must also have read and write access to *Refractory Memory* so that *Refractory Memory* elements may be deleted when corresponding elements are removed from *Working Memory*. The details of this are explained further below.

Exercise 3.1: Create a new research programme for the models of this chapter, and create a new root model within that research programme. Draw the box and arrow diagram from Figure 3.1 in that model, making sure that all boxes are of the appropriate type and labelled correctly. ◇

The Initial Contents of Buffers

A production system's behaviour on any particular task is determined by the contents of *Working Memory* and *Production Memory*. *Working Memory* should initially contain a representation of the information on which the system is required to act. In the case of multicolumn addition, this will be a representation of the two numbers to be added. *Production Memory* should contain a representation of the rules or procedures of the task (i.e., in the current case, the rules or procedures for multicolumn addition).

For present purposes it is useful to specify contents for the two buffers so that the production system may be tested as it is developed. Box 3.1 shows suitable contents. The figure gives two initial elements for each buffer. The elements for *Working Memory* represent digits (5 and 3). The elements for *Production Memory* represent a simple addition rule (that $3 + 5 = 8$) and a rule to output the sum of two digits, once that sum has been calculated. The details of the rules will be discussed further in Section 3.2.5, where the initial contents of both buffers will be refined. For present purposes it is sufficient to note that *Production Memory* contains elements of the form `production(Conds, Acts)`, where `Conds` is a list

Element: *Initial (dummy) element*
`digit(5)`
Element: *Initial (dummy) element*
`digit(3)`

a) Initial contents for *Working Memory*

Element: *The sum of 3 and 5 is 8*
`production([digit(3), digit(5)], [+sum(8)])`
Element: *Output a sum and its answer*
`production([digit(X), digit(Y), sum(Z)], [output(X + Y = Z)])`

b) Initial contents for *Production Memory*

Box 3.1: Initial contents for the two principal production system buffers

of conditions and `Acts` is a list of actions. The list notation for conditions and actions is important because it allows us to represent rules with some, none, or many conditions or actions, should we need to do so.

The other buffers, *Match Memory* and *Refractory Memory*, should initially be empty. These buffers will have elements added to and deleted from them as processing proceeds.

Exercise 3.2: Add the elements given in Box 3.1 to the relevant buffers of the production system model. Initialise the model and check that the initial contents of the two buffers are visible in their **Current Contents** views. ◇

Production Matching: The Recognise Phase (Part 1)

The function of the *Match Productions* process is to ensure that at all times *Match Memory* contains all and only instances of productions whose conditions are satisfied by the contents of *Working Memory*. This function can be achieved with two rules, one to add valid production instances to *Match Memory*, and one to remove invalid production instances from *Match Memory*. Box 3.2 shows suitable rules.

Rule 1 fires for each production instance whose conditions are satisfied and which is not already in *Match Memory*. It adds the production instance to *Match Memory*. The user-defined condition `match_conditions_in_wm/1` is used to test if the production's conditions are satisfied by *Working Memory*. This condition also ensures that any variables in the production's conditions are bound. Rule 2 is a kind of inverse of Rule 1. It looks for elements in *Match Memory* whose

Rule 1 (unrefracted): *Add new matching productions to match memory*
IF: `production(Conds, Acts)` is in *Production Memory*
`match_conditions_in_wm(Conds)`
not `production(Conds, Acts)` is in *Match Memory*
THEN: add `production(Conds, Acts)` to *Match Memory*

Rule 2 (unrefracted): *Delete unmatching productions from match memory*
IF: `production(Conds, Acts)` is in *Match Memory*
not `match_conditions_in_wm(Conds)`
THEN: delete `production(Conds, Acts)` from *Match Memory*

Condition Definition: `match_conditions_in_wm/1`: *Test condition list*
```
match_conditions_in_wm([]).
match_conditions_in_wm([H|T]) :-
    condition_is_satisfiable(H)
    match_conditions_in_wm(T)
```

Condition Definition: `condition_is_satisfiable/1`: *Test one condition*
```
condition_is_satisfiable(H) :-
    H is in Working Memory
condition_is_satisfiable(not H) :-
    not H is in Working Memory
```

Box 3.2: Rules and a condition definition from *Match Productions*

conditions are not satisfied by *Working Memory* (using the negation of the user-defined condition used by Rule 1), and removes them from *Match Memory*.

Rules 1 and 2 are both marked as unrefracted. This means that both rules may fire multiple times with the same variable bindings. Thus, Rule 1 may add a production instance to *Match Memory* more than once, and Rule 2 may delete a production instance from *Match Memory* more than once. To see why this is important consider the following scenario: An element is added to *Working Memory*. The element matches the conditions of a production, and the resulting production instance is added to *Match Memory* (by Rule 1). The element is then removed from *Working Memory*. The corresponding production instance is removed from *Match Memory* (by Rule 2). At some later point another element that is identical to the first is added to *Working Memory*. Another copy of the production instance should be added to *Match Memory*. However, if Rule 1 was refracted, it would not apply again, and the system would not function as intended.

The user-defined condition `match_conditions_in_wm/1` requires additional comment. It tests if a production's conditions are satsified, and generates a production instance in the process. The definition uses a common list processing trick for applying functions to elements of lists: a function can be applied to all elements of a list by applying it to the first element of the list (sometimes called the *head* of the list) and then applying it to the remainder of the list (sometimes called the *tail* of the list).

The first clause of the definition of `match_conditions_in_wm/1` deals with the case of an empty condition list: if a production rule has an empty condition list (i.e., no conditions), its conditions are necessarily satisfied. The second clause deals with non-empty condition lists. It breaks the list into its head and tail, and tests that the head condition is satisfiable (via a further user-defined condition) and that the tail condition list matches in working memory, through a recursive call to `match_conditions_in_wm/1`.

It is important to understand the functioning of recursion. If, in the above case, the condition list consisted of just one element, the second clause would break this list into its head (the element) and its tail (the empty list), and test the appropriate user-defined conditions on each. The test on the tail (the empty list) would succeed because of the first clause of the definition of `match_conditions_in_wm/1`. Each additional element of the condition list will result in an additional recursive call of `match_conditions_in_wm/1`.

The second user-defined condition, `condition_is_satisfiable/1`, also requires comment. Production systems differ with respect to the complexity of the conditions that they allow, but most production systems allow negated conditions — conditions of the form *not X* — which are true if and only if the embedded condition, *X*, is false. `condition_is_satisfiable/1` has been designed to work with productions that may have such negated conditions. Its first clause deals with standard (non-negated) conditions, while its second clause deals with negated conditions.

Exercise 3.3: Add the contents of Box 3.2 to *Match Memory* and step through execution of the model. After initialisation, Rule 1 of *Match Productions* should transfer one element to *Match Memory*. Processing should then terminate. ◇

Conflict Resolution: The Recognise Phase (Part 2)

Conflict resolution is the process of selecting one applicable production instance from the set of matching instances. The selected instance is then fired or applied. Conflict resolution ensures that only one production is fired at a time. While conflict resolution is not present in all production systems (see Hajnal *et al.*, 1989, and Meyer & Kieras, 1997, for examples without conflict resolution), it is part of the vast majority, and provides a convenient mechanism to ensure serial behaviour.

A simplified form of conflict resolution can be achieved within the present system with a single rule (see Box 3.3) and appropriate access settings for *Production Memory* and *Working Memory*. The conditions of the rule match one production instance in *Match Memory* that is not also in *Refractory Memory*. The rule's

Rule 1 (unrefracted; once): *Fire and refract matching production*
IF: `Instance` is in *Match Memory*
not `Instance` is in *Refractory Memory*
THEN: add `Instance` to *Refractory Memory*
send `Instance` to *Fire Production*

Box 3.3: The conflict resolution rule (from *Resolve Conflicts*)

actions add the matched instance to *Match Memory* (thus preventing the same instance from being matched by the rule later) and send it to *Fire Production*, which should apply the production instance.

Crucially, the rule is marked as once. This ensures that the rule doesn't fire multiple times on the same processing cycle, and hence that only one production instance is applied at a time. The rule is also marked as unrefracted, but the effect of refraction is achieved through the use of *Refractory Memory* to store instances of rules that have been applied and prevent those instances from being applied again. A similar effect could be obtained by marking the rule as refracted, but the solution here is more flexible: it allows production rules to be temporarily refracted, but to be reactivated if the refractory record is ever removed. Such cases may occur when an element is removed from *Working Memory*, as described below.

The once marking ensures that multiple possible instantiations of the rule are ignored, but if multiple instantiations exist, the one selected will depend upon the settings of the Access properties of *Production Memory*, *Working Memory* and *Match Memory*. If *Match Memory* has LIFO (Last-In First-Out) access, for example, then the production instance chosen by Rule 1 of Box 3.3 will be that which was most recently added to *Match Memory*. This is generally what is required, but this means that if multiple matches are added to *Match Memory* on the same processing cycle, less favourable matches should be added before more favourable matches. Thus, if the top-to-bottom ordering of productions in *Production Memory* is to be favoured then *Production Memory* should also have LIFO access, so that the top-most elements in *Production Memory* are tested last. In contrast, if recency in *Working Memory* is to be favoured, then *Working Memory* should have FIFO (First-In First-Out) access, so that the elements that have been in *Working Memory* for many cycles are matched before elements that have just entered *Working Memory*.

With all of these settings, Rule 1 of Box 3.2 will still result in *Production Memory* access having priority over *Working Memory* access, because the rule tests *Production Memory* before it tests *Working Memory*. More complex approaches to conflict resolution may prioritise *Working Memory* access over *Pro-*

duction Memory access, and may ensure that productions with many conditions are favoured over productions with few conditions. Such complications are not considered here.

Exercise 3.4: Add the conflict resolution rule to *Resolve Conflicts* and set all buffer access properties appropriately. Examine the messages generated by each process as the resulting model is executed. After a couple of cycles of processing, *Resolve Conflicts* should now select one production instance to fire, add it to *Refractory Memory*, and send it to *Fire Productions*. ◇

Production Firing: The Act Phase

The final stage of the production system's operation consists of the application or firing of the production instance selected by *Resolve Conflicts*. The rules given in Box 3.4 assume that productions may perform three distinct types of action: additions to *Working Memory*, deletions from *Working Memory*, and output operations. Different production systems allow different actions. While virtually all production systems allow productions to add elements to working memory, some do not allow deletion of working memory elements, and some provide alternative means for output.

Each of the first three rules in Box 3.4 has the same basic form. They are all triggered by the receipt of a production instance of the form `production(Conds, Acts)`. `Acts` is assumed to be a list of actions to be performed. Rule 1 adds an element of the form `X` to *Working Memory* for each element of the form +`X` in `Acts`. Rule 2 deletes an element of the form `X` from *Working Memory* for each element of the form −`X` in `Acts`. Rule 3 outputs an element of the form `X` to *Output* for each element of the form `output(X)` in `Acts`. All three rules are unrefracted because a production system may need to perform a particular action multiple times in the service of a task.

The one wrinkle in the above is that if a production fires based on the matching of an element in *Working Memory*, and the element is subsequently deleted and then added again, the production should in principle be able to fire a second time. Rule 4 (and the second action of Rule 2, which triggers Rule 4) ensures that this is possible. If an element is deleted from *Working Memory* Rule 4 removes any *Refractory Memory* elements that matched that element, thus allowing identical production instances to again enter into conflict resolution.

Exercise 3.5: Add the rules for applying productions and test the model. In particular track the passing of messages between processes, and the accumulation of output in *Output*. How does the model's behaviour differ from that described above? Can you identify why the model behaves incorrectly? ◇

Rule 1 (unrefracted): *Make additions to working memory*
TRIGGER: `production(Conds, Acts)`
IF: `+X` is a member of `Acts`
THEN: add `X` to *Working Memory*

Rule 2 (unrefracted): *Make deletions from working memory*
TRIGGER: `production(Conds, Acts)`
IF: `−X` is a member of `Acts`
THEN: delete `X` from *Working Memory*
send `tidy(X)` to *Fire Productions*

Rule 3 (unrefracted): *Send output*
TRIGGER: `production(Conds, Acts)`
IF: `output(X)` is a member of `Acts`
THEN: send `X` to *Output*

Rule 4 (unrefracted): *Keep refractory memory up to date*
TRIGGER: `tidy(X)`
IF: `production(Conds, Acts)` is in *Refractory Memory*
`X` is a member of `Conds`
THEN: delete `production(Conds, Acts)` from *Refractory Memory*

Box 3.4: Rules for applying a production (from *Fire Productions*)

Ensuring Sequential Operation

There are two undesirable aspects of the behaviour of the system as it stands. First, the output includes statements that are both true (e.g., $3 + 5 = 8$) and false (e.g., $3 + 3 = 8$). This is because the second production rule is unable to distinguish between the two digits. It is essentially a representational problem. Second, if *Match Memory* contains multiple production instances that have not previously been applied, then *Resolve Conflicts* will select one production instance and forward it to *Fire Productions* (as it should), but *Resolve Conflicts* will continue to select another production instance on the very next processing cycle, before the previously selected instance has been performed by *Fire Productions*.

This second problem is serious, for it means that the production system is not really acting sequentially — it is not selecting one production instance, applying it, and then selecting a second production instance on the basis of the consequences of applying the first instance. Rather, it is selecting several production instances, effectively at the same time, and then applying all of them. To see why this is not what is required consider the following production rules:

Rule 1 (unrefracted; once): *Fire and refract matching production*
TRIGGER: `system_quiescent`
IF: `Instance` is in *Match Memory*
not `Instance` is in *Refractory Memory*
THEN: add `Instance` to *Refractory Memory*
send `Instance` to *Fire Production*

Box 3.5: The revised conflict resolution rule (from *Resolve Conflicts*)

```
1:  production([a, b], [+c, -b])
2:  production([a, b], [+d, -b])
3:  production([a, c], [+e, -c])
4:  production([a, d], [+e, -d])
```

If *Working Memory* initially contains `a` and `b`, then both production 1 and production 2 might apply. Conflict resolution should select one of these productions, apply it, and then, on the basis of the resultant state of *Working Memory* select the next production. Consequently, if production 1 is selected by conflict resolution, production 3 will fire on the next production cycle. If production 2 is selected by conflict resolution, production 4 will fire on the next production cycle. However, with the model developed thus far, production 1 and production 2 will fire on successive COGENT processing cycles, leading to both production 3 and production 4 also firing.

Fortunately there is a simple solution to this problem. The conflict resolution rule (Rule 1 of Box 3.3) must be modified so that it only fires when all other processing by the production system has ceased. This point is known as quiescence. COGENT detects quiescence and automatically sends a message of the form `system_quiescent` to each process whenever the system is quiescent. Thus, the conflict resolution rule may be prevented from firing inappropriately by modifying it so that it is triggered by `system_quiescence`, as in Box 3.5. With this modification, the basic production system is complete.

Exercise 3.6: Modify the conflict resolution rule as described above, and ensure that conflict resolution now only occurs when all other processing has ceased. ◇

Exercise 3.7: Try to find a way of representing the digits, sums, and production rules used in this section so that the production system does not generate false statements (i.e., so that it does not generate statements such as $3 + 3 = 8$). ◇

1. Focus on the right-most column first.
2. To process the focus column, recall the sum of its digits.
3. If a column's digits have been summed and there remains an unprocessed carry, add that too.
4. If a column's digits have been summed and there's no unprocessed carry and the answer is less than 10, write it under the column
5. If there's no carry to be processed, and the answer is 10 or more, then write the units digit under the focus column and carry the tens digit to the next column.
6. If an answer has been written in the focus column, shift focus one column to the left.

Figure 3.2: Semi-formal condition-action rules for multicolumn addition

3.2.2 Rules and Representations for Multicolumn Addition

The production system described above is a general processing system that may be applied to a range of tasks or cognitive skills. To apply the system to a specific task requires supplementing the system with task knowledge in the form of a set of production rules.

The six semi-formal rules in Figure 3.2 summarise the standard procedure for multicolumn addition in semi-formal terms. The rules depend on the concept of a focus column, and provide instructions for setting the focus column, processing it, and shifting focus when the focus column has been processed. In addition, the rules take the form of condition-action pairs: if the conditions of any rule hold then the actions of that rule may be performed. In other words, the rules have the same form as production rules.

The addition rules can be fully formalised by re-representing their conditions and actions in terms of symbolic propositions. For example, the first rule might be re-represented as:

If	`goal(mca)` and
	not `answer(C, A)` and
	not `processing(C)`
then	`+processing(column1)`

The propositional form of the rule may be translated as: "if the goal is to perform a multicolumn addition (i.e., working memory contains `goal(mca)`), and there are no answers under any columns (working memory does not contain anything of the form `answer(C, A)`), and no column is currently being processed (working memory does not contain anything of the form `processing(C)`), then begin processing the first column (by adding `processing(column1)` to the working memory).

The first rule is relatively straightforward to represent in terms of symbolic propositions, but the other rules raise difficulties. The second and third rules, for example, require recall of the sum of two digits. How might such recall be handled? The fourth and fifth rules require comparing the sum of digits in a column with ten, and decomposing that sum into tens and units digits if it is not less than ten. The sixth rule, for shifting focus, requires knowing which column comes next, but if the columns are labelled 1, 2, 3, ..., then even this requires knowledge of counting.

There are four ways of addressing each of the above problems: by extending the production rule language (e.g., allowing arithmetic comparison and simple addition within rules), by augmenting the production rule set with many special purpose rules, by augmenting working memory with many special purpose facts, or by choosing a representation that is conducive to the relevant operation.

To illustrate the issues raised by each of these possibilities, consider the focus shifting rule:

```
If   goal(mca) and
     processing(Column) and
     answer(Column, AnyAns)
then −processing(Column)
     +processing(NextColumn)
```

The difficulty is in relating `NextColumn` to `Column`. If the production language were extended to allow addition, and columns were labelled by integers increasing from right to left, then this could be achieved by extending the production rule with a further action:

```
NextColumn is Column + 1
```

This is the simplest of the modifications, but it requires that actions within a production may perform basic arithmetic. This in turn requires modification of the rules within *Fire Production* (Box 3.4).

Alternatively, a separate production rule could be used for shifting from each column:

```
If   goal(mca) and
     processing(1) and
     answer(1, AnyAns)
then −processing(1)
     +processing(2)
```

The difficulty with this solution is its lack of generality. Three production rules will be needed for a three column problem, but five production rules will be needed for a five column problem, and however many production rules are supplied, they will never capture the general rule of shifting focus one column to the left.

A better solution involves using a single production rule to capture the idea of shifting focus to the left by augmenting working memory with facts about column layout. For example, if working memory were to contain propositions such as:

```
next_column(column1, column2)
next_column(column2, column3)
⋮
```

then focus shifting could be achieved by a single production rule of the form:

```
If    goal(mca) and
      processing(Column) and
      answer(Column, AnyAns) and
      next_column(Column, NextColumn)
then  −processing(Column)
      +processing(NextColumn)
```

This does not require that columns be labelled with integers. Instead it requires a series of propositions in working memory.

A fourth solution is to represent columns in a form that is conducive to the requirements of focus shifting. For example, column labels may be represented using *successor* notation. Successor notation is a way of representing order within labels. With this notation, the first column might be labelled `c1`. The second column may then be labelled `s(c1)`, indicating that it is the successor of `c1`. Similarly the third column may then be labelled `s(s(c1))`, indicating that it is the successor of the second label. Using successor notation, the focus shifting rule can be expressed as:

```
If    goal(mca) and
      processing(Column) and
      answer(Column, AnyAns) and
then  −processing(Column)
      +processing(s(Column))
```

Any of these four solutions could be applied to each of the three representational problems raised by the semi-formal rules in Figure 3.2. For example, Section 3.3 discusses how the production rule language might be extended, in the context of multicolumn subtraction, to allow simple arithmetic operations within production rules. However, the approach adopted here in the case of multicolumn addition is to use additional production rules for recall of basic arithmetic facts because these facts correspond to long-term knowledge and such knowledge is

Element: *The top-level goal is multicolumn addition (mca)*
`goal(mca)`
Element: *In the first column is 2 and 3*
`column(c1,2,3)`
Element: *In the second column is 8 and 2*
`column(s(c1),8,2)`
Element: *In the third column is 7 and 4*
`column(s(s(c1)),7,4)`
Element: *In the fourth column is 5 and 7*
`column(s(s(s(c1))),5,7)`
Element: *In the fifth column is 4 and 1*
`column(s(s(s(s(c1)))),4,1)`
Element: *In the sixth column is 3 and 8*
`column(s(s(s(s(s(c1))))),3,8)`

Box 3.6: A representation of a multicolumn addition problem, with successor notation used for column labels

normally represented via production rules. Additional production rules are also used for decomposing a number into tens and units. Arguably this decomposition should be supported by the representation, in a way analogous to the way successor notation supports shifting focus, rather than encoded as long-term knowledge. For example, if 26 were represented as $(2 \times 10) + 6$, then decomposition could be achieved by matching the tens or units parts of the representation. The treatment adopted here is based on convenience and simplicity. Finally, successor notation is used for representing column labels, as such labels are assumed to be implicit in the representation of a multicolumn addition problem.

3.2.3 Representing a Multicolumn Addition Problem

Box 3.6 shows a representation of the multicolumn addition problem shown on page 84, with successor notation used for column labels. Each column is represented by a `column/3` term whose first element is the column label and whose second and third elements are the digits in that column.

Exercise 3.8: Replace the contents of *Working Memory* in the basic production system with the elements in Box 3.6. Initialise the model and examine the Current Contents view of *Working Memory*. Each element from Box 3.6 should appear in the view. ◇

3.2.4 Display Rules for Working Memory

The *Working Memory* representation of multicolumn addition problems shown in Box 3.6 is entirely equivalent to the standard diagrammatic representation shown on page 84. However, the use of successor notation and the representation of the problem in terms of rows rather than columns is slightly obscure. COGENT provides a mechanism for specifying *display rules*, which improve visualisation of a model's behaviour by mapping propositional representations of buffer contents to diagrammatic representations. The mechanisms involve defining a set of rules for mapping between representations. The user may then examine the diagrammatic representation of a propositional buffer's contents in place of its propositional representation.

Display rules are similar to standard COGENT rules except that 1) they can only match elements in the buffer that contains them and 2) their actions all take the form "show x", where x specifies a graphical object (e.g., some text or line segments). Display rules have no effect on model execution: they only map between internal proposition representations manipulated by the COGENT model and a diagrammatic representation that is more convenient for monitoring the model's behaviour.

Box 3.7 shows a complete set of rules for converting the kind of propositional representation shown in Box 3.6 to diagrammatic form. Display Rule 1 displays each digit from the addition problem. It uses a user-defined condition, `x_column/2`, to work out a reasonable X co-ordinate for each column. The first row is placed at Y co-ordinate 50 and the second at Y co-ordinate 75. Each time the rule fires it displays two `text/3` items. The arguments of a `text/3` item specify an arbitrary label for the item, the text and its co-ordinates, and a list of secondary properties, in this case indicating the colour of the text.

Display Rules 2 and 3 draw "syntactic sugar" — the plus sign to the right of the top-most row and the line beneath two numbers respectively. Note that the plus sign is surrounded by space characters and the whole thing is enclosed in single quotation marks. This is essential to make COGENT treat the plus sign as text rather than as an arithmetic operator. Display Rule 2 should fire just once to draw the plus sign. Display Rule 3 will fire once for each column, drawing a line segment under each column. This will yield a continuous line under the complete addition problem.

Display Rule 4 is designed to display the answer under each column. It will only apply when the model has begun to perform its calculations. Display Rule 5 is similarly of interest when the model is performing its calculations. It draws a red box around the focus column.

Exercise 3.9: Add the rules from Box 3.7 to the Display Rules view of *Working Memory*. Reinitialise the model and examine the Current Display view. The

Display Rule 1: *Display the digits in each column*
IF: `column(C, A1, A2)` is in *Working Memory*
`x_column(C, X)`
THEN: show `text(column(C), A1 at (X, 50), [colour(black)])`
show `text(column(C), A2 at (X, 75), [colour(black)])`

Display Rule 2: *Display a plus sign*
IF: `goal(mca)` is in *Working Memory*
`x_column(c1, X)`
`X2` is `X + 15`
THEN: show `text(stx, ' + ' at (X2, 50), [colour(black)])`

Display Rule 3: *Display the line beneath the addenda (in each column)*
IF: `column(C, _, _)` is in *Working Memory*
`x_column(C, X)`
`X1` is `X − 10`
`X2` is `X + 15`
THEN: show `line(stx, (X1, 85) to (X2, 85), [colour(black)])`

Display Rule 4: *Display the answer for each column*
IF: `answer(C, S)` is in *Working Memory*
`x_column(C, X)`
THEN: show `text(column(C), S at (X, 100), [colour(black)])`

Display Rule 5: *Display a focus box*
IF: `processing(C)` is in *Working Memory*
`x_column(C, X)`
`X0` is `X − 7`
THEN: show `box(focus, (22, 45) at (X0, 82), [colour(red)])`

Condition Definition: `x_column/2`: *Get X co-ordinate of column's location*

```
x_column(c1, 400).
x_column(s(C), X1) : −
    x_column(C, X)
    X1 is X − 25
```

Box 3.7: Display rules for multicolumn addition (from *Working Memory*)

problem should now be displayed in the familiar multicolumn addition format.

◇

Element: *1. Start by processing the first column*

```
rule([goal(mca), not answer(_,_), not processing(_)],
     [+processing(c1)])
```

Element: *2. Process a column: Initiate recall of arithmetic fact*

```
rule([goal(mca), processing(C), column(C, A, B)],
     [+recall(A + B)])
```

Element: *3. Arithmetic fact has been recalled: Remove trigger*

```
rule([goal(mca), processing(C), recall(X + Y), sum(Sum)],
     [-recall(X + Y)])
```

Element: *4. Add the carry to the partial column sum*

```
rule([goal(mca), processing(C), sum(Sum), carry(C, X)],
     [-sum(Sum), -carry(C, X), +recall(Sum + X)])
```

Element: *5. Split the answer once the carry has been processed*

```
rule([goal(mca), processing(C), sum(A), not carry(C, _)],
     [-sum(A), +split(A)])
```

Element: *6. Determine the answer for the current column*

```
rule([goal(mca), processing(C), split(A), tens_units(T, U)],
     [+answer(C, U), +carry(s(C), T), -split(A), -tens_units(T, U)])
```

Element: *7. Output a column's answer*

```
rule([goal(mca), processing(C), answer(C, Sum)],
     [output(C = Sum), -processing(C)])
```

Element: *8. Process the next column*

```
rule([goal(mca), answer(C, _), not answer(s(C), _), not processing(_)],
     [+processing(s(C))])
```

Element: *9. Finish processing: write any remaining carry*

```
rule([goal(mca), processing(C), not column(C, _, _), carry(C, X)],
     [+answer(C, X), -carry(C, X)])
```

Element: *10. Finish processing: terminate the "mca" goal*

```
rule([goal(mca), processing(C), not column(C, _, _), not carry(_, _)],
     [-goal(mca), -processing(C)])
```

Box 3.8: Production system rules for multicolumn addition (from *Production Memory*)

3.2.5 Production Rules for Multicolumn Addition

It remains to formalise the rules for multicolumn addition given in Figure 3.2 and provide the system with appropriate knowledge of arithmetic facts. Box 3.8 shows a set of suitably formalised rules. Each rule is given in the form of a *Production Memory* element, but the correspondence between the semi-formal rules of Figure 3.2 and the productions is loose.

The first production is an initialisation rule that results in a `processing/1` element being added to *Working Memory*. The second production prompts recall of an arithmetic fact. It is assumed that this recall results in the creation of a new *Working Memory* element of the form `sum(S)`. The third production removes the recall prompt once this element has been added, and the fourth production prompts another cycle of arithmetic fact recall to process any digits carried from a previous column.

The fifth production prompts splitting the sum obtained for the current column into tens and units. It is assumed that other productions perform this splitting, and add an appropriate element of the form `tens_units(T,U)` to *Working Memory*. Once the sum has been split, the sixth production determines that the units digit is the answer for the current column and that the tens digit should be carried to the next column. The seventh production then outputs the answer for the current column. The eighth production shifts focus to the next column once an answer has been obtained.

The ninth and tenth productions only apply near the end of processing. The ninth production deals with any carry from the last column, setting this as the answer for a new column to the left of the sum. The tenth production recognises when processing is complete and terminates the multicolumn addition goal.

Exercise 3.10: Add the ten production rules from Box 3.8 to *Production Memory*. Be sure to enter the rules in the same order as they appear in the figure. Initialise the production system and run a few cycles. The first production rule should fire, initialising the focus to the right-most column. On the next cycle of production firing the second rule should fire, entering a recall prompt into *Working Memory*. Processing in the system should then halt, as no further production rules should be applicable. ◇

The production rules of Box 3.8 embody knowledge of the procedure for multicolumn addition. As noted above, knowledge of arithmetic facts is also required. Box 3.9 illustrates these facts. Three types of fact are needed: the result of splitting each number from `0` to `19` into tens and units, the result of adding any two single digit numbers, and the result of adding `0` or `1` to any number from `0` to `18`. The last of these is required when processing numbers that have been carried from one column to the next.

Exercise 3.11: Extend *Production Memory* with production rules that embody the necessary arithmetic facts, as in Box 3.9. One hundred and forty additional elements are required for the full multicolumn system. Entering all facts is very tedious, so attempt to enter just those needed for one simple problem (e.g., the

Element: *Split 0 into 0 * 10 + 0*
`rule([split(0)], [+tens_units(0, 0)])`
Element: *Split 1 into 0 * 10 + 1*
`rule([split(1)], [+tens_units(0, 1)])`

⋮

Element: *Split 19 into 1 * 10 + 9*
`rule([split(19)], [+tens_units(1, 9)])`
Element: *Basic arithmetic fact: 0 + 0 = 0*
`rule([recall(0 + 0), not sum(_)], [+sum(0)])`
Element: *Basic arithmetic fact: 0 + 1 = 1*
`rule([recall(0 + 1), not sum(_)], [+sum(1)])`

⋮

Element: *Basic arithmetic fact: 9 + 9 = 18*
`rule([recall(9 + 9), not sum(_)], [+sum(18)])`
Element: *Basic arithmetic fact: 10 + 0 = 10*
`rule([recall(10 + 0), not sum(_)], [+sum(10)])`
Element: *Basic arithmetic fact: 10 + 1 = 11*
`rule([recall(10 + 1), not sum(_)], [+sum(11)])`
Element: *Basic arithmetic fact: 11 + 0 = 11*
`rule([recall(11 + 0), not sum(_)], [+sum(11)])`

⋮

Element: *Basic arithmetic fact: 18 + 1 = 19*
`rule([recall(18 + 1), not sum(_)], [+sum(19)])`

Box 3.9: Some of the additional arithmetic knowledge required for multicolumn addition (from *Production Memory*)

problem on page 84, which requires $2 + 3$ for the first column, $8 + 2$ for the second column, and so on). ◇

3.2.6 Discussion

The production system model of multicolumn addition illustrates how a basic production system architecture can be applied to a simple cognitive skill. The representational issues arising from this application have already been discussed (see Section 3.2.2). The application also illustrates the different types of knowledge required by the skill (knowledge of the procedure and knowledge of arithmetic facts), the distinction between knowledge and use of that knowledge, the interaction of parallel and sequential processing within a production system, and the complexities of conflict resolution.

Production systems draw a clear distinction between knowledge and use of that knowledge. Each production represents one unit of long-term knowledge, and the production system interpreter provides a general mechanism for applying this knowledge. Notice though that the production system interpreter is not able to directly access or reflect upon the contents of its production memory. That is, while the production system might "know" that $2 + 2 = 4$, it can't know that it knows this.

At one level there is no distinction within the production system between knowledge of the multicolumn addition procedure and knowledge of arithmetic facts: both are represented as production rules and both are used in the same way by the general production system interpreter. The only difference between the rules is that those relating to the procedure include `goal(mca)` among their conditions. Hence, the rules of multicolumn addition will only apply when the goal is to complete a multicolumn addition problem. None of the arithmetic facts test this goal, so they may apply in other situations (e.g., in multicolumn multiplication or in any other task requiring arithmetic). In general, including a goal test within a production rule allows different rule sets, for different goals, to sit alongside each other in production memory. Rule sets will only become relevant when the appropriate goal enters working memory.

It is a common misconception that symbolic models are inherently serial in nature. This is not true, and aspects of parallel symbolic processing are shown by the production system model. In particular, the recognise phase — determining which production instances might fire — is a fully parallel process. It is only the act phase — firing one of those productions — that is serial.

The recognise phase terminates with the process of conflict resolution. The implementation of conflict resolution described above relies upon the interaction of Access properties of three buffers. This interaction is potentially complex, and judicious order of production rules in *Production Memory* is required in order to ensure that the system functions as intended. Arguably this is an unsatisfactory aspect, not of this particular model, but of the standard production system conflict resolution procedure.

Lack of control over conflict resolution has led to several innovations in production system design. For example, ACT-R (Anderson, 1993) uses an activation-based mechanism to ensure that only one production instance fires at a time. Production instances accumulate activation over time, and the instance that accumulates sufficient activation first is the one that fires. In Soar (Laird *et al.*, 1987), by constrast, multiple production instances may fire in parallel, but production firing does not directly change working memory. Instead it generates "preferences" for working memory changes, and these preferences are then evaluated, yielding a single most preferred working memory change.

Exercise 3.12: Explore the production system model by altering the properties of the buffers. In particular, try varying the **Access** property of the three buffers that control the match order of production rules. Try to explain any effects observed. Also experiment with decay and capacity limitations on *Refractory Memory* and *Working Memory*. How does this affect the system's performance? ◇

3.2.7 Project: Extending the Model

The basic multicolumn addition procedure can be applied to addition problems consisting of more than two numbers. Thus, in the three number case we have:

$$
\begin{array}{ccccccc}
 & 3 & 4 & 5 & 7 & 8 & 2 & + \\
 & 9 & 2 & 1 & 8 & 0 & 7 & \\
 & & {}_{1}1 & {}_{2}7 & {}_{1}4 & {}_{1}2 & 3 & \\
\hline
1 & 2 & 8 & 5 & 0 & 1 & 2 &
\end{array}
$$

Modify the production system to perform multicolumn addition for more than two numbers. Try to develop a single, general solution that applies for any number of rows. Your solution should involve specifying a representation, initial contents for *Working Memory* and suitable production rules for *Production Memory*.

Multicolumn multiplication is another cognitive skill with some similarities to multicolumn addition. Develop a production system for multicolumn multiplication.

3.3 Multicolumn Subtraction

The previous section demonstrated that production systems are able to perform the steps from a multi-step task in sequence. This appears to be a computational requirement of the cognitive skill of multicolumn addition. However, no attempt was made in the previous section to evaluate the production system model against human performance. This section develops a more sophisticated model of a related task, multicolumn subtraction, that is informed by the errors made by children when learning the task.

3.3.1 Some Empirical Findings

Children frequently make errors when learning the cognitive skill of multicolumn subtraction. Some of these errors appear to result from number-fact errors —

faulty knowledge of basic arithmetic — such as thinking that $7 - 5 = 3$. However, many errors appear not to be of this form. Yet there are strong regularities that hold over these other errors. These regularities may be understood as reflecting characteristic faults in the application of the procedure or algorithm for multicolumn subtraction. The following examples, adapted from Young and O'Shea (1981) and taken from children's workbooks, are illustrative:

$$\begin{array}{cc}6 & 3\ - \\ 4 & 4 \\ \hline 2 & 1\end{array} \qquad \begin{array}{cc}{}^{8}\not{9} & {}^{1}6\ - \\ 4_1 & 2 \\ \hline 3 & 4\end{array} \qquad \begin{array}{cc}7 & 0\ - \\ 4 & 7 \\ \hline 3 & 0\end{array}$$

In the first example, the child appears to have incorrectly taken the difference of the digits in the right-most column, instead of borrowing. In the second example, another child has borrowed from the second column when it it was not necessary. He or she has then carried the tens digit of the answer into the second column. The third example illustrates an error that sometimes occurs when zero is present in a column: the child has simply copied the other digit, instead of borrowing and taking the difference.

Young and O'Shea (1981) analysed a corpus of 1549 subtraction problem attempts obtained from 33 10-year old children. The attempts contained 344 errors, including 127 which could be interpreted as number-fact errors and 178 which could be interpreted as algorithm errors. Young and O'Shea were unable to classify the remaining 39 errors. Further analysis of the algorithm errors suggested that there were just nine error types. The consistency with which individual children produced the different error types led Young and O'Shea to argue that the behaviour of individual children was best understood in terms of "faithfully executing a faulty algorithm, rather than wrongly following a correct one" (Young & O'Shea, 1981, p. 154). In order to demonstrate this, they developed a production system account of children's behaviour on multicolumn subtraction. The production system (described below) was able to account for correct multicolumn subtraction with 12 production rules. Each of the nine algorithm errors could be accounted for by removing rules from the production system or by adding extraneous rules to the production system.

3.3.2 The Production System Interpreter

Young and O'Shea were primarily interested in the procedure of multicolumn subtraction. They were not interested in errors in recall of basic arithmetic facts. They therefore used a slightly more powerful production system interpreter than that introduced in Section 3.2.1. The interpreter (OPS2: Forgy & McDermott, 1977) could perform a variety of basic actions beyond simple modification of working memory and output. These actions included arithmetic, input, and focus shifting.

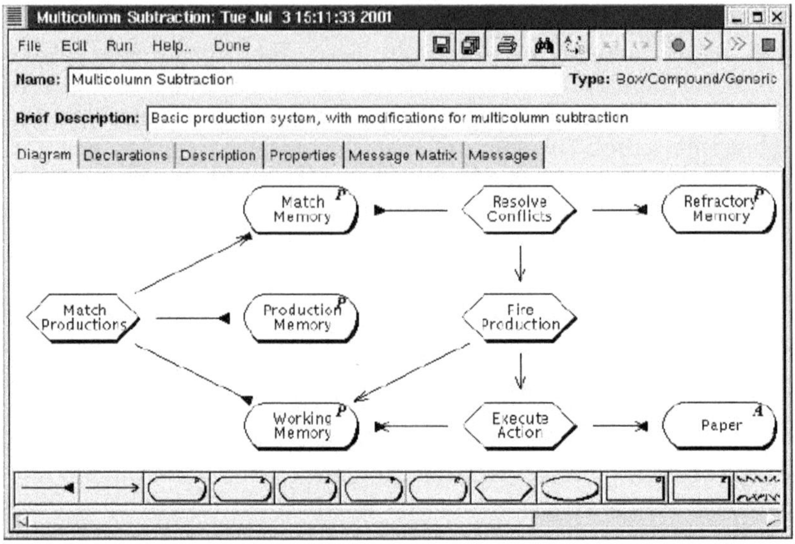

Figure 3.3: The box and arrow structure of the production system for multicolumn subtraction

Functional Components

Figure 3.3 shows a box and arrow diagram of a production system equivalent to that used by Young and O'Shea (1981). It differs from Figure 3.1 in three respects:

1. There is a new process, *Execute Action*, which may be triggered by *Fire Production*. This allows production rules to perform the necessary basic actions. Thus, if a production requires that the difference between two digits be calculated, *Fire Productions* will send an appropriate message to *Execute Actions*, and *Execute Actions* will perform the calculations and add the result to *Working Memory*.
2. *Output*, a data sink in the previous system, has been replaced by *Paper*, an analogue buffer. *Paper* will be used for a diagrammatic representation of the subtraction problem. It will be modified by *Execute Action* as processing proceeds.
3. *Fire Production* no longer has read or write access to *Refractory Memory*. Young and O'Shea's production rules do not delete elements from *Working Memory*. Thus *Fire Production* does not need to remove elements from *Refractory Memory*. This means that another solution must be found to the problems caused to the refraction process by *Working Memory* elements that are added, deleted, and then added again.

Exercise 3.13: Create a copy of the previous multicolumn addition model and modify its box and arrow diagram to yield the diagram shown in Figure 3.3. Clear all initial elements from *Working Memory* and *Production Memory*. ◇

The Recognise Phase

As noted above, Young and O'Shea's production rules for multicolumn subtraction do not delete elements from *Working Memory*. They do, however, rely on elements such as `process_column` and `next_column` which may be added to *Working Memory* multiple times during processing of a subtraction problem. Each time these items are added they should trigger production rules for processing a column or for moving to the next column. However, the standard refractory test ensures that instances of production rules only fire if the same instance has not previously fired.

In the multicolumn addition model this problem was addressed by removing production instances from *Refractory Memory* when elements matched by those instances were removed from *Working Memory*. This meant that a later instance of the working memory element could cause a production instance to fire again. An alternative approach to this problem is to make all elements of *Working Memory* distinct by tagging each one with a unique symbol. This approach is superior to that employed in the multicolumn addition model because it does not rely upon the previous instance of an element being removed from *Working Memory*.

The multicolumn subtraction model therefore assumes that all elements of *Working Memory* take the form `wme(Token,Tag)`, where `Token` is the content of the working memory element and `Tag` is a tag associated with this particular instance. This modification requires a slight adjustment to the COGENT rules for recognising matching productions. Appropriately adjusted rules are shown in Box 3.10.

Notice that the rules assume that *Production Memory* elements are `rule/3` terms and that `MatchMemory` elements are `rule/4` terms. All production rules in the multicolumn subtraction model are named for easier reference. The name is the first argument of the `rule/3` and `rule/4` terms. The second and third arguments of each are the production rule's condition list and action list. The final argument of a `rule/4` term is the list of tagged working memory elements matched by the production instance. This list is constructed during the matching process by `match_conditions_in_wm/2`, which has been appropriately modified. It is this list of tagged elements that will allow production instances that match against different instances of the same working memory tokens to be differentiated.

Exercise 3.14: Modify the rules in *Match Productions* to take account of tagging of *Working Memory* elements, as shown in Box 3.10. ◇

Rule 1 (unrefracted): *Add new matching productions to match memory*
IF: `rule(N, C, A)` is in *Production Memory*
`match_conditions_in_wm(C, M)`
not `rule(N, C, A, M)` is in *Match Memory*
THEN: add `rule(N, C, A, M)` to *Match Memory*

Rule 2 (unrefracted): *Delete unmatching productions from match memory*
IF: `rule(N, C, A, M)` is in *Match Memory*
not `match_conditions_in_wm(C, _)`
THEN: delete `rule(N, C, A, M)` from *Match Memory*

Condition Definition: `match_conditions_in_wm/2`: *Test conditions*

```
match_conditions_in_wm([], []).
match_conditions_in_wm([H|T], [wme(H, N)|MT]) : −
    wme(H, N) is in Working Memory
    match_conditions_in_wm(T, MT)
match_conditions_in_wm([notH|T], MT) : −
    not wme(H, N) is in Working Memory
    match_conditions_in_wm(T, MT)
```

Box 3.10: Rules for maintaining *Match Memory* for the multicolumn subtraction model (from *Match Productions*)

The second aspect of the recognise phase, conflict resolution, does not need adjustment for the multicolumn subtraction model. The single conflict resolution rule developed for the multicolumn addition model and presented in Box 3.5 is appropriate, provided also that the Access properties of all relevant buffers are set as previously described.

The Act Phase

Several details of the act phase of the production system for multicolumn subtraction differ from that for multicolumn addition. First, production rules are limited such that they cannot delete elements from *Working Memory*. Rules 2 and 4 from Box 3.4 are therefore not required. Second, when elements are added to *Working Memory*, they must be tagged as described above. Third, production rules may include a variety of operations amongst their actions. Each of these details is incorporated in the revised rule set for *Fire Production* given in Box 3.11.

These rules assume that production actions take two forms: `add(X)` where `X` is a token to be added to *Working Memory* or `do(X)` where `X` is an action that may be performed by *Execute Action*. In both cases the current processing cycle is used as a tag. This will not necessarily be unique (as several elements may be added to

Rule 1 (unrefracted): *Make additions to working memory*
TRIGGER: `rule(Name, Conditions, Actions, Matches)`
IF: the current cycle is `N`
`add(X)` is a member of `Actions`
THEN: add `wme(X, N)` to *Working Memory*

Rule 2 (unrefracted): *Execute an action*
TRIGGER: `rule(Name, Conditions, Actions, Matches)`
IF: the current cycle is `N`
`do(X)` is a member of `Actions`
THEN: send `do(X, N)` to *Execute Action*

Box 3.11: Rules for executing a production rule's actions in the multicolumn subtraction model (from *Fire Production*)

Working Memory on a single cycle), but it is sufficient for present purposes.

Actions of the form `do(X)` are passed by *Fire Production* to *Execute Action*, which must include triggered rules for each action required by the multicolumn subtraction production rules. These are described further in Section 3.3.5.

3.3.3 Young and O'Shea's Production Rules

Young and O'Shea's rules for correct multicolumn subtraction are shown in Figure 3.4. The rules are justified in part with reference to contemporary teaching practices. To illustrate the intended interpretation consider the first rule, *Initialise Column*. This is applicable when about to process a new column (i.e., working memory contains `process_column`). If the rule fires it triggers an action (`read_m_and_s`) within *Execute Action*. This action should read the digits in the minuend row and subtrahend row of the current column into *Working Memory*. (The minuend is the top-most number, the number from which the other, the subtrahend, is subtracted.) At least two rules may then fire on the next production cycle: *Compare* and *Find Difference*. In this instance *Compare* will fire because it occurs in *Production Memory* before *Find Difference*.

As in the case of multicolumn addition, each rule from Figure 3.4 must be encoded as a separate item within *Production Memory*. The COGENT rules given above assume that each production rule consists of three components: its name, a list of conditions, and a list of actions. Thus, the *Compare* rule might be represented as:

```
rule(comp, [minuend(X), subtrahend(Y)], [do(compare)])
```

Young and O'Shea's production rules make use of a variety of actions. Most are context sensitive, in that they depend upon the column that is currently in

Initialise Column	process_column ⇒ do(read_m_and_s)
Compare	minuend(X) & subtrahend(Y) ⇒ do(compare)
Find Difference	minuend(X) & subtrahend(Y) ⇒ add(find_difference), add(next_column)
Borrow 2a	greater(subtrahend, minuend) ⇒ add(borrow)
Borrow from Subtrahend 2	borrow ⇒ do(decrement)
Borrow from Subtrahend 1	borrow ⇒ do(add_ten_to_minuend)
Find Absolute Difference	find_difference ⇒ do(take_abs_diff)
Write Answer	result(X) ⇒ do(write(X))
Next Column	next_column ⇒ do(shift_left), add(process_column)
Done	no_more ⇒ do(halt)
B2C	equal(subtrahend, minuend) ⇒ add(result(0)), add(next_column)
Add Carry	result(1, X) ⇒ do(carry), add(result(X))

Figure 3.4: Production rules for multicolumn subtraction (adapted from Young & O'Shea, 1981)

focus. Several, such as compare and add_ten_to_minuend, correspond to basic arithmetic operations. Others, such as read_m_and_s and write/1, correspond to input and output operations. One, shift_left, alters the focus column by shifting attention one column to the left.

Exercise 3.15: Enter the initial contents of *Production Memory* based on the production rules in Figure 3.4. Recall that the order of elements in *Production Memory* may affect the order in which production instances are fired (if multiple production instances can fire on the same cycle). This has been taken into account in the ordering of production rules in the figure. Therefore be sure to enter the production rules in the same order as they appear in the figure.

The *Initialise Column* rule assumes that *Working Memory* initially contains a symbol to trigger processing of the first (right-most) column. To test the partial

Element: *Goal: multicolumn subtraction*
`text(goal, ' − ' at (325, 50), [colour(black)])`
Element: *Syntax: the line beneath the subtrahend and minuend*
`line(stx, (270, 80) to (315, 80), [colour(black)])`
Element: *First column*
`text(minuend, 4 at (300, 50), [colour(black)])`
Element: *Second column*
`text(minuend, 7 at (275, 50), [colour(black)])`
Element: *First column*
`text(subtrahend, 8 at (300, 75), [colour(black)])`
Element: *Second column*
`text(subtrahend, 2 at (275, 75), [colour(black)])`

Box 3.12: The initial contents of *Paper*

model, create the following initial element in *Working Memory*:

`wme(process_column, 0)`

Initialise and run the model. It should run for several cycles, selecting an initial rule to fire and stopping when *Execute Action* is required to read the minuend and subtrahend. ◇

3.3.4 The Paper

The multicolumn subtraction model uses *Paper*, an analogue buffer, for input and output. This allows the model's interactions with the world to be shown in the same form as a child's interactions when he or she is attempting a multicolumn subtraction problem.

Box 3.12 shows the initial contents of *Paper* for a simple subtraction problem (74 − 28). Each element represents either a digit or a piece of syntax representing the subtraction problem. The *Paper* representation may be used by COGENT rules within *Execute Action*, such as that for `read_m_and_s`, when obtaining information about the subtraction problem or when writing an answer beneath a column.

Exercise 3.16: Enter the elements from Box 3.12 into the **Initial Contents** view of *Paper*. Initialise the model and examine the **Current Image** view of *Paper*. It should show the subtraction problem in the standard diagrammatic format. ◇

3.3.5 Execute Action

Execute Action contains a set of special purpose COGENT rules for performing the actions used by the production system. As noted above, the rules, which are given in full in an appendix to this chapter, perform a variety of arithmetic and input/output functions. They are essential if the model is to be able to perform correctly, but are not of central interest.

Exercise 3.17: Enter the rules from the chapter appendix (Section 3.6) into *Execute Action* and run the model. It should now be able to perform a complete multicolumn subtraction task. Test the model on a variety of problems, including some with more than two columns, by altering the initial contents of *Paper*. ◇

3.3.6 Accounting for Errors

With the production rule set of Figure 3.4 the model is able to correctly complete all two digit multicolumn subtraction problems. Young and O'Shea (1981) argue that algorithm errors result from incorrect or missing rules. Thus, the error in the first example on page 105 will occur if either the *Compare* or the *Borrow 2a* rules are omitted. The error in the second example may be attributed to inappropriate conditions on *Borrow 2a*, such that the rule applies regardless of the relative sizes of the subtrahend and minuend digits. Finally, the error in the third example requires an additional rule that applies when the minuend digit is zero.

Figure 3.5 shows the additional rules used by Young and O'Shea (1981) to account for the errors in their corpus. Thus, they assumed that children who always borrowed had somehow acquired either rule *Borrow 2b* or rule *Borrow 1* (i.e., an incorrect version of rule *Borrow 2a*). Similarly, children who produced errors in response to patterns associated with zero were assumed to possess one or more of the last six "pattern" rules. By associating different rule sets with different children, Young and O'Shea were able to account for, on average, 90% of each child's errors (though with some minor over-prediction). These results strongly support the view that most children were following an algorithm in their attempts at multicolumn subtraction, but that children who were making errors were following an erroneous algorithm.

Exercise 3.18: Explore the effects of selectively ignoring each production rule on the model's behaviour. (To temporarily ignore a COGENT buffer element right-click on the element and select **Ignore**. Use **Reinstate** to reinstate an ignored element.) Also explore the effects of adding each production rule from Figure 3.5. Attempt to characterise the errors that occur in each case. Can you reproduce the errors described in Section 3.3.1? ◇

Borrow 2b	`less(subtrahend, minuend) ⇒ add(borrow)`
Borrow 1	`minuend(X) & subtrahend(Y) ⇒ add(borrow)`
N minus Zero is N	`minuend(M) & subtrahend(0) ⇒ add(result(M)), add(next_column)`
Zero minus N is N	`minuend(0) & subtrahend(S) ⇒ add(result(S)), add(next_column)`
N minus Zero is Zero	`minuend(M) & subtrahend(0) ⇒ add(result(0)), add(next_column)`
Zero minus N is Zero	`minuend(0) & subtrahend(S) ⇒ add(result(0)), add(next_column)`
S minus M is Zero	`greater(subtrahend, minuend) ⇒ add(result(0)), add(next_column)`
N minus N is N	`minuend(N) & subtrahend(N) ⇒ add(result(N)), add(next_column)`

Figure 3.5: Additional production rules for multicolumn subtraction algorithm errors (adapted from Young & O'Shea, 1981)

3.3.7 Discussion of the Model

The Young and O'Shea (1981) model provides a good illustration of many of the strengths of production systems and production system modelling. The production system interpreter provides a domain general system for executing or enacting the production rules, each of which specifies a unit of task knowledge. The knowledge units are self-contained in the sense that they may be added or deleted to yield different behaviours. This clarifies how algorithm errors may arise. It also clarifies how rules from one task might intrude upon the performance of a related task. Thus, although not discussed above, Young and O'Shea (1981) describe errors that appear to involve some rules from multicolumn addition intruding upon the multicolumn subtraction procedure.

The model also demonstrates how production systems allow flexible control in which different strategies may be mixed. Modifying the set of production rules need not result in a system that halts when it encounters an error or that cannot function. Rather, provided a minimal set of rules is present, the system will work through a problem until it is complete, continuing in the face of adversity. This sits well with the general tendency of children when solving multicolumn subtraction to continue to some semi-logical end even after error.

This also demonstrates that a common claim in some literatures — that symbolic models are "brittle" in the sense that they fail to function in situations not explicitly anticipated by the programmer — need not be true. This claim is generally made when contrasting symbolic models with connectionist models that show graceful degradation (see, for example, Bechtel & Abrahamsen, 1991), and is intended to suggest that symbolic models are inferior to connectionist models. Production system models in general, and Young and O'Shea's model in particular, show that the claim is a fallacy. Symbolic models can be developed that sensibly extrapolate behaviour to situations beyond those relating to normal functioning of the model.

Young and O'Shea's work also has clear educational utility. The authors suggest that their model and analysis of children's errors may help target those children who have faulty multicolumn subtraction algorithms, and may allow the fault in those algorithms to be clearly identified and then rectified. They also suggest that their model, together with current teaching practices, provides an account of why one particular error, that of always borrowing even when it is not necessary, is very common. Children are generally initially taught subtraction problems that don't require borrowing. Once they have mastered this, they are taught the borrowing method, and given extensive practice of problems that require borrowing. This practice generally does not include problems that don't require borrowing (as it is assumed that children can solve such problems). The result is that children are unable to learn the precise conditions in which the borrow rule should apply, because they do not get practice of when not to use the rule. Hence, they overapply the rule. The modelling work therefore suggests that multicolumn subtraction (and teaching more generally) should focus on discrimination training (i.e., training when procedures do and don't apply), rather than purely on consolidation training (i.e., training on the procedure itself).

3.3.8 Project: Encapsulation of Subject Functions

Embed the multicolumn subtraction model within *Subject* and *Experimenter* compound boxes as described in Section 2.7.1 of Chapter 2. The *Experimenter* module should administer a block of multicolumn subtraction problems to the *Subject* module, with one problem presented on each trial. The problems should be presented on *Paper*, which should be initialised at the beginning of each trial. The *Experimenter* should also examine the paper once the *Subject* has completed the trial, and classify the *Subject*'s solution as correct or incorrect.

3.4 General Discussion

This chapter has presented two production system models of basic cognitive skills involving arithmetic. The production system model of multicolumn addition is intended as an illustration of the production system approach rather than as a realistic model of the cognitive processes involved in multicolumn addition. No empirical support for the model is provided. As such, the model does little more than demonstrate that the production system approach is sufficient for multicolumn addition. The model's main claim is that production systems provide a plausible account of the control of cognitive skills with a sequential component. Other computational approaches may be equally plausible.

In contrast, the model of multicolumn subtraction is grounded in empirical findings. It is intended as a psychologically plausible model of children's behaviour. It claims that children who can perform multicolumn subtraction successfully possess rules that correspond to those in Figure 3.4, and apply those rules in much the same way as the production system model. This is a strong claim, but it is supported by a reasonable body of evidence: a large corpus of children's errors.

Two significant limitations are evident in the models. First, while both models view arithmetic as a cognitive skill, neither model includes an account of how the skill might be acquired. In the case of multicolumn addition, the model might demonstrate the sufficiency of a production system approach to the application of a cognitive skill, but it fails to demonstrate that such approaches are also sufficient for the acquisition of a cognitive skill. This limitation is harder to ignore in the case of multicolumn subtraction, where the emphasis is on modelling the errors of children who have failed to learn the full multicolumn subtraction procedure. An obvious question for this model is, if children's errors do indeed reflect incorrect knowledge of the multicolumn subtraction procedure, how or why do they learn this incorrect knowledge? Young and O'Shea (1981) do not ignore this question, but argue that it is beyond the remit of their investigation.

As it happens, there are several production system models of learning (e.g., Klahr *et al.*, 1987; Newell, 1990; Anderson, 1993; Anderson & Lebiere, 1998). These models post-date the work of Young and O'Shea (1981), but they are of particular interest to educationalists for they promise to answer two important questions: why is it that we sometimes learn incorrect algorithms, and once we have learnt an incorrect algorithm, what is the most effective way of rectifying the mistake?

A further use of production system models of cognitive skill acquisition is in the evaluation of different approaches to teaching the cognitive skill. Thus, Ohlson (1990) has used such a model to compare the demands of two teaching approaches (conceptual and mechanical) and two different algorithms (regrouping and augmenting) in the domain of multicolumn subtraction.

A second limitation of the models is that separate models, using slightly different production systems, are employed for the two tasks. In principle, a single production system should be able to account for performance of a range of cognitive skills, with different skills corresponding to different sets of production rules. This limitation is artificial: Young and O'Shea's (1981) production system could easily be converted to model multicolumn addition by providing appropriate production rules.

A final issue raised by the models in this chapter concerns the psychological reality of production system models. There are two extreme views that might be adopted. At one extreme, one may argue that production systems are nothing more than a framework for describing cognitive functioning. On this view, the contents of a production system model's working memory after each production cycle approximate the contents of a human's working memory at various stages in processing (modulo representation), but there may be little or no relation between the processes that transform the information in the two systems. At the other extreme, one might suggest that production rules are cognitively real, that is, that production rules really are the currency of cognition, that our knowledge of cognitive skills consists of packets that are directly equivalent to production rules, and that the mind/brain is a production rule interpreter. Newell and Simon (1972), in their use of production systems to model problem solving behaviour (discussed further in Chapter 4), suspect the latter, but even on the former more cautious interpretation, production systems provide cognitive modellers with a very useful tool.

3.5 Further Reading

The opening chapters of Anderson (1993) provide a good introduction to production systems and their application in modelling cognitive skills. Anderson also uses multicolumn addition to illustrate production system concepts, and the production rules employed in this chapter are very similar to those he describes. An alternative model of multicolumn addition, developed within COGENT, is described by Cooper (1996). Further details on the production system model of multicolumn subtraction, including additional motivation and discussion of the relation between the model and the children's behaviour, are best obtained from the original source (Young & O'Shea, 1981).

Learning and the application of production systems to multiple tasks are discussed by Klahr *et al.* (1987), Newell (1990), and Anderson and Lebiere (1998). Klahr *et al.* (1987) is primarily concerned with theoretical issues arising from production systems that learn or develop. Both Newell (1990) and Anderson and Lebiere (1998) describe production system architectures that include a learning mechanism and that have been applied to a range of tasks. One chapter of Anderson and Lebiere (1998) deals specifically with cognitive arithmetic. All three of these texts are quite advanced.

3.6 Appendix: Rules for Execute Action

Rule 1 (refracted): *Set up problem and focus box*
IF: `text(goal, ' − ' at (X, Y), Props)` is in *Paper*
`X0` is `X − 35`
`Y0` is `Y + 60`
THEN: add `wme(process_column, 0)` to *Working Memory*
add `box(focus, (25, 80) at (X0, Y0), [colour(red)])` to *Paper*

Rule 2 (unrefracted): *Read the minuend – not decremented*
TRIGGER: `do(read_m_and_s, N)`
IF: not `borrow_coordinates(X, _)`
`text(dec, M at (X, Y), P)` is in *Paper*
`x_coordinate(column, X)`
`text(minuend, M at (X, Y), P)` is in *Paper*
THEN: delete all `wme(minuend(_), _)` from *Working Memory*
add `wme(minuend(M), N)` to *Working Memory*

Rule 3 (unrefracted): *Read the minuend – decremented*
TRIGGER: `do(read_m_and_s, N)`
IF: `borrow_coordinates(X, _)`
`text(dec, M at (X, Y), P)` is in *Paper*
THEN: delete all `wme(minuend(_), _)` from *Working Memory*
add `wme(minuend(M), N)` to *Working Memory*

Rule 4 (unrefracted): *Read the subtrahend – no carry*
TRIGGER: `do(read_m_and_s, N)`
IF: not `x_coordinate(carry, Xc)`
`text(carry, C at (Xc, Yc), P)` is in *Paper*
`x_coordinate(column, X)`
`text(subtrahend, S at (X, Y), P)` is in *Paper*
THEN: delete all `wme(subtrahend(_), _)` from *Working Memory*
add `wme(subtrahend(S), N)` to *Working Memory*

Rule 5 (unrefracted): *Read the subtrahend – carry*
TRIGGER: `do(read_m_and_s, N)`
IF: `x_coordinate(carry, Xc)`
`text(carry, C at (Xc, Yc), P)` is in *Paper*
`x_coordinate(column, X)`
`text(subtrahend, S at (X, Y), P)` is in *Paper*
`S1` is `S + C`
THEN: delete all `wme(subtrahend(_), _)` from *Working Memory*
add `wme(subtrahend(S1), N)` to *Working Memory*

Rule 6 (unrefracted): *Is the minuend equal to the subtrahend?*
TRIGGER: `do(compare,N)`
IF: `wme(subtrahend(X),_)` is in *Working Memory*
`wme(minuend(X),_)` is in *Working Memory*
THEN: add `wme(equal(subtrahend,minuend),N)` to *Working Memory*

Rule 7 (unrefracted): *Is the subtrahend greater than the minuend?*
TRIGGER: `do(compare,N)`
IF: `wme(subtrahend(S),_)` is in *Working Memory*
`wme(minuend(M),_)` is in *Working Memory*
`S` is greater than `M`
THEN: add `wme(greater(subtrahend,minuend),N)` to *Working Memory*

Rule 8 (unrefracted): *Is the subtrahend less than the minuend?*
TRIGGER: `do(compare,N)`
IF: `wme(subtrahend(S),_)` is in *Working Memory*
`wme(minuend(M),_)` is in *Working Memory*
`S` is less than `M`
THEN: add `wme(less(subtrahend,minuend),N)` to *Working Memory*

Rule 9 (unrefracted): *Add 10 to the minuend*
TRIGGER: `do(add_ten_to_minuend,N)`
IF: `wme(minuend(M),_)` is in *Working Memory*
`M1` is (`M`) + (`10`)
`borrow_coordinates(Xm,Ym)`
THEN: delete `wme(minuend(M),_)` from *Working Memory*
add `wme(minuend(M1),N)` to *Working Memory*
add `text(borrow,1 at (Xm,Ym),[colour(black)])` to *Paper*

Rule 10 (unrefracted): *Decrement the next column of the minuend*
TRIGGER: `do(decrement,_)`
IF: `x_coordinate(column,X0)`
`X` is `X0` − 25
`text(minuend,M at (X,Y),P)` is in *Paper*
`borrow_coordinates(Xb,Ydec)`
`Xdec` is `Xb` − 25
`M1` is `M` − 1
`strike_deltas(Xd1,Yd1,Xd2,Yd2)`
`Xs1` is `X` + `Xd1`
`Ys1` is `Y` + `Yd1`
`Xs2` is `X` + `Xd2`
`Ys2` is `Y` + `Yd2`
THEN: add `line(strike,(Xs1,Ys1) to (Xs2,Ys2),P)` to *Paper*
add `text(dec,M1 at (Xdec,Ydec),P)` to *Paper*

Condition Definition: strike_deltas/4: *Geometry specification for slash*
strike_deltas(0, −10, 7, 0).

Comment: *The above rule assumes that next column exists and is not 0!*

Rule 11 (unrefracted): *Carry 10 (Add 1 to subtrahend in next column)*
TRIGGER: do(carry, _)
IF: x_coordinate(carry, Xc)
Xc2 is Xc − 25
THEN: add text(carry, 1 at (Xc2, 65), [colour(black)]) to *Paper*

Rule 12 (unrefracted): *Put the absolute difference into working memory*
TRIGGER: do(take_abs_diff, N)
IF: wme(minuend(M), _) is in *Working Memory*
wme(subtrahend(S), _) is in *Working Memory*
R is the absolute value of S − M
THEN: add wme(result(R), N) to *Working Memory*

Rule 13 (unrefracted): *Shift attention one column left*
TRIGGER: do(shift_left, _)
IF: box(focus, Size at (X0, Y), P) is in *Paper*
x_coordinate(next, X1)
THEN: delete box(focus, Size at (X0, Y), P) from *Paper*
add box(focus, Size at (X1, Y), P) to *Paper*

Rule 14 (unrefracted): *Shift attention, but no more columns!*
TRIGGER: do(shift_left, N)
IF: box(focus, Size at (X, Y), P) is in *Paper*
not x_coordinate(next, X1)
THEN: add wme(no_more, N) to *Working Memory*
delete box(focus, Size at (X, Y), P) from *Paper*

Rule 15 (unrefracted): *Write an answer*
TRIGGER: do(write(N), _)
IF: x_coordinate(column, X)
y_coordinate(answer, Y)
THEN: add text(answer, N at (X, Y), [colour(black)]) to *Paper*

Rule 16 (unrefracted): *Stop processing*
TRIGGER: do(halt, _)
IF: True
THEN: send stop to *Multicolumn Subtraction*

Condition Definition: `x_coordinate/2`: *X co-ordinate of various elements*

```
x_coordinate(column, X) :-
    box(focus, Size at (Xf, Yf), P) is in Paper
    X is Xf + 10
x_coordinate(carry, Xc) :-
    box(focus, Size at (Xf, Yf), P) is in Paper
    Xc is Xf + 16
x_coordinate(next, Xc) :-
    box(focus, Size at (Xf, Yf), P) is in Paper
    X is Xf - 15
    exists text(Any, T at (X, Y), _) is in Paper
    Xc is Xf - 25
```

Condition Definition: `y_coordinate/2`: *Y co-ordinate of various elements*

```
y_coordinate(answer, Y0) :-
    once text(subtrahend, M at (X, Y), P) is in Paper
    Y0 is Y + 25
```

Condition Definition: `borrow_coordinates/2`: *X,Y co-ordinates of borrow*

```
borrow_coordinates(Xb, Yb) :-
    box(focus, Size at (Xf, Yf), P) is in Paper
    Xb is Xf + 2
    once text(minuend, M at (X, Y), P) is in Paper
    Yb is Y - 7
```

Chapter 4

Problem Solving

Richard P. Cooper

Overview: The psychology of problem solving is surveyed from an historical perspective. Associationist, Gestalt, and information processing accounts are outlined. The chapter then adopts the view of problem solving as the sequential application of moves to a problem state, transforming that state from the initial state to a goal state. Two heuristics that govern move selection are then outlined. The bulk of the chapter illustrates these heuristics through a series of models of two standard problem solving tasks (Missionaries and Cannibals and the Tower of Hanoi). We conclude by considering structural and psychological regularities that hold across the problem solving domain, and discuss how such regularities might feed into the development of a general problem solver.

4.1 The Psychology of Problem Solving

Much mental activity can be classified as problem solving: working out how to achieve one's desires and goals when a solution is not immediately apparent. Problem solving of this sort is involved in a range of tasks, including planning and scheduling (e.g., how to perform several tasks on a limited budget and in limited time), trouble-shooting (e.g., how to find and fix a malfunction in a piece of equipment), game-playing (e.g., playing chess or noughts-and-crosses), and puzzle-solving (e.g., how to generate appropriate words for crossword clues). The ability to perform such tasks, and to solve the problems that they raise quickly or to produce novel or "insightful" solutions, is generally taken as a key indicator of intelligence. How, though, do we solve problems? More specifically, what cognitive machinery is required for competent problem solving?

4.1.1 Productive and Reproductive Problem Solving

The psychological investigation of problem solving extends back to the early twentieth century. Since then, several schools of problem solving research have emerged and research has focused on several distinct types of problem. Early work focused on so-called reproductive problems. In these problems, people were required to reproduce (and possibly modify) a solution to a previous task. Thorndike (1911), for example, developed the puzzle box, a small cage with many levers and pulleys, that could only be opened by pushing the correct lever or pulling the right string attached to a pulley. Thorndike observed how hungry cats learnt to escape from such boxes, and argued from this behaviour that problem solving involved the application of "habit families". A habit family was a set of responses available to an individual (human or other animal) in a given situation. Habits within a family were argued initially to be tried randomly, but learning was held to lead to the reorganisation of habit families, with successful responses being strengthened or promoted (and hence becoming more likely with practice) and unsuccessful responses being weakened or demoted (and hence becoming less likely with practice).

Thorndike's view, which was characteristic of the associationist school of thought, provided little room for thought processes. Problem solving was reduced to the application of stimulus-response pairs. Further research suggested that this view was incomplete. Kohler (1925) examined the problem solving abilities of apes. When faced with novel problems (e.g., a number of crates, a stick and a bunch of tasty-looking bananas hanging from the ceiling of the enclosure), the apes sat, apparently in thought, for some time before carrying out a complete solution (e.g., building a stack of crates, and then climbing up the stack and using a stick to obtain the bananas). Kohler argued that this could not be explained by the direct application of habit families.

Associationists were unmoved by Kohler's observations. They maintained the view that problem solving was the application of habit families by suggesting that habit families could be applied covertly (in one's head, as it were). According to this view Kohler's apes assembled random sequences of responses in their heads until a sequence was found that solved the problem. This sequence was then applied in full.

In the 1940s Gestalt psychologists developed a different view. They focused on productive problems — problems whose solutions involved more than simply reproducing an earlier response. These included so-called insight problems, such as Dunker's (1945) X-ray problem. This problem involved finding a way of using X-rays to destroy a tumour without damaging the surrounding healthy tissue. A strong dose of X-rays would destroy the tumour, but this dose would also kill surrounding tissue. The solution is to project several weak X-ray sources from different directions so they all intersect at the tumour site, producing a concentration of X-rays at the tumour but not at surrounding tissue.

Gestalt psychologists viewed problem solving as a process of imposing an appropriate structure on the problem solving task. It was argued that once the appropriate structure was found (in a moment they termed "illumination", and corresponding in the X-ray problem to the realisation or insight that converging X-rays could be used) the solution would be straightforward. As such, Gestalt psychologists were particularly interested in what prevented successful problem solving. One of the most robust findings was that prior problem solving performance could create in people a "mental set" in which they were predisposed towards a particular solution strategy, even if that strategy was inappropriate for the problem under consideration (Luchins, 1942; Dunker, 1945).

Neither the associationist nor the Gestalt view of problem solving provides an adequate account of the complexities of human problem solving. This much is obvious from the fact that the views focus on different types of problems (i.e., reproductive versus productive problems respectively). Notwithstanding this difference in focus, however, both views fail to provide adequate accounts at the cognitive level of problem solving. The associationist school, with its concentration on stimulus-response associations, cannot account for the effects of knowledge (both general strategic knowledge and task-specific knowledge) on problem solving. The Gestalt school, with its emphasis on structure and its appeal to incompletely specified processes such as illumination, fails to provide an adequately concrete account of the processes between stimulus (the presentation of a problem) and response (problem solving behaviour).

4.1.2 Well-Defined, Knowledge-Lean Problems

More recently human performance on problems and puzzles such as chess, the Missionaries and Cannibals problem (discussed below), the Tower of Hanoi (also discussed below), and arithmetic puzzles has been studied intensively, and general findings concerning problem solving in these domains have emerged. This work has focused on a class of problems that possess two simplifying properties: they are "well-defined" and "knowledge-lean". A well-defined problem is one in which the given information (e.g., in the case of chess, the initial configuration of pieces on the board), the problem-solver's options (i.e., the legal chess moves), and the desired state of affairs (a configuration of pieces in which the opponent is check-mated) can be unambiguously and completely specified. A knowledge-lean problem is one for which the solution depends on only limited knowledge (e.g., knowledge of the possible chess moves) and does not depend upon extensive general knowledge. Knowledge-lean problems are self-contained, in that the knowledge required to solve them can be specified completely and succinctly.

Well-defined, knowledge-lean problems like chess contrast with ill-defined, knowledge-rich problems such as becoming a millionaire or achieving world domination. Such problems are discussed further in section 4.1.3.

State Spaces and Problem Spaces

Work on problems that are both well-defined and knowledge-lean typically characterises those problems in terms of the transformation of problem states. A state is simply a snapshot of the problem solving situation. It is a complete description of all objects relevant to the problem, including features of those objects and relations between objects, at a given point in time. The state of a game of chess at the beginning of the game, for example, is a specification of the position and colour of each piece on the board, together with the information that it is the turn of the person who is playing white to move.

Problem solving on this view is just the transformation of the initial state, via a series of moves, to a desired state. In chess, each move transforms one state into a subsequent state. Certain states are desirable (notably those in which your opponent is check-mated). The problem solving task of chess is therefore to make appropriate moves such that one of these desirable states is achieved. Of course it is also necessary, along the way, to avoid certain undesirable states (those in which you are check-mated).

Frequently, the moves available within a well-defined knowledge-lean problem fall into a number of classes. Returning to the chess example, one class of moves consists of advancing a pawn by one square. Another class consists of moving a bishop diagonally. A third class involves moving the king one space in any direction. These classes of moves are referred to as operators. Formally, well-defined knowledge-lean problems consist of three elements: a completely specified initial state, a finite set of operators, and either a complete specification of the desired (or goal) state or a specification of a condition which is true of all and only goal states.

The set of states for any problem, together with the moves that transform those states, form the problem's state space. State spaces can be shown diagrammatically as a set of nodes joined by arrows (i.e., as a directed graph), where the nodes correspond to states and the arrows correspond to moves that transform one state into another. To illustrate, consider the Missionaries and Cannibals problem. In this problem three missionaries and three cannibals must cross a river using a small boat. The boat can only hold two people, and so it is necessary to make several crossings of the river in order to transport everyone to the other side. However, if at any stage the number of cannibals on one bank exceeds the number of missionaries on that bank, the cannibals will eat the missionaries. This is to be avoided. The problem then is how to get the six people to the other side of the river.

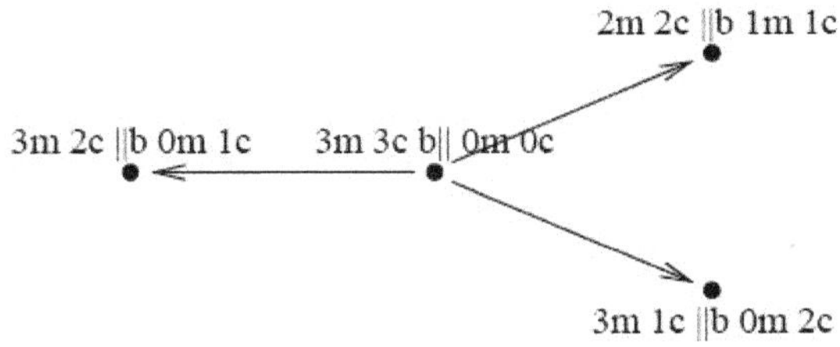

Figure 4.1: Initial moves in the Missionaries and Cannibals problem. The initial state is represented by the central node in the structure. State labels are interpreted as follows: the river is represented by two vertical lines. Elements to the left of those lines correspond to individuals on the left bank. Elements to the right of the lines correspond to individuals on the right bank. Missionaries are represented by the letter "m", cannibals by the letter "c", and the boat by the letter "b". Thus, "3m 2c ||b 0m 1c" represents a state with three missionaries and two cannibals on the left bank, and zero missionaries, one cannibal, and the boat on the right bank.

States in the Missionaries and Cannibals problem consist of positional information for each of the people and the boat. In the initial state, all people and the boat are on one bank. (We'll assume they start on the left bank.) Since the boat may hold up to two people, two operators are applicable: move one person to the right bank or move two people to the right bank. There are two different moves licensed by the first of these operators: move a missionary to the right or move a cannibal to the right. There are three different moves licensed by the second operator: move two cannibals, move two missionaries, or move a missionary and a cannibal. Two of these five moves lead to states in which the number of cannibals on the left bank exceeds the number of missionaries. (Moving one missionary to the right will leave three cannibals and two missionaries on the left, and moving two missionaries to the right will leave three cannibals and one missionary on the left.) They are therefore not valid moves. Given this, Figure 4.1 represents the initial state, the initially available moves, and the states that would arise if each move were made.

Figure 4.1 may be extended by considering all possible moves from each of the states arising after the first move. In fact, there is only one move possible from the left-most state of Figure 4.1 — moving the cannibal in the boat from the right bank back to the left bank. This move returns all people to their original positions (and hence returns us to the initial state). The right-most states each have two possible moves. In both cases one of these leads to the initial state. The remaining moves both lead to the same state: having one cannibal on the right bank and the boat and all other people on the left bank. Several repetitions of this process leads to the complete state space as shown in Figure 4.2.

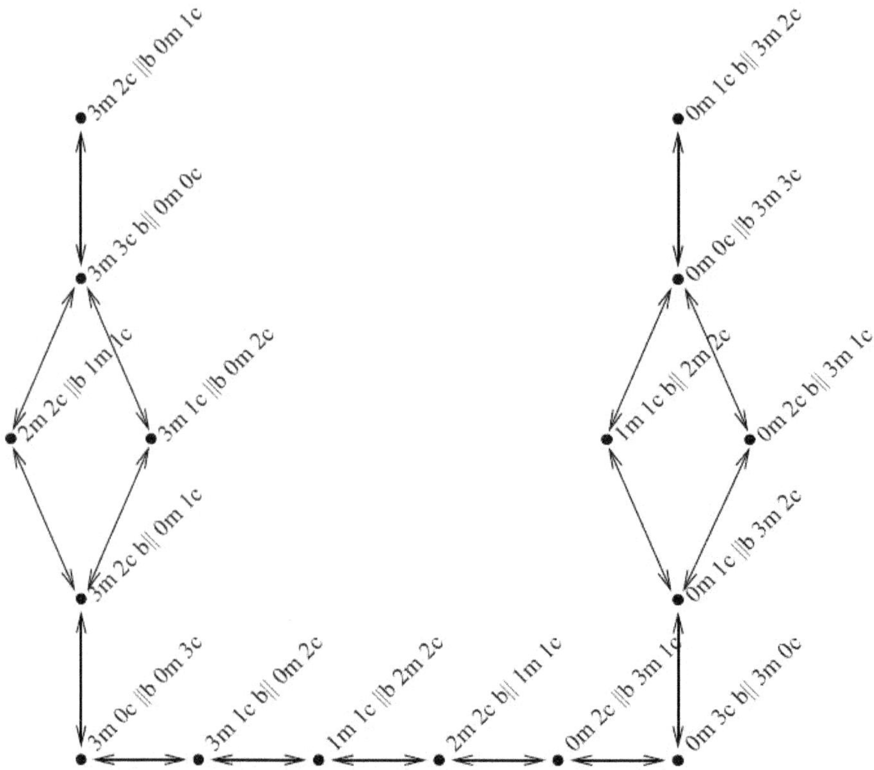

Figure 4.2: The complete state space for the Missionaries and Cannibals problem

The Missionaries and Cannibals problem is somewhat unusual in having a small state space. The 16 nodes in Figure 4.2 represent each of the 16 possible states, and the 17 double-ended arrows represent each of the 34 possible moves. However, state spaces often contain many more states and moves, and it is not always possible to draw complete state space diagrams. The state space for chess, for example, contains many thousands of millions of states, and for many problems the state space is actually infinite. Nevertheless, representation of a problem in terms of its state space (even when it is not practical to draw the complete state space) provides a conceptual tool which may be used to analyse problem solving behaviour.

Figure 4.2 shows all states of the Missionaries and Cannibals problem, but does not distinguish the initial state and the desired state from the other states. The initial and desired states are only special when the state space is considered with respect to a specific problem. In the figure the initial state of the standard Missionaries and Cannibals problem corresponds to the second node from the top on the left, and the desired state corresponds to the second node from the top on the right.

When a state space is augmented with information concerning the problem's initial and desired states it is referred to as a problem space. Within the problem space perspective, successful problem solving is simply a matter of selection of moves, in sequence, which transform the initial state of the problem into a desired state. If a problem space is small (as in the Missionaries and Cannibals problem) the diagrammatic representation of the problem space generally makes the solution to the problem obvious — it is just a matter of following the arrows in the graph from the initial state to the desired state.

Problem Solving as Search within a Problem Space

Figure 4.2 raises some interesting questions. There are only 16 states in the problem, and in most states there are just two moves available, one which moves back to the previous state and one which moves to a new state. The only exceptions to this rule are cases where different sequences of moves lead to the same state (the diamond shapes on the left and right of the figure). It would therefore seem that problem solving in this task should be straightforward. This is not so. Empirical evidence shows that people do find the problem difficult, and in particular that some moves are more difficult than others (e.g., Thomas, 1974; Greeno, 1974).

Adopting the problem space view of problem solving makes clear that the principal issue in solving a problem concerns the selection, in an appropriate sequence, of a series of moves. Two questions arise. Typically several moves are applicable in any state. Given a particular state, then, how do we determine which moves are applicable? Secondly, once a set of applicable moves has been determined, how do we select from that set one move to apply?

The above formal analysis of problems in terms of problem spaces has led many researchers to view problem solving as *search* within a problem space. That is, to solve a problem it is necessary to search for a path from the initial state to a desired state. The "most efficient" solution is the one corresponding to the shortest path. There are numerous formal procedures which are guaranteed to find such a path if one exists (assuming that the number of moves applicable from any state is finite). The simplest such procedure is to consider all possible paths from the initial state of length one. (There are three such paths in the Missionaries and Cannibals problem described above.) If none of these terminate at a desired state then consider all possible paths from the initial state of length two. Repeat the procedure extending the length of the path by one each time until a path that terminates at the desired state is found. If the problem can be solved in a finite number of moves, this procedure is guaranteed to terminate with a solution.

The above procedure is known as breadth-first search. In order to investigate whether people use this or other approaches to problem solving psychologists developed the method of protocol analysis (Ericsson & Simon, 1984). This requires people to verbalise their thought processes during problem solving. Protocol analysis has revealed that people do not generally solve problems by breadth-first search. Instead, people appear to use rules of thumb, or heuristics, to help guide the search. One simple heuristic is hill-climbing. This heuristic is applicable when there is some measure of "distance" between states. In the case of Missionaries and Cannibals the distance between any state and the end state might be the number of cannibals remaining on the left bank of the river.

The hill-climbing heuristic guides the selection of moves as follows: no matter what problem state you are currently in, consider all possible moves from that state. Each move will lead to a new state. For each new state, calculate or estimate the distance between that state and the desired state (or the nearest desired state, if there are multiple such states). Select the move which leads to the state that is closest to a desired state.

Hill-climbing may be a good heuristic for some problems if an appropriate distance measure is used. However, it can also lead to problems. In particular, it can lead to dead-ends: states which are not a desired state but for which each move appears to lead further away from a desired state. Thus, heuristics are not infallible. However, heuristics tend to be more efficient than exhaustive search procedures (such as breadth-first search), and frequently they lead to a satisfactory solution.

Problem solving research has revealed several distinct heuristics that appear to be employed in certain situations (beyond simple hill-climbing, which appears to be used by some people when attempting to solve the Missionaries and Cannibals problem), including: backward chaining (working backwards from a desired state towards the initial state); Means-Ends Analysis or operator subgoaling (setting intermediate milestones, such as identifying an essential state or move and working towards that, instead of the true desired state); and progressive deepening (exploring paths in the state space of a given length, ruling out some of those paths as dead-ends, and then repeating this process but considering progressively longer paths).

Many of the empirical findings concerning knowledge-lean problem solving have been explored and replicated within computational models of the problem solving process. Of greatest historical importance are the Logic Theorist (LT), developed by Newell *et al.* (1958), the General Problem Solver (GPS), developed by Ernst and Newell (1969), and the "Universal Weak Method" embodied in Soar (Laird *et al.*, 1987). The third of these systems was capable of solving a variety of problems using general heuristics and strategies similar to those discussed above. The system was based on the use of a production system (see Chapter 3) — a set of structures and processes developed in order to model sequential rule-based processing, similar to that apparently exhibited by people.

4.1.3 Ill-Defined and Knowledge-Rich Problems

Some classes of problem do not map neatly onto problem space concepts. Insight problems, as studied by Gestalt psychologists, are one such class. A second class consists of ill-defined problems. Consider the problem of designing a toy aeroplane, as discussed by Goel, Grafman, Tajik, Gana, and Danto (1997). A problem space analysis of this problem might take the initial state to be a blank sheet of paper, and the goal state to be the same piece of paper but with a drawing of a design for the toy. However, it is unclear what might constitute operators within the problem, and the specification of the goal state is vague in comparison with that of chess or the Missionaries and Cannibals problem. Reitman (1964) referred to problems such as this, where one or more of the initial state, goal state, or possible operators were incompletely specified, as ill-defined problems. It has been argued that the cognitive processes underlying the solution of ill-defined problems differ from those involved in well-defined problems (e.g., Goel *et al.*, 1997; Goel & Grafman, 2000), although this view is not universal (see, e.g., Newell, 1990). While many, perhaps most, problems encountered in everyday life are arguably ill-defined, ill-defined problems will not be considered further in this chapter.

A third class of problem that arguably does not sit well with a problem space view of problem solving is that of knowledge-rich problems: problems whose solution involves the use of a large body of knowledge, possibly including substantial general knowledge. Many knowledge-rich problems are also ill-defined, and many ill-defined problems are also knowledge rich. Newell (1990), however, discusses one problem — configuring a VAX mainframe computer system — that is both well-defined and knowledge-rich (see also Rosenbloom, Laird, McDermott, Newell, & Orciuch, 1985). This configuration problem is essentially one of finding the most cost-effective configuration of sub-components that satisfies multiple constraints (including user-requirements, compatibility between sub-components, power demands of sub-components, etc.). The solution described by Newell (1990) includes a knowledge-base containing over 10,000 facts. Clearly the solution involves use of a large body of knowledge. On the basis of this, Newell suggests that the processes employed in knowledge-rich problem solving are continuous with those employed in knowledge-lean problem solving. This may justify introducing problem solving concepts with knowledge-lean problems (as is done below), but caution should still be exercised in generalising these concepts to knowledge-rich problems, where empirical support for the use of a problem space approach is generally weak.

4.2 The Missionaries and Cannibals Problem

We saw above that the state space of the Missionaries and Cannibals problem is relatively simple. There are just 16 states, with at most 3 moves possible from any state. Nevertheless, most people find the Missionaries and Cannibals problem difficult. We thus begin our attempt at modelling problem solving behaviour within COGENT with a series of models of behaviour on the Missionaries and Cannibals problem.

4.2.1 Some Empirical Findings

There have been several studies of human performance on the Missionaries and Cannibals problem. Thomas (1974) found that participants made disproportionately many errors (selecting invalid moves) at two key points: early in the task when one cannibal had been moved to the right bank and the boat was back on the left bank (i.e., state 3m 2c b|| 0m 1c), and mid-way through the task, after moving two missionaries and two cannibals to the right bank (i.e., state 1m 1c ||b 2m 2c). Thomas was unable to explain the early errors, but suggested that errors in the middle of the task arose because participants thought they were following a blind alley: both moves from state 1m 1c ||b 2m 2c appear to be moving away from the goal. This may suggest that participants use a hill-climbing strategy, selecting moves that move them closer to their goal. Consistent with this interpretation, the difficulty was less pronounced (though still apparent) when participants were informed during the task that they were on the right track.

Many of Thomas's participants were not maximally efficient in their solution of the Missionaries and Cannibals problem, and consequently they frequently encountered the same state more than once. Thomas (1974) analysed moves made in these situations, and found that participants avoided reselecting moves that they had previously tried. Thus, experience gained during the task has a strong effect upon subsequent problem solving.

A third result reported by Thomas (1974) concerned the existence of two to four problem solving "stages". On the basis of an analysis of solution times, Thomas argued that participants did not solve the problem by making a series of independent moves. Rather, moves were clustered into higher-level solution stages. Similar findings were reported by Greeno (1974). (The work of Thomas and Greeno was actually carried out using the Hobbits and Orcs problem. This is equivalent to the Missionaries and Cannibals problem, with hobbits replacing missionaries and orcs replacing cannibals. Analogous rules apply: orcs will eat hobbits if given the chance.)

A further study of problem solving on a related problem was carried out by Simon and Reed (1976), who investigated a version of the Missionaries and Cannibals problem involving five missionaries, five cannibals, and a boat with a ca-

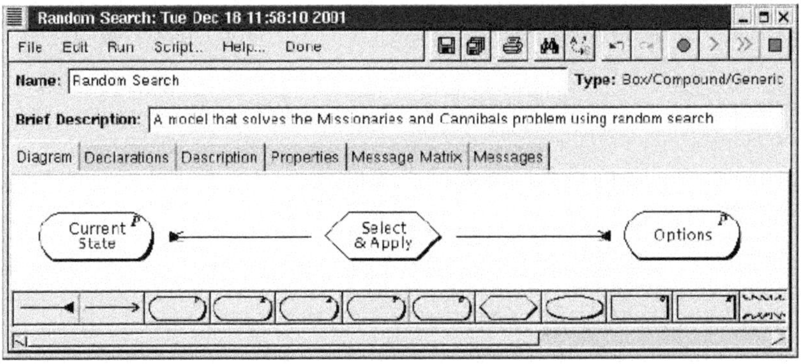

Figure 4.3: The box and arrow diagram for the initial (Random Search) Missionaries and Cannibals model

pacity of three. This version of the problem is substantially more difficult than the traditional version. Simon and Reed argued that participants initially used simple strategies that relied upon attempting to balance the number of missionaries and cannibals on each bank. Only when prompted did participants switch to more complex strategies (such as Means-Ends Analysis, as briefly described above) that were necessary to solve the problem.

4.2.2 A First Model: Random Search

The first step in developing any COGENT model consists of conducting an analysis of the functional components of the system that is being modelled. In this case, at least three components are required:

- a propositional buffer to contain the current state;
- a propositional buffer to contain the current set of possible moves; and
- a rule-based process for selecting, comparing, and applying moves.

The rule-based process must be able to read from and write to both buffers. The model should therefore have the diagrammatic structure shown in Figure 4.3. *Current State* will hold a representation of the positions of the missionaries, cannibals, and boat throughout the task. *Select & Apply* will examine the state and determine the set of moves possible from each state. These moves will be stored temporarily within *Options*. *Select & Apply* will also choose one move from *Options* and apply it to *Current State*, transforming that state to produce a new state. This will lead to a new set of possible moves, the subsequent selection of a further move, and so on. *Select & Apply* must also detect when the problem has been solved (i.e., when *Current State* matches the desired state), and terminate processing.

Element: *Three missionaries and three cannibals on the left bank*
`position(left, 3 : 3)`
Element: *No missionaries or cannibals on the right bank*
`position(right, 0 : 0)`
Element: *The boat is initially on the left bank*
`boat(left)`

Box 4.1: The initial contents of *Current State*

Representing the Problem

Before fleshing out the details of the three boxes it is necessary to fix upon a suitable representation for the state, *viz*, the number of missionaries and cannibals on each bank and the position of the boat. One possibility would be to represent the situation as a series of `position/2` terms, such as `position(missionary, left)` or `position(boat, right)`, with multiple terms used to represent the multiple missionaries and cannibals.

It turns out to be more convenient to represent the number of missionaries and cannibals on each bank in numerical terms, and to represent the people on each bank within one term. Thus, a more convenient representation consists of two terms of the form:

`position(left, 3 : 1)`

where the first argument represents a bank (`left` or `right`) and the second argument represents the number of missionaries and cannibals on that bank (in this case 3 missionaries and 1 cannibal). Box 4.1 shows the initial state of the problem using this representation, together with a representation of the boat's position as a `boat/1` term. The rules in *Select & Apply* (detailed below) will query and manipulate the contents of *Current State* using this representational scheme.

Exercise 4.1: Create a model with the box and arrow structure shown in Figure 4.3 and enter the specification of the initial state (as in Box 4.1) into *Current State*. ◇

Proposing Moves

The general problem solving strategy that has been described is cyclic. On each cycle: all possible moves are proposed; the most appropriate move is selected; and the selected move is performed. The cycle then repeats.

Given the size and the possible positions of the boat, there are at most five moves that must be considered at each state: move two missionaries to the other

Rule 1 (unrefracted): *Propose moving one missionary*
IF: not `option(AnyMove, AnyStatus)` is in *Options*
`boat(Bank)` is in *Current State*
`position(Bank, NM : NC)` is in *Current State*
`NM` is greater than `0`
THEN: add `option(move(Bank, 1 : 0), possible)` to *Options*

Box 4.2: A rule to propose moving one missionary and zero cannibals from the current bank (from *Select & Apply*)

bank, move two cannibals to the other bank, move one missionary and one cannibal to the other bank, move one missionary to the other bank, or move one cannibal to the other bank. Each move may be proposed by a separate COGENT rule within *Select & Apply*. Not all moves are available at each stage in the problem, however. For example, if there are fewer than two missionaries on the bank with the boat then two missionaries cannot be moved to the other side. The rules for proposing moves must therefore be sensitive to the position of the missionaries, cannibals, and boat, and only propose moves when the preconditions of those moves (i.e., the conditions that must be true in order to make the move) are true.

A second issue arises with moves that lead to illegal states — states in which the cannibals on one bank out-number the missionaries on that bank. These were ignored in the description given earlier in the chapter, but introspection suggests that we consider all moves of one or two people, and then rule out moves that lead to these illegal states. This introspection is backed up by empirical studies (such as those of Thomas, 1974, and Greeno, 1974, cited above) in which participants suggest, and then reject, such moves. We will therefore propose all possible moves, and leave rejection of illegal moves to a separate move selection phase.

Box 4.2 shows a suitable rule for proposal of moving one missionary. The first condition of this rule prevents the rule from firing when other moves are being considered. The second condition ensures that `Bank` is bound to `left` or `right`, depending on the position of the boat. The third condition then determines the number of missionaries and cannibals currently on `Bank`. If the number of missionaries (`NM`) is greater than zero, the rule will fire, and add a representation of the move as a possible option to *Options*.

The representation of moves added to *Options* by Rule 1 parallels the representation of the position of missionaries and cannibals: it consists of a `move/2` term in which the first argument represents the bank from which the move begins (`left` or `right`) and the second argument represents the number of missionaries to move and the number of cannibals to move. The `move/2` term is itself the first argument of an `option/2` term. The second argument of this term indicates the status of the proposed move. This status is initially set to `possible` by Rule 1. Other COGENT rules will transform this status into `valid`, `selected`, etc. as problem solving progresses.

Rule 1, and the four other move proposal rules, must be marked as **unrefracted**. This is to ensure that the rule may fire multiple times with exactly the same variable instantiations. This is necessary because we want the rule to fire whenever it is possible to move a missionary, and not just on the first such occasion.

Exercise 4.2: Add Rule 1 from Box 4.2, and four other rules to propose the four other possible moves, to *Select & Apply*. Run the partial model while examining the **Current Contents** view of *Options*. If the rules are specified correctly they should fire on the first cycle, adding five options to the buffer. The model will then terminate, as no further processing will be possible. ◇

Avoiding Invalid Moves

After the initial burst of firing of the above move proposal rules *Options* will contain the set of all possible moves, including some that lead to invalid states (i.e., states in which the missionaries are out-numbered by the cannibals on one of the banks). Such moves must be ruled out. Thus, a filtering phase is required following move proposal.

Filtering of moves that lead to invalid states requires an element of "look-ahead": one must effectively apply the move and then check that the resultant state is valid. Rule 6 of Box 4.3 checks valid moves by doing just this. If a move is possible, and that move transforms the current state into some resultant state, and that resultant state is valid, then the move itself is valid. A companion rule, to remove possible but invalid moves from *Options*, is also given in the figure (Rule 7).

Rules 6 and 7 make use of three user-defined conditions: `current_state`/1, `apply`/3, and `valid_state`/1. These conditions allow the manipulation and testing of current and future states. Appropriate definitions are given in Box 4.3. Note that it is necessary to represent the current state as a single structure so that it can be manipulated and so the effects of hypothetical moves can be determined. The representation used here consists of a term with three sub-terms, representing (respectively) the number of missionaries and cannibals on the left bank, the boat's position, and the number of missionaries and cannibals on the right bank.

Further user-defined conditions are employed in the definitions of `apply`/3 and `valid_state`/1. `add_state`/3 and `subtract_state`/3 manipulate state representations. `add_state`/3 takes a representation of the people on one bank and a representation of the people in the boat and adds them (e.g., when given `2 : 0` and `1 : 1` for its first two arguments it yields `3 : 1` as its third argument). `subtract_state`/3 is analogous, but it subtracts the two representations. Neither definition is

Rule 6 (unrefracted): *If a possible move leads to a valid state, it is valid*
IF: `option(Move, possible)` is in *Options*
`current_state(CurrentState)`
`apply(CurrentState, Move, ResultantState)`
`valid_state(ResultantState)`
THEN: delete `option(Move, possible)` from *Options*
add `option(Move, valid)` to *Options*

Rule 7 (unrefracted): *If a possible move leads to an invalid state, remove it*
IF: `option(Move, possible)` is in *Options*
`current_state(CurrentState)`
`apply(CurrentState, Move, ResultantState)`
not `valid_state(ResultantState)`
THEN: delete `option(Move, possible)` from *Options*

Condition Definition: `current_state/1`: *Get the current state*
`current_state(state(Left, Boat, Right)) :-`
`position(left, Left)` is in *Current State*
`position(right, Right)` is in *Current State*
`boat(Boat)` is in *Current State*

Condition Definition: `apply/3`: *Apply a move to a state*
`apply(state(LB, left, RB), move(left, MC), state(LA, right, RA)) :-`
`add_state(RB, MC, RA)`
`subtract_state(LB, MC, LA)`
`apply(state(LB, right, RB), move(right, MC), state(LA, left, RA)) :-`
`subtract_state(RB, MC, RA)`
`add_state(LB, MC, LA)`

Condition Definition: `valid_state/1`: *Are the missionaries safe?*
`valid_state(state(Left, Boat, Right)) :-`
`missionaries_safe(Left)`
`missionaries_safe(Right)`

Condition Definition: `missionaries_safe/1`: *Is an M/C combination safe?*
`missionaries_safe(0 : C).`
`missionaries_safe(M : C) :-`
not `C` is greater than `M`

Box 4.3: Rules and condition definitions for rejecting invalid moves (from *Select & Apply*)

shown. `missionaries_safe/1` is true if the number of missionaries represented by the first argument is either zero, or not exceeded by the number of cannibals

Rule 8 (unrefracted; once): *Select one valid move*
IF: not `option(AnyMove, selected)` is in *Options*
`option(Move, valid)` is in *Options*
THEN: add `option(Move, selected)` to *Options*

Rule 9 (unrefracted): *If a move has been selected, remove all others*
IF: exists `option(Move, selected)` is in *Options*
`option(AnyMove, valid)` is in *Options*
THEN: delete `option(AnyMove, valid)` from *Options*

Box 4.4: Rules to select one possible move and discard all others (from *Select & Apply*)

represented by its second argument.

Like the first five rules, Rules 6 and 7 are unrefracted, allowing them to fire multiple times with the same variable instantiations. Unlike the first five rules, however, Rules 6 and 7 are allowed to (and indeed must) fire multiple times on any cycle. Rule 6 will fire once for each valid move. Rule 7 will fire once for each invalid move.

Exercise 4.3: Enter Rules 6 and 7 and the user-defined conditions from Box 4.3 into *Select & Apply*. Run the partial model. On the first cycle it should propose five moves (as before). It should then carry on and, on the second cycle, mark those moves that lead to valid states as `valid` and remove all others. ◇

Selecting Moves

The simplest approach that one might take to the Missionaries and Cannibals problem, once invalid moves have been ruled out, is to select randomly from the remaining moves. In this section we implement this "random choice" strategy in order to explore its feasibility. It turns out that the random choice strategy yields behaviour that is very dissimilar to that of experimental participants solving the problem. In subsequent sections we therefore consider more elaborate move selection strategies, along with relevant empirical evidence.

Two rules are required to implement the random choice strategy. Rule 8 of Box 4.4, which is marked to fire only once per cycle, selects a valid move from *Options*. It relies upon the Access property of *Options*, which should be set to the default value of Random, to enforce random choice. Rule 9 of Box 4.4 discards all other moves, once one has been selected. Both rules are unrefracted, as it may be necessary to make the same move more than once (on different cycles) or to discard the same move multiple times.

Rule 10 (unrefracted): *Make a move (modifying Current State)*
IF: `option(Move, selected)` is in *Options*
`position(left, LB)` is in *Current State*
`position(right, RB)` is in *Current State*
`apply(state(LB, BB, RB), Move, state(LA, BA, RA))`
THEN: delete `option(Move, selected)` from *Options*
delete `position(left, LB)` from *Current State*
add `position(left, LA)` to *Current State*
delete `position(right, RB)` from *Current State*
add `position(right, RA)` to *Current State*
delete `boat(BB)` from *Current State*
add `boat(BA)` to *Current State*

Box 4.5: The rule for performing a move (from *Select & Apply*)

Exercise 4.4: Add Rules 8 and 9 to *Select & Apply* and run the model. It should now run for two further cycles, selecting and discarding moves on the last two cycles. Reinitialise and run the model a few times to ensure that it doesn't always choose the same initial move. If it does, ensure that the **Access** property of *Options* is set appropriately. ◇

Performing Moves

Once a move has been selected, performing or executing the move is a matter of adjusting *Current State* to reflect changes in the positions of the various people and the boat. Rule 10 (Box 4.5) performs these adjustments. The rule's conditions ensure that it only fires when a move is selected. The conditions also match all state information and use the user-defined condition `apply/3` (from Box 4.3) to determine the new state. The rule's actions delete the selected move from *Options* and update the position information of all entities involved in the problem. The rule is unrefracted so that it can apply over and over with the same variable instantiations. This is necessary because solving the problem may require carrying out the same move multiple times.

Once Rule 10 has been applied, and the selected move has been deleted, *Options* will be empty. The move proposal rules (Rules 1 to 5) will then be able to fire on the next cycle, thereby continuing the processing loop.

Exercise 4.5: Add Rule 10 to *Select & Apply* and run the resultant model. It should now make a sequence of moves, with different combinations of people moving back and forth across the river. (In fact, if you run the model using the **Run** button it will continue processing until it is interrupted with the **Stop** button.

Rule 11 (unrefracted): *Stop processing when everybody is on the right bank*
IF: `position(right, 3 : 3)` is in *Current State*
THEN: send `stop` to *Random Search*

Box 4.6: A rule to detect task completion (from *Select & Apply*)

If it doesn't — if it terminates after a few cycles, or a few tens of cycles — check that all rules are set to unrefracted.) ◇

Halting on Task Completion

One final rule is necessary to complete the model. We must detect when the problem has been solved (i.e., when everybody is on the right bank) and stop processing. Otherwise the model will continue shuffling people back and forth, *ad infinitum*. A single rule, Rule 11 in Box 4.6, suffices. This rule monitors *Current State*, and fires when all three missionaries and all three cannibals are on the right bank.

Exercise 4.6: Add Rule 11 to *Select & Apply* and run the model a number of times. Observe that the model can now solve the Missionaries and Cannibals problem, but that it can take several hundred moves to do so. From Figure 4.2 we can see that the problem can in fact be solved in just 11 moves. The simple random choice strategy is very inefficient. Often moves are made and then reversed, even when only one additional move is required to solve the problem. This characteristic does not feature in human attempts at the problem. ◇

Exercise 4.7: An alternative approach to halting on task completing is to modify the move proposal rules so that rules are only proposed when the goal state has not been achieved. Modify Rules 1 to 5 (the move proposal rules) so that they check for task completing and fire only when the goal state has not been achieved. ◇

The previous exercises have demonstrated that the random choice strategy can lead to solution of the Missionaries and Cannibals problem. However, random choice is not a valid model of human performance on this task: as discussed above, humans show characteristic difficulties at specific points in the solution of the task. Their behaviour is clearly not entirely random. Below we consider how the model may be improved through the addition of psychologically plausible problem solving strategies.

Displaying the Current State

The representation of the state in the random choice model via `position/2` and `boat/1` clauses is appropriate for the computational requirements of the Missionaries and Cannibals problem, but the intended interpretation of the information is unnecessarily obscure. The task lends itself to a diagrammatic representation in which the various elements (river, banks, boat, and people) and their relations are more directly apparent. This section provides such a representation of the state of the problem by augmenting *Current State* with display rules. These rules play no part in the behaviour of the model. Instead, they specify graphical representations corresponding to elements in *Current State*. These representations simplify the assessment of the behaviour of the model.

Recall that display rules are similar to the rules that normally inhabit processes, except that: they are contained within buffers; they can only match elements in the buffer that contains them; they may not be triggered, refracted, or marked to fire only once on a cycle; and their actions must all take the form "show x", where x specifies a graphical object of the kind normally contained within an analogue buffer (e.g., a point, some text, a circle, a box, etc.).

Three display rules (shown in Box 4.7) are sufficient for the present model. Display Rule 1 enters blue and green boxes on the display, corresponding to the river and its banks. Display Rule 2 places text showing the number of missionaries and cannibals on each bank. It uses `x_location` to determine the x-coordinate for each piece of text. Display Rule 3 draws a representation of the boat. It uses a black polygon, with coordinates dependent upon whether the boat is on the left or right bank.

Exercise 4.8: Enter the display rules from Box 4.7 into the Display Rules panel of *Current State*. Initialise the model and switch *Current State* to its Current Display panel. The display should appear as in Figure 4.4. Now run the model. The display should update as missionaries, cannibals and the boat move from side to side. ◇

4.2.3 Proposal and Evaluation of Moves

There are many differences between the behaviour of the random search model and that of most people. Two of particular concern are the model's tendency to backtrack (i.e., the tendency of the model to select a move that undoes its previous move) and its tendency to continue to move randomly when only one step away from its goal (and hence to frequently backtrack even when only one move away from the solution). Both of these short-comings may be addressed by making move selection more "intelligent". The general idea is that all possible moves should be given an evaluation prior to selection, and selection should in-

Display Rule 1: *The river and its banks...*
IF: `H is 250`
THEN: show `box(r, (400, H) at (120, H), [colour(blue), filled(yes)])`
show `box(b, (120, H) at (0, H), [colour(green), filled(yes)])`
show `box(b, (120, H) at (520, H), [colour(green), filled(yes)])`

Display Rule 2: *The people...*
IF: `position(Bank, NM : NC)` is in *Current State*
`x_location(Bank, X)`
THEN: show `text(m, (missionaries : NM) at (X, 90), [colour(black)])`
show `text(c, (cannibals : NC) at (X, 130), [colour(black)])`

Display Rule 3: *The boat...*
IF: `boat(Bank)` is in *Current State*
`boat_graphic(Bank, Coords)`
THEN: show `polygon(boat, Coords, [colour(black), filled(yes)])`

Condition Definition: `x_location`/3: *X coordinate for each bank*
`x_location(left, 20).`
`x_location(right, 530).`

Condition Definition: `boat_graphic`/2: *A boat-shaped polygon...*
`boat_graphic(left, [(100, 100), (180, 100), (170, 110), (110, 110)]).`
`boat_graphic(right, [(470, 100), (550, 100), (540, 110), (480, 110)]).`

Box 4.7: Display rules for *Current State*

volve choosing the move that receives the highest evaluation. Moves that undo previous moves can be given a low evaluation. Moves that achieve the desired state can be given a high evaluation. Other moves can be given intermediate evaluations, perhaps determined by some measure of how close they move the state to the desired state. Such a measure results in the hill-climbing strategy discussed above. There is therefore good psychological reason to pursue a model that makes use of this kind of evaluation phase.

Rules 6 and 7 of the random search model described above already perform a simple kind of move evaluation: they divide possible moves into valid moves (i.e., those that are legal) and invalid moves. The first step in improving move evaluation is therefore to adjust these rules to yield numerical values for moves (e.g., $+1$ for valid moves and -1 for invalid moves). In fact, the rules can be merged into a single rule by calling upon an additional user-defined condition that calculates the numerical evaluation of a given state. This is illustrated by Rule 6 of Box 4.8, which, with the addition of the definition of `evaluate_state`/2, may replace the previous two rules.

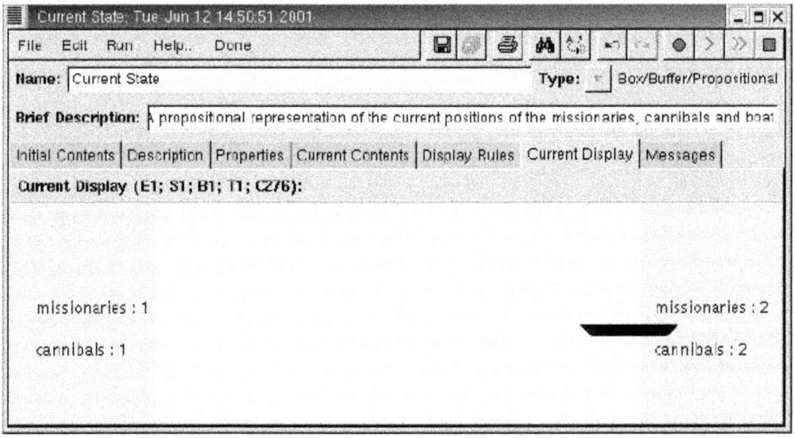

Figure 4.4: The display of *Current State* part-way through solution of the Missionaries and Cannibals problem

Rule 6 (unrefracted): *Evaluate all possible moves*
IF: `option(Move, possible)` is in *Options*
`current_state(CurrentState)`
`apply(CurrentState, Move, ResultantState)`
`evaluate_state(ResultantState, Value)`
THEN: delete `option(Move, possible)` from *Options*
add `option(Move, value(Value))` to *Options*

Condition Definition: `evaluate_state/2`: *Version 1: favour valid states*
`evaluate_state(State, +1) :-`
`valid_state(State)`
`evaluate_state(State, -1).`
not `valid_state(State)`

Rule 7 (unrefracted; once): *Select one of the best moves*
IF: not `option(AnyMove, selected)` is in *Options*
`option(Move, value(X))` is in *Options*
not `option(OtherMove, value(Y))` is in *Options*
`Y` is greater than `X`
THEN: add `option(Move, selected)` to *Options*

Box 4.8: Rules and condition definitions for evaluating possible moves (from *Select & Apply*)

Condition Definition: `evaluate_state/2`: *Version 2: favour goal states*

```
evaluate_state(State, +2) :-
    goal_state(State)
evaluate_state(State, +1) :-
    not goal_state(State)
    valid_state(State)
evaluate_state(State, -1) :-
    not goal_state(State)
    not valid_state(State)
```

Condition Definition: `goal_state/1`: *Is the given state the goal state?*

```
goal_state(state(0 : 0, right, 3 : 3)).
```

Box 4.9: An improved definition of `evaluate_state/2` (from *Select & Apply*)

Corresponding adjustments are required in rules 8 and 9 (which, because of the merger of Rules 6 and 7 become Rules 7 and 8). Rule 7 (Box 4.8) must select one move whose evaluation is not less than any other move's evaluation. The rule is marked to fire once per cycle, so if several moves have equal high evaluations selection from amongst those moves will be determined by the Access property of *Options*. Unless explicitly modified this will lead to random selection from amongst moves with equally high evaluations.

Exercise 4.9: Carry out the revisions to the move selection rules as described above. Convince yourself that the model's behaviour is unchanged. ◇

We are now in a position to add genuine evaluation of moves. This may be achieved by elaborating the definition of `evaluate_state/2`. As a first step, note that if a move leads directly to the goal state, then that move should receive the highest evaluation. A minimal modification that embodies this principle is shown in Box 4.9. With this revision to `evaluate_state/2` the model will at least make the correct final move whenever possible.

Exercise 4.10: Explore different state evaluation functions. First consider giving high evaluations to moves that increase the number of people on the right bank. What effect does this have on the model's behaviour? Why is this evaluation function flawed? Next consider favouring moves that tend to balance the number of missionaries and cannibals on each bank. Again, what effect does this evaluation function have on the model's behaviour and why is it flawed? Do the empirical findings discussed above provide any support for the use of either evaluation function? Neither evaluation function leads to a model that can solve the

Rule 11 (unrefracted): *Record the state before making a move*
IF: `option(AnyMove, selected)` is in *Options*
`current_state(State)`
THEN: add `State` to *Prior State*

Condition Definition: `evaluate_state/2`: *Version 3: avoid prior states*

```
evaluate_state(State, +2) :-
    goal_state(State)
evaluate_state(State, +1) :-
    not goal_state(State)
    valid_state(State)
    not State is in Prior State
evaluate_state(State, 0) :-
    not goal_state(State)
    valid_state(State)
    State is in Prior State
evaluate_state(State, -1) :-
    not goal_state(State)
    not valid_state(State)
```

Box 4.10: Augmentations necessary for recording states and using that information to bias move selection (from *Select & Apply*)

Missionaries and Cannibals problem efficiently. Can you suggest any evaluation functions that address the problems raised by the two approaches? If so, explore their behaviour. Consider, in particular, evaluation functions that look ahead to subsequent states. ◇

The effectiveness of simple evaluation functions (i.e., those that do not attempt to look ahead beyond the given state) can be increased substantially by allowing them access to information gained whilst attempting the task. At a minimum, we may maintain a record of the previous state, and give low evaluations to moves that lead from the current state back to the previous state. Such an approach will reduce the tendency of the model to select moves that undo previous moves. To implement this approach we augment the model with a new propositional buffer, *Prior State*, which may be read and written to by *Select & Apply*. We only need to store a single prior state, so the buffer's properties should be set to limit its capacity to one.

Select & Apply requires one additional rule to keep *Prior State* up to date. Rule 11 of Box 4.10 achieves this. If the capacity limit properties of *Prior State* are set correctly, it will not be necessary for the rule to clear the contents of *Prior*

State: the new element will over-write any previous element.

With Rule 11, the definition of `evaluate_state/2` may be modified to use *Prior State* information, as in Box 4.10. The definition gives an evaluation of zero to moves that undo the effects of the last move. This ensures that, in situations where no other valid moves are applicable, moves that undo the previous move will still be preferred to moves that lead to illegal states (i.e., states in which the missionaries on one bank are outnumbered).

There is some evidence to suggest that strong negative evaluations may be given to undesirable, but valid, moves (such as those that undo the previous move) — people sometimes suggest invalid moves in preference to valid undesirable moves. Although we have avoided such evaluations in the above model, it is straightforward to incorporate them.

Exercise 4.11: Add Rule 11 to *Select & Apply* and make the appropriate revisions to the definition of `evaluate_state/2` so that the model avoids moves that undo the effects of the most recent move. The model's solution time should be substantially reduced. Describe the behaviour of the model. Do any oddities remain? ◇

Exercise 4.12: Although the current model avoids backtracking where possible, it can still cycle aimlessly around some parts of the problem space. Only chance prevents it, for example, from performing the following four moves *ad infinitum*: move two cannibals to the right, move one cannibal to the left, move one missionary to the right, move one missionary and one cannibal to the left. This is not consistent with the finding of Thomas (1974) discussed above concerning participant's reluctance to retry moves that have previously failed. In order to address this failing it is necessary to keep track of previous moves and the states from which they were made (rather than just previous states), and give low evaluations to moves that have previously been tried. Change the name of *Prior State* to *Prior Moves* and use the renamed buffer to store more detailed information about problem solving "history". In particular, store clauses of the form `previous_move(State, Move)`. Modify the move evaluation procedure to use these clauses so that novel moves are favoured over moves that have previously been tried. ◇

Exercise 4.13: The performance of the final version of the model is, if anything, too good. Unlike a real person, it always solves the problem in the minimum number of moves, never violates the rules, and never backtracks. While the model is a poor model of human *performance*, it may still be a good model of human *competence*. That is, it may be a good model of what behaviour would be like if the human information processing system was not subject to performance limitations such as decay of buffer contents. To investigate the competence/performance distinction evaluate the model's behaviour when performance limitations (e.g., buffer decay in either or both of *Options* and *Prior Moves*) are added. Is the resultant behaviour more plausible? ◇

4.2.4 Project: Serial Proposal of Moves

The model developed above proposes all possible moves in parallel. It then evaluates all proposed moves, again in parallel. Introspection suggests that this is incorrect: both processes appear to be serial processes. That is, people propose and evaluate moves in sequence. Modify the above model to produce a serial implementation.

Hint: Merge the move proposal rules into a single rule, and set the flag on this rule to ensure it fires at most once on any cycle. Make sure the rule only fires when a) no moves are being considered, or b) all considered moves have been evaluated. You will also need to store move evaluations and delay selection of the best move until no more moves can be proposed.

Question 1: How do we select which move to propose and evaluate first? Using the once flag to limit firing of the move proposal rule will result in a system in which the order of move proposal is governed by the Access property of *Current State*. Experiment with different values of this property to see how they affect the order of move proposal.

Question 2: Do we evaluate all possible moves before making a move? Evidence from a variety of domains suggest that people are not this systematic. In the related domain of decision making, Simon (1957) suggests that we typically adopt a strategy of "satisficing". That is, rather than carrying out an exhaustive serial search of all possible options, we choose the first option that is good enough. How might the model be modified to satisfice?

4.2.5 Project: The Jealous Husbands Problem

A problem that is analogous on many levels to the Missionaries and Cannibals problem is the Jealous Husbands problem. Reed, Ernst, and Banerji (1974, p. 438) state the problem as follows:

> Three jealous husbands and their wives having to cross a river at a ferry find a boat, but the boat is so small that it can contain no more than two persons. Find the simplest schedule of crossings that will permit all six people to cross the river so that none of the women

> shall be left in company with any of the men, unless her husband is present. It is assumed that all passengers on the boat unboard before the next trip and that at least one person has to be in the boat for each crossing.

Reed *et al.* (1974) were particularly interested in the possible transfer of solution patterns between this problem and the Missionaries and Cannibals problem. They found little evidence of spontaneous transfer between the problems, but when the relation between the problems was explained to participants transfer was observed in one direction (from the Jealous Husbands problem to the Missionaries and Cannibals problem) but not the other. They suggested that the asymmetry in transfer arose because of an asymmetric relation in the problem spaces: in the Jealous Husbands problem it is necessary to represent husband/wife relations within the state. Thus for each state in the Missionaries and Cannibals problem there are multiple states in the Jealous Husbands problem. The mapping from Jealous Husbands to Missionaries and Cannibals is therefore many-to-one. In contrast the mapping from Missionaries and Cannibals to Jealous Husbands is one-to-many.

Develop a COGENT model that is able to solve the Jealous Husbands problem (in the minimum number of moves). When developing the model keep in mind the fact that there exists a single problem solving apparatus (i.e., the human mind) that is able to solve both the Jealous Husbands problem and the Missionaries and Cannibals problem. What are the differences between the Jealous Husbands model and the Missionaries and Cannibals model? Can you develop a combined model, capable of solving both problems?

4.3 The Tower of Hanoi

The Missionaries and Cannibals problem is one of the simpler problems that psychologists have investigated, and the relatively simple heuristic of hill-climbing provides a reasonable account of many people's performance on the problem. Hill-climbing fails to account, however, for the findings of Thomas (1974) and Greeno (1974) of distinct stages in solution attempts. Furthermore, and as noted above, hill-climbing has its limitations, especially in cases were there is no clear evaluation metric for determining the distance between two problem states. More complex heuristics are required in such cases. In this section we consider the Tower of Hanoi problem, another classic, and the powerful heuristic of Means-Ends Analysis (MEA).

In some problem solving situations a plausible approach to a solution is to break the problem into simpler problems and solve the simpler problems. This "divide and conquer" approach is the basis of MEA. In its raw form, MEA involves comparing the current state with the goal state, finding a difference between the two, and then attempting to reduce or eliminate that difference. The process may then be repeated: the problem solver may compare the (revised) current state and the goal state, find a second difference, and reduce or eliminate this difference. Problem solving terminates when there are no remaining differences between the current state and the goal state. The elimination of a difference is a sub-problem (or subgoal).

MEA is a heuristic, rather than an algorithm, because for any particular problem it does not specify how to determine appropriate subgoals. It is also not guaranteed to find a solution even if one exists. Successful use of MEA requires intelligent selection of subgoals. The factors that influence subgoal selection when using MEA are therefore of considerable interest. They are also under-researched.

One well-studied problem for which MEA is an appropriate strategy is the Tower of Hanoi problem. The three-disk version of the problem is shown in Figure 4.5. The task is to move the tower of disks from the left peg to the right peg by moving disks, one at a time, from one peg to another and subject to one constraint: no disk can be placed on top of a smaller disk. The task can be made more difficult by increasing the number of disks (while keeping just three pegs).

Figure 4.5: The "standard" three-disk Tower of Hanoi problem

The Tower of Hanoi provides a very clear illustration of the utility of the MEA approach. From a formal perspective, the problem can be broken into a series of sub-problems: move the largest disk to the right peg; move the intermediate-sized disk to the right peg; and move the smallest disk to the right peg. The problem constraints (concerning stacking order and disk size) mean that these three sub-problems must be solved in order, so the problem has a clear and unambiguous decomposition. Once this decomposition is determined we may direct attention to each sub-problem in turn. In particular we may focus on the first sub-problem (moving the largest disk to the right peg) and on achieving a state in which that problem can be solved in a single move (i.e., one in which there are no other disks on the big disk and no disks on the right peg). To achieve this state we must move the two-disk tower that sits upon the big disk from the left peg to the middle peg. This is just an easier version of the problem we started with, and the same MEA principles may be used to solve it.

4.3.1 Empirical Findings

The problem space for the four-disk version of the Tower of Hanoi consists of 81 states. The task itself can be completed in just fifteen moves, though few people are this efficient on their first attempt. Simon (1975) performed an analysis of possible solution strategies for the problem and identified four classes of strategy, including the strategy described above, two simpler strategies phrased in terms of moving disks (rather than smaller towers) and with moves triggered by perceptual features of the changing state, and a strategy of rote learning. The strategies have different properties in terms of generalisation (to problems involving different numbers of disks) and processing requirements.

Anzai and Simon (1979) demonstrated that Simon's (1975) strategies have some psychological significance. They present a detailed analysis of the behaviour of one person over four attempts at the five-disk version of the problem. The analysis, based on verbal protocols, demonstrates that the approach adopted by the person evolved over successive attempts. At first she showed little sign of strategy, moving disks subject to simple constraints (basically the task constraints, supplemented with an avoidance of backtracking and an avoidance of moving the same disk twice in succession). By the third attempt a sophisticated recursive strategy, involving subgoals of moving disks of various sizes to various pegs, had developed. On the final attempt, this strategy evolved further, with subgoals involving the movement of pyramids of disks. Anzai and Simon were particularly interested in what is learnt when solving the problem, and developed an adaptive production system to simulate the acquisition and evolution of the person's strategies.

Studies of transfer of solution strategy between different versions of the Tower of Hanoi problem have also been carried out. Thus, Gagné and Smith (1962) looked at the effects of verbalisation on generalisation from two-, three-, four-, and five-disk versions of the problem to the six-disk version. Subjects who verbalised their solution attempts at simpler problems were significantly better at solving the six-disk version, completing the problem in less time and with fewer unnecessary moves. The data suggest that people who were instructed to verbalise acquired a general, and efficient, strategy (such as that of the person studied by Anzai and Simon). The poor performance of people who were not instructed to verbalise suggests that mere experience with the problem does not guarantee acquisition of such strategies.

4.3.2 A First Model: Selection without Search

We begin by developing a "naïve" model, with the aim of replicating the behaviour of the person studied by Anzai and Simon (1979) on her first attempt at the five-disk problem. We take up where we left off with the Missionaries and Cannibals problem. That is, we employ the same basic information processing architecture

a) Initial State	b) Goal State
`disk(30,left,5)`	`disk(30,right,5)`
`disk(40,left,4)`	`disk(40,right,4)`
`disk(50,left,3)`	`disk(50,right,3)`
`disk(60,left,2)`	`disk(60,right,2)`
`disk(70,left,1)`	`disk(70,right,1)`

Figure 4.6: A representation of the initial and goal states of the five-disk Tower of Hanoi problem

shown in Figure 4.3, consisting of the *Select & Apply* process coupled to two propositional buffers: *Current State* and *Options*. The contents of each of these components will, of course, need to be adjusted for the Tower of Hanoi task. We therefore start with each initially empty.

The state of the Tower of Hanoi is fully determined by the positions of the various disks. Three features of each disk are significant: its size, the peg it is on, and the position on that peg. Thus, the initial state and goal state of the five-disk problem may be represented as the two sets of propositions in Figure 4.6. In each proposition, disk size is represented by the first argument (ranging from `30` units to `70` units), peg (which may be `left`, `middle` or `right`) is represented by the second argument, and position is represented by the third argument (with position `1` being at the foot of the peg, position 2 being above that, and so on).

Exercise 4.14: Create a new model and populate it with the three boxes as described above. Enter the propositional representation of the initial state as the initial contents of *Current State*, and write rule(s) and/or condition definitions for *Select & Apply* that determine, by querying *Current State*, a set of possible moves. The rule(s) should add these moves to *Select & Apply*, mirroring Rules 1 to 5 in the random search model of the Missionaries and Cannibals task described earlier in the chapter. Represent moves by propositions of the form `move(Width,FromPeg,ToPeg)`. It is not necessary to include a specification of position on each peg in the representation of the move, as this information is available from *Current State*. At this stage do not worry about ensuring that the moves meet the constraints of disk size.

Note: A single rule can be written for move proposal if judicious use is made of three user-defined conditions that determine 1) if the goal has been achieved, 2) the size of the top-most disk on a peg, and 3) the names of other pegs. ◇

Operator evaluation may proceed in a way analogous to that of the Missionaries and Cannibals problem: moves that break the task constraint (by placing one disk on another that is smaller) should be given a negative evaluation (e.g., -1). For present purposes all other moves can be assumed to receive a positive evaluation (e.g., $+1$).

Exercise 4.15: Extend the model by adding a move evaluation rule as described above. In order to test the model, specify different initial states (e.g., with one or two disks on each peg). Ensure that all and only correct moves are proposed in each case, and that all proposed moves then receive appropriate evaluations. ◇

Exercise 4.16: Add move selection rules (such as the pair used in the Missionaries and Cannibals problem) to select one move from those with the highest evaluation (and delete all other moves). Also add a rule for executing moves. This rule should transform *Current State* to reflect the effects of moving the appropriate disk. The model should now be able to move disks between the pegs, subject to the disk size constraint. If the model stops after a few tens of cycles, ensure that all rules are marked as unrefracted. ◇

Exercise 4.17: As with the Missionaries and Cannibals problem, the Tower of Hanoi is naturally represented in pictorial form. The current implementation may be extended to provide such a representation by augmenting *Current State* with appropriate display rules. Create such display rules. ◇

On her first attempt at the Tower of Hanoi, Anzai and Simon's (1979) participant avoided two types of moves: backtracking (i.e., undoing the previous move) and moving the same disk twice. Her evaluation function therefore made reference to her previous move. In order to implement such an evaluation function we must therefore keep a record of the prior move (as in the Missionaries and Cannibals problem).

Exercise 4.18: Extend the model by adding a further propositional buffer, *Previous Move*. When a move is executed, store the move in this buffer. Use the buffer contents to give low evaluations (e.g., 0) to moves that move the same disk twice in succession. (Recall that if such moves were given the same evaluation as illegal moves, then illegal moves could be selected in suitably unfavourable circumstances.) How does the model perform now? ◇

Anzai and Simon (1979) noted one further aspect of their participant's behaviour on her first attempt at the problem: whenever she moved the small disk, it was never back to the peg it was on two moves previously. If one adopts this additional constraint, all moves are fully determined by the initial move.

Exercise 4.19: Modify your model so that moves in which the small disk is returned to the peg it was on two moves previously receive low evaluations. Do this by renaming *Previous Move* to *Previous Moves* and setting its capacity to 2. Be sure that the On Excess property is set to Oldest, so that the oldest elements are deleted when the capacity is exceeded. Note that it is necessary to index previous moves, so that the evaluation function can explicitly refer to either the previous move or the move prior to that. Represent the previous move in *Previous Moves* by a proposition of the form `history(Move, -1)` and the move prior to that by a proposition of the form `history(Move, -2)`. You will need another rule to update the indices each time a move is made. Extend the evaluation function to use the information in *Previous Moves* accordingly. ◇

4.3.3 A Second Model: Goal-Directed Selection

The previous model is able to solve the Tower of Hanoi problem, and sometimes it is able to do so efficiently, but it requires some good fortune. If it makes the wrong first move, it is doomed to charge through an unproductive region of the problem space. In fact, Anzai and Simon's (1979) participant did make the wrong first move on her first attempt at the problem, but she quickly realised her mistake. After six moves she began expressing doubts, and after nine moves she abandoned her attempt and began afresh. On her second attempt at the problem, she explicitly avoided making the same first move, and subsequently solved the problem. Her protocol during the second attempt shows further signs of learning. In particular, she began to talk of intermediate goals (such as moving the largest disk to the right peg). In this section we therefore develop a model that incorporates goal-directed move selection. We consider the relation between the two models below.

Simon's (1975) perceptual strategy involves identifying the largest disk that is not in its correct position (call this the focus disk), and setting a goal of moving this disk to its correct position. This goal may not be directly achievable, either because the focus disk has other disks on top of it or because there is a smaller disk on the target peg. In either case, a subgoal may be created to move smaller disks either from above the focus disk or from the target peg to the third peg. The most efficient form of this strategy is to set a subgoal of moving the largest blocking disk to the third peg. This subgoal may also not be directly achievable. In this case, however, the process can be repeated, with the creation of a further subgoal to move another (yet smaller) disk to another peg. This setting of subgoals is guaranteed to terminate when we get to the smallest disk.

In order to perform this strategy it is necessary to maintain a goal stack: an ordered set of goals in which behaviour at any moment is controlled by the top-most element. When processed, the top-most element may be removed or "popped" from the stack if it is directly achievable. Alternatively, processing of the top-most element may lead to other elements being "pushed" onto the top of the stack, tem-

Rule 1 (unrefracted): *Find the next goal, and push it*
IF: not `AnyGoal` is in *Goal Stack*
`biggest_difference(Size, TargetPeg)`
THEN: send `push(move(Size, TargetPeg))` to *Goal Stack*

Rule 2 (unrefracted): *If possible, apply a move and pop it*
IF: `move(Size, TargetPeg)` is in *Goal Stack*
`disk(Size, SourcePeg, SourcePos)` is in *Current State*
`move_is_possible(SourcePeg, Size, TargetPeg)`
`get_target_position(TargetPeg, TargetPos)`
THEN: delete `disk(Size, SourcePeg, SourcePos)` from *Current State*
add `disk(Size, TargetPeg, TargetPos)` to *Current State*
send pop to *Goal Stack*

Rule 3 (unrefracted): *If a desired move is blocked, push a subgoal*
IF: `move(Size, TargetPeg)` is in *Goal Stack*
`disk(Size, SourcePeg, SourcePos)` is in *Current State*
not `move_is_possible(SourcePeg, Size, TargetPeg)`
`biggest_blockage(move(SourcePeg, Size, TargetPeg), Disk)`
`other_peg(SourcePeg, TargetPeg, OtherPeg)`
THEN: send `push(move(Disk, OtherPeg))` to *Goal Stack*

Box 4.11: Rules for using a goal stack to aid move selection within the Tower of Hanoi task (from *Select & Apply*)

porarily obscuring the previous goal. This strategy requires a rule such as Rule 1 of Box 4.11 to set basic goals.

Exercise 4.20: Create a copy of the previous Tower of Hanoi model and modify it in preparation for development of a goal-directed model. This will entail replacing *Select & Apply* with *Goal Stack*, a stack buffer, and removing all rules from *Select & Apply*. Defined conditions within *Select & Apply* may be retained as they may be useful later. *Current State* should also be retained. Add Rule 1 of Box 4.11 to *Select & Apply* and define a condition within the process that identifies the largest disk that is not in its desired location (i.e., the condition `biggest_difference/2` referenced in Rule 1). Ensure that the proto-model runs for one cycle after initialisation, and that on this cycle the goal to move the largest disk to the right peg is pushed onto *Goal Stack*. ◇

The goal-directed strategy requires two more rules: one to move a disk if the top-most goal is possible and one to create an appropriate subgoal if the top-most goal is blocked. Rules 2 and 3 of Box 4.11 perform these functions.

Exercise 4.21: Enter the above rules (and appropriate defined conditions) into *Select & Apply*. Run the resulting model and note how the goal stack grows and shrinks during problem solving. The model's goal stack can grow to be very large. This is cognitively implausible. What happens if you limit the size of the goal stack (by setting the appropriate properties of *Goal Stack*)? What is the relation between the complexity of Tower of Hanoi problems that may be solved and the size of the goal stack? ◇

4.3.4 Generalised Means-Ends Analysis

Anzai and Simon (1979) suggested that their participant was able to develop an MEA solution to the Tower of Hanoi problem because MEA is a general problem solving strategy that the participant had acquired earlier in her life. (See also Ernst & Newell, 1969, and Newell & Simon, 1972, for comments on MEA as a general problem solving strategy.) The model developed in the previous section does not use such a general purpose strategy. Rather, it uses a specialisation of MEA appropriate to the Tower of Hanoi problem. This section demonstrates how the general principles of MEA may be abstracted as a small set of rules. These rules may then be instantiated in different ways for different problems.

In its raw form, MEA involves first locating the largest difference between the current state and the desired state, and selecting a move to eliminate this difference. Assuming this move is then pushed onto a stack, this general rule can be expressed as Rule 1 of Box 4.12.

Rule 1 assumes two user-defined conditions — `biggest_difference`/1 and `appropriate_move`/2 — that detect differences and select appropriate moves accordingly. We have also replaced the goal stack by a move stack, because we are stacking moves and not goals. (There is little of significance in this step.) Rule 1 will fire whenever *Move Stack* becomes empty. It will then determine the next difference to be addressed, and add an appropriate move to address this difference to *Move Stack*.

If *Move Stack* is not empty, and if the preconditions of the top-most move on *Move Stack* are satisfied (i.e., the move is not blocked), then the top-most move can be performed and popped off the stack. For reasons discussed below, full generality in COGENT requires that these two processes are allocated to separate rules. The simpler of the two rules, Rule 2 of Box 4.12, pops a move off *Move Stack* if it is not blocked. The second rule, Rule 3 of Box 4.12, applies a non-blocked move by changing the state.

Separate rules are required because a move may, in general, lead to multiple changes to a state. Thus, Rule 3 may fire several times (in pseudo-parallel) for a single move, with each firing dealing with a single change to the state. Rule 2, by contrast, should only fire once, popping just the top-most move from *Move Stack*, when a move is made.

Rule 1 (unrefracted): *If the move stack is empty, push the next subgoal*
IF: not `AnyMove` is in *Move Stack*
`biggest_difference(Difference)`
`appropriate_move(eliminate(Difference),Move)`
THEN: send `push(Move)` to *Move Stack*

Rule 2 (unrefracted): *If a move exists that achieves the top-most goal, pop it*
IF: `Move` is in *Move Stack*
not `move_is_blocked(Move,Blockage)`
THEN: send `pop` to *Move Stack*

Rule 3 (unrefracted): *If a move exists that achieves the top-most goal, do it*
IF: `Move` is in *Move Stack*
not `move_is_blocked(Move,Blockage)`
`move_changes_state(Move,Before,After)`
`Before` is in *Current State*
THEN: delete `Before` from *Current State*
add `After` to *Current State*

Rule 4 (unrefracted): *If the top-most goal is blocked, create a subgoal*
IF: `Move` is in *Move Stack*
`move_is_blocked(Move,Blockage)`
`appropriate_move(eliminate(Blockage),SubMove)`
THEN: send `push(SubMove)` to *Move Stack*

Box 4.12: Rules for generalised Means-Ends Analysis

One further rule is required. If a move is blocked, a subgoal to eliminate that blockage must be created. Rule 4 of Box 4.12 performs this function. The rule uses `move_is_blocked`/2 to determine, for any blocked move, that aspect of the state that must be eliminated for the move to apply. It then selects a move that will eliminate the blockage, and pushes the new move onto the stack.

The four rules of Box 4.12 embody MEA as a general problem solving strategy. Use in any particular situation requires appropriate definitions for the four conditions.

Exercise 4.22: Create a new version of the model using the above general MEA rules. Write appropriate condition definitions (based on the condition definitions in the previous model) and run the resulting model. Ensure that its behaviour is identical to that of the model developed in the previous section. ◇

Of course, if MEA is a general strategy available to all mature problem solvers, then one is left with the question of why Anzai and Simon's participant doesn't use the strategy on her first attempt at the problem. Two possibilities present themselves. First, she may have assumed that simpler general solution strategies (such as selection without search) would be sufficient. Second, she may have lacked the necessary knowledge of the problem space (in terms of the operators and the differences that they could be used to eliminate) needed to perform MEA. This suggests that one of the things acquired by the participant during her first attempts at the problem was an understanding of how to decompose the problem into subgoals (corresponding to moving disks of successively smaller sizes to the right peg). This is consistent with the fact that the explicit mention of subgoals became progressively more common as she gained experience with the task.

4.3.5 Project: Macro-Operators and Moving Pyramids

Two further aspects of the behaviour of Anzai and Simon's (1979) participant have not been considered: as she gained experience with the problem she began to behave as if certain common sequences of moves could be treated as a single move; and on her fourth attempt at the task her strategy was reconceptualised in terms of moving pyramids of disks.

The first point is initially most apparent in the movement of a two-disk pyramid from one peg to another in three moves: move the small disk to the third peg, move the second smallest disk to the target peg, move the small disk from the third peg to the target peg. These higher order operators, assembled out of basic operators, are frequently referred to as macro-operators.

The second point is clear from her verbal protocol, in which she decomposes the goal of moving the five-disk pyramid from the left peg to the right peg into three subgoals: move the four-disk pyramid to the centre peg, then move the largest disk to the right peg, and finally move the four-disk pyramid from the centre peg to the right peg. This reconceptualisation in terms of pyramids can also be seen as resulting from the use of macro-operators. Here though the macro-operators are more complex, being built out of both basic operators (move a disk) and simpler macro-operators (move a pyramid of lesser size). Extend the above model to use macro-operators.

Hint: Add a propositional buffer and initialise it with some macro-operators. To start with, enter only simple macro-operators for moving pyramids consisting of just two disks. You will need to represent macro-operators in terms of their pre-conditions (i.e., what must be true of the state before they can be applied), their post-conditions (i.e., what is true after they have been applied), and their component operators. You will then need to detect when a macro-operator might be usefully applied (with reference to the current goal and the macro-operator's preconditions). Assuming that such macro-operators are then pushed onto the stack (as a list of moves), you will need to modify the rules for processing the top-most stack element to deal with macro-operator moves appropriately. Once the model works with simple macro-operators, try adding complex macro-operators (e.g., for moving a pyramid of three disks).

Question: How might macro-operators be acquired? What would be required to extend the model so that, with practice, it could acquire and use such operators?

4.3.6 Performing the Generalised Task

The Tower of Hanoi task may be generalised by allowing different start and goal states. That is, rather than starting from a tower configuration on the left peg with a goal of reconstructing the tower on the right peg, one might be required to go from one intermediate configuration to another, as in Figure 4.7.

Figure 4.7: A generalised Tower of Hanoi problem, with a "partial tower" initial state and a "flat" ending

Klahr and Robinson (1981) compared young children's attempts at tower-ending and flat-ending Tower of Hanoi problems. Superior performance was found in the tower-ending problems. Klahr and Robinson suggested that tower-ending problems are easier than flat-ending problems because in tower-ending problems there is a fixed order in which the various disks must reach the final peg. This is not true of flat-ending problems.

Exercise 4.23: The strategy embodied in the model developed above (without macro-operators) is able to solve the generalised task. At each stage of processing the same general principle applies: detect the largest disk that is not in its desired position, and set a goal to move the disk to its desired position. The model requires some modification, however, to explore its behaviour on the generalised task. Specifically, a mechanism for specifying different goal configurations must be added, and the definition of `biggest_difference`/2 must be adjusted to make use of this specification. Add a second buffer to the model (called *Desired State*) in which the desired state may be specified, and perform the necessary modification to `biggest_difference`/2. Test the model on both tower-ending and flat-

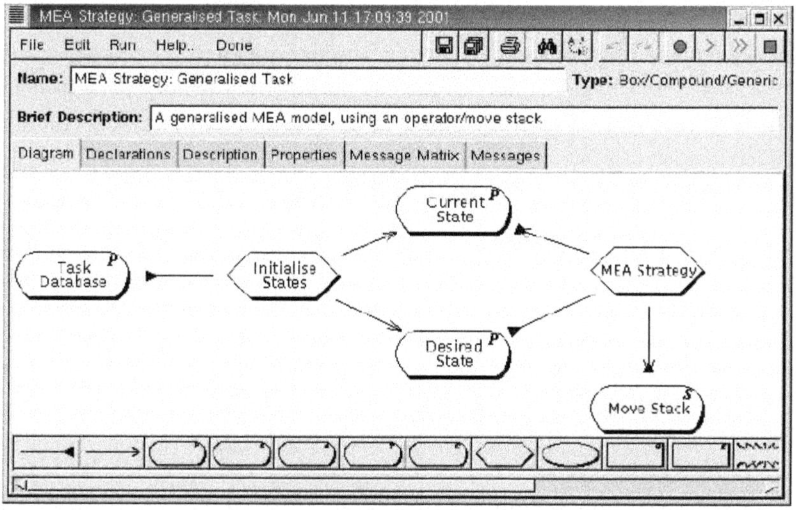

Figure 4.8: A box and arrow diagram for the Generalised MEA Tower of Hanoi model

ending problems. How does the inclusion of macro-operators affect the model's behaviour on each type of problem? ◇

Exercise 4.24: In order to thoroughly evaluate any model it is necessary to run it on a range of tasks. It is possible to use the box types provided by COGENT to simplify this process. Add two additional boxes to the model: a propositional buffer in which a range of tasks can be stored, and a process that selects one task and initialises *Current State* and *Desired State* accordingly. You should end up with a box/arrow diagram similar to that in Figure 4.8. Use a simple general representation of tasks in *Task Database*, such as:

$$\texttt{task}(1, \texttt{state}([1,3],[2],[]), \texttt{state}([2],[1],[3]))$$

to represent task 1, in which the initial state and goal state are as in Figure 4.7. Write rules for *Initialise States* to select a task from *Task Database* and add the correct elements to the two state representations. ◇

Exercise 4.25: Goel, Pullara, and Grafman (2001) report data from patients with frontal lobe damage performing several versions of the generalised five-disk problem. They argue that frontal lobe damage affects "working memory" — the ability to hold and manipulate task-relevant information in the absence of external cues. In developing their argument, Goel *et al.* (2001) compare patient behaviour with simulation results from a "lesioned" model of the Tower of Hanoi task. The model is lesioned by adding random decay to its working memory. Explore how adding random decay to the goal stack affects the generalised model's performance. Is the model still able to solve any five-disk problem? ◇

4.3.7 Project: MEA Using Goal States

The treatment of MEA above has emphasised the operator subgoaling aspects of the strategy. This is apparent in the use of a move stack, rather than a goal stack. It is also apparent in the relatively infrequent use of the rule that detects differences and selects moves to reduce such differences (i.e., Rule 1 above). However, some would argue that the strategy discussed above is not true MEA at all, and that true MEA involves using the stack to store goal states rather than moves. This true MEA strategy works as follows:

If the goal stack is empty, compare the current state and the desired state:

- If they differ, then push a representation of the desired state onto the goal stack.
- If they do not differ, then the problem has been solved. Cease processing.

If the goal stack is not empty, compare the current state with the top-most state on the goal stack:

- If they do not differ, then the current goal state has been achieved. Pop it from the top of the stack.
- If they do differ, detect the most significant difference between the two and select a move that will reduce or eliminate this difference. Determine a precondition state for the selected move. If this precondition state is the same as the current state, then perform the move. If the precondition state differs from the current state, push the precondition state onto the goal stack. It then becomes the new goal state.

The first eight cycles of processing on the five-disk problem with this strategy (using the above representation of state) would consist of the following:

Cycle 1:

current state:	`state`([1, 2, 3, 4, 5], [], [])
goal state:	`state`([], [], [1, 2, 3, 4, 5])
biggest difference:	disk 5 on left; should be on right
precondition state to eliminate difference:	`state`([5], [1, 2, 3, 4], [])
Hence:	push `state`([5], [1, 2, 3, 4], [])

Cycle 2:

current state:	`state([1, 2, 3, 4, 5], [], [])`
goal state:	`state([5], [1, 2, 3, 4], [])`
biggest difference:	disk 4 on left; should be on middle
precondition state to eliminate difference:	`state([4, 5], [], [1, 2, 3])`
Hence:	push `state([4, 5], [], [1, 2, 3])`

Cycle 3:

current state:	`state([1, 2, 3, 4, 5], [], [])`
goal state:	`state([4, 5], [], [1, 2, 3])`
biggest difference:	disk 3 on left; should be on right
precondition state to eliminate difference:	`state([3, 4, 5], [1, 2], [])`
Hence:	push `state([3, 4, 5], [1, 2], [])`

Cycle 4:

current state:	`state([1, 2, 3, 4, 5], [], [])`
goal state:	`state([3, 4, 5], [1, 2], [])`
biggest difference:	disk 2 on left; should be on middle
precondition state to eliminate difference:	`state([2, 3, 4, 5], [], [1])`
Hence:	push `state([2, 3, 4, 5], [], [1])`

Cycle 5:

current state:	`state([1, 2, 3, 4, 5], [], [])`
goal state:	`state([2, 3, 4, 5], [], [1])`
biggest difference:	disk 1 on left; should be on right
precondition state to eliminate difference:	`state([1, 2, 3, 4, 5], [], [])`
precondition state = current state. Hence:	move disk 1 from left to right

Cycle 6:

current state:	`state([2, 3, 4, 5], [], [1])`
goal state:	`state([2, 3, 4, 5], [], [1])`
biggest difference:	none: current state = goal state
Hence:	pop current goal state

Cycle 7:

current state:	`state([2, 3, 4, 5], [], [1])`
goal state:	`state([3, 4, 5], [1, 2], [])`
biggest difference:	disk 2 on left; should be on middle
precondition state to eliminate difference:	`state([2, 3, 4, 5], [], [1])`
precondition state = current state. Hence:	move disk 2 from left to middle

Cycle 8:

current state:	`state([3, 4, 5], [2], [1])`
goal state:	`state([3, 4, 5], [1, 2], [])`
biggest difference:	disk 1 on right; should be on middle
precondition state to eliminate difference:	`state([3, 4, 5], [2], [1])`
precondition state = current state. Hence:	move disk 1 from right to middle

Develop a model of the Tower of Hanoi that uses this true MEA strategy. Compare its behaviour on a range of problems, including tower-ending and flat-ending ones.

4.3.8 Project: The Tower of London

Shallice (1982) developed a modified version of the three-disk Tower of Hanoi in order to investigate the breakdown of planning processes in neurologically impaired individuals. He referred to the modified task as the Tower of London. The apparatus is illustrated in Figure 4.9. There are three pegs, like the Tower of Hanoi, but the pegs are of different length, and three coloured balls are used in place of the three disks of the Tower of Hanoi. The smallest peg can hold only a single ball, the middle peg can hold two balls, and the third peg can hold three balls. The task involves transforming an initial configuration of balls into a goal configuration, subject to the constraints that only one ball may be moved at a time, and that balls cannot be moved onto the table.

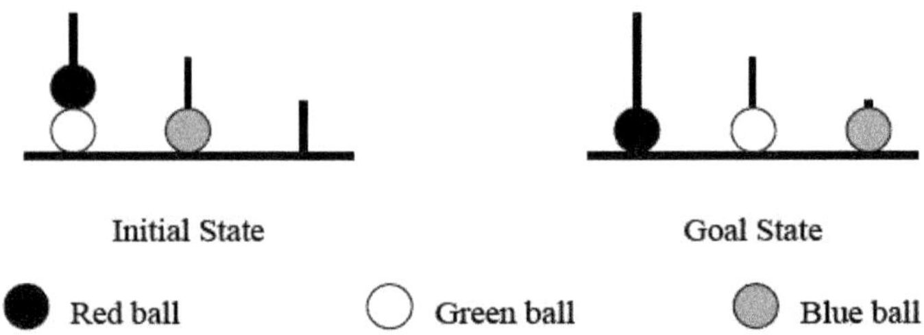

Figure 4.9: The Tower of London apparatus, showing a sample initial state and final state

Despite the similarities between the two problems, there are significant differences. The Tower of London has a larger problem space (with 36 states, as opposed to only 27 in the three-disk Tower of Hanoi). The recursive MEA approach that worked so well in the Tower of Hanoi is also not appropriate for the Tower of London. Finally, the Tower of London does not generalise (through the addition of balls) in the way that the Tower of Hanoi generalises (through the addition of disks), although Ward and Allport (1997) have developed a five-ball version of the Tower of London in which the three pegs are all of equal length.

Develop a model capable of solving any Tower of London problem (i.e., for any initial state and any desired state). What are the differences between your Tower of London model and the Tower of Hanoi models developed above? Can you develop a single model capable of solving both problems?

4.4 Toward a General Problem Solver

We have seen that problem solving can be understood in terms of traversal of a problem space — moving from an initial state to a goal state via the application of a series of operators — and that this traversal may be aided by the application of one or more heuristics such as hill-climbing or Means-Ends Analysis. However, different problems appear to require (or induce the use of) different heuristics. General intelligence, as exhibited by most human problem solvers, requires use of a range of heuristics, and selection of an appropriate heuristic from those available. There is therefore considerable scientific interest in developing integrated or general problem solving systems. Ernst and Newell (1969) were the first to create such a system. Subsequent work by Newell and colleagues led to the development of Soar (Laird *et al.*, 1987; Newell, 1990), an extremely powerful general problem solver capable of solving a wide range of problems by intelligently selecting from an array of heuristics. In this section, we consider the basic requirements of a general problem solver by reviewing the strengths and weaknesses of the models developed earlier in the chapter, and considering how they might be incorporated into a single problem solving system.

The most obvious feature shared by most of the above models is the operator proposal/evaluation/selection cycle. This was shared by all but the more complex models of the Tower of Hanoi problem. In fact, the processing of these more complex Tower of Hanoi models could be subsumed within the same operator-based processing cycle. It would therefore appear that a generalised system for problem solving should be based around rules to implement this cycle.

A general problem solver must also be goal directed. Heuristics such as MEA suggest that it must be able to set subgoals when necessary, and to detect when a goal has been achieved. This suggests that the basic operator cycle must be employed within a context specified by the current goal, and that an additional mechanism (possibly in the form of specialised operators) must be included for setting goals.

Full use of MEA also requires maintenance of a goal stack. There is no strong evidence, however, that people are able to employ a stack of unlimited depth in their problem solving, and while the recursive approach to the six-disk version of the Tower of Hanoi might require a stack of depth 5, there are other (less efficient but more psychologically plausible) approaches to such complex tasks (e.g., in which the top element of the goal stack is effectively reconstructed from scratch as and when necessary). Thus, it appears that a general problem solver must be able to represent multiple goals, and relations between these goals (e.g., one goal is a subgoal of another), but it is not clear that a general problem solver must have access to a goal stack.

Further requirements related to the application of even simple heuristics such as hill-climbing concern the representation of states. In order to apply either MEA or hill-climbing it is necessary to represent both the current state and some possible future state, and to compare those states to determine similarities and differences. State comparison is, of course, also required in order to detect when a goal state has been achieved.

Finally, a uniform representation language is required. It is necessary to represent all problems in a consistent manner, so that generic operator proposal, goal setting, and state comparison functions can be employed across tasks. Representation has not been a major theme of this chapter. We have assumed a propositional representation of all mental information, and this representation has proved to be sufficient, but other, equally suitable, symbolic representation languages exist (e.g., feature-based languages).

The above requirements address the principal issues arising in the solution of well-defined, knowledge-lean problems. The extent to which they address the issues arising from other classes of problem is unclear. Ill-defined problems certainly seem to require something more, at least in deriving a suitable problem space from the problem specification. Knowledge-rich problems, on the other hand, can be argued to involve nothing more than more knowledge. Although this was the position of Newell (1990), it is not clearly true. Knowledge-rich problems may present new difficulties in the integration of multiple knowledge sources. The third class of problem discussed at the beginning of this chapter, that of insight problems, seems qualitatively different. The intuition pursued by Gestalt psychologists was that these problems were normally solved through a flash of inspiration or a moment of insight. There appears to be little room in the problem space conceptualisation of problem solving for such insight. However, recent work by MacGregor, Ormerod, and Chronicle (2001) provides empirical support for the claim that people do employ a problem space approach even with insight problems. What makes insight problems special, on this account, is the difficulty in determining appropriate operators.

4.5 Further Reading

The classic work on human problem solving remains Newell and Simon's 1972 opus *Human Problem Solving*. This lengthy volume (with almost 1000 pages) focuses on problem solving in three specific domains (number/word puzzles, chess, and mathematical logic), and provides analyses of individual participant protocols together with a unifying theory. More manageable works worth reading include many of the papers by Simon, Newell, and colleagues. Although many of these appeared 30 to 40 years ago, they are of more than historical interest. Newell *et al.* (1958), for example, describe the Logic Theorist, one of the earliest systems capable of proving theorems of mathematical logic. The Logic Theorist was developed in order to explore the basic elements required of a theory of human problem solving, and the article ends by relating the elements employed by the Logic Theorist to the work of Selz, an early pioneer of the Gestalt school of problem solving.

Work towards theoretical unification of problem solving is well illustrated by Laird *et al.*'s (1987) presentation of Soar as a "universal weak method". Laird *et al.* show how Soar embodies a range of domain-independent problem solving methods (or heuristics), and how its knowledge of a problem determines the methods it employs.

Newell (1990) takes Soar one step further in *Unified Theories of Cognition*. Newell argues that our knowledge of cognitive processes is sufficient to allow the development of theories that span domains (e.g., problem solving, memory, and language), and that Soar is in fact such a theory. Specifically, Newell argues that all cognitive processing is problem solving, and that Soar, as a theory of problem solving, is also a general or unified theory of cognition. Newell covers far more than just problem solving, and his position is not entirely uncontroversial, but the book is well worth reading in its entirety.

Chapter 5

Deductive Reasoning

Peter Yule and Richard P. Cooper

Overview: Deductive reasoning is introduced and contrasted with other types of reasoning. Basic findings relating to human deductive reasoning are then reviewed, with special emphasis on findings from studies on syllogistic reasoning. A highly influential theory of deductive reasoning — Johnson-Laird's Mental Models theory — is then presented, and a model of the theory as it applies to syllogistic reasoning is developed. The model forces consideration of several issues that are under-specified in most verbal accounts of the theory. Following this, an alternative theory of syllogistic reasoning — one based on Euler Circles — is introduced, together with a model of the theory. The chapter concludes by comparing the strengths and weaknesses of the two theories.

5.1 Introduction

Reasoning is the process of making inferences or drawing conclusions from some information. Logicians distinguish three kinds of reasoning:

Inductive reasoning involves generalising from a set of cases to a rule that holds of those cases (e.g., generalising from a number of observations of swans, all of which happen to be white, that all swans are white). Inductive reasoning is not foolproof — it can lead to false conclusions (as in the case of white swans), even if the information on which it is based is true.

Deductive reasoning involves drawing conclusions from a set of facts or given information in a way such that, if the given information is true, the conclusion is necessarily true. Thus, given that *Aristotle is a man* and *all men are mortal* we may deduce that *Aristotle is mortal*. It is not possible for the given information to be true and the conclusion to be false.

Abductive reasoning involves reasoning from a conclusion or effect to an explanation or possible cause. If, for example, a normally mediocre athlete produces an outstanding performance, one might abduce that the athlete has started taking performance enhancing drugs. Like inductive reasoning, abductive reasoning leads to conclusions that may be invalid.

Inductive reasoning has mainly been studied by psychologists interested in learning. It is touched on in Chapters 1 and 6. Deductive reasoning, the focus of this chapter, is of interest to psychologists because most people find some deductive reasoning problems more difficult than others, and because when people err on deductive reasoning problems, they generally err in predictable ways. Abductive reasoning has received little attention from psychologists (though it is of considerable interest to AI researchers: Charniak & McDermott, 1985), and is not considered in this book.

5.2 Basic Effects in Human Deductive Reasoning

Mayer (1992) reviews psychological work on deductive reasoning in terms of three types of reasoning problem and two experimental paradigms that have been applied to each of these types of problem. The types of problems are:

Transitive reasoning: These problems involve reasoning about transitive relations (e.g., *taller than*). In a transitive inference task a participant might be told that *A is taller than B* and *C is shorter than B* and required to generate a conclusion relating *A* and *C*.

Conditional reasoning: These problems involve reasoning with statements containing conditionals. A typical task might require a participant to generate a conclusion from statements such as *If it is dark then the street lights will be on* and *The street lights are on*.

Syllogistic reasoning: These problems involve reasoning with statements relating categories, such as *All lions are savage animals* and *All lions are cats*. The participant might be required, given these statements, to infer the relation, if any, that holds between *savage animals* and *cats*.

Each of these problems involves making an inference from two premises to a conclusion. Conditional reasoning tasks involve two terms (the antecedent and consequent terms). Transitive and syllogistic reasoning tasks involve three terms, with a middle term (e.g., *B* in the above transitive reasoning case) mediating a relation between two end terms (*A* and *C* in the above case).

The two experimental paradigms differ in whether participants are given two premises and required to verify a possible conclusion, or whether they are required to generate valid conclusions from premises. Dependent variables in both paradigms may include both time to respond and accuracy.

5.2.1 Transitive Reasoning

Two primary issues have emerged from the transitive reasoning literature: whether transitive reasoning is visual or verbal (i.e., based on building a mental image of the entities and the relations between them and then "reading off" a conclusion, or based on manipulation of the premises by rules such as *if "C is shorter than B" then "B is taller than C"*), and whether transitive reasoning involves creation of an integrated representation involving all entities or whether each entity is considered only in relation to one other entity at a time.

Thus, DeSotto *et al.* (1965) argued that people form a visual image of the premises that integrates all information, subject to two principles: that people "end-anchor" the image, and that people learn one order of representation better than another. End-anchoring is the tendency to base the integrated representation on an end term, and for integration of each premise to involve extending the representation with respect to the previously integrated term (effectively building a sequence from left-to-right, or top-to-bottom, rather than integrating terms in an *ad hoc* way). Different orders of representation are illustrated by *A is better than B* and *B is worse than A*. It is argued that, in this case, people are more familiar with the *better than* ordering than the *worse than* ordering, and hence find it easier to work with the former representation than the latter.

DeSotto *et al.* (1965) motivated end-anchoring by the fact that participants found *A is better than B and C is worse than B* easier than *B is worse than A and B is better than C*. In this case, *A* is a better anchor than *B* because the problem requires finding a relation between *A* and another term (*C*) and not between *B* and another term. Order is similarly motivated: participants found *C is worse than B and B is worse than A* harder than *A is better than B and B is better than C*.

A different perspective on transitive reasoning was presented by Clark (1969), who argued that the order effect was related to lexical marking. There are often pairs of words that correspond to a single relation, where, other things being equal, one word is generally used instead of the other. One such pair is *tall* and *short*: the neutral way of asking someone's height is *How tall are you?*, and not *How short are you? Short* is said to be lexically marked, because its use indicates a non-neutral way of referring to the comparative height relation.

Clark (1969) found that transitive reasoning was more difficult with lexically marked relations than with lexically unmarked relations. He argued that transitive reasoning involved a verbal strategy in which linguistic terms were encoded as logical relations, with marked linguistic terms requiring more effort to encode. Clark explained apparent end-anchoring in terms of his principle of congruence: that participants may, if necessary, reformulate the hypothesis to make it congruent with their mental representation.

5.2.2 Conditional Reasoning

Order effects are possible within transitive reasoning tasks because the premises and the conclusions all relate two terms. Such effects are not possible in simple conditional reasoning tasks, such as the generation or verification of conclusions given one conditional statement (of the form *if P then Q*) and one further statement concerning the truth or falsity of either the antecedent or the consequent (e.g., *P is false* or *Q is true*). However, conditional reasoning tasks have shown that human reasoning is also prone to other types of error. (See Mayer, 1992, or Johnson-Laird, Byrne, & Schaeken, 1992, for a review.)

One source of error in conditional reasoning tasks appears to be in the interpretation of conditional statements: people frequently appear to interpret statements of the general form *if P then Q* as if they were of the form *if P then Q and if Q then P*. Such a mis-interpretation can account for why, when given *if P then Q* and *Q is true*, people may incorrectly deduce that *P is true*.

Mis-interpretation of conditionals is not sufficient to explain all data from conditional reasoning experiments, however. People are also faster at deducing from *if P then Q* and *P is true* that *Q is true* than at deducing from *if P then Q* and *Q is false* that *P is false*. Both deductions are valid. The first corresponds to the general reasoning schema of *modus ponens* and the second to the general schema of *modus tollens*. It is possible that people are simply more familiar with *modus ponens* than with *modus tollens*, but it has also been argued that the relative difficulty of *modus tollens* is indicative of the mental procedures used when reasoning (Johnson-Laird & Byrne, 1991). Evidence for the form of such procedures has been adduced from performance on syllogistic reasoning tasks.

5.2.3 Syllogistic Reasoning

Syllogisms (or categorical syllogisms) are inferences from two premises to a conclusion, where the premises and conclusion express well-defined set-theoretic relations between categories. For example, given the premises:

Some artists are beekeepers,
No beekeepers are chemists

we can conclude that

Some artists are not chemists

This follows because the artists who are beekeepers cannot be chemists. As with all deductive reasoning problems, the conclusion is not derived from experience with particular artists, beekeepers, and chemists, but from the meaning and arrangement of the set-theoretic relations in the premises themselves. Thus, if the premises are true, so must be the conclusion, even if we replace the artists by aardvarks, the beekeepers by bookworms, and the chemists by chiropodists.

The structure of the syllogism is quite simple. Each premise must have one of four *quantifiers* (all, no, some and some... not), relating two *terms*, one of which, the *middle term*, appears in both premises. Conclusions must also have one of the four quantifiers, and should relate the remaining two terms, the *end terms*, in the premises. The terms refer to categories, and the quantifiers express well-defined set-theoretic relations between those categories.

Syllogisms come in four varieties (known as *figures*), depending on where in the premises the middle term comes in relation to the end terms. When the middle term comes second in the first premise and first in the second premise (as in the beekeepers example above), the figure is said to be ab/bc. Here, b denotes the middle term and a and c denote the end terms. When the middle term comes first in both premises (as in the lions example earlier), the figure is said to be ba/bc. Two other figures, ba/cb and ab/cb, are possible.

The syllogism has the distinction of being the first ever system of logic. The system was invented by Aristotle (384–322 BC), who developed methods for determining the validity of every syllogism (and invented variables in order to do so). The early excitement has since faded, and the Aristotelian syllogism is no longer considered an important branch of logic, but as logicians grew bored with it after the 19th century, psychologists began to take an interest.

From a psychological point of view, syllogisms are interesting for several reasons. First, because they are expressed in something close to natural language, little training is required to tackle them. This makes them suitable for the experimental study of natural reasoning. Second, they are interesting because human performance on them exhibits several robust effects. There are wide variations in difficulty: some syllogisms are easy enough for young children to solve correctly (it is easy, given *all A are B* and *all B are C*, to conclude *all A are C*), whereas others are so difficult that few non-specialists can tackle them correctly (what, if anything, follows from *no A are B* and *all B are C*?). Furthermore, within single problems, some valid conclusions are more readily produced than others, and these systematic biases can be related to the structure of the problems. Such effects, which are quite robust, may be able to tell us something about the mechanisms underlying human reasoning.

One important psychological bias is towards producing conclusions whose end-term order is related to the figure of the premises. This bias is similar to the order biases present in transitive reasoning. For example, from the premises *some A are B* and *all B are C*, most people will correctly conclude *some A are C*. The conclusion *some C are A* is equally valid, but is rarely drawn by human reasoners in experimental situations. This bias is called the Figural Effect (Johnson-Laird & Steedman, 1978; Johnson-Laird & Bara, 1984; Stenning & Yule, 1997). In the ab/bc figure, the bias is towards ac conclusions, in the ba/cb figure, it is towards ca conclusions, and in the other figures the numbers of ac and ca conclusions are roughly equal.

5.3 Syllogistic Reasoning with Mental Models

One of the most influential theories within the domain of deductive reasoning is the "Mental Models" theory of Johnson-Laird and colleagues (e.g., Johnson-Laird, 1983; Johnson-Laird & Byrne, 1991; Johnson-Laird *et al.*, 1992). The original application of the theory was to data gathered from syllogistic reasoning tasks. This section introduces Mental Models theory within the context of syllogistic reasoning and presents an initial COGENT model of the theory.

Early theories of human syllogistic reasoning, such as the atmosphere hypothesis (Woodworth & Sells, 1935; Sells, 1936) and the theory of illicit conversion (Chapman & Chapman, 1959; Revlis, 1975), presented simple systems that could account for some overall patterns of performance reasonably well, but could not account for competence, the ability to get the conclusions right, maybe all of the time. Nowadays such restricted approaches are considered to be unsatisfactory. More recent approaches have tended to concentrate on model-theoretic approaches (e.g., Johnson-Laird, 1983; Johnson-Laird & Byrne, 1991) or on rule-based theorem provers (e.g., Braine, 1978; Rips, 1983, 1994).

Model-based theories use models such as diagrams of circles, or arrangements of symbols in an array, to model the possible interpretations of the premises so as to attempt to refute candidate conclusions, whereas rule-based theories use a theorem proving approach derived from logical natural-deduction or axiom systems, and derive conclusions by a series of syntactic operations. Both types of systems are typically sound and complete for syllogisms. That is, they only draw valid conclusions, and they can draw all of them. Thus, they can account for competence. Non-optimal performance, such as that exhibited by typical undergraduate students, is typically explained by postulating memory limitations that restrict the number of models which can be considered, or by postulating strategic biases that systematically restrict the range of conclusions that are likely to be produced.

Mental Models theory (Johnson-Laird, 1983; Johnson-Laird & Byrne, 1991; Johnson-Laird *et al.*, 1992) postulates both memory limitations and strategic biases. The theory is intended to apply more widely than merely to the simple syllogism, but its account of syllogistic reasoning has been a centre-piece of the theory for many years, and in several rather different versions. The relations and differences between these versions are beyond the scope of this chapter. Concepts will therefore be discussed in general terms, with primary reference to the most recent version of the theory (Johnson-Laird & Byrne, 1991). However, this version is not fully explicit about all details, so sometimes reference will be made to earlier versions, particularly when discussing the Figural Effect.

The Mental Models approach to syllogistic reasoning involves the construction of a model of the situation described by the syllogistic premises, allowing a conclusion to be read off. The model represents a set of individuals with various combinations of properties. To illustrate, consider the syllogism *some A are B* and *all B are C*. A model of the first premise, *some A are B*, might be represented as follows:

$$\begin{array}{cc} a & b \\ a & b \\ \multicolumn{2}{c}{\ldots} \end{array} \tag{5.1}$$

The model contains two rows, each representing an individual which is both an *A* and a *B*; the exact number of each type of individual is unimportant. The row of dots beneath indicates that other types of individuals, so far unspecified, are also possible.

The model may be extended with information from the other premise, *all B are C*:

$$\begin{array}{ccc} a & b & c \\ a & b & c \\ & \ldots & \end{array} \tag{5.2}$$

Each row containing an individual who is *B* has been extended to show that the individual is also a *C*. Several conclusions are true of this model: *all A are C*, *some A are C*, *all C are A*, and *some C are A*. However, the only valid conclusions of the syllogism are the *some* conclusions. Mental Models theory postulates two other processes: "fleshing out" and revision of the model. These processes add more possible individual types, or change the types of individuals present, to produce different models that are still consistent with the premises. Only those conclusions that are true of all possible models of the premises are valid conclusions.

An example of a "fleshed out" model of the above premises is:

$$\begin{array}{ccc} a & b & c \\ a & b & c \\ & b & c \\ a & & \\ & & c \end{array} \tag{5.3}$$

On the basis of the first premise, *some A are B*, it is possible to have *A*s that are not *B*s, and *B*s that are not *A*s. On the basis of the second premise, *all B are C*, the *B*s that are not *A*s must be *C*s, but also, *C*s that are not *B*s are possible. The only conclusions that hold in both models are *some A are C* and *some C are A*.

Johnson-Laird and Byrne (1991) are not clear about the distinction, if any, between "fleshing out" a model and revising it. However, they make use of a type of annotation of the model that indicates terms that are "exhaustively represented" in the model, with respect to some other term. What this means is that any new types of individual cannot use a different configuration of these terms from those already in the model. Thus the annotated version of the initial model above is:

$$\begin{array}{ccc} \text{a} & [\text{b} & \text{c}] \\ \text{a} & [\text{b} & \text{c}] \\ & \ldots & \end{array} \tag{5.4}$$

The square brackets indicate that *B* is exhaustively represented with respect to *C*; this constraint derives from the *all* premise, and it implies that any new *B*s that are entered into the model must also be *C*s. However, *C* is not exhaustively represented with respect to *B*, so *C*s that are not *B*s are permitted. Although Johnson-Laird and Byrne (1991) use square brackets to indicate exhaustive representation, they are not sufficient to indicate the direction of this asymmetric relation. Johnson-Laird and Byrne (1991) further cloud the waters by using the notation in inconsistent ways. In the implementation developed below, these difficulties are avoided by not trying to represent exhaustive representation graphically, but by using a different memory buffer for storing exhaustive representation information. This is consistent with one interpretation of Johnson-Laird and Byrne (1991), since they postulate that the memory decay characteristics of this information are different from the decay characteristics of the representation of individuals.

A further key theoretical assumption of Mental Models theory is that mental models are constructed in a buffer that has first-in first-out (FIFO) access characteristics. Johnson-Laird (1983) (see also Johnson-Laird & Bara, 1984) argues that the Figural Effect is a consequence of this feature of the model construction buffer. Specifically, it is argued that, when solving syllogisms with ab/bc figure, a terms are entered into the model before c terms, and so reading conclusions from the FIFO model buffer yields a strong preference for ac-type conclusions, even when corresponding ca-type conclusions are equally valid. However, when solving syllogisms with ba/cb figure, it is supposed that construction begins with the second premise, so c terms are entered into the model before a terms, and so reading conclusions from the FIFO model buffer yields a strong preference for ca-type conclusions, even when corresponding ac-type conclusions are equally valid. In these cases, only one premise has an end term in subject position, so their representations are constructed in a deterministic, end-anchored way. For the other two figures, either both premises have an end term in subject position (ab/cb), or neither do (ba/bc), so construction can begin with either premise, and the other must be reversed (as described below) before being integrated into the model.

Johnson-Laird and Byrne (1991) augment earlier versions of Mental Models theory by introducing a "principle of truth". This principle stipulates that, at least in initial representations, individuals are not explicitly marked as lacking a property. In other words, only positive properties are explicitly represented. Explicit marking of negatives may only be introduced while fleshing out the model. In the implementation below, negative marking is avoided altogether, as it is not required to get a working model up and running, but the model that is produced should not be interpreted as a faithful implementation of all aspects of the Mental Models theory. The reader is encouraged to treat it as a starting point for exploration of a range of possible model theories.

5.4 Building a Mental Model

From the preceding discussion it should be clear that the Mental Models theory of syllogistic reasoning involves a number of distinct processes (including building an initial model of the premises, drawing conclusions from a model, and revising a model) and buffers (including separate buffers for the model and any annotations). Figure 5.1 shows a COGENT box and arrow diagram for a preliminary arrangement of possible components. Within this implementation, input of premises and output of conclusions are both via *Problem Buffer*, which is an ordinary propositional buffer. It is both read and written by *Scheduler*, which sequences the various subtasks of the problem solution process: building models of each of the premises in turn, and then initiating the conclusion drawing process. *Scheduler* makes no direct use of the *Mental Model*. Instead, there is a process to build and integrate models of premises (*Build Initial Model*), and another to draw conclusions (*Draw Conclusions*). In Section 5.5 a third process, *Revise Model*, will be added. This process will make use of the information stored in *Annotations* to revise the initial model of the premises in a search for counterexamples to candidate conclusions.

Exercise 5.1: Create a new research programme for this chapter, and a new model within that research programme. Create *Subject* and *Experimenter* compound boxes within the new model, and link them so *Experimenter* may read and send to *Subject*. Populate *Subject* with boxes and arrows as in Figure 5.1, and populate *Experimenter* with a single data source that sends to *Problem Buffer* within *Subject*. ◇

5.4.1 The Scheduler

Scheduler handles sequential aspects of the model construction and manipulation process. Its main task is to identify the middle and end terms of the premises, to trigger construction of an appropriate initial mental model (based on one end term), and then to add each premise in turn to the mental model representation via

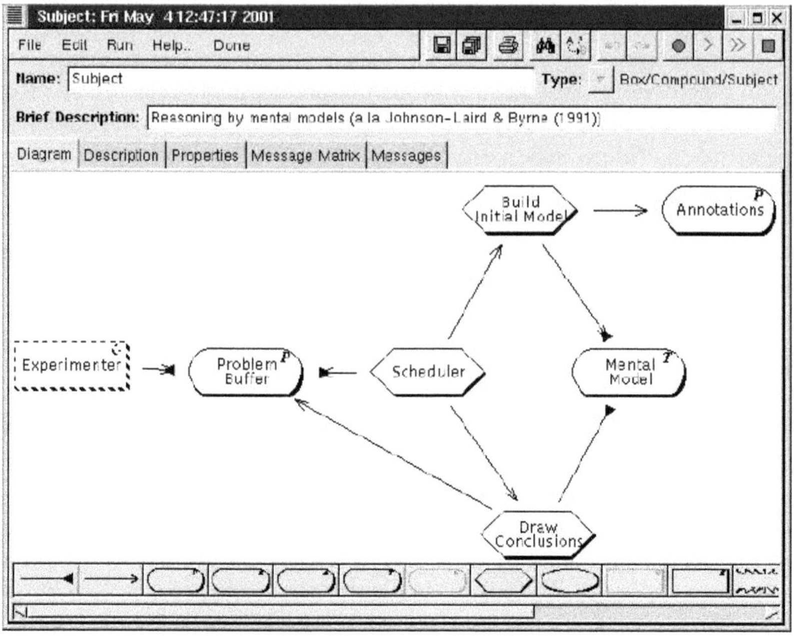

Figure 5.1: A box and arrow diagram of a subject box for Mental Models

Build Initial Model. Once the model has been constructed, *Scheduler* initiates the drawing of conclusions by sending an appropriate message to *Draw Conclusions*.

Box 5.1 shows the rules and partial condition definitions from *Scheduler*. The rules assume that a pair of premises appears in *Problem Buffer* at the beginning of each trial. Rule 1 imposes an order on the two premises, determines the initial term which should be entered in the model, triggers construction of an initial model based on that term, and records that the model has been initialised. The initial term which should be entered in the model depends on the figure of the syllogism being attempted. For the ab/bc figure, the initial term corresponds to a. For the ba/cb figure, it corresponds to c. For the remaining ab/cb and ba/bc figures, the initial term depends on which premise is integrated first, as described in the following paragraph.

One subtlety in Rule 1 is that for non-diagonal figures (ab/cb and ba/bc) the mapping of the premises to the premise variables (`Premise1` and `Premise2`) is under-specified. That is, the premise which, according to *Experimenter*, is the first premise need not be considered by *Scheduler* as the first premise. For non-diagonal figures, either premise may map to either variable. (This is why the rule is marked to fire at most once.) This indeterminacy in premise selection is critical because Mental Models theory dictates that, with such figures, the initial mental

Rule 1 (refracted; once): *Initialise the model*
IF: not `initialised(_,_)` is in *Problem Buffer*
`premise(Premise1)` is in *Problem Buffer*
`premise(Premise2)` is in *Problem Buffer*
`Premise1` is distinct from `Premise2`
`extract_term(Premise1, Premise2, initial, X)`
THEN: send `initialise(X)` to *Build Initial Model*
add `initialised(Premise1, Premise2)` to *Problem Buffer*

Rule 2 (refracted): *Integrate the next premise*
IF: `initialised(Premise1, Premise2)` is in *Problem Buffer*
`extract_integration_order(Premise1, Premise2, Order)`
`premise_to_integrate(Order, Premise)`
`extract_direction(Premise1, Premise2, Premise, Direction)`
THEN: send `premise(Premise, Direction)` to *Build Initial Model*
add `integrated(Premise)` to *Problem Buffer*

Rule 3 (refracted): *Trigger conclusion drawing*
IF: `initialised(Premise1, Premise2)` is in *Problem Buffer*
`integrated(Premise1)` is in *Problem Buffer*
`integrated(Premise2)` is in *Problem Buffer*
`extract_term(Premise1, Premise2, middle, Middle)`
THEN: send `initial_concs(Middle)` to *Draw Conclusions*

Condition Definition: `extract_term/4`:
`extract_term([Q1, A, B], [Q2, B, C], initial, A).`
...

Condition Definition: `extract_integration_order/3`:
`extract_integration_order([Q1, A, B], [Q2, B, C], [[Q1, A, B], [Q2, B, C]]).`
...

Condition Definition: `extract_direction/4`:
`extract_direction([Q1, A, B], [Q2, B, C], [Q1, A, B], forward).`
...

Condition Definition: `premise_to_integrate/2`: *Select next premise*
`premise_to_integrate([P1, P2], P1) :-`
`initialised(_,_)` is in *Problem Buffer*
not `integrated(P1)` is in *Problem Buffer*
`premise_to_integrate([P1, P2], P2) :-`
`integrated(P1)` is in *Problem Buffer*
not `integrated(P2)` is in *Problem Buffer*

Box 5.1: Rules and partial condition definitions from *Scheduler* model may be based on either premise. Since the mental model buffer is hypothesised to have FIFO access, the premise that is integrated first determines whether ac-type conclusions or ca-type conclusions are favoured. If an ab-type premise is integrated before a cb-type premise, ac-type conclusions will be preferred, but if the reverse integration order is selected ca-type conclusions will be preferred. The indeterminacy of integration order for non-diagonal figures means that, on average, there will be no bias to ac-type or ca-type conclusions, and this is consistent with empirical work (see Johnson-Laird, 1983).

Rule 2 of Box 5.1 selects a premise and triggers integration of that premise into the mental model. Several factors must be taken into account by the rule. First, the order of integration depends on the figure. For ab/bc, ab/cb, and ba/bc figures, the first premise should be integrated before the second premise. For the remaining ba/cb figure, the integration order is opposite: the second premise must be integrated before the first premise. `extract_integration_order/3` and `premise_to_integrate/2` combine to give the desired effect. The former returns a list consisting of the premises in the appropriate order, and the latter selects one premise from that list. The premise selected depends upon the stage of processing. If the mental model has not been initialised, or if both premises have been integrated, the condition will fail. If the mental model has been initialised but the first premise has not been integrated, the condition will return the first premise. If the first, but not the second, premise has been integrated, the condition will return the second premise.

A further complication in Rule 2 concerns the direction of integration. Basically, each premise must be integrated into the mental model so as to extend the existing model. Since each premise relates two terms, a subject term and a predicate term, there are two cases to consider: when the subject term is contained in the prior model or when the predicate term is contained in the prior model. The two cases must be treated differently by the model integration rules. `extract_direction/4` provides a case-by-case statement of the direction of integration (`forward` or `reversed`) for each premise in each figure.

Rule 3 of Box 5.1 fires when both premises have been integrated. It sends a trigger containing the middle term to *Draw Conclusions*. *Draw Conclusions* needs to be able to distinguish the middle term from the end terms, because it must only draw conclusions that relate the end terms. One way of enabling this is to provide *Draw Conclusions* with the identity of the middle term.

Exercise 5.2: Populate *Scheduler* with the rules and condition definitions given in Box 5.1. Complete the definitions of the partially defined conditions:

- The definition of `extract_term/4` should consist of eight cases, corresponding to `initial` and `middle` terms for each figure. The `middle` term should always be `B`. The `initial` term should normally be `A`, except in the ba/cb figure, when it should be `C`.

- The definition of `extract_integration_order/3` should consist of four cases, corresponding to the four figures. The integration order should follow the order of the premises, except in the ba/cb figure, when the second premise should be integrated before the first.
- The definition of `extract_direction/4` should consist of eight cases, corresponding to the first and second premises for each of the four figures. For most cases the integration direction should be `forward`, except in the cases of the second premise of ab/cb figure and the first premise of the bc/ba figure, when it should be `reversed`.

Test the arrangement by adding a suitable pair of premises to the data source within *Experimenter*, such that on the first processing cycle those premises are added to *Problem Buffer* within *Subject*. Ensure that *Scheduler* then sends appropriate messages to *Build Initial Model* and *Draw Conclusions* in turn. Repeat the testing with a range of premise pairs covering all figures. ◇

5.4.2 Build Initial Model

The *Build Initial Model* process contains rules that integrate individual premise representations into a mental model. The mental model itself is held in *Mental Model*, a tabular buffer with a FIFO access setting. A tabular buffer is used to provide an array-like representation analogous to the standard graphical representation of a mental model, with each row of the table representing a separate individual. The FIFO access setting is motivated by the Figural Effect, as discussed above.

Build Initial Model contains nine rules: one to build an initial model based on the first term and two rules for each of the four quantifier types, allowing integration of any premise in forward and reversed directions. Box 5.2 shows a selection of these rules. Rule 1 is the model initialisation rule. It enters individuals of the category given by `Term` into two rows of the mental model. (Both individuals are entered in the same column, because they are of the same category, and the category name is used as the label for the column.) The rule uses a built-in condition, "`X` is a new symbol with base `Y`", to generate new symbols for the names of new rows. The first time it is called with base `'I'`, it will generate the symbol `'I1'`. The second time it is called with base `'I'`, it will generate the symbol `'I2'`, and so on. The condition is available under the **miscellaneous** sub-menu when creating and editing rules and condition definitions.

Rules 2 and 3 in Box 5.2 are premise integration rules for *all* premises, for forward and reversed directions respectively. The rules work by creating new entries in the mental model that positively link every individual of a given category with the second category. Thus, Rule 2 states, for the forward integration of a premise of the form *all* `X` *are* `Y`, that each row in the model that contains an `X` should be extended with a `Y` (which is entered in a new column). The rule applies

Rule 1 (unrefracted): *Initialise the model buffer with selected terms*
TRIGGER: `initialise(Term)`
IF: `Ind1` is a new symbol with base `'I'`
`Ind2` is a new symbol with base `'I'`
THEN: add `data(Ind1, Term, Term)` to *Mental Model*
add `data(Ind2, Term, Term)` to *Mental Model*

Rule 2 (unrefracted): *Positive links for "all" forward*
TRIGGER: `premise([all, X, Y], forward)`
IF: `data(Ind, X, X)` is in *Mental Model*
THEN: add `data(Ind, Y, Y)` to *Mental Model*
add `exhaust(X, Y)` to *Annotations*

Rule 3 (unrefracted): *Positive links for "all" reversed*
TRIGGER: `premise([all, X, Y], reversed)`
IF: `data(Ind, Y, Y)` is in *Mental Model*
THEN: add `data(Ind, X, X)` to *Mental Model*
add `exhaust(X, Y)` to *Annotations*

⋮

Rule 6 (unrefracted): *New individuals for "no" forward*
TRIGGER: `premise([no, X, Y], forward)`
IF: `data(_, X, X)` is in *Mental Model*
`NewInd` is a new symbol with base `'I'`
THEN: add `data(NewInd, Y, Y)` to *Mental Model*
add `exhaust(X, Y)` to *Annotations*
add `exhaust(Y, X)` to *Annotations*

Rule 7 (unrefracted): *New individuals for "no" reversed*
TRIGGER: `premise([no, X, Y], reversed)`
IF: `data(_, _, Y)` is in *Mental Model*
`NewInd` is a new symbol with base `'I'`
THEN: add `data(NewInd, X, X)` to *Mental Model*
add `exhaust(X, Y)` to *Annotations*
add `exhaust(Y, X)` to *Annotations*

⋮

Box 5.2: Selected rules from *Build Initial Model*

to all instances of `X`, and hence, once it has been applied, `X` will be exhaustively represented with respect to `Y`.

Exercise 5.3: Enter Rules 2 and 3 into *Build Initial Model* and test the system on the four syllogisms with *all* in both premises (one for each of the four figures). While testing the system, examine the contents of *Mental Model* and *Annotations*. The system should build an integrated representation of the premise pair, and depending on the premises, `exhaust/2` items may accumulate in *Annotations*. Ensure that the Sort property of *Mental Model* is set to Primacy. This will ensure that the left-right and top-bottom order of the display reflects the order in which rows and columns are added to the model. At this stage, each syllogism should yield a model containing two individuals (i.e., two rows), each of which is a, b, and c. ◇

Exercise 5.4: Rules 4 and 5, for *some*, are similar to those for *all*, except they do not exhaustively represent any categories, and so should not record any annotation. Specify them yourself and test the mental model generation properties of the system on syllogisms that include both *some* and *all* premises. ◇

The rules for integrating negative premises (*no* and *some not*) do not extend existing rows of a model. Instead they create new rows (corresponding to new individuals) with positive instances of the new term. Thus, a premise such as *no A are B* would result in a model containing as being extended with representations of new individuals that were b but not a. Rules 6 and 7 in Box 5.2 allow integration of *no* premises in forward and reversed directions. Note that the order of conditions within the rules is critical. The first condition will succeed once for each entry of the given type already in the model (and so will normally succeed twice). Each time, the second condition will be called to generate a new row label. Hence, and in Rule 6, if `X` occurs twice in the mental model, two individuals of category `Y` will be added. If the rule's conditions had been specified in the reverse order, one row label would be created and two entries inserted in this row. Note also that *no* premises lead to exhaustive representations of `X` with respect to `Y` and `Y` with respect to `X`.

Exercise 5.5: Enter Rules 6 and 7 into *Build Initial Model* and test the system on syllogisms with *no* premises. Ensure that *Mental Model* is extended appropriately with new rows. ◇

Exercise 5.6: The rules for *some... not*, again, create the same new individuals as do those for *no*, but paralleling the difference between *some* and *all*, the two negative premise types are annotated differently. Specifically, *some* `X` *are not* `Y`, when integrated in either direction, results in `Y` being exhaustively represented with respect to `X` (i.e., in `exhaust(Y,X)` being added to `Annotations`). Specify the rules for *some... not* and test the complete premise integration rules on a range of syllogisms. ◇

Models created by the premise integration rules are not comprehensive representations of the semantics or true meaning of the premises; for positive premises, all the rows (corresponding to individuals) are positively linked, even though the existence of unlinked cases would be consistent with the premises' semantics. That is, for a premise such as *all A are B*, the rules create representations only of individuals that are both *A* and *B*, even though the existence of other individuals that are *B* but not *A* is consistent with the premise. Other possible models will be created later, by the model revision process and using the `exhaust/2` terms stored in the *Annotations* buffer. These annotations constrain the ways in which the model revision process may "flesh out" initial representations.

Readers familiar with Johnson-Laird and Byrne (1991) may have noticed that the representation for *some... not* differs from that given there, in that optional positively linked individuals are not represented in the initial model. This is to avoid certain technical difficulties with such individuals in models of *some... not* premises. The model revision procedure presented below side-steps these difficulties.

5.4.3 Draw Conclusions

Having created an initial mental model of a pair of premises, the next stage is to generate conclusions from the model. This is the task of the *Draw Conclusions* process, which is triggered by *Scheduler* after integration of both premises. The triggering message takes the form `initial_concs(B)`, where `B` is bound to the middle term.

Box 5.3 shows rules and condition definitions for *Draw Conclusions*. When Rule 1 is triggered it generates and tests possible conclusions. If a conclusion is found to hold of the current mental model, it is added to *Problem Buffer* and the rule is triggered again. Only when all conclusions have been tested will the conclusion drawing process terminate.

It is important that the rule is marked to fire once per cycle and that generation of possible conclusions is sensitive to the order of terms in *Mental Model*. This ensures that conclusions are generated in sequence and in an order consistent with the Figural Effect (i.e., so figural conclusions are drawn before counter-figural ones). This order is achieved by a combination of the order of conditions within the definition of `generate_conclusion` and the FIFO access properties of *Mental Model*.

Conclusions are tested by `truth_condition/1`, which is a multi-clause user-defined condition that succeeds if and only if the given conclusion is true in the model. Thus, *all* `S` *are* `P` holds if and only if there are no individuals that are `S` and not `P`, whereas *no* `S` *are* `P` holds if and only if there are no individuals that are both `S` and `P`. Note that according to the traditional interpretation of sentences in the syllogism, the condition should also check that instances of the subject term

Rule 1 (refracted; once): *Generate conclusions (in FIFO order)*

```
TRIGGER: initial_concs(B)
IF:      generate_conclusion(B, Conc)
         truth_condition(Conc)
THEN:    add conclusion(Conc) to Problem Buffer
         send initial_concs(B) to Draw Conclusions
```

Condition Definition: generate_conclusion/2: *Find a possible conclusion*

```
generate_conclusion(Mid, [Quant, Subj, Pred]) :-
    get_end_term(Mid, Subj)
    get_end_term(Mid, Pred)
    Subj is distinct from Pred
    Quant is a member of [all, no, some, somenot]
```

Condition Definition: get_end_term/2: *Get any end term*

```
get_end_term(Mid, T) :-
    data(_, _, T) is in Mental Model
    T is distinct from Mid
```

Condition Definition: truth_condition/1: *Truth conditions for sentences*

```
truth_condition([all, S, P]) :-
    not data(Ind, _, S) is in Mental Model
        not data(Ind, _, P) is in Mental Model
truth_condition([no, S, P]) :-
    not data(Ind, _, S) is in Mental Model
        data(Ind, _, P) is in Mental Model
truth_condition([some, S, P]) :-
    exists data(Ind, _, S) is in Mental Model
        data(Ind, _, P) is in Mental Model
truth_condition([somenot, S, P]) :-
    exists data(Ind, _, S) is in Mental Model
        not data(Ind, _, P) is in Mental Model
```

Box 5.3: Rules and condition definitions from *Draw Conclusions*

(S) exist, whereas here we simply check for the absence of individuals that violate the generalisation. In practice, this makes no difference to the set of conclusions drawn by the system, since the models have all been constructed with instances of all three terms anyway.

Exercise 5.7: Add the rules and condition definitions to *Draw Conclusions* and examine the behaviour of the system. When given a pair of premises, it should now construct an initial model and draw all conclusions that hold of that model.

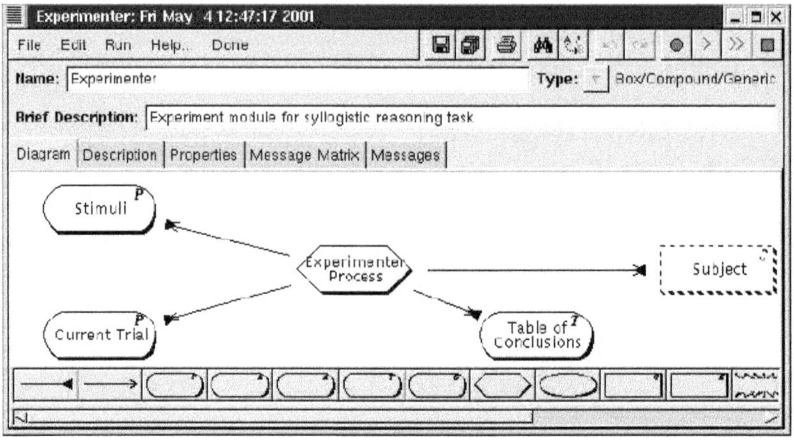

Figure 5.2: A box and arrow diagram of the Mental Models *Experimenter* box

The conclusions should appear in sequence in *Problem Buffer*. ◇

5.4.4 Adding an Experimenter Module

The syllogistic reasoning model developed thus far is incomplete with respect to Mental Models theory in that it does not include a model revision process. It therefore does not attempt to refute putative conclusions. However, the model is capable of generating conclusions for all syllogisms. While it is possible to test the model on all syllogisms by setting appropriate premise pairs within the *Experimenter*'s data source (as outlined in Exercise 5.2), such an approach is tedious. A more effective solution to testing the model is to develop appropriate model evaluation infrastructure (within *Experimenter*).

Figure 5.2 shows the box and arrow representation of a simple *Experimenter* module. The module comprises four boxes:

- *Experimenter Process*, a process that enters premise pairs into *Subject*'s *Problem Buffer* at the beginning of each trial and reads conclusions from *Subject*'s *Problem Buffer* at the end of each trial, recording them in a suitable format;
- *Stimuli*, a propositional buffer with random access that is initialised at the beginning of each block with all 64 premise pairs;
- *Current Trial*, a propositional buffer, initialised at the beginning of each trial, in which the premise pairs for the current trial are stored; and
- *Table of Conclusions*, a tabular buffer that is initialised at the beginning of each experiment and that is used to construct a table of conclusions drawn for each premise pair.

Rule 1 (unrefracted; once): *Pick premises at the start of a trial*
IF: not `Premises` is in *Current Trial*
`problem(Prem1, Prem2)` is in *Stimuli*
`filter_premises(Prem1, Prem2)`
THEN: add `premise(1, Prem1)` to *Subject:Problem Buffer*
add `premise(2, Prem2)` to *Subject:Problem Buffer*
delete `problem(Prem1, Prem2)` from *Stimuli*
add `[Prem1, Prem2]` to *Current Trial*

Condition Definition: `filter_premises/2`: *Select premise pairs to test*
```
filter_premises(_, [all, _, _]).
filter_premises([all, _, _], _).
```

Box 5.4: Selected rules and condition definitions from *Experimenter Process*

Box 5.4 shows partial possible contents of *Experimenter Process*. Rule 1 fires only if *Current Trial* is empty and there is a pair of premises in *Stimuli* that satisfy `filter_premises/2`. `filter_premises/2` is not strictly necessary, but it is a convenient way of controlling the form of syllogism tested in any run of the model. The definition given in the box ensures that only syllogisms that involve an *all* premise (either as the first premise, the second premise, or both) will pass the filter. When Rule 1 fires, it copies the premise pair to *Subject*'s *Problem Buffer* and to the *Current Trial* buffer (thus ensuring that the rule doesn't fire again until *Current Trial* is cleared), and deletes the premise pair from *Stimuli* (thus ensuring that the premise pair will not be selected again until *Stimuli* is reinitialised). The once marking on the rule ensures that, when the rule fires, only one premise pair is selected.

Rule 1 of Box 5.4 assumes that premise pairs are represented in *Stimuli* in the form of `problem/2` terms, as in Box 5.5. If *Stimuli* is to to be initialised at the beginning of each block of trials, then on each trial within a block, Rule 1 of *Experimenter Process* will remove one premise pair from *Stimuli* and present it to *Subject*. After 64 trials, *Stimuli* will be empty. It will then be reinitialised with all 64 premise pairs at the beginning of the next block. *Stimuli* should also have random access, so that premise pairs are selected from it in a random order.

Exercise 5.8: Add Rule 1 from Box 5.4 to *Experimenter Process* and specify a generic filter condition (i.e., ensure `filter_premises/2` succeeds for all premise pairs). Also add all premise pairs to *Stimuli* (by analogy with Box 5.5). Be sure that there are 64 problems in all, with all combinations of four first premise quantifiers × four second premise quantifiers × four figures. Adjust the number of repetitions of the Trial script to 64, so that a single run of the model will complete

Element: *Premise pair*
`problem([all, a, b], [all, b, c])`
Element: *Premise pair*
`problem([all, a, b], [some, b, c])`
Element: *Premise pair*
`problem([all, a, b], [no, b, c])`
Element: *Premise pair*
`problem([all, a, b], [somenot, b, c])`
Element: *Premise pair*
`problem([some, a, b], [all, b, c])`
⋮

Box 5.5: Selected buffer elements from *Stimuli*

64 trials. Initialise the model and run it over all 64 premise pairs. ◇

Experimenter should also record conclusions drawn from each premise pair. For this, *Experimenter Process* requires one further rule. Rule 2 of Box 5.6 is triggered at the end of each trial by the `system_end(trial)` trigger, which is automatically generated by COGENT at the end of each trial. The rule maintains a table whose rows correspond to the various syllogistic problems and whose columns correspond to possible conclusions. Entries in the table cells are counts of how frequently each conclusion has been drawn for each problem. The rule matches a conclusion in *Subject*'s *Problem Buffer* and updates the corresponding counter.

Exercise 5.9: Extend *Experimenter Process* so that it counts conclusions for all problems. Run the system over the entire set of problems, while monitoring *Table of Conclusions*. The system should never fail to draw conclusions on the basis of the initial model. In fact, for all premise pairs, four initial conclusions should always be drawn. ◇

The system as developed thus far will draw four conclusions for all premise pairs because, on the basis of the initial model, it is unable to discriminate between *all* and *some* premises, or between *no* and *some... not* premises: their initial representations are the same. To make the system discriminate, and to make it produce all and only the valid conclusions, it will be necessary to add a model revision process. This is considered in Section 5.5.

Exercise 5.10: Rule 2 of *Experimenter Process* will only record data if the subject model draws one or more conclusions. However, researchers usually accept

Rule 2 (unrefracted): *Update table of conclusions*
TRIGGER: `system_end(trial)`
IF: `conclusion(Conc)` is in *Subject:Problem Buffer*
`Problem` is in *Current Trial*
`count_concs(Problem, Conc, N)`
`N1` is `N + 1`
THEN: add `data(Problem, Conc, N1)` to *Table of Conclusions*

Condition Definition: `count_concs/3`: *Return table entry, or zero*
`count_concs(Problem, Conc, 0) : -`
not `data(Problem, Conc, _)` is in *Table of Conclusions*
`count_concs(Problem, Conc, N) : -`
`data(Problem, Conc, N)` is in *Table of Conclusions*

Box 5.6: Additional items from *Experimenter Process*

another response: "No Valid Conclusion". In the present model, this can be signalled by the absence of conclusions in *Problem Buffer* at the end of the trial. Write a further rule to record such situations. Since this rule makes the table much larger, it might be helpful to switch it on and off as required, by using the **Ignore/Reinstate** mechanism available from the menu that appears when the user right-clicks on an item within a **Rules & Condition Definitions** view. ◇

Exercise 5.11: Many syllogistic reasoning experiments require participants to draw at most one conclusion for each problem. *Experimenter Process* may be adjusted to count just one conclusion by marking Rule 2 of Box 5.6 such that it fires at most once on any processing cycle. Modify Rule 2 to record just one conclusion and re-run the system on all problems. ◇

Exercise 5.12: One difficulty with the subject model as it stands is that the first conclusion recorded by *Experimenter* is not necessarily the first one produced by *Subject*. This is because *Subject* accumulates the conclusions in *Problem Buffer*, which is configured with random access (the default) in order to randomise model construction order in the non-diagonal figures. In order for *Experimenter* to record conclusions in the order they are generated by *Subject*, it is necessary for the buffer that receives conclusions to be configured with **FIFO** access. There are two possible approaches to handling this: a separate buffer could be used for recording conclusions, or *Problem Buffer* could be configured as having **FIFO** access and an alternative way of randomising construction order for non-diagonal figures used (e.g., by defining a condition in *Scheduler* to randomise premise order). Try to implement either of these alternatives. ◇

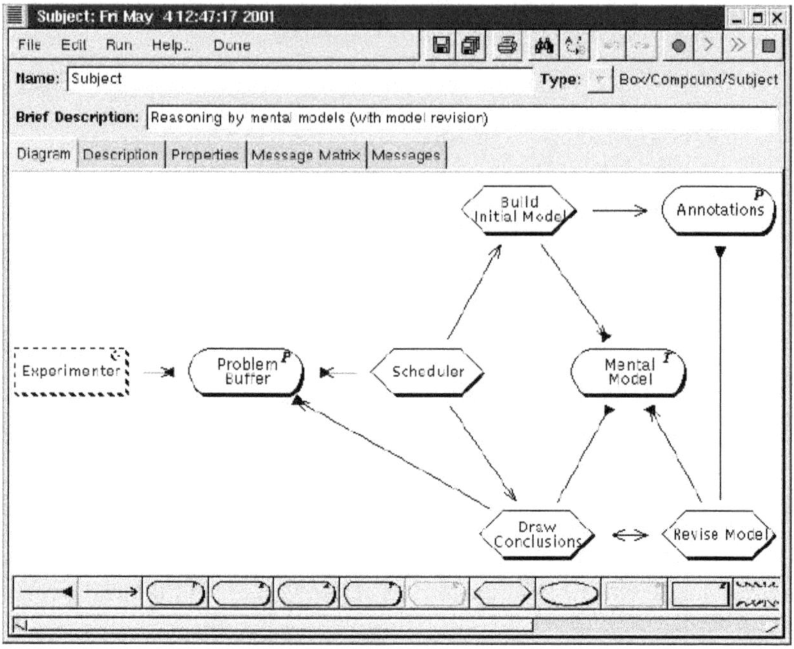

Figure 5.3: The Mental Models *Subject*, extended for model revision

5.5 Revising a Mental Model

If the system is to draw all and only the valid conclusions, it must be able to revise initial models, and to retest its initial conclusions and delete them from *Problem Buffer* if appropriate. This requires a further process (*Revise Model*) that is triggered after the initial conclusions have been drawn. The process requires read and write access to *Mental Model* (so it can examine and modify the model) and read access to *Annotations* (so that model revisions are consistent with any annotations). When the process has revised the model, it must be able to trigger testing of existing conclusions. Figure 5.3 shows a suitably augmented box and arrow diagram (compare Figure 5.1). The figure assumes that conclusion testing is performed by *Draw Conclusions*, and *Draw Conclusions* has accordingly been given read access to *Problem Buffer*.

5.5.1 Control of Model Revision

Model revision should be initiated after all conclusions have been drawn from a model. It is therefore natural that model revision should be triggered by *Draw Conclusions*. Box 5.7 shows additional rules for this process. Rule 2 is a com-

Rule 2 (refracted; once): *If no more conclusions, trigger model revision*
TRIGGER: `initial_concs(B)`
IF: exists `conclusion(Any)` is in *Problem Buffer*
not `generate_conclusion(B, Conc)`
`truth_condition(Conc)`
not `conclusion(Conc)` is in *Problem Buffer*
THEN: send `revise(B)` to *Revise Model*

Rule 3 (unrefracted): *Retract falsified conclusions*
TRIGGER: `revised(B)`
IF: `conclusion(Conc)` is in *Problem Buffer*
not `truth_condition(Conc)`
THEN: delete `conclusion(Conc)` from *Problem Buffer*

Rule 4 (unrefracted): *If conclusions remain, try further model revision*
TRIGGER: `revised(B)`
IF: exists `conclusion(Conc)` is in *Problem Buffer*
`truth_condition(Conc)`
THEN: send `revise(B)` to *Revise Model*

Box 5.7: Additional control rules for *Draw Conclusions*

panion rule to the previous conclusion drawing rule (Box 5.3). Like that rule, it is triggered when the process receives an `initial_concs`/1 message, and like that rule it fires at most once in response to that message. However, unlike the previous rule, this rule fires only when no further conclusions can be drawn, and hence, when model revision should be initiated. The rule's single action is to send a model revision triggering message to *Revise Model*. (The rule also requires that some conclusions exist. If no conclusions exist then model revision is unnecessary, and the rule will not fire.)

It is assumed that *Revise Model* responds to the `revise`/1 trigger issued by Rule 2 and, if it is successful in revising the model, replies to *Draw Conclusions* with a `revised`/1 trigger. The argument of each trigger is the middle term, which is used by both processes.

Rules 3 and 4 of Box 5.7 respond to any `revised`/1 triggers received by *Draw Conclusions*. Rule 3 uses `truth_condition`/1 (as previously defined) to test if each existing conclusion holds in the revised model. Those that do not are retracted. Rule 4 triggers another attempt at model revision if one or more unfalsified conclusions remain. Processing within the system therefore passes between *Draw Conclusions* and *Revise Model*, terminating when either no conclusions remain or no further model revisions are possible.

The logical soundness of this procedure depends upon keeping a complete record of unrefuted conclusions in *Problem Buffer*. After being generated on the basis of the initial model, conclusions are then eliminated. New conclusions are not generated for revised models, so any conclusion in *Problem Buffer* must have been tested against all model variants that have been considered so far. If the generation of "new" conclusions from revised models were to be allowed, more comprehensive records, detailing which conclusions have already been refuted, would be required to ensure soundness.

5.5.2 The Revise Model Process

The model revision process comprises several mutually exclusive model revision rules. Each rule has the same general form: it responds to a trigger of the form `revise(B)`, it makes some modification to *Mental Model*, and it then sends the trigger `revised(B)` to *Draw Conclusions*. The model revision rules must be capable of generating models that falsify all invalid conclusions for each possible syllogism, without producing models that violate the semantics of the premises. The rules are mutually exclusive because each rule encapsulates a different way in which an existing model may be modified. Each time the process is triggered, the existing model should be modified in one and only one way, with different modifications attempted each time the process is triggered.

Johnson-Laird and Byrne (1991) do not give a detailed description of putative model revision processes, so the processes described below are based on the functional requirement of model revision (i.e., that revised models refute invalid conclusions). Johnson-Laird and Byrne (1991) also assume an additional process of "fleshing out" models, which they distinguished from model revision. The distinction between these processes is subtle, and not considered in the first approximation to the Mental Models theory presented here.

The full model revision process contains many subtleties and complexities. The discussion therefore begins with a simpler problem: that of generating revised models for pairs of positive premises (i.e., those containing the quantifiers *all* and *some*). Model revision is then extended to deal with negative premises.

Revision Rules for Positive Syllogisms

Consider the syllogism *all A are B* and *all C are B*: the initial model consists of two rows (each representing an individual), each of which has positive instances of all three terms, like this:

$$\begin{array}{ccc} a & b & c \\ a & b & c \end{array} \tag{5.5}$$

This arrangement in the initial model is due to the overall bias exhibited in model construction, to create fully positive rows if possible. The model supports *all* and *some* conclusions with both possible end-term orders (i.e., *all A are C*, *some A are*

C, all C are A, and *some C are A*). However, a moment's reflection reveals that the premises could be true even if none of the as that are bs are cs, and hence if none of the cs are as, as below:

	b	c
	b	c
a	b	
a	b	

(5.6)

Furthermore, the same initial model will be generated for any combination of positive premises, so it isn't possible just to create a rule that transforms the first model above into the second, since the second would violate the semantics of many such premise pairs. Thus, model revision must be performed with due consideration for the meaning of the premises.

One possible approach would be to give *Revise Model* read-access to *Problem Buffer*, for it to reread the premises whenever required, and for it to use them somehow to constrain model revision. However, the relevant information about the premises has already been stored in *Annotations* (by the initial model construction rules). This information may be used to constrain model revision within appropriate semantic limits.

All information in *Annotations* is represented by `exhaust/2` terms. A term of the form `exhaust(Term1,Term2)` represents the fact that "`Term1` is exhaustively represented with respect to `Term2`". It means that all permissible combinations of `Term1` with `Term2` are already represented in the model, so new combinations cannot be introduced. These relations are represented only for the pairs of terms in premises, so one of the arguments will always be the middle term, and they never relate both end terms.

Reconsider the problem described above. In the initial model, a is exhaustively represented with respect to b, and c is exhaustively represented with respect to b, but b is not exhaustively represented with respect to either of the end terms. So, given the initial model, new individuals that are only a cannot legitimately be added to the model. Similarly an a term cannot legitimately be moved from one individual into a new row. Both operations would violate the concept of exhaustive representation (and the semantics of *all A are B*). However, a new individual that is both a and b (but not c) can legitimately be added to the model, and an a can legitimately be deleted from one of the original rows to leave b and c, resulting in the following model:

	b	c
a	b	c
a	b	

(5.7)

Repeating this operation on Model 5.7 will yield Model 5.6.

Rule 1 of Box 5.8 implements the above operation. It identifies a row in the model that is suitable for transformation, and applies the transformation, one row

Rule 1 (refracted; once): *Move exhaustively represented pair of terms*
TRIGGER: `revise(B)`
IF: `positive_exhaust_move(B, T, OldInd)`
`NewInd` is a new symbol with base `'I'`
THEN: delete `data(OldInd, T, T)` from *Mental Model*
add `data(NewInd, T, T)` to *Mental Model*
add `data(NewInd, B, B)` to *Mental Model*
send `revised(B)` to *Draw Conclusions*

Condition Definition: `positive_exhaust_move/3`: *See Rule 1*
`positive_exhaust_move(B, ET, Ind) :-`
`exhaust(ET, B)` is in *Annotations*
not `exhaust(B, _)` is in *Annotations*
`data(Ind, ET, ET)` is in *Mental Model*
`data(Ind, B, B)` is in *Mental Model*
`positive_throughout(Ind)`

Box 5.8: Model revision via movement of exhaustively represented terms (from *Revise Model*)

at a time. The rule uses the user-defined condition `positive_exhaust_move/3`, which expects the first argument to be the middle term. This is supplied within the rule's trigger. The condition identifies an end term (which will be moved) and a middle term (which will be copied), both of which occur in a row with three positive terms, such that the end term is exhaustively represented with respect to the middle term, but the middle term is not exhaustively represented with respect to anything. Effectively, two applications of the rule will map a model such as Model 5.5 to Model 5.6, via Model 5.7.

`positive_exhaust_move/3` makes use of a second user-defined condition `positive_throughout/1`. This tests that the row specified by its argument contains all three terms. The definition of the condition is left as an exercise.

Exercise 5.13: Enter the rule and condition definition from Box 5.8 into *Revise Model*, providing a suitable definition of `positive_throughout/1`. Test the model on suitable premises. In order to do this, it is useful to adjust the definition of `filter_premises/2` in *Experimenter Process* such that only syllogisms with *all* or *some* quantifiers are presented.

Step through all positive syllogisms, while watching *Mental Model* and *Problem Buffer* to see how model revision interacts with the rest of the system. In most cases the revision rule will have no effect, but where it does, check that it is correctly applied. Notice that this revision rule applies not only to the above *all/all* problem, but also to some of the *all/some* and *some/all* problems. If all is well, you should also see, after some applications of the model revision rule, conclusions that were drawn on the basis of the initial model being refuted by a revised model and removed from *Problem Buffer*. ◇

A second revision rule is required to address cases of breaking positive links when the end term to be moved is not exhaustively represented with respect to anything. Consider the case of *some A are B* and *some B are C*. The initial model constructed from these premises will be the same as for all positive premise pairs (Model 5.5), but there will be no annotations on the model. The model may therefore be transformed by moving, for example, an a to a new row (corresponding to one of the as being neither b nor c):

$$\begin{array}{ccc} & \mathrm{b} & \mathrm{c} \\ \mathrm{a} & \mathrm{b} & \mathrm{c} \\ \mathrm{a} & & \end{array} \tag{5.8}$$

A c individual may also be moved to a new row, yielding (from Model 5.5):

$$\begin{array}{ccc} \mathrm{a} & \mathrm{b} & \\ \mathrm{a} & \mathrm{b} & \mathrm{c} \\ & & \mathrm{c} \end{array} \tag{5.9}$$

Furthermore, both model modifications may be carried out in succession, yielding:

$$\begin{array}{ccc} \mathrm{a} & \mathrm{b} & \\ & \mathrm{b} & \mathrm{c} \\ & & \mathrm{c} \\ \mathrm{a} & & \end{array} \tag{5.10}$$

This model satisfies both premises, but refutes all four conclusions that could be drawn from the initial model.

This second model revision operation is implemented by Rule 2 of Box 5.9. The first condition of the rule (testing that `positive_exhaust_move/3` fails) ensures that the rule can only fire when Rule 1 cannot fire. (To put it another way, Rule 1 has priority over Rule 2.)

Rule 2 identifies nonexhaustively represented end terms and moves them to a new row, provided no other "free" instances of that end term (i.e., without the middle term) already exist. This breaks positive links associated with *some* premises, as described above. The condition `free_end_term/2` is required to identify instances of the end term that occur without the middle term. The rule should not apply to such instances.

Exercise 5.14: Test Rule 2 by adding it, and its user-defined condition, to *Revise Model* and testing the model on all four *some/some* syllogisms. ◇

Rule 2 (refracted; once): *Move nonexhaustively represented pair of terms*
TRIGGER: `revise(B)`
IF: not `positive_exhaust_move(B, _, _)`
`positive_nonexhaust_move(B, T, OldInd)`
`NewInd` is a new symbol with base `'I'`
THEN: delete `data(OldInd, T, T)` from *Mental Model*
add `data(NewInd, T, T)` to *Mental Model*
send `revised(B)` to *Draw Conclusions*

Condition Definition: `positive_nonexhaust_move/3`: *See Rule 2*
`positive_nonexhaust_move(B, T, Ind) :-`
`data(Ind, T, T)` is in *Mental Model*
`T` is distinct from `B`
`positive_throughout(Ind)`
not `free_end_term(B, T)`
not `exhaust(T, B)` is in *Annotations*
not `exhaust(B, T)` is in *Annotations*

Condition Definition: `free_end_term/2`: *Term occurs without B?*
`free_end_term(Mid, T) :-`
`data(Ind, T, T)` is in *Mental Model*
not `data(Ind, Mid, Mid)` is in *Mental Model*

Box 5.9: Model revision via movement of nonexhaustively represented terms (from *Revise Model*)

One further model revision rule is required to handle all valid revisions to models of positive premises. Consider *all B are A* and *all B are C*. The initial model will, as usual, be:

```
a  b  c
a  b  c        (5.11)
```

In this case, b is exhaustively represented with respect to both a and c. New as and cs, that are not bs, may be added, extending the model to:

```
a  b  c
a  b  c        (5.12)
a
```

or:

```
a  b  c
a  b  c        (5.13)
      c
```

Rule 3 (refracted; once): *Move nonexhaustively represented pair of terms*
TRIGGER: `revise(B)`
IF: not `positive_exhaust_move(B, _, _)`
not `positive_nonexhaust_move(B, _, _)`
`positive_nonexhaust_copy(B, T)`
`NewInd` is a new symbol with base `'I'`
THEN: add `data(NewInd, T, T)` to *Mental Model*
send `revised(B)` to *Draw Conclusions*

Condition Definition: `positive_nonexhaust_copy/2`: *See Rule 3*
`positive_nonexhaust_copy(B, T) :-`
`data(Row, B, B)` is in *Mental Model*
`data(Row, T, T)` is in *Mental Model*
`T` is distinct from `B`
not `exhaust(T, B)` is in *Annotations*
not `free_end_term(B, T)`

Box 5.10: Model revision via copying of nonexhaustively represented terms (from *Revise Model*)

or even:

$$\begin{array}{ccc} a & b & c \\ a & b & c \\ a & & \\ & & c \end{array} \tag{5.14}$$

Thus, if an end term occurs in the same row as a middle term, but is not exhaustively represented with respect to the middle term, and is not free in the middle, then a new individual, corresponding to a free instance of the end term, may be added. Rule 3 of Box 5.10 implements this form of transformation. The rule is specified to apply only if neither Rule 1 nor Rule 2 may apply.

The three model revision rules given are sufficient for all positive syllogisms. However, they do not produce all possible alternative models that are consistent with the premises. For example, there is no rule to create "optional" b terms, even where they might exist. This is because such terms don't help to refute any conclusions.

Exercise 5.15: Extend *Revise Model* with Rule 3 and its corresponding condition. The model revision procedure may now be tested on the full set of positive syllogisms. Set `filter_premises/2` accordingly and examine the behaviour of the model on all sixteen positive syllogisms. In each case, the model revision rules should take each initial model through a succession of transformations, producing a range of alternative models that refute all but the valid conclusions. ◇

Exercise 5.16: The correct operation of Rule 2 requires that at least two identical fully-linked individuals are in the model. If the initial model were built with fewer instances of each type of individual this rule would produce models that violate the semantics of the *some* premise. Attempt to develop and implement a solution to this problem. What issues arise? ◇

Revision Rules for *No*

A convenient way to begin tackling the revision of models of negative syllogisms is to consider the negative problem given by Johnson-Laird and Byrne (1991): *no A are B* and *no B are C*. The initial model is:

a		
a		
	b	
	b	
		c
		c

(5.15)

Each end term is exhaustively represented with respect to the middle term, and the middle term is exhaustively represented with respect to each end term.

Model 5.15 supports both *no* and *some... not* conclusions, in both end-term orders. All such conclusions can be refuted by constructing the alternative model:

a		c
a		c
	b	
	b	

(5.16)

Johnson-Laird and Byrne (1991) claim that it is necessary to add negated terms to flesh out the gaps in Model 5.16, but give no indication of why they think this should be required. The idea behind the revision, however, is to take free end terms and merge them into a single individual, without an instance of the middle term (since this combination is ruled out by the exhaustive representation relations). Rather than explicitly representing negative information, it is sufficient to identify a free instance of one end term, find a free instance of the other end term, then add the second end term to the individual with the first. This should be done for all distinct pairings of available free terms.

Rule 4 of Box 5.11 implements the operation that transforms Model 5.15 to Model 5.16. Unlike the previous three rules, it does not need to be restricted to fire once per cycle. Also, it can apply at any time, and does not need to be prioritised

Rule 4 (refracted): *Overlap free end terms*
TRIGGER: `revise(B)`
IF: `negative_move(B, T, Ind)`
THEN: add `data(Ind, T, T)` to *Mental Model*
send `revised(B)` to *Draw Conclusions*

Condition Definition: `negative_move/3`: *See Rule 4*
```
negative_move(B, ET1, Ind) :-
    free_end_term(B, ET1)
    singleton_term(Ind, ET2)
    ET2 is distinct from ET1
    ET2 is distinct from B
```

Condition Definition: `singleton_term/2`: *Find solitary terms*
```
singleton_term(Row, ST) :-
    data(Row, ST, ST) is in Mental Model
    not data(Row, OT, OT) is in Mental Model
        OT is distinct from ST
```

Box 5.11: Model revision via overlapping free end terms (from *Revise Model*)

relative to the other rules. The condition definition used by the rule ensures that the rule only fires when one end term is free and the other is a "singleton" term (that is, it appears in a row without the middle term or the first end term). If the condition holds, the rule augments the model by adding the first end term to (what was) the singleton row.

Exercise 5.17: Examine how Rule 4, in combination with Rules 1 to 3, handles syllogisms that have at least one *no* premise by incorporating the rule and its condition definitions into *Revise Model* and defining an appropriate filter in *Experimenter Process*. ◇

The revision rules should now be able to refute all but the valid conclusions for every problem containing a *no* premise, as well as those composed of combinations of *all* and *some* premises. Only problems containing *some... not* premises are not adequately covered.

Revision Rules for *Some... Not*

Problems containing the *some... not* quantifier are always among the most difficult ones to handle, for theories of syllogistic inference as well as for human reasoners. By way of introduction, consider *some A are B* and *some B are not C*. The model

Rule 5 (refracted): *Negative nonexhaustively represented pair swap*
TRIGGER: `revise(B)`
IF: not `positive_exhaust_move(B,_,_)`
`negative_nonexhaust_move(B,ET,Ind1,Ind2)`
THEN: delete `data(Ind1,ET,ET)` from *Mental Model*
add `data(Ind2,ET,ET)` to *Mental Model*
add `data(Ind2,B,B)` to *Mental Model*
send `revised(B)` to *Draw Conclusions*

Condition Definition: `negative_nonexhaust_move/4`: *See Rule 5*
`negative_nonexhaust_move(B,ET,Ind1,Ind2) :-`
`data(Ind1,ET,ET)` is in *Mental Model*
`data(Ind1,B,B)` is in *Mental Model*
`ET` is distinct from `B`
not `positive_throughout(Ind1)`
`singleton_term(Ind2,ET2)`
not `ET2` is a member of `[ET,B]`
not `exhaust(B,_)` is in *Annotations*
not `singleton_term(_,B)`

Box 5.12: Model revision via copying negative nonexhaustively represented terms (from *Revise Model*)

construction rules from Section 5.4.2 yield Model 5.17 as an initial model of these premises:

```
a b
a b
    c        (5.17)
    c
```

This model may be revised to yield Model 5.18:

```
  b
  b
a b c        (5.18)
a b c
```

Rule 5 (Box 5.12) implements this form of model revision.

Rule 5 is rather like the opposite of Rules 1 and 2, in that it tries to build positive links instead of destroying them. Rule 5's condition searches for an end term and middle term pair that do not occur with the other end term. The middle term should not be exhaustively represented, and should not already occur in the model as a singleton. The condition then locates a singleton instance of the other

Rule 6 (refracted): *Add free end term to nonexhaustively represented middle*
TRIGGER: `revise(B)`
TRIGGER: `revise(B)`
IF: not `positive_exhaust_move(B, _, _)`
not `negative_nonexhaust_move(B, _, _, _)`
not `positive_nonexhaust_move(B, _, _)`
not `positive_nonexhaust_copy(B, _)`
not `negative_move(B, _, _)`
`negative_build(B, T, Ind)`
THEN: add `data(Ind, T, T)` to *Mental Model*
send `revised(B)` to *Draw Conclusions*

Condition Definition: `negative_build/3`: *See Rule 6*
`negative_build(B, ET, Ind) : −`
`free_end_term(B, ET)`
`data(Ind, B, B)` is in *Mental Model*
`exhaust(B, ET)` is in *Annotations*
not `data(Ind, ET, ET)` is in *Mental Model*
not `exhaust(ET, B)` is in *Annotations*

Box 5.13: Model revision via building new negative terms (from *Revise Model*)

end term. If the condition holds Rule 5 moves the original pair of terms to the row with the second end term, leaving a singleton middle term in place of the original pair. Like Rule 4, Rule 5 fires as many times as it can on a single cycle. Thus, Rule 5 can transform Model 5.17 to Model 5.18 in a single cycle.

The priority of Rule 5 is critical to the correct functioning of the model revision process, as Rule 5 can generate models to which Rule 2 can apply, and Rule 2 can generate models to which Rule 5 can apply. If Rule 5 has lower priority than Rule 2, then model revision can in some cases fall into an infinite loop, with new terms being added to the model *ad infinitum*. In order to avoid this, it is essential that Rule 5 has higher priority than Rule 2 (and Rule 3). The addition of Rule 5 therefore requires adjustment of the conditions of Rules 2 and 3.

Exercise 5.18: Augment *Revise Model* with Rule 5 and the definition of its condition. Also modify the priority of Rules 2 and 3 by ensuring they only fire when `negative_nonexhaust_move/4` fails. Explore the behaviour of the system on syllogisms containing at least one *some... not* premise. Can you identify syllogisms which are still beyond the system's competence? ◇

It has already been mentioned that the initial representation for *some...not* premises presented here differs from that given by Johnson-Laird and Byrne (1991); crucially, if *some A are not B*, the current initial representation does not represent the possible *a*s that are *b*s. The difficulty is that when individuals of this type are represented, they tend to support existential conclusions that are hard to eliminate. Instead, the approach adopted here is to introduce these possible *a*s that are *b*s through model revision. This is the purpose to the final rule (Rule 6). Note that, although this approach works, it does appear to violate the conventional sense of the exhaustive representation relation. It is therefore less than perfectly satisfactory.

Rule 6 (Box 5.13) is applicable when there is a free end term that is exhaustively represented with respect to the middle term and when the middle term is not exhaustively represented with respect to that end term. In such cases each instance of the middle term may be augmented with the end term (hence the rule is not restricted to firing once on a given cycle). This effectively augments a mental model of, for example, *some A are not B*, with *a*s that are *b*s. The rule has the lowest priority of all model revision rules.

Exercise 5.19: Add Rule 6 and its condition definition to *Revise Model*. Test the system on the full set of 64 syllogisms, paying particular attention to those with *some...not* premises. ◇

With Rule 6 in place, the model revision process is complete. The system should now produce all and only the valid conclusions for each syllogism.

5.5.3 Discussion of the Extended Model

This model successfully captures many of the principal aspects of the Johnson-Laird and Byrne (1991) Mental Models account of syllogistic reasoning. Initial models are constructed in broadly the same fashion as specified by the theory, without using explicit optional terms. Exhaustive representation information is also recorded, and used to constrain model revision. The FIFO access property of the *Mental Model* buffer interacts with the model construction process to produce a Figural Effect.

However, there are some major differences too. There is no counterpart of the "fleshing out" process, and explicitly negated terms are never used. As a consequence, the model currently produces too many conclusions on the basis of each initial model. Although some "single-model problems" exist (i.e., problems which do not involve or require model revision), they are relatively rare, and restricted to a single family of problems equivalent to *all A are B* and *no B are C*. A true Mental Models theory approach should include a number of other types of problem, such as *all A are B, all B are C* among the single-model problems.

The revision process also typically produces sequences of alternative models that are much longer than the two or three usually claimed by Mental Models theory. This is a consequence of the lack of a fleshing out process; fleshing out allows a single representation to abstract across several possible logical models of the premises, and in the case of single-model problems at least, this should be sufficient to cover all the relevant alternatives, so that explicit revision of these models would not be required.

As we have seen, the system implements the Figural Effect by interaction of the scheduling of model construction and the FIFO access property of the *Mental Model* buffer. In the original theory (e.g., Johnson-Laird & Bara, 1984; Johnson-Laird, 1983), the reason for this arrangement is that the end terms should be "brought together" to create an integrated model. Mental models are therefore built only in *abc* and *cba* orders. However, there is little real motivation for this requirement, since the order of terms within individuals (i.e., rows) is completely immaterial from a logical point of view. The revision and conclusion-drawing processes in the present implementation do not require that middle terms be brought together either, so the models could be constructed in different orders without impairing the system's deductive performance.

In fact, several studies have found evidence to suggest that in certain circumstances (especially the *ba*/*bc* figure), human reasoners appear to construct their mental models (if indeed they do construct mental models at all) with the middle term first (Stenning & Yule, 1997; Bucciarelli & Johnson-Laird, 1999). Within the context of the current model, this could be implemented by having *Scheduler* always integrate its first premise forward (having initialised *Mental Model* with the subject term of that premise instead of the end term), and then integrating the second premise forward or backward as required. This would produce *bac* and *bca* orders in *Mental Model* in *ba*/*bc* problems, but would not affect term order in other figures, and it would have no effect on term order in conclusions, since only end terms occur in conclusions.

Exercise 5.20: Modify *Scheduler* so that it constructs *bac* and *bca* orders in the *ba*/*bc* figure. *Mental Model* should be initialised with the *b* term, then one premise should be integrated forward, and the other should be integrated reversed. ◇

Exercise 5.21: One unsatisfactory aspect of the system developed here is that the revision rules for positively linked models are always constrained to fire once per cycle, whereas those for negatively linked models are free to fire as many times as they can on each cycle. When a revision rule fires multiple times on one cycle it introduces or moves multiple terms in a single revision of the model. When a rule is restricted to firing once, it may need to fire on multiple successive cycles to fully achieve the intended revision. In fact, it is only Rule 2 that must be performed sequentially, and Rule 5 that must be performed multiple times in a single application. Investigate the consequences of changing the firing behaviour (i.e., once or multiple firings per cycle) of these two rules. Attempt to improve the model revision process so that these rules are not sensitive to their firing behaviour. Be sure that possible improvements do not compromise the deductive competence of the system. ◇

Exercise 5.22: As noted above, the complete system, with processes of initial model construction, conclusion drawing, model revision, and conclusion refutation, is capable of perfect deductive competence — it can generate all and only the correct conclusions for every syllogism. Human reasoners rarely show such perfect performance. Johnson-Laird and Byrne (1991) suggest that one source of error is decay of annotations. Investigate the effects of such performance factors by adding Half-Life decay to *Annotations*. How does the rate of decay impact upon performance? Which, if any, syllogisms are immune to annotation decay? ◇

5.6 Project: Reasoning as Problem Solving

The various model revision rules bear strong similarities to operators that license transitions between states within a problem space, as introduced in Chapter 4. The rules for model construction may also be treated as operators. Explore this approach by developing another implementation of Mental Models theory. Processing within the implementation should follow the standard operator proposal, evaluation, selection, and application cycle, as introduced in Chapter 4. The state should consist of representations of the premises, the current mental model, and any annotations. There should be several sets of operator proposal rules, with operators for model construction, conclusion drawing, model revision, and conclusion refutation. The model revision operator evaluation rules should take advantage of the operator evaluation mechanism to achieve the effect of prioritising the revision rules in the above model.

A problem solving approach to reasoning also requires consideration of the goals of reasoning. The three phases of syllogistic reasoning with mental models (constructing an initial model, drawing conclusions from that model, and revising the model) correspond to different subgoals of the reasoning process. However, adopting a goal-directed approach suggests that the model revision phase might be treated instead as a conclusion refutation phase. Consider how shifting the emphasis from model revision to conclusion refutation affects both the model that you develop and the behaviour of that model. (For more on reasoning as problem solving see Polk & Newell, 1995.)

5.7 Syllogistic Reasoning with Euler Circles

Another method for solving syllogisms using a different kind of model is the method of Euler Circles. The method depends on drawing diagrams composed of circles, each representing the set of individuals that have one of the properties denoted by the terms of the syllogism. Although attributed to the Swiss mathematician Leonhard Euler (1707–1783), the method seems to have been invented by Gottfried Wilhelm von Leibniz (1646–1716). Either way, the details of how the method can be effectively used have not been widely understood in the psychology of reasoning.

5.7.1 The Method of Euler Circles

The basic defining characteristic for methods based on Euler Circles is that the circles are arranged in such a way that only individuals which could possibly exist are represented in the diagram. Such individuals are represented as subregions, and individuals which cannot exist are not represented at all. This characteristic distinguishes methods based on Euler Circles from those based on Venn Diagrams (see Johnson-Laird, 1983). However, beyond this point there are different methods for using Euler diagrams, corresponding to different interpretations of the semantics of the diagrams. Euler diagrams have usually been taken to represent logical models of the premises (e.g. Erickson, 1974; Guyote & Sternberg, 1981), so that each topologically distinct diagram represents a different logical model of the premises, and each region in that diagram represents an individual which exists in that logical model. On this interpretation, given that many logical models are possible for any premise combination, the number of distinct diagrams to be considered can become large, and this makes the method unwieldy to use (see Johnson-Laird, 1983).

However, as Stenning and Oberlander (1995) and Stenning and Yule (1997) have shown, it is possible to solve all syllogisms effectively by using only one diagram, provided that the most general diagram is chosen (i.e., the one with the greatest possible number of subregions). This corresponds to a different way of interpreting the diagrams, in which the regions in the diagram represent individuals which are possible given the premises, and the diagram represents the entire space of possible individuals; the presence of a region no longer means that the corresponding individual exists, but instead means that the individual *possibly* exists, that is, the individual exists in at least one logical model. An additional notation, the placing of a mark in certain regions, indicates that individuals corresponding to that region necessarily exist, that is, they exist in all logical models. So a single diagram can abstract across the entire space of logical models.

Figure 5.4 shows Euler diagrams for each of the premise types using this approach. Marks show which types of individual must exist given the truth of the

Figure 5.4: Euler diagrams for each premise type, with regions representing necessary individuals marked with "×"

premise. Thus, in the case of *some A are not B*, the mark in the left circle indicates the existence of an individual that is an *a* but not a *b*.

The diagram for a pair of premises is formed by taking the appropriate diagram for each of the premises, and unifying the circles corresponding to the middle term. While this combined diagram may be free to take any of several topological forms, the rule that the number of subregions should be maximised always results in a topologically unique arrangement.

Now, the marked regions in the original diagrams may or may not have been cut in two by the arc of another circle in creating the integrated diagram; if they have, then the mark should be removed. This can be rationalised as follows: such a region represents a conjunction of properties which must exist, given one of the premises. Either the other premise constrains how the third term can be added to the individual, or it does not. For example, suppose we have a region representing the conjunction of properties *a* and *b* (as in the premise for *some A are B*). For convenience we indicate the conjunction as [a, b]. If the region is entirely contained inside the circle representing *c*, then all the [a, b] individuals must in fact be [a, b, c], and if the [a, b] region is entirely outside the *c* circle, then all the [a, b] individuals must be [a, b, −c] (where −c indicates *not* c). But if a region containing a mark is cut in two by the addition of a new circle, this tells us that both completions of the [a, b] individual are semantically possible, and so neither is necessary — there might be either [a, b, c] or [a, b, −c] individuals. Since marks represent necessary individuals in the context of their diagrams, and neither subregion corresponds to a necessary individual in the completed diagram, the mark must be removed.

When the process is complete all marks that remain correspond to individuals that are necessary given the premises. From these, particular conclusions (i.e., concerning *some* and *some... not*) follow directly, since, for example, if there is

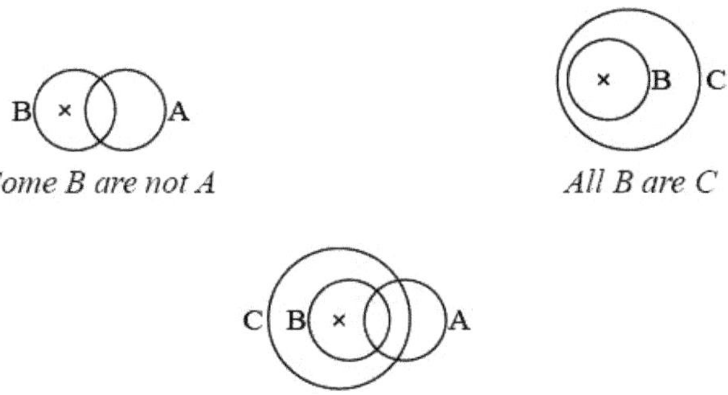

Some B are not A and *all B are C*
Therefore there is a b that is a c and not an a
That is, *some C are not A*

Figure 5.5: The Euler Circles solution to *some B are not A* and *all B are C*

at least one individual of type [a, b, c], then *some A are C*. Universal conclusions (concerning *all* and *no*) follow provided they pass another test: that the marked region is an unbroken circle representing the subject term of the conclusion. The fact that the circle is unbroken implies that the necessary individual could be any member of the set represented by the circle, so the conclusion applies to all members of that set.

The method is illustrated in Figure 5.5, which shows the diagrams corresponding to *some B are not A*, *all B are C*, and to the conjunction of these two premises. The $\times$-mark is not removed when the diagrams are merged, because the circle corresponding to C does not cut through the marked region. Instead, the $\times$-mark indicates one or more individuals that are b and c but not a. Furthermore, the marked region is not an unbroken circle. Therefore the conclusion is particular. Thus, it follows from the diagram that *some C are not A*.

5.7.2 The Individuals Task

Stenning and Yule (1997) investigated a variant syllogistic inference task called the Individuals Task. The objective of this task was to describe types of individuals that must exist given the truth of the premises (i.e., necessary individuals, corresponding to marks in Euler diagrams). For example, given the premises *all A are B* and *all B are C*, and the traditional syllogistic "no empty sets" assumption (that there is at least one a, one b, and one c), then there must be an a who is also b and c. Similarly, given *some A are not B* and *all C are B*, there are as who are neither b nor c. It should be stressed that the existence of necessary individuals in no way depends on the use of Euler Circles; individual conclusions are logical consequences of the premises, just like quantified conclusions.

As we have seen above, every conventional syllogistic conclusion depends on the existence of a necessary individual, but there are also cases where a premise pair has an individual conclusion, but no conventionally expressible quantified conclusion relating the end terms. These cases only occur with pairs of negative premises, such as *no A are B* and *no B are C*, and *no A are B* and *some B are not C*. In both cases individuals must exist who are *b*, but neither *a* nor *c*. This corresponds to the conclusion *some not-A are not-C*, but the traditional syllogism does not permit negated subject terms, so these problem types ordinarily have no valid conclusions.

Individual conclusions are interesting because they are fully convertible, that is, their term order is logically unconstrained, since they are just conjunctions of atomic (ground or negated) terms. This raises the possibility of using the Individuals Task to investigate the Figural Effect, free of the logical constraints that tend to distort it in the standard, quantified conclusion task.

One interesting prediction of the Euler Circles method depends on the way the marks are used in inference. We have seen that a marked region represents a type of individual that one or another premise has asserted to exist. Stenning and Yule (1997) showed that human reasoners tend to mention terms from this premise in their conclusions before mentioning the remaining term from the other premise. Furthermore, the order in which the end terms occur in individual conclusions closely parallels the conventional Figural Effect for quantified conclusions — the subject term in a quantified conclusion generally comes from the premise which originally asserts the existence of the individual, provided that the semantics of quantification do not force another order.

5.7.3 An Implementation of Euler Circles

The structure of processing within an Euler Circles approach to syllogistic reasoning is quite similar to that of Mental Models. Figure 5.6 shows an appropriate box and arrow diagram (compare Figure 5.1). *Problem Buffer* holds the premises, some intermediate data, and any conclusions. Its contents are monitored by *Scheduler*, which controls the construction of an integrated model of the premises, and the drawing of conclusions on the basis of that model. However, in this case the model is a geometrical diagram, composed of circles and ×-markers. It is therefore held in an analogue buffer (*Diagram*), rather than a tabular buffer, as in the Mental Models case. There are also separate processes for constructing diagrams (*Construct Diagram*), and drawing conclusions (*Draw Conclusions*). There is no revision process, since no model revision is required. Instead, there is a separate process (*Update Marks*), which keeps the ×-marks consistent as the premise representations are integrated into the model.

For present purposes, *Problem Buffer* should have random access and *Diagram*

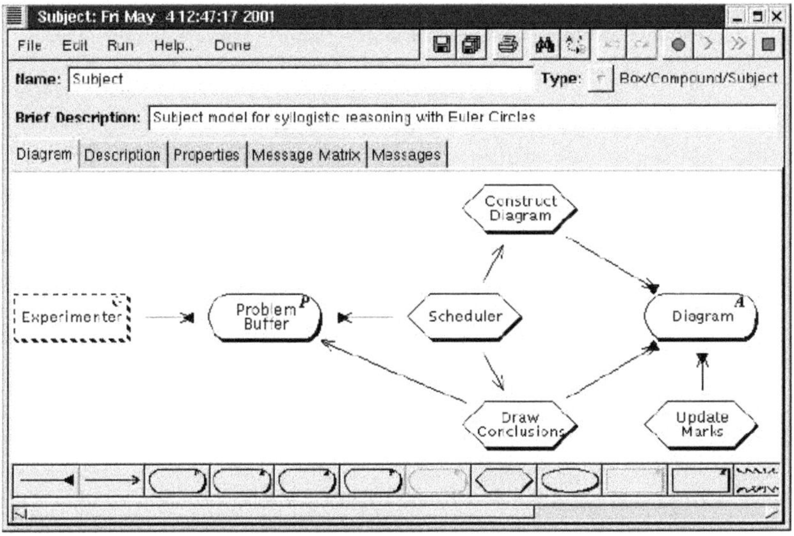

Figure 5.6: A box and arrow diagram for the subject box using Euler Circles

should have FIFO access. This reflects the access characteristics of the equivalent buffers in the implementation of Mental Models theory, where they were essential in the generation of the Figural Effect. Below it will be seen that the Euler Circles model's behaviour is less sensitive to buffer access characteristics.

Exercise 5.23: Create a new model with *Subject* and *Experimenter* boxes as in the implementations of Mental Models theory. Copy the contents of the Mental Models' *Experimenter* to the new model's *Experimenter*, and recreate the box and arrow configuration from Figure 5.6 within *Subject*. Ensure that all buffer Access properties are set appropriately. Test the set-up: on each new trial, two premises should be added by *Experimenter* to *Problem Buffer*. ◇

The Scheduler

The tasks of the Euler Circles' *Scheduler* are similar to those of *Scheduler* in the Mental Models model, and its rules are generally analogous (see Box 5.14). Rule 1 initialises construction of circles by identifying the middle and end terms, and by triggering processing in *Construct Diagram*. The once marking ensures that, if multiple solutions to `identify_end_terms/2` exist, only one is adopted. Whether this has an effect depends upon the complete definition of `identify_end_terms/2`. (The simplest definition will yield two solutions for non-diagonal figures.)

Rule 1 (refracted; once): *Locate the end terms and initialise the model*
TRIGGER: `system_quiescent`
IF: not `end_terms(_)` is in *Problem Buffer*
`identify_terms(MiddleTerm, EndTerms)`
THEN: add `end_terms(EndTerms)` to *Problem Buffer*
send `initialise(MiddleTerm)` to *Construct Diagram*

Rule 2 (refracted; once): *Integrate one premise*
TRIGGER: `system_quiescent`
IF: `end_terms(_)` is in *Problem Buffer*
`premise(Premise)` is in *Problem Buffer*
THEN: send `premise(Premise)` to *Construct Diagram*
delete `premise(Premise)` from *Problem Buffer*

Rule 3 (refracted; once): *Trigger conclusion drawing*
TRIGGER: `system_quiescent`
IF: not `premise(_)` is in *Problem Buffer*
`end_terms(EndTerms)` is in *Problem Buffer*
THEN: send `drawconc(EndTerms)` to *Draw Conclusions*

Condition Definition: `identify_terms/2`: *Identify middle/end terms*
`identify_terms(B, [A, C]) :-`
`premise([Quant1, A, B])` is in *Problem Buffer*
`premise([Quant2, B, C])` is in *Problem Buffer*
`A` is distinct from `C`
...

Box 5.14: Scheduling rules for syllogistic reasoning with Euler Circles (from *Scheduler*)

Rule 2 only fires once the end terms have been identified. It selects a premise and integrates it with the current diagram by sending the premise to *Construct Diagram*. The once marking is again critical. It ensures that the premises are integrated in sequence, rather than in parallel. The rule also removes each premise from *Problem Buffer* as it is integrated, so the same premise will not be integrated twice. Note that, by contrast with Mental Models, construction order does not depend on figure, so there is no need to explicitly annotate premises before constructing the diagram.

Rule 3 initiates conclusion drawing once all premises have been integrated. The once marking has no effect (as there is only one solution to the rule's conditions), but the refracted marking ensures that the rule does not continue to fire on subsequent processing cycles.

All three rules are triggered by `system_quiescence`. The quiescence trigger ensures that each phase is complete before the next phase is begun. It could equally have been used by the rules within the Mental Models' scheduler. In this model it primarily serves to delay the drawing of conclusions until all changes to *Diagram* have been completed.

Exercise 5.24: Add the rules from Box 5.14 to *Scheduler*, and complete the definition of `identify_terms/2` to handle all figures. Test scheduling on a range of figures. The scheduler should generate at most one message on each cycle, and precisely four messages over the course of a complete trial: three to *Construct Diagram* followed by one to *Draw Conclusions*. ◇

Construct Diagram

Construct Diagram has two functions: to initialise *Diagram* for a given term (when triggered by `initialise/1`) and to integrate a premise into the existing diagram (when triggered by `premise/1`). Initialising is straightforward: it is a matter of adding a circle of arbitrary radius at an arbitrary position to the (initially empty) diagram, and placing a mark within the circle to indicate the existence of individuals of the given type. Rule 1 of Box 5.15 is sufficient. The rule creates a circle of radius 50 units at coordinates (200,150) and places an ×-mark at its centre. The circle is labelled with `circle(Term)`. This allows other rules to extract the term represented by any circle in *Diagram* from its label. The ×-mark is labelled `mark([Term])`. The list representation is used within the mark's label because it generalises to marks that represent individuals belonging to multiple categories (e.g., *a*s that are also *b*s).

The integration of premises is more complicated. The initialisation rule is only ever used by *Scheduler* to create the diagram corresponding to the middle term, so integration of any premise requires addition of another circle in such a way as to capture the semantics of the premise. For *all* premises, this means adding a circle either inside the one that is already present (the forward case, as when given *B* and integrating *all A are B*), or surrounding it (the reversed case, as when given *B* and integrating *all B are A*). Rules 2 and 3 of Box 5.15 illustrate the two cases. For both rules, the first condition locates a circle currently on *Diagram* (the circle created by Rule 1). The user-defined condition `geometry_parameters/4` then specifies radius and location parameters of the second circle given the type of premise, and `new_circle/5` constructs the appropriate circle representation from these parameters. The rules' actions add the new circle, and an appropriately labelled ×-mark at the circle's centre, to *Diagram*.

There are several aspects of Rules 2 and 3 that require additional comment. The geometry parameters specify the new circle in relation to the existing circle. In the case of *all* premises, the new circle should be larger for the forward direction and smaller for the reversed direction. Hence, in Rule 3 it is the reciprocal of

Rule 1 (unrefracted): *Represent a single set*
TRIGGER: `initialise(Term)`
IF: True
THEN: add `circle(circle(Term), 50 at (200, 150))` to *Diagram*
add `x_mark(mark([Term]), (200, 150))` to *Diagram*

Rule 2 (unrefracted): *Integrate "all" premise (forward)*
TRIGGER: `premise([all, X, Y])`
IF: `circle(circle(X), Xcircle)` is in *Diagram*
`geometry_parameters(all, RadRat, Cdist, Angle)`
`new_circle(Xcircle, Cdist, RadRat, Angle, Yrad at Ycentre)`
THEN: add `circle(circle(Y), Yrad at Ycentre)` to *Diagram*
add `x_mark(mark([Y]), Ycent)` to *Diagram*

Rule 3 (unrefracted): *Integrate "all" premise (reversed)*
TRIGGER: `premise([all, X, Y])`
IF: `circle(circle(Y), Ycircle)` is in *Diagram*
`geometry_parameters(all, RadRat, Cdist, Angle)`
`new_circle(Ycircle, Cdist, 1/RadRat, Angle, Xrad at Xcentre)`
THEN: add `circle(circle(Y), Xrad at Xcentre)` to *Diagram*
add `x_mark(mark([Y]), Xcentre)` to *Diagram*

⋮

Condition Definition: `geometry_parameters/4`: *Rad ratio; Dist; Angle*

```
geometry_parameters(all, 1.667, 0.100, -pi).
geometry_parameters(no, 1, 2.150, -pi/4).
geometry_parameters(some, 1, 1.300, -pi/3).
...
```

Condition Definition: `new_circle/5`: *Get new circle parameters*

```
new_circle(Rad at (Xx, Xy), Dist, Rat, Angle, NewCirc) : -
    count_circles(1)
    NewCirc = Rad * Rat at (Xx + Dist * Rad, Xy)
new_circle(Rad at (Xx, Xy), Dist, Rat, Angle, Rad * Rat at New) : -
    count_circles(2)
    cartesian (Xx + Dist * Rad, Xy) <=> polar [L, Th] (with origin (Xx, Xy))
    cartesian New <=> polar [L, Th + Angle] (with origin (Xx, Xy))
```

⋮

Condition Definition: `midpoint/3`: *Find midpoint between two circles*

```
midpoint(Rad1 at (X1, Y1), Rad2 at (X2, Y2), (XMid, YMid)) : -
    XMid is X1 + (X2 - X1)/2
    YMid is Y1 + (Y2 - Y1)/2
```

Box 5.15: Selected rules and condition definitions from *Construct Diagram* the radius ratio that is passed to `new_circle`/5 (resulting in the new circle being smaller than the original circle when integration order is reversed). The other geometry parameters specify a horizontal offset between the centre of the new circle and the original circle, and an angular offset between the centres. The value `−pi` (equivalent to 180 degrees) ensures that the centres of both circles lie on a single horizontal line.

The way that `new_circle`/5 uses the geometry information that it is given to determine the centre and radius of the new circle depends on how many circles there are already on *Diagram*. If there is only one circle, the angle is ignored. If there are two circles, the condition translates the cartesian centre of the original circle to polar coordinates, applies the distance translation and angular rotation, and then translates the polar result back to cartesian coordinates.

Exercise 5.25: Add Rules 1, 2, and 3 and associated condition definitions to *Construct Diagram*. Include an appropriate definition for `count_circles`/2 that counts the number of circles in *Diagram* (e.g., by finding the length of a list containing all such circles). Test the system by ensuring that it builds appropriate diagrams for each of the four *all*/*all* syllogisms. ◇

The rules for *no* premises parallel those for *all* premises. Each rule adds a circle of the same size as the first, but in such a position that neither circle overlaps or is contained within the other. (Recall Figure 5.4.) The geometry parameters shown in Box 5.15 ensure this. Like the rules for *all*, an ×-mark is always placed in the centre of the new circle.

Exercise 5.26: Using the geometry parameters given in Box 5.15, construct rules for integration of *no* premises in both forward and reversed directions. Note that for *no* premises the size of the new circle is not dependent upon the direction of integration, so the radius ratio is 1 for both forward and reversed integration directions. Test the diagram construction rules on premises involving both *all* and *no*. Ensure that the rules interact appropriately. ◇

The rules for *some* require that a new circle of the same size as the first is placed in such a position as to overlap the first. An ×-mark, labelled with both premise terms (e.g., `mark([a, b])`), should be placed in the intersection.

Exercise 5.27: Create rules for integrating *some* premises (in both directions). The user-defined condition `midpoint`/3, from Box 5.15, may be used to determine the location for the ×-mark. Be sure that the ×-mark's label is a list consisting of the two premise terms. Test the rules on a range of premise pairs including *some*, *all* and *no* quantifiers. ◇

The rules for integration of *some... not* premises may use the same geometry parameters as those used by the rules for *some*. However, the rules require that the ×-mark is placed in the circle corresponding to the subject term, but not in the intersection with the other circle. With the parameters given in Box 5.15, it is sufficient to place the ×-mark at the centre of the subject circle. The mark corresponding to *some A are not B* must also be labelled to reflect *A* and not *B*. This can be achieved with a label such as `mark([a, -b])`, provided that other rules are written to correctly interpret the `-b` notation.

Exercise 5.28: Create rules for integrating *some... not* premises (in both directions). Ensure that in each case the mark is appropriately labelled. Test the rules, and their interaction with other model integration rules, on all premise pairs. ◇

Update Marks

Recall that appropriate use of Euler Circles requires that, when a new circle is added to a diagram, any ×-marks in regions cut by the new circle must be removed. The diagram construction rules in *Construct Diagram* do not ensure this. Instead, *Update Marks* consists of a single autonomous rule that monitors *Diagram* as it is constructed, identifies ×-marks corresponding to regions of *Diagram* that have been cut by the arc of another circle during construction, and deletes them.

Box 5.16 shows the update rule and some associated condition definitions. As in the case of *Construct Diagram*, the complexity is in the geometry required to make the process work. The first three conditions of the rule identify a mark and a circle that is not mentioned in the mark's label. The condition to test for this (`mentioned/2`) examines each element of the label in turn. The complexity comes in `check_bisection/2`, which checks for bisection of the mark's region by the circle. Like `mentioned/2`, this is a recursive condition that examines each element of the mark's label in turn. The condition succeeds if all positive terms correspond to circles that are bisected by the circle under consideration, and all negative terms correspond to circles that are not inside that circle.

Exercise 5.29: Add the rule and condition definitions from Box 5.16 to *Update Marks*. Also give definitions for `circle_inside/2` and `circle_outside/2`. The former should succeed if the circle given by its first argument is entirely within that given by the second argument. This will be true if and only if the difference between the circles' radii is greater than the distance between their centres. The latter should succeed if the circle given by its first argument is entirely outside of that given by the second argument. This will be true if and only if the distance between the circles' centres is greater than the sum of their radii. (It is probably

Rule 1 (refracted): *Delete marks for bisected regions*
IF: `x_mark(mark(Marks), Centre)` is in *Diagram*
`circle(circle(Q), Qcircle)` is in *Diagram*
not `mentioned(Q, Marks)`
`check_bisection(Marks, Qcircle)`
THEN: delete `x_mark(mark(Marks), Centre)` from *Diagram*

Condition Definition: `mentioned/2`: *Is circle name in mark descriptor?*

```
mentioned(X, [-X|_]).
mentioned(X, [X|_]).
mentioned(X, [_|T]) :-
    mentioned(X, T)
```

Condition Definition: `check_bisection/2`: *Does circle bisect region?*

```
check_bisection([P|T], Qcircle) :-
    circle(circle(P), Pcircle) is in Diagram
    bisects(Qcircle, Pcircle)
    check_bisection(T, Qcircle)
check_bisection([-P|T], Qcircle) :-
    circle(circle(P), Pcircle) is in Diagram
    not circle_inside(Qcircle, Pcircle)
    check_bisection(T, Qcircle)
check_bisection([], Qcircle).
```

Condition Definition: `bisects/2`: *P bisects Q*

```
bisects(P, Q) :-
    circle_inside(P, Q)
bisects(P, Q) :-
    not circle_inside(P, Q)
    not circle_outside(P, Q)
    not circle_inside(Q, P)
```

Box 5.16: Selected rules and condition definitions from *Update Marks*

simplest to define these two conditions in terms of a third, `distance/3`, that determines the distance between two points.) When complete, run the system over several premise pairs. It should now construct an appropriate diagram in all cases. In doing this, *Update Marks* should delete all ×-marks except those corresponding to necessary individuals. ◇

Rule 1 (unrefracted): *Draw individual conclusions*
TRIGGER: `drawconc(_)`
IF: `x_mark(mark(X), Point)` is in *Diagram*
`draw_ind_conc(X, Point, IndConc)`
THEN: add `conclusion(IndConc)` to *Problem Buffer*

Condition Definition: `draw_ind_conc/3`: *Read off individual conclusions*
`draw_ind_conc(Label, Mark, Conclusion) :-`
`Conclusion` is the list of all `T` such that `ind_pol(Label, Mark, T)`

Condition Definition: `ind_pol/3`: *Find all term polarities for a given mark*
`ind_pol(Label, Mark, T) :-`
`T` is a member of `Label`
`ind_pol(Label, Mark, PT) :-`
`circle(circle(T), Tcircle)` is in *Diagram*
not `mentioned(T, Label)`
`polarity(Mark, Tcircle, T, PT, _)`

Condition Definition: `polarity/5`: *Is term plain or negated?*
`polarity(Mark, Circle, Name, Name, positive) :-`
`point_inside(Mark, Circle)`
`polarity(Mark, Circle, Name, -Name, negative) :-`
not `point_inside(Mark, Circle)`

Box 5.17: Selected rules and condition definitions from *Draw Conclusions*

Draw Conclusions

Conclusions concerning individuals (as in the Individuals Task) may be read directly from *Diagram*. A syllogism has one or more valid individual conclusions if and only if at least one mark, indicating the existence of a necessary individual, remains in *Diagram*. These individuals may be fully characterised by taking the label of the mark, which specifies one or two of the three terms, and determining the values of the remaining term(s) by checking whether the mark lies inside or outside the relevant circles. Conclusions of the standard form (with quantifiers relating end-terms) require slightly more effort.

Rule 1 of Box 5.17 draws individual conclusions. It is triggered by *Scheduler* once both premises have been integrated and the system has reached quiescence (and so no model updates remain). The first condition finds any marks on *Diagram* and the second elaborates the label to include all three terms. This is achieved with the subcondition `ind_pol/3`, which, given the mark label and position, returns the polarity of each term (i.e., `T` or `-T`, to indicate the individual is a `T` or not a `T`). `ind_pol/3` does this in such a way as to preserve the order of terms, drawing first from the label and then from other circles, with other circles being used in the order they were added to the diagram. As noted above, Stenning and Yule (1997) argue that this is the order normally given by human participants completing the Individuals Task.

The `polarity/5` condition tests whether a given point is inside or outside a given circle, and returns either the term for the circle (if the point is within the circle) or the negative term (otherwise). The fifth argument gives the same information in a different form, and is not used in `ind_pol/3`. It is included for use by the rules for drawing quantified conclusions discussed below. `polarity/5` uses `point_inside/2`, whose definition is similar to that of `circle_inside/2` (from *Update Marks*). `point_inside/2` is true if the point given by its first argument is within the circle given by its second (or equivalently, if the distance between the point and the circle's centre is less than the circle's radius).

Exercise 5.30: Add the rules and condition definitions given in Box 5.17 to *Draw Conclusions*. Also provide a suitable definition for `point_inside/2`. Test the system by running it on all premise pairs. It should now generate all valid individual conclusions from all problems. ◇

It remains to show how to draw conventional, quantified conclusions from an Euler diagram. There are two approaches. One is to draw an individual conclusion and transform it (if possible) into quantified form. The second is to refer more directly to the diagram: universal conclusions (with *all* and *no* quantifiers) are valid when the marked region is an unbroken circle corresponding to an end term, while particular conclusions (with *some* and *some not* quantifiers) are valid if the marked region is the intersection of circles. In both cases it is necessary that the subject of the conclusion is an unnegated end term. (Recall that particular conclusions of the form *some not A are not C* cannot be expressed with conventional quantifiers.)

Rule 2 of Box 5.18 draws conventional conclusions using the second of the above approaches. It finds an ×-mark on *Diagram*, and attempts to use this, together with the geometry of the marked region and previous knowledge of which are the end terms, to determine the subject and the mood (universal or particular) of the conclusion. If that succeeds, the predicate is selected from the end terms and its polarity determined. `get_quant/3` is then used to determine the conclusion's quantifier from the polarity and mood.

The complexity in Rule 2 stems from the difficulty of extracting the subject of the conclusion from the diagram. `get_subject/5` achieves this with three cases:

1. where the ×-mark is labelled with a single, non-negated, end term (in which case the mood of the conclusion is universal);
2. where the ×-mark is labelled with a list of terms, one of which is a non-negated end term (in which case the mood of the conclusion is particular, and the non-negated end term is the subject); and

Rule 2 (refracted): *Draw quantified conclusions*
TRIGGER: `drawconc(EndTerms)`
IF: `x_mark(mark(Mark), Point)` is in *Diagram*
`get_subject(Mark, Point, EndTerms, Subj, UorP)`
select `Pred` from `EndTerms` leaving `[Subj]`
`circle(circle(Pred), PredCirc)` is in *Diagram*
`polarity(Point, PredCirc, Pred, _, Polarity)`
`get_quant(UorP, Polarity, Quant)`
THEN: add `conclusion([Quant, Subj, Pred])` to *Problem Buffer*

Condition Definition: `get_subject/5`: *get subject for conclusion*
`get_subject([Subj], _, EndTerms, Subj, universal) :-`
`circle(circle(Subj), Scircle)` is in *Diagram*
`get_subject(Marks, _, EndTerms, Subj, particular) :-`
`Subj` is a member of `Marks`
`Subj` is a member of `EndTerms`
`get_subject(Marks, Point, EndTerms, Subj, particular) :-`
`circle(circle(Subj), Scircle)` is in *Diagram*
not `mentioned(Subj, Marks)`
`polarity(Point, Scircle, _, _, positive)`

Condition Definition: `get_quant/3`: *Quantifier definitions*
`get_quant(universal, positive, all).`
...
`get_quant(particular, negative, somenot).`

Box 5.18: Selected rules and condition definitions from *Draw Conclusions*

3. where the subject is any end term, and the conclusion is particular, provided also that the ×-mark is within the subject's circle.

Note that universal conclusions licensed by the first case of this definition (e.g., *No A are C*) will always yield particular conclusions via the second case (e.g., *some A are not C*). The third case is more general. It can draw counter-figural particular conclusions. It is also able to draw some of the same figural conclusions licensed by the second case. However, as the rule is refracted, only one copy of each possible conclusion is ever drawn.

Exercise 5.31: Add the rule to draw conventional conclusions to *Draw Conclusions*, together with the necessary condition definitions. Ensure that *Experimenter* records only the first conclusion drawn for each syllogism, for example by adjusting the conclusion drawing rules to fire only once. Deactivate the individual conclusion drawing rule (Rule 1 from Box 5.18) and run the system over the complete set of syllogisms a number of times, accumulating the results. You should see an overall association between term order in conclusions and figure, in the diagonal figures. Some problems will show no overall bias, whereas others will show systematic biases. Compare the biases shown by this system with those shown by the Mental Models system developed earlier in the chapter. ◇

Exercise 5.32: Experiment with the Access properties of the buffers. Try setting *Diagram* for Random access, and compare the Figural Effect it generates with that generated by FIFO access. You should find that it is unaffected. Now compare term order in Individual conclusions with both settings. How is the model's operation affected by changing *Problem Buffer*'s Access property? Attempt to explain the pattern of sensitivity to buffer access properties. ◇

5.7.4 Discussion of the Euler Circles Model

The Euler Circles model can account for human competence in syllogistic reasoning adequately. The model is relatively simple: its semantics are transparent, and its implementation details relate to geometry, rather than specifics of initial model construction and model revision rules. However, the soundness of the model's inferences depends on the fact that suitable geometry parameters are chosen to ensure that each constructed diagram is the maximal diagram required by the semantic theory. The model does not check that its diagram is maximal, nor does it represent, and attempt to achieve, the goal of drawing a maximal diagram.

The model's main empirical predictions concern term order in conclusions. It generates systematic term-order biases for both individual and quantified conclusions, which Stenning and Yule (1997) have shown to fit the human Figural Effect for valid conclusions of both types fairly well. The model's biases do not depend greatly on construction order or buffer access properties, since they are based on semantic differences between premises. However, because the model implemented here draws all and only valid conclusions, it cannot account for human reasoning errors, or for Figural Effects in invalid conclusions, as observed in human reasoning.

Perhaps the most obvious source of error for a performance-limited Euler Circles model is failure to draw a maximal diagram. Such an error will result in the failure to appropriately bisect all possible marked regions and consequently in the failure to refute putative individual conclusions. It is interesting to note that the problems in which such errors are possible are exactly those identified by Johnson-Laird and his co-workers as "multiple-model" problems. This is because in the Johnson-Laird and Bara (1984) account of Mental Models theory, as applied to the syllogism, the representations of individual premises are semantically equivalent to the Euler Circles theory's graphical representations of individual premises, even to the extent that they explicitly distinguish necessary from merely possible individuals. Consequently, the only source of difference between the theories is in creating integrated representations (i.e., the way the models of the individual premises are combined to form an integrated model of both premises). If the representations of individual premises under-determines the final integrated configuration, the problem is, within Mental Models theory, a multiple-model one, or, within Euler Circles theory, one for which several non-maximal Euler Circle configurations are also possible.

A system that builds non-maximal diagrams will only produce extra, invalid conclusions (i.e., conclusions that are valid in one, but not all, diagrams). It will not fail to draw valid conclusions if valid conclusions exist, yet human reasoners make such errors. Different types of modification to the system are required if it is to produce such errors. One approach is to allow marks to decay independently of the rest of the diagram. This is similar in some ways to the decay of annotations from a model within Mental Models theory. Another approach is to limit the conclusion drawing process by, for example, modifying `get_subject/5` such that it fails to extract all possible conclusions from a diagram.

5.7.5 Project: Performance Factors in the Euler Circles Model

The preceding paragraphs identified three factors that could impair the deductive competence of a reasoner that uses Euler Circles for syllogistic reasoning. Explore each of the factors and attempt to characterise the types of errors that might be attributed to each. Specifically, attempt to address the following issues:

1. *Non-maximal diagram construction:* Experiment with different layouts of circles by changing geometry parameters in the model construction process. The model should sometimes produce invalid conclusions when the final diagram is non-maximal. Does the modified model still predict Figural Effects in its (invalid) conclusions?
2. *Decay of marks:* Add a rule to *Update Marks* that randomly deletes marks. (Note that decay of marks cannot be modelled simply by adding decay to *Diagram*, as then circles may also decay.) In what ways do the predictions of this variant model differ from that of a model which fails to build maximal diagrams?
3. *Difficulties in extracting a conclusion from the final diagram:* The third case of the definition of `get_subject/5` handles situations when the subject term is not included in the mark label. It is used in drawing some of the harder counter-figural conclusions. How does the model behave when this case is omitted? Explore other reasonable cases that might be included in the definition of `get_subject/5` in place of this case.

As a more challenging project, reconsider issue 1 above and attempt to develop a model-construction process that does not depend on arbitrary geometry parameters, and that does not bias the types of conclusions drawn in a systematic, but arbitrary, manner. What issues must such a model-construction process address?

5.8 General Discussion

Detailed COGENT models of two approaches to deductive reasoning have been presented in this chapter. The models, and the theories underlying them, share some similarities, but there are also fundamental differences. The models also illustrate several issues that arise within computational modelling. This discussion compares the two theories before highlighting the computational issues and attempting to draw more general lessons for computational modelling from those issues.

5.8.1 Mental Models and Euler Circles: A Comparison

The Mental Models and Euler Circles approaches to syllogistic reasoning differ in several respects. Most obviously, Mental Models involves an array-like representation of possible interpretations of the premises, whereas Euler Circles uses a diagrammatic representation that reflects the most general interpretation of each premise. One consequence of this is that Mental Models involves a model revision process, which is absent from Euler Circles. There are also similarities between the approaches, however. From a logical perspective, both are model-theoretic — they are both based upon the construction of models that reflect the semantics, or meaning, of the premises, and the subsequent reading off of conclusions from such models. As such, both theories differ from straightforwardly proof-theoretic theories of deductive reasoning (e.g., Braine, 1978; Rips, 1983, 1994), which involve the application of inference schemas (e.g., *modus ponens* and *modus tollens*) to the premises in a purely syntactic fashion (but see Stenning & Yule, 1997, and Yule, 1997, for alternative rule-based methods with close similarities to the Euler Circles model).

A fundamental difference between the theories is in their explanation of the Figural Effect. Mental Models theory attributes the Figural Effect to the first-in, first-out access characteristics of the buffer in which the mental model is developed. Within the Euler Circles approach, the Figural Effect is effectively an artifact of the problem structure. The Individuals Task, which has not been addressed within Mental Models theory, provides a different way of exploring Figural Effects, and appears to support the predictions of the Euler Circles approach.

A further difference concerns the integration of premises. The Euler Circle approach constructs a single, maximal model that integrates both premises. It does this while maintaining a consistent interpretation of the representation. It could be argued that Mental Models theory fails to acknowledge that there is a "best" way of combining premises that maintains a consistent interpretation of the representation. Instead, the Johnson-Laird and Bara (1984) version assumes the reasoner is capable of understanding the semantics of individual premises perfectly, but is usually incapable of integrating them properly, to the extent that it posits integrative biases away from the normative semantics of the basic-level representations it uses (e.g., towards making positive links wherever possible). It would be possible to create the most general Mental Model representation at the first attempt, if we knew that this was the best thing to do, and we knew how to use the resulting integrated representation to draw conclusions.

More recent versions of Mental Models theory (e.g. Johnson-Laird & Byrne, 1991) have extended the presumed bias towards positive links to the representation of premises — reasoners are supposed only to produce models with positive links between positive properties (unless otherwise prompted) and then forget (how) to revise these models afterwards. This is intended to apply both to single premise representations and to combinations. While this step reduces the arbitrariness of the theory, a comprehensive account of the semantics of Mental Model representations has yet to be developed. Such an account would be highly desirable, if only as a backdrop against which the "psychological" principles of the theory could properly be assessed.

A further dimension along which Mental Models theory and the Euler Circles approach differ is that of generality. Mental Models theory has been applied in a range of situations, including conditional inference, transitive inference (Johnson-Laird & Byrne, 1991), reasoning with multiple quantifiers (Johnson-Laird, Byrne, & Tabossi, 1989), and propositional reasoning (Johnson-Laird *et al.*, 1992). Euler Circles has not been applied so broadly, though the extension to conditional reasoning would appear straightforward (e.g., by effectively interpreting *if A then B* as *all A are B*). Mental Models may therefore appear to provide a superior account of human deductive reasoning. However, there is little consistency in the way Mental Models theory has been extended across reasoning tasks. The unifying aspects seem to be the use of an array-like representation for models of the premises and the principle of truth for constructing representations, but the explanatory power of these aspects is unclear. Furthermore, many researchers use the term "mental model" in an even broader range of senses (e.g. Gentner & Stevens, 1983; Knauff, Rauh, & Schlieder, 1995), making it hard to discern any overall commonalities between the representations so described, other than that they are all, in some sense, analogues of the situation under consideration. Despite this vagueness of definition, the idea that much reasoning is accomplished using models, whether logical, mental or otherwise, is intuitively attractive, has wide descriptive applicability, and has stimulated a great deal of research.

5.8.2 Project: Propositional Reasoning with Mental Models

Johnson-Laird *et al.* (1992) demonstrate how Mental Models theory could be extended to propositional reasoning (i.e., reasoning with statements involving *if/then*, *and*, and *or*). Using Johnson-Laird *et al.* (1992) as a source, develop an implementation of the extended theory.

5.8.3 Some Issues for Computational Modelling

The models developed in this chapter illustrate two different systems for solving syllogistic reasoning problems. When performance factors are excluded, the systems produce the same outputs (i.e., the same set of conclusions that are valid) for each pair of inputs (i.e., each pair of premises). At the level of input/output, the systems are therefore indistinguishable. It is only when one considers how the systems work — the representational and algorithmic assumptions of the systems — that differences emerge. The models therefore illustrate two issues: indistinguishability of models and description of a theory at the level of representation and algorithm. An awareness of these issues is important because the data against which models are evaluated generally takes the form of a set of input/output pairs. Model evaluation must therefore look beyond such simple data if competing algorithmic accounts are to be discriminated. Issues arising from this are discussed in detail in Chapter 9.

A third issue raised concerns the representational assumptions of the Euler Circles model. These are of particular interest for the model illustrates how graphical representations may be employed within a symbolic system. Graphical objects (circles and marks within those circles) are created and manipulated via a set of propositional rules. One could argue that the graphical objects themselves could have been stored as propositions within a propositional buffer, and that the model uses an analogue buffer merely to provide a convenient pictorial view of the reasoning process, but equally one could argue that this view misses a fundamental claim of the Euler Circles approach: that the underlying representation is graphical and not propositional.

The resolution of this tension between propositional and graphical representations is far from straightforward. The argument for non-propositional representations is as follows: one must distinguish between the elements of the representation and the implementation of the processes that manipulate those elements. The Euler Circles model employs a number of graphical or geometrical functions for testing geometrical properties of a diagram. These functions are implemented as user-defined conditions (e.g., `circle_inside/2`, `circle_outside/2` and `check_bisection/2`). While the implementation of these conditions within the model involves calculating distances between points, other, graphical, implementations may be envisaged. For example, one might determine the truth of `circle_inside/2` by scanning the pixels within one circle on the image to ensure that the second circle is entirely contained within the first. By declaring the implementation of the geometrical functions to be an implementation detail, one may remain agnostic about the nature of mental representation. Alternatively, one may go further and argue that the true nature of mental representation is underdetermined by available data: methods rooted in graphical and propositional representations may be indistinguishable. (For debate about the nature of mental representation, see Pylyshyn, 1981, 1984, and Kosslyn, 1980, 1987.)

Implementation details are also apparent in the Mental Models model. There is a level at which Mental Models theory is relatively simple: when premises are given, an integrated mental model of those premises is constructed and possible conclusions are read off from the mental model. Some reasoners attempt to refute possible conclusions by revising their models (i.e., developing alternative models of the premises) and testing the possible conclusions drawn from their initial model against their revised models. The implementation of Mental Models theory, however, reveals hidden subtleties. These concern the precise specification of initial models for each premise, the details of combining premise representations, and the rules governing model revision. Only the drawing of conclusions from complete mental models is relatively straightforward. The model therefore illustrates how implementation of psychological theory, whether it be a theory of deductive reasoning or a theory in any other psychological domain, requires detailed specification of all elements of the theory. This level of detail is essential if a working model that embodies the theory is to be developed. Johnson-Laird is clear in most of his writing that many of the details of initial model construction, model integration, and model revision are part of Mental Models theory. These details have changed with successive revisions of the theory, however, and so should be understood within a framework of theory change (such as that of Lakatos, 1970). They might therefore best be viewed as peripheral assumptions: working assumptions that are being refined with a view to eventual integration into the "core" of the theory. Implementation details beyond such peripheral assumptions remain, however. Specifically, Johnson-Laird and colleagues repeatedly argue that the number of tokens in a mental model (e.g., whether there are two individuals or four individuals represented in a model of *some A are B*) is not relevant. The use of two tokens is thus an implementation detail.

Exercise 5.33: Return to the Mental Models model and examine the behaviour of the model when initial models are constructed with three or more instances of a term. (This will involve modification of Rule 1 of Box 5.2.) Are the model's predictions independent of the number of tokens in the initial model? If not, why not? ◇

A final issue raised in this chapter is the relation between deductive competence — idealised reasoning behaviour — and deductive performance — the patterns of conclusions favoured and errors produced in actual behaviour. Both models can account for deductive competence. Performance is accounted for in each model by incorrect functioning of one or more components of the reasoning system. Thus, in both cases the performance theory consists of a competence theory together with a set of performance factors. Both elements (the competence theory and the performance factors) are essential to the extraction of behavioural predictions from the models.

5.9 Further Reading

General cognitive texts with useful chapters on deductive reasoning include Mayer (1992) and Gilhooly (1996), and user-friendly texts specifically devoted to reasoning include Evans, Newstead, and Byrne (1993) and Manktelow (1999). Each of these provides good introductory material on the psychology of human reasoning, including the major experimental paradigms and theoretical approaches.

The Mental Models theory was introduced by Johnson-Laird (1983), and although more up-to-date presentations of the theory exist (e.g., Johnson-Laird & Byrne, 1991), the earlier text remains of interest for its positioning of reasoning with respect to other higher mental faculties (including language and, rather speculatively, consciousness). Johnson-Laird and Byrne (1991) provides a more highly focused account of Mental Models as it applies to a variety of deductive reasoning tasks.

Arguably both of the above sources on Mental Models suffer from a lack of logical rigour. Hodges (1977) provides an excellent introduction to the background formal logic. A briefer account, more focused towards human deductive reasoning, is contained in Rips (1995). This introduction focuses on the principal issue that has served to guide much work in human reasoning: that of the distinction between rule-based and model-based approaches to reasoning tasks. Rips favours rule-based accounts, and Rips (1994) provides a detailed description of his theory of reasoning via rules (together with criticisms of Mental Models and diagrammatic approaches). Rips (1995) is also of interest for his presentation of an account of problem solving in terms of reasoning. It serves as a useful counterpoint to other general accounts of cognitive processing in which reasoning is under-pinned by problem solving.

Lastly, a further COGENT model of performance on another reasoning task, that of Allen Inferences (see Knauff *et al.*, 1995; Berendt, 1996), is described in Cooper, Yule, Fox, and Sutton (1998). Readers seeking further details of the application of COGENT to reasoning tasks may find this of interest.

Chapter 6

Decision Making

Richard P. Cooper and Peter Yule

Overview: Decision making is defined and some of the principal findings and approaches surveyed. The chapter then focuses on one particular variety of decision making: medical diagnosis. Two models that learn to classify symptom patterns as indicating one of several diseases are developed. The models adopt different approaches to the task: the first employs a mathematically optimal approach based on probability theory; the second learns to associate symptoms with diseases via a simple connectionist network. The initial models assume that complete symptom information is available prior to making their diagnoses. This is unrepresentative of situations in which the information required for a decision must be explicitly obtained. We therefore extend the models to include symptom querying (i.e., querying symptoms in sequence and making a decision when sufficient information is available), and develop a third model of the task that adopts a hypothesis generation/testing approach. The chapter concludes by highlighting the general methodological strategy of comparative modelling, whereby several competing models are evaluated against multiple dependent measures gathered from a single task.

6.1 The Psychology of Decision Making

Decision making may be defined as the act of deliberately choosing one option from a number of alternatives. When defined in this general form, decision making is ubiquitous in higher cognition. Examples include: choosing whether to buy a lottery ticket (and other forms of gambling); consumer choice (ranging from selecting a brand of soap powder to choosing a car or house); medical and other forms of fault diagnosis (i.e., deciding which disease or fault is affecting a system); classification; choosing an operator when solving a problem; and even selecting a partner. In all interesting cases of decision making, the decision maker has some information about the desirability or possible consequences of each of the alternatives, and the decision maker's task is to select the alternative that is in some way the best.

Early work on decision making (e.g., von Neumann & Morgenstern, 1944; Edwards, 1954; Ledley & Lusted, 1959) was heavily influenced by economic theory and probability theory. Expected Value Theory (EVT) provides a means of determining the mathematically optimal alternative from a set, when the probabilities and values (or desirability) of all outcomes for each alternative are known. In such cases the decision maker may calculate the average long-term gain or loss — the expected value — for each alternative, and select the alternative with the highest average gain.

To illustrate, consider the case of buying a lottery ticket, where we have two alternatives: we could buy a ticket or we could not buy a ticket. If we buy a ticket, there are several possible outcomes. We could correctly match all numbers and win a huge sum. This is very unlikely. Alternatively we could match fewer numbers and win a modest sum. This is somewhat more likely. Finally we may match hardly any numbers and win nothing. Normally this is the most likely outcome. In fact, in the third case, one actually loses the cost of the ticket. The mathematics depends on the details of the lottery, but on average one typically loses between one quarter and one half of the cost of the ticket. The expected value of choosing to purchase a ticket might therefore be as low as -50 cents (assuming a \$1 ticket price). If one does not buy a ticket, one gains nothing and one loses nothing. The expected value of not purchasing a ticket is therefore 0 cents. EVT therefore tells us that the best alternative is not to buy lottery tickets — on average this choice will leave us better off.

EVT is not a good psychological theory of decision making because in this simple form it fails to account for lottery ticket buying behaviour. Controlled empirical work has also shown it to be unsatisfactory. For example, Kahneman and Tversky (1984) offered participants the choice between two gambles: an \$8 win with a probability of 1/3 or a \$3 win with a probability of 5/6. The expected values of the options are \$2.67 and \$2.50 respectively, yet participants reliably preferred the second option. The basic difficulty with EVT is that it is prescriptive rather than descriptive: it prescribes what people should do, without describing what people actually do. However, a series of studies such as the above led Kahneman and Tversky to propose that participants employed a "subjective" version of EVT, in which the objective probabilities and values employed in the mathematical calculation of expected values were replaced by subjective equivalents. Kahneman and Tversky (1984) went on to describe the relationships between objective and subjective probabilities and values. For example, losses have greater negative subjective value than equivalent gains, events of low objective probability are over-weighted, and events of high objective probability are under-weighted (see also Edwards, 1954).

A different tradition in decision making research focuses on limitations imposed by time, available information, and information processing resources on the decision making process. Many decisions must be made on the basis of incomplete information and under time constraints. For example, how should a fire chief respond to a blazing house when the structure is unstable and it is unknown if people remain in the house? In other cases, the alternatives available to a decision maker may change with time, and the decision maker may have to commit to one alternative before all alternatives are known. Thus, in selecting a partner or buying a house, one cannot be sure when highly desirable options might appear on the market, but one cannot delay a decision on any particular alternative indefinitely, as one cannot know for how long the alternative will remain available. (The situation with selecting a partner is complicated further by the requirement that both parties must agree to the decision!)

Working in this second tradition, Simon (1957) introduced the concepts of bounded rationality and satisficing. The context of Simon's work was a debate on human rationality: is human decision making rational? By the normative standards set by the mathematical approaches of EVT (and the Bayesian approach to probabilistic reasoning discussed later) the answer would appear to be in the negative. Much human decision making appears to be irrational. Simon argued, however, that the normative approaches failed to take into account the bounds or limitations on human decision making imposed by working with finite processing and memory resources. EVT requires, for example, the calculation of the expected value of each alternative. In doing this, the decision maker must consider all possible outcomes for each alternative. For example, for the alternative of buying a lottery ticket, the decision maker must consider the outcome of correctly selecting all winning numbers, the outcome of selecting all but one of the winning numbers, the outcome of selecting all but two of the winning numbers, and so on. Frequently decisions must be made under time constraints and the time required to perform all of the calculations is not available. This is most clearly true when there are infinitely many possible alternatives or outcomes. Bounded rationality is the term used by Simon (1957) to describe a system that is rational with respect to the constraints operating on that system's decision making processes.

Satisficing goes hand-in-hand with bounded rationality. A decision maker who satisfices is one who considers alternatives in sequence and selects the first alternative that is both satisfactory and sufficient, i.e., the first alternative that is good enough, even if it is not necessarily the best. A classic example of satisficing concerns house purchasing. As noted above, one cannot consider all houses and select the one with the greatest expected value because houses may come on to the market, or be withdrawn from the market, at any time. A satisficing approach to house buying involves setting criteria and selecting the first house that is satisfactory and sufficient with respect to those criteria.

Psychological evidence for the use of non-normative approaches such as satisficing has been provided by Payne, Bettman, and Johnson (1988), who compared participant behaviour with that predicted by various normative and non-normative approaches (including satisficing) on a range of choice tasks and under two conditions: with and without time constraints. Two results were of particular interest.

First, on the purely computational side, they found that normative procedures were not always the most effective of strategies when time constraints were imposed. Several non-normative procedures yielded choice performance that was superior to that of the normative procedures when the procedures were terminated prior to their natural completion point. Similar simulation results using several non-normative approaches have been reported by Gigerenzer and Goldstein (1996).

Second, on the psychological side, Payne *et al.* (1988) found that participant behaviour was close to that predicted by normative theory when there were no time constraints, but that when time constraints were imposed participant behaviour shifted towards that of the non-normative approaches. However, no single non-normative approach could account for participant behaviour in all conditions, and Payne *et al.* (1988) concluded that participants selected decision making strategies on a task-by-task basis. Similar conclusions have been reached by Gigerenzer and Todd (1999), who provide a catalogue by "fast and frugal" decision making heuristics and discuss the use of such heuristics in a variety of domains.

6.2 Medical Diagnosis

Choice tasks involving gambling are one of a number of prototypical tasks that have been considered by researchers in decision making. Another strand of decision making research has focused on tasks like medical diagnosis which involve categorisation (see, for example Fox, 1980; Gluck & Bower, 1988; Medin & Edelson, 1988; Estes, Campbell, Hatsopoulos, & Hurwitz, 1989; Kruschke, 1996; Ross, 1997). Medical diagnosis is a popular area of research not only because the basic task — of assigning a diagnosis to a set of symptoms — is of considerable practical interest, but because it provides a semi-naturalistic domain in which a number of factors that may influence generic decision making behaviour may be investigated. Such factors include the relative frequency of categories or diseases, the order of presentation of cue or symptom information, learning, and fatigue.

6.2.1 Bayes' Theorem, Base-Rates, and Base-Rate Neglect

Consider the following question (due to Casscells, Schoenberger, & Grayboys, 1978):

> If a test to detect a disease whose prevalence is 1/1000 has a false-positive rate of 5%, what is the chance that a person found to have a positive result actually has the disease, assuming you know nothing about the person's symptoms or signs?

Most participants queried by Casscells *et al.* answered 95%, apparently arguing as follows: Since the test has a false-positive rate of 5%, it will yield correct results on 95% of cases. This reasoning fails to take into account the fact that only one in 1000 people have the disease. If we were to test 1000 people chosen at random, we would expect one person to have the disease (because the prevalence is 1/1000), but we would also expect 50 people (5%) who did not have the disease to yield positive results. Thus, the chances of someone with a positive test result having the disease are actually nearer one in 50 (or 2%). Only 12% of participants queried by Casscells *et al.* gave this answer.

Probability theory provides a mathematically correct approach to problems such as the above through application of Bayes' theorem. This theorem allows one to calculate the probability of a hypothesis given some evidence. This is termed the posterior probability and denoted by P(H | E). In order to calculate this, we need to know three other pieces of information:

1. P(H), the prior probability of the hypothesis,
2. P(E), the probability of the evidence, and
3. P(E | H), the probability of the evidence given the hypothesis.

Note that P(E | H) and P(H | E) are not the same. Suppose E is that someone has a limp and H is that that person has a broken toe. The probability of a person having a limp given that they have a broken toe (P(E | H)) is very near one (almost everyone with a broken toe will have a limp) but the probability of a person having a broken toe given that they have a limp (P(H | E)) is much closer to zero, since very few people who have a limp also have a broken toe.

Bayes' theorem may be stated as:

$$\mathrm{P(H \mid E)} = \frac{\mathrm{P(H)} \times \mathrm{P(E \mid H)}}{\mathrm{P(E)}} \tag{6.1}$$

That is, the probability of a hypothesis given some evidence is the prior probability of the hypothesis times the probability of the evidence given the hypothesis divided by the probability of the evidence.

The probability of the evidence (the denominator term in Equation 6.1) is the sum over all possible hypotheses, H_i, of the probability of H_i being true times the probability of the evidence given that H_i is true. That is:

$$P(E) = \sum_i P(H_i) \times P(E \mid H_i) \tag{6.2}$$

In the above problem, the hypothesis is that a person who is tested actually has the disease. There is only one other hypothesis (call it H_a): that a person who is tested does not have the disease. The evidence is that the person tests positive for the disease. Assuming that the test correctly detects the disease when it is present, we have:

$$\begin{aligned}
&P(H) = 0.001 \text{ (i.e., } 1/1000) \\
&P(H_a) = 0.999 \text{ (i.e., } 1 - P(H)) \\
&P(E \mid H_a) = 0.05 \text{ (i.e., } 5\%) \\
&P(E \mid H) = 1
\end{aligned}$$

Substituting into Equation 6.2:

$$\begin{aligned}
P(E) &= P(E \mid H) \times P(H) + P(E \mid H_a) \times P(H_a) \\
&= 1 \times 0.001 + 0.05 \times 0.999 \\
&= 0.05095
\end{aligned}$$

Substituting into Equation 6.1:

$$P(H \mid E) = \frac{0.001 \times 1}{0.05095} \approx 0.01963$$

This compares well with our approximate answer of 2% (or 0.02) as estimated above.

The probability of a hypothesis being true in the absence of any evidence is known as the base-rate (P(H) in the above example), and the tendency for people to ignore base-rate information as demonstrated in Casscells *et al.*'s experiment is known as *base-rate neglect*. Base-rate neglect has been demonstrated in a number of situations (see also Tversky & Kahneman, 1980), and it is often presented as a fundamental bias affecting human probabilistic decision making. However, several experiments have shown that in certain circumstances base-rate information can be used effectively (e.g., Gigerenzer & Hoffrage, 1995; Evans, Handley, Perham, Over, & Thompson, 2000; Giorotto & Gonzalez, 2001), and Koehler (1996) goes so far as to suggest that base-rate neglect is a fallacy.

Arguably, base-rate neglect only occurs in artificial and abstract mathematical situations. Gigerenzer and Hoffrage (1995) have argued that base-rate neglect is a consequence of the use of non-natural representational formats (involving probabilities or percentages), and that it may be substantially reduced through the use of frequency formats (e.g., 1 out of 20, rather than 5%) in information presentation. Others have argued that even frequency formats can be artificial, and that the essential requirement for correct use of base-rate information is that the information be presented in a format that facilitates reasoning about subset relations (see Evans *et al.*, 2000; Giorotto & Gonzalez, 2001).

6.2.2 Medin and Edelson's Diagnosis Task

Participants in Casscells *et al.*'s experiment did not have direct experience with base-rate information. That is, while they were told the statistical facts, they did not have the opportunity to experience those statistical facts first hand through exposure to hundreds or thousands of applications of the test. Providing participants with such first-hand experience has been shown also to reduce or eliminate base-rate neglect.

Medin and Edelson (1988) demonstrated this by training participants on a diagnosis task in which the diseases varied in frequency. Participants were presented with pairs of symptoms, and required to select one of six diseases. They were then given feedback, allowing them to learn symptom/disease associations. Several symptoms were imperfect predictors, in that they could occur with multiple diseases. Base-rates were manipulated by ensuring that some diseases occurred more frequently than others. When participants had achieved perfect diagnostic accuracy for two complete blocks of training trials the task was modified. In some transfer trials, only one symptom was presented. When this symptom was an imperfect predictor (i.e., when it had previously been associated with more than one disease), participants tended to select the disease most frequently associated with that symptom. Thus, participants correctly applied base-rate information. Medin and Edelson (1988) examined a number of other experimental manipulations, and found that in some situations base-rates did appear to be neglected, and that in other situations over-compensation of base-rates occurred, with participants reliably selecting the least common disease.

The formal structure of Medin and Edelson's task was as follows:

> Participants completed a sequence of blocks of trials (12 trials per block) in which they were presented with two symptoms (e.g., back pain, skin rash) and six fictional diseases (terrigitis, coralgia, etc.). They were required to select one disease as their diagnosis. After selecting a diagnosis, they were given feedback indicating either that they were correct, or what the correct disease was. They then moved on to the next trial. Trials were self-paced. The 12 trials within each block had the abstract form shown in Table 6.1. Thus, on three out of 12 trials symptoms a and b were presented and the correct diagnosis was disease 1, and on one out of 12 trials symptoms a and c were presented and the correct diagnosis was disease 2. (The 12 trial forms were randomised within each block.) Symptom a was therefore an imperfect predictor (occurring with either disease 1 or disease 2). Symptoms b and c were perfect predictors (of disease 1 and disease 2 respectively), but disease 2 was rare in comparison to disease 1. A transfer test was given once participants had achieved perfect diagnostic accuracy for two consecutive blocks (at worst this occurred

Table 6.1: The abstract structure of trials within each block of Medin and Edelson's (1988) diagnosis task. The nine symptoms are indicated by letters. The six diseases are indicated by numbers.

Symptoms	Disease	No. of Trials per Block
a & b	1	3 trials
a & c	2	1 trial
d & e	3	3 trials
d & f	4	1 trial
g & h	5	3 trials
g & i	6	1 trial

after 14 blocks of training trials). The transfer test consisted of 33 randomly ordered trials consisting of symptom patterns that had not previously been presented. Nine of these trials involved presenting a single symptom. Others involved presentation of two or even three conflicting symptoms.

The results from the transfer phase were as follows: when the presented symptom was a high frequency perfect predictor (such as b), 81.2% of responses were for the appropriate disease (1, in the case of b). When the symptom was a low frequency perfect predictor (such as c), 92.7% of responses were for the appropriate disease (2, in the case of c). These figures indicate that participants had acquired good knowledge of symptom/disease associations. When the symptom was an imperfect predictor (such as a), 78.1% of responses were for the appropriate high frequency disease (1, in the case of a) and 14.6% of responses were for the appropriate low frequency disease (2, in the case of a). These figures indicate that the majority of participants were able to make correct use of base-rate information acquired through differential exposure to the stimulus materials. The results from when several conflicting symptoms were presented are more complex. We return to these below.

6.2.3 A Bayesian Model of Medical Diagnosis

A Bayesian approach to Medin and Edelson's (1988) task might work as follows. During the training phase participants would acquire knowledge of the base-rates of all diseases (e.g., disease 1 occurs on 25% of cases, disease 2 occurs on 8.33% of cases, and so on) and the conditional probabilities of symptoms given diseases (e.g., the probability of having symptom a given that a patient has disease 1 is 1.0). This information can then be substituted into Bayes' theorem to give a system that is able to calculate the probability of each disease given any set of presenting symptoms, and then offer the disease that is mathematically most likely as its diagnosis. The situation of Medin and Edelson is slightly complicated by the fact that participants were presented with two pieces of evidence in the training trials and up to three pieces in the transfer phase. Knowledge of each symptom corresponds to one piece of evidence. Bayes' theorem must be applied several times in succession if the multiple pieces of evidence are to be used.

The Experimenter Module

In order to develop and evaluate a model of Medin and Edelson's diagnosis task, it is necessary also to develop infrastructure to support the presentation of stimuli to the model and the collation of the model's responses. We follow the approach adopted in earlier chapters by which these functions are implemented within a separate compound box (*Experimenter*) that communicates with a second compound box (*Subject*) that implements the task model.

On each trial *Experimenter* should send the set of symptoms that are present to *Subject*. *Subject* should then respond by sending its diagnosis to *Experimenter*. For simplicity *Experimenter*'s two functions may be handled by separate processes (one sending to an input/output process within *Subject* and the other receiving from the same input/output process).

Exercise 6.1: Create a new research programme (for a series of medical diagnosis models) and create a new model within that research programme for the first attempt at a model of Medin and Edelson's task. Create appropriately connected *Experimenter* and *Subject* modules within that model and populate them with processes as described above. In developing the *Experimenter* module further it is helpful to have a mock-up of the *Subject*'s functionality. Therefore, populate *Subject* with a single *Input/Output* process containing a triggered rule that sends a random diagnosis (e.g., a signal of the form `diagnosis(X)`, where `X` is a digit randomly drawn from $\{1,2,3,4,5,6\}$), on receipt of a list of symptoms. Assume this list of symptoms takes the form `symptoms(L)`, where `L` is a list of letters (corresponding to the symptoms in Table 6.1). This rule will be replaced once sufficient *Experimenter* functionality has been implemented. ◇

Experimenter must be able to function in two phases, corresponding to the two types of block administered to participants (blocks of training trials and blocks of transfer trials). When in training phase, each trial should correspond to a case from Table 6.1, with the relative frequency of cases equal to their relative frequency in that table. The order of presentation of cases should be randomised.

Figure 6.1 shows a possible arrangement of components for *Experimenter*. *Trial Database* contains a set of terms that define the trials for the different types

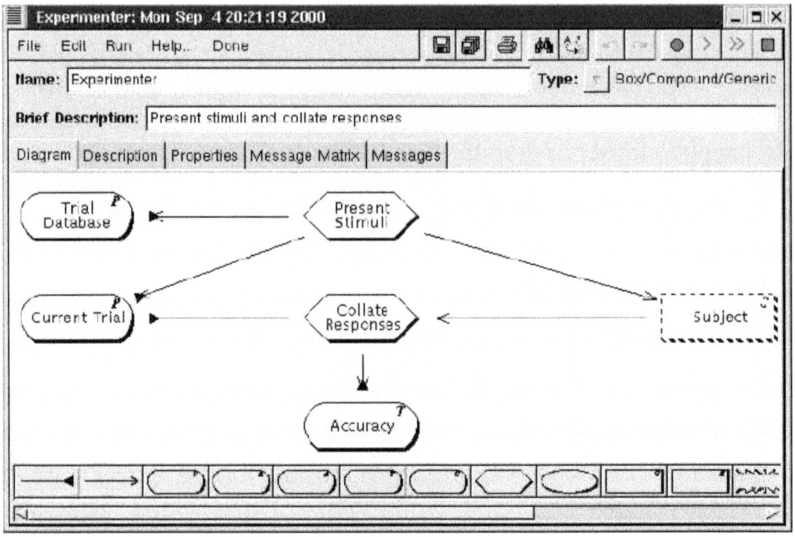

Figure 6.1: The organisation of a possible *Experimenter* module for Medin and Edelson's diagnosis task

of block. The terms all have the form: `trial(Phase, SymptomList, Disease)`, where `Phase` is either `train` or `transfer`, and `Disease` is uninstantiated for transfer trials. *Current Trial* is used for temporary storage of the details of case from *Trial Database* on each trial. At the beginning of each trial, a rule in *Present Stimuli* moves the data specifying one trial from *Trial Database* to *Current Trial*, and sends the symptom information for that trial to *Subject*. The type of trial selected by the rule (`train` or `transfer`) depends on the type of block. This is determined by a user-defined property of *Present Stimuli*. The initialisation property of *Trial Database* is set to Each Block, and for *Current Trial* it is set to Each Trial. This ensures that each trial is self-contained but that the full database of trials is reinitialised on each block. *Collate Responses* contains two triggered rules that tabulate responses from *Subject*, as in Figure 6.2.

Exercise 6.2: Fully specify all components of *Experimenter*. Also create two scripts: one to run a block of 12 training trials and one to run a block of 9 transfer trials. Test the infrastructure by running the model over several trials. (In order to test *Experimenter*, *Subject* must produce a response when presented with a set of symptoms. The rule described in the Exercise 6.1 should ensure this.) ◇

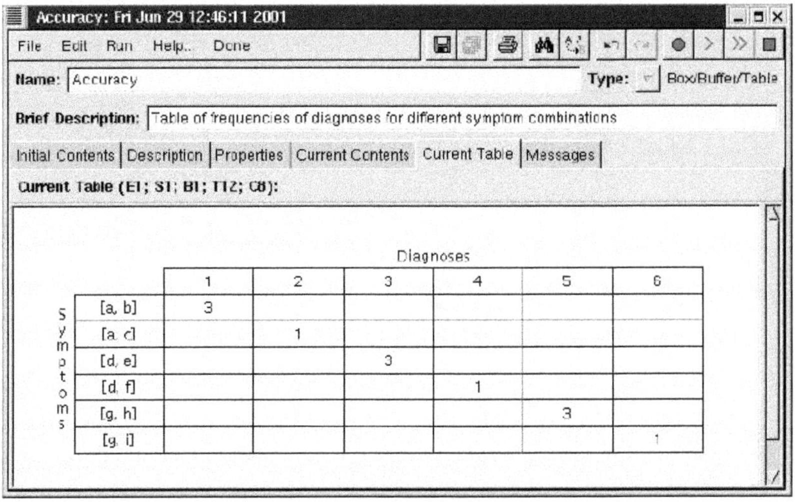

Figure 6.2: A tabulation of diagnoses against symptoms presented

The Subject Module

The Bayesian approach assumes that, during the training phase, participants acquire knowledge of base-rates and conditional probabilities of symptoms given diseases. We begin by developing an account of the use of this knowledge as it occurs in later trials of the experiment. This account is founded on the assumption that the knowledge can be acquired in earlier trials. The actual mechanisms of acquisition are considered below. The initial model is therefore a model of the "expert" participant.

The expert Bayesian participant requires a long-term store containing knowledge of base-rates and conditional probabilities, a temporary store in which probabilities of various hypotheses may be manipulated, and a process that calculates the probabilities of each possible hypothesis given the symptom information communicated by *Experimenter*. Figure 6.3 shows an appropriate arrangement.

Exercise 6.3: *Oracle*, in Figure 6.3, contains the necessary base-rate and conditional probability information. (It is implemented as a tabular buffer, rather than a propositional buffer, because its contents are best viewed in tabular form.) Elements of *Oracle* might take the form:

```
data(disease(1), prevalence, 0.25)
data(disease(1), symptom(a), 1.00)
```

Specify the contents of *Oracle* (with reference to Table 6.1). Many table entries will be zero (e.g., the conditional probability of symptom c given disease 1). Do

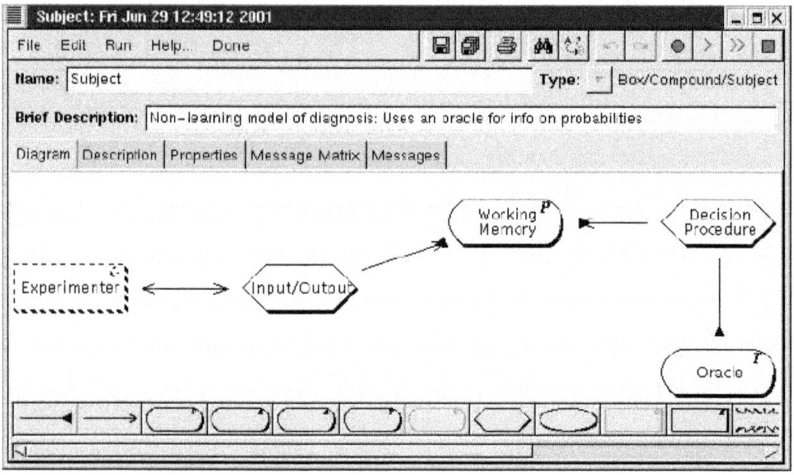

Figure 6.3: The box and arrow diagram for the expert Bayesian subject

not specify such entries. (There are 42 of them, and specifying them in full is highly repetitious.) *Decision Procedure* will adopt the convention that any conditional probability that is not specified in *Oracle* is zero. ◇

Working Memory within the Bayesian *Subject* may contain three types of information: known symptoms, probabilities of diseases given the presence of specified symptoms, and, near the end of each trial, a diagnosis. Known symptoms may be represented by terms such as `symptom(a)`. Diagnoses may similarly be represented by terms such as `diagnosis(1)`. The representation of probabilities of hypothesised diseases given symptoms requires more complex terms. The presentation here assumes that such information is represented as triples of the form:

`probability(disease(D), given(SymptomList), P)`

This representation makes the given information explicit and uses a list to represent known symptom information. It is therefore sufficiently flexible to handle cases where any number of symptoms (including zero) are given.

Processing begins with the initialisation of *Working Memory* with base-rate information (determined with reference to *Oracle*). After the first cycle *Working Memory* should contain elements of the form:

`probability(disease(1), given([]), 0.25)`

for each of the six diseases. Shortly after this, *Input/Output* should receive symptom information from *Experimenter*. This information should immediately be forwarded to *Working Memory*.

Exercise 6.4: Create a rule in *Decision Procedure* to initialise *Working Memory* with base-rate information. This rule should just match against appropriate elements in *Oracle* and add appropriate `probability`/3 terms to *Working Memory*. Also modify the mock-rule in *Input/Output* so that it forwards symptom information to *Working Memory*. Ensure that each known symptom is represented in *Working Memory* as a separate element. That is, if several symptoms are known to be present, each symptom should be entered individually in *Working Memory*. ◇

The next phase in processing is the sequential application of Bayes' theorem. The theorem allows the information about only one symptom to be processed at a time. The order of processing symptoms is not important, provided given information is correctly tracked. The representation of the probabilities of hypotheses in *Working Memory*, as described above, ensures that this is the case. *Decision Procedure* requires one rule to select an unprocessed symptom for processing, and a second rule to calculate posterior probabilities of all hypotheses given the selected symptom. The pair of rules given in Box 6.1 is appropriate.

Two rules are required because the first should fire at most once on any cycle (i.e., for just one symptom), while the second rule should fire once for each disease (i.e., six times in the current task). The first rule randomly selects a symptom that is known to be present but that hasn't been processed. It triggers the second rule to process the selected symptom and records that the symptom has been processed. The two rules do not actually apply Bayes' theorem. Rather, they control the application of the theorem. The critical aspect of this control is the way the rules sequentially process symptoms, updating `probability`/3 clauses in *Working Memory* and extending the list of given symptoms on each processing cycle.

The control rules draw upon `probability_of_disease_given_symptom`/4, a user-defined condition, to perform the actual calculations required of Bayes' theorem. This condition takes a disease, a new symptom and a list of previously given symptoms, and returns the probability of the disease given all of the symptoms. It embodies Equation 6.1, and may be defined as in Box 6.1.

In the above `conditional_probability`/3 is assumed to consult *Oracle* to determine the conditional probability of a symptom given a disease, and to return a conditional probability of zero if there is no appropriate entry in *Oracle*. The calculations required of Equation 6.2 are assumed to be performed by `probability_of_symptom`/3, which takes the current context — i.e., the given symptoms that have already been processed — into account. A suitable definition is given in Box 6.1.

Exercise 6.5: Add the above rules and condition definitions to *Decision Procedure*. Complete the specification by defining `conditional_probability`/3 and

Rule 2 (unrefracted; once): *Select an unprocessed symptom and process it*
IF: `symptom(Symptom)` is in *Working Memory*
`not processed(Symptom)` is in *Working Memory*
THEN: send `process(Symptom)` to *Decision Procedure*
add `processed(Symptom)` to *Working Memory*

Rule 3 (unrefracted): *Process a symptom by applying Bayes' theorem*
TRIGGER: `process(S)`
IF: `probability(D, given(G), Prior)` is in *Working Memory*
`probability_of_disease_given_symptom(D, S, given(G), Post)`
THEN: delete `probability(D, given(G), Prior)` from *Working Memory*
add `probability(D, given([S|G]), Post)` to *Working Memory*

`probability_of_disease_given_symptom(D, S, G, Post) :-`
`probability(D, G, Prior)` is in *Working Memory*
`conditional_probability(D, S, CP)`
`probability_of_symptom(S, G, PS)`
`Post` is `(Prior) * (CP/PS)`

`probability_of_symptom(S, G, Prob) :-`
`L` is the list of all `X` such that `conditional_probability(D, S, C)`
`probability(D, G, P)` is in *Working Memory*
`X` is `C * P`
`Prob` is the sum of the elements of `L`

Box 6.1: Selected rules and condition definitions for applying Bayes' theorem (from *Decision Procedure*)

test the resulting partial model. If the rules are correct, *Working Memory* should be initialised with probabilities reflecting base-rates. On successive cycles these probabilities should be revised to incorporate given symptom information. ◇

Once all symptoms have been processed, the model must produce a diagnosis. The simplest approach to diagnosis is to select the most likely hypothesis (i.e., that with the greatest probability). A second common approach is to use the probabilities of the various hypotheses to bias selection. For example, if the evidence were to yield a 0.75 probability of disease 1 and a 0.25 probability of disease 2, then disease 1 would be offered as the diagnosis on 75% of occasions and disease 2 would be offered on 25% of occasions.

Exercise 6.6: Create rules in *Decision Procedure* that implement each of the approaches to diagnosis. Both rules should apply when all known symptoms have been processed, and both rules should result in the addition of a `diagnosis/1` element to *Working Memory*. However, only one of the two rules should be present in the model at a time. (Right-click on one of the rules and select **Ignore** or **Reinstate** to temporarily ignore the rule.) ◇

Exercise 6.7: The model requires one final rule (in *Input/Output*) to detect when a diagnosis has been reached and to forward that diagnosis to *Experimenter*. Add an appropriate rule and test the model over the full set of training trials by running the training script developed above. Training trails should be presented to the subject model in random order. The subject model should then perform the appropriate calculations and produce the correct diagnosis, with the probability of one diagnosis given the symptom information always being one and the probability of all other diagnoses given the symptom information always being zero. The model can therefore account for participant performance in the final blocks of the training phase (when participants achieve perfect accuracy). Also test the model on those transfer trials in which just one symptom is given. The model should diagnose in accordance with base-rates (again, in line with participant performance). What is the effect of the different diagnosis rules on diagnostic performance? ◇

In the transfer phase of Medin and Edelson's experiment participants were presented with three types of trials: single symptom trials (for each of the nine symptoms), pairs of conflicting symptoms (e.g., b, c), and triples of symptoms (e.g., a, b, c). Participants had not seen any of the conflicting pairs or triples in the training phase. Medin and Edelson were interested in the diagnoses given to such novel symptom combinations. Given a symptom combination of b and c, in which b had been seen (with a) with the relatively common disease 1 and c had been seen (with a) with the relatively rare disease 2, would participants show a preference towards the relatively common disease or the relatively rare disease? In this situation, participants favoured the relatively rare disease. Medin and Edelson's results are summarised in Table 6.2. Medin and Edelson argued that participant responses when two conflicting symptoms were presented conflicted with the underlying base-rates. The base-rate conflict was not present, however, when triples of conflicting symptoms were presented.

Exercise 6.8: Augment *Experimenter* with transfer trials consisting of conflicting pairs of symptoms (e.g., b, c; b, d) and the three symptom triples (a, b, c; d, e, f; g, h, i). Why does the Bayesian model fail when presented with conflicting symptoms? Adjust condition definitions as necessary to ensure that division by zero errors do not occur. ◇

Bayes' theorem uses cues in a maximally informative way. Thus, in the Medin and Edelson task, when symptoms b and c are present, the presence of symptom

Table 6.2: The proportion of responses for possible diagnoses given different symptom presentation conditions. Adapted from Medin and Edelson (1988).

Symptoms	Diagnosis		
	Common (e.g., 1)	Rare (e.g., 2)	Other
Conflicting pairs (e.g., b, c)	0.323	0.584	0.094
Triples (e.g., a, b, c)	0.708	0.281	0.010

b rules out disease 2, while the presence of symptom c rules out disease 1. A true Bayesian response in this case would therefore be to assert that the symptom configuration corresponds to none of the observed diseases. Alternatively, Medin and Edelson (1988) and Kruschke (1996) imply that the near normative response when symptom information conflicts is to select the most common of the two possible categories.

Exercise 6.9: Modify the model so that it responds appropriately when conflicting symptoms are presented. ◇

6.2.4 Learning in the Bayesian Model

In order to extend the basic Bayesian model of expert diagnostic performance to a model capable of learning it is necessary to add a mechanism for acquiring disease base-rate information and the conditional probabilities of symptoms given diseases. Both of these may be estimated from experience by counting disease cases and the co-occurrence of symptoms and diseases. Thus, the base-rate of a specific disease can be estimated by counting the number of cases of that disease and the total number of cases. The base-rate is approximated by the former divided by the latter. Similarly, for a given disease the conditional probabilities of symptoms given that disease may be estimated by counting the number of times a symptom is present for the disease and the total number of occurrences of the disease. The conditional probability will be approximated by the former divided by the latter. In both cases the approximation will improve as the number of observed cases of each disease increases.

Figure 6.4 shows a box and arrow diagram for a Bayesian subject module with learning. *Oracle* (from Figure 6.3) has been renamed *Knowledge Base*, and a further process, *Learning Mechanism*, has been added. *Knowledge Base* serves the same function as *Oracle*, but contains base-rate and co-occurrence information in a frequentistic format:

```
data(Disease, cases, P)
```

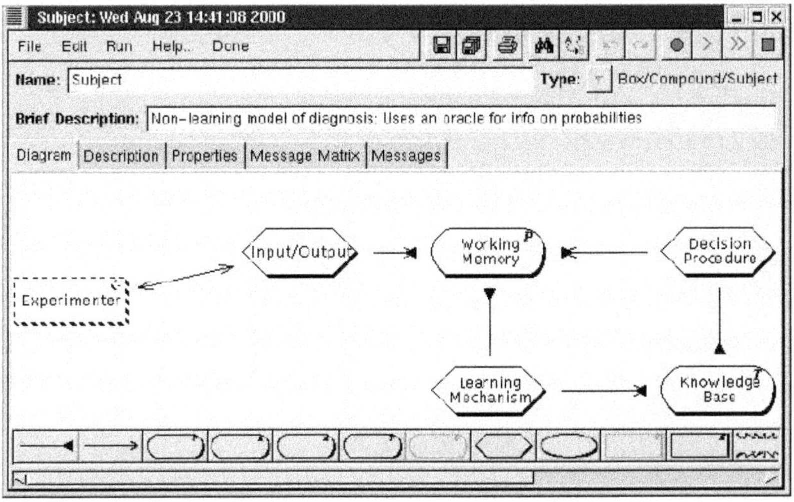

Figure 6.4: The box and arrow diagram for the Bayesian subject with learning

data(Disease, Symptom, N)

where P and N are integers. The first of these terms is interpreted as P cases of Disease have been observed. The second is interpreted as Disease has been observed to occur with Symptom on N occasions.

Exercise 6.10: Create a new version of the Bayesian model and modify the *Subject* box and arrow diagram as described above. Specify the initial contents of *Knowledge Base* (e.g., data(1, cases, 0), data(1, a, 0), data(1, b, 0), etc.). The rules and condition definitions in *Decision Procedure* that refer to *Knowledge Base* must also be modified to make use of the frequentistic representation. Modify the rules and condition definitions accordingly. Take care to avoid arithmetic division by zero errors. ◇

Exercise 6.11: Learning requires that the participant is given feedback of the correct diagnosis at the end of each training trial. Adjust *Experimenter* to give appropriate feedback to *Subject*. This will require addition of an arrow from *Collate Responses* (within *Experimenter*) to *Subject* and an additional rule in *Collate Responses* that sends the diagnosis to *Input/Output* (within *Subject*). ◇

Learning Mechanism must respond to the appearance of feedback in *Working Memory* and increment the appropriate frequencies in *Knowledge Base*. The three rules given in Box 6.2 are sufficient. Rule 1 detects feedback and triggers learning.

Rule 1 (refracted): *Trigger learning of current disease associations*
IF: `feedback(D)` is in *Working Memory*
THEN: send `learn(D)` to *Learning Mechanism*

Rule 2 (unrefracted): *Increment frequency counter for the current disease*
TRIGGER: `learn(disease(D))`
IF: `data(D, cases, X)` is in *Knowledge Base*
`X1` is `X + 1`
THEN: delete `data(D, cases, X)` from *Knowledge Base*
add `data(D, cases, X1)` to *Knowledge Base*

Rule 3 (unrefracted): *Increment frequency counter of disease/symptom pair*
TRIGGER: `learn(disease(D))`
IF: `symptom(S)` is in *Working Memory*
`data(D, S, N)` is in *Knowledge Base*
`N1` is `N + 1`
THEN: delete `data(D, S, N)` from *Knowledge Base*
add `data(D, S, N1)` to *Knowledge Base*

Box 6.2: Learning rules for the Bayesian model (from *Learning Mechanism*)

It is refracted because it should fire just once for any piece of feedback. Rule 2 updates the count of cases for the current disease. It fires once when triggered by Rule 1. Rule 3 updates the count for each symptom of the current disease. It is also triggered by Rule 1, but fires once for each known symptom.

Exercise 6.12: Add the above rules to *Learning Mechanism*. Ensure that the Initialisation property of *Knowledge Base* is set to Each Subject, so that base-rate and co-occurrence information is accumulated in *Knowledge Base* across trials and blocks. Test the model by running a series of blocks. Check that *Knowledge Base* correctly accumulates frequency statistics on each trial. Categorisation accuracy should also improve from approximately 60% on the first block to 100% on the second block. ◇

Exercise 6.13: Augment *Experimenter* with graph facilities to show diagnostic accuracy as a function of block. ◇

6.2.5 An Associationist Model of Medical Diagnosis

Background

A rather different approach to categorisation and medical diagnosis stems from the associationist tradition (Hull, 1920). From this perspective, categorisation is based on the summation of weighted cues, where cue weights approximately reflect the correlation between cues and categories. Thus, in the case of medical diagnosis, a symptom that is strongly positively correlated with one disease, uncorrelated with a second disease, and strongly negatively correlated with a third disease, would have a high positive weight for the first disease, zero weight for the second disease, and a high negative weight for the third disease. Associationist models of this sort may be implemented through the use of a two-layer feed-forward network that maps cues to categories, as shown in Figure 6.5.

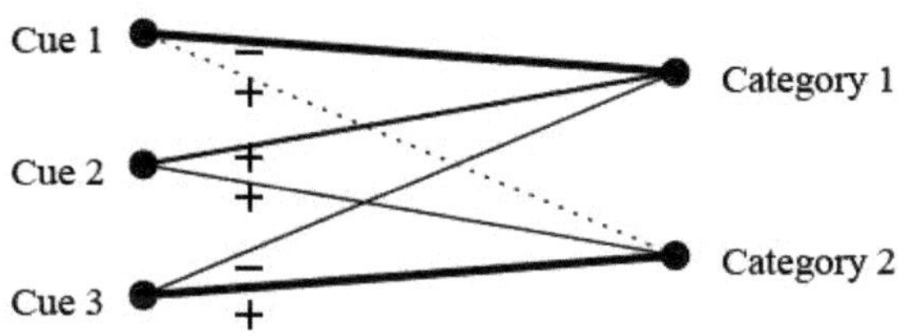

Figure 6.5: A two-layer feed-forward network mapping three cues (or symptoms) to two categories (or diseases). The thickness of lines reflects the strength of weighting. The sign of weighting is indicated by the '+' and '−' annotations. Thus, there is a strong negative association between Cue 1 and Category 1, and a weak positive association between Cue 1 and Category 2. Processing in the network is initiated by presentation of a pattern of activations representing given cues at the left. Activation then flows from left to right, resulting in activation of one (or more) category nodes.

One advantage of two-layer feed-forward networks is that simple learning rules with well-understood convergence properties exist. These learning rules (the Hebbian learning rule and the delta-rule: see Hertz *et al.*, 1991) allow mappings from cues to categories to be acquired through exposure to a set of cases. Associationist models, like Bayesian models, can therefore provide an account of both the training and the transfer phase of Medin and Edelson's task. More importantly, however, the rate of learning in associationist models can be varied. Such models can therefore provide an account of individual differences in learning. For example, the best of Medin and Edelson's participants required 5 blocks to learn the task, but some participants required as many as 13 blocks. This difference may be attributed to differences in participants' learning rates. (Note that the Bayesian learning model achieves perfect performance on the second block of the task, but there is no simple way of adjusting or slowing learning in the Bayesian model.)

An associationist model should also provide a more reasonable account of behaviour when conflicting symptoms are presented. Such cases should not be possible if the training stimuli cover all possible symptom/disease combinations. In the Bayesian model this leads to division by zero errors in the application of Bayes' theorem, and strictly speaking the Bayesian model is therefore unable to predict human behaviour in these cases. The associationist model works by summing the weighted cues. Consequently it is able to produce an answer no matter what symptom combination is presented.

There are disadvantages, however, with the associationist approach. First, there are limits on the complexity of cue-category mappings that may be represented within a two-layer network. While these limits do not apply to networks with "hidden layers" that mediate between the input and output layers, such networks (and mappings) require more complex learning algorithms. These algorithms generally require thousands of exposures to the complete set of cases (see Hertz *et al.*, 1991) and are generally regarded as psychologically and biologically implausible (e.g., Crick, 1989). A second disadvantage of the associationist approach concerns the place of base-rate information. It is not immediately clear how different base-rates of categories can be represented by weighted cue-category associations. We will see, however, by developing an associationist model of Medin and Edelson's task, that this disadvantage is only apparent: associationist models can show base-rate effects.

The Associationist Experimenter Module

The *Experimenter* module developed in the previous sections embodies the stimulus presentation and response collation functions required of the Medin and Edelson task. It is not specific to the Bayesian approach to the task. In developing an associationist model of the task within COGENT it is therefore appropriate to copy the complete Bayesian model and modify the copy by adding and deleting components within *Subject*.

Exercise 6.14: Use the "copy model" function within the research programme manager to create a copy of the Bayesian model. Rename it in preparation for modification to an associationist model. ◇

The Associationist Subject Module

Figure 6.6 shows the box and arrow structure of an associationist *Subject* module. Much of the basic structure is shared with the Bayesian model (Figure 6.4). *Working Memory* is still required to hold information on the symptoms present and the eventual diagnosis. *Input/Output* is still required to enter information into

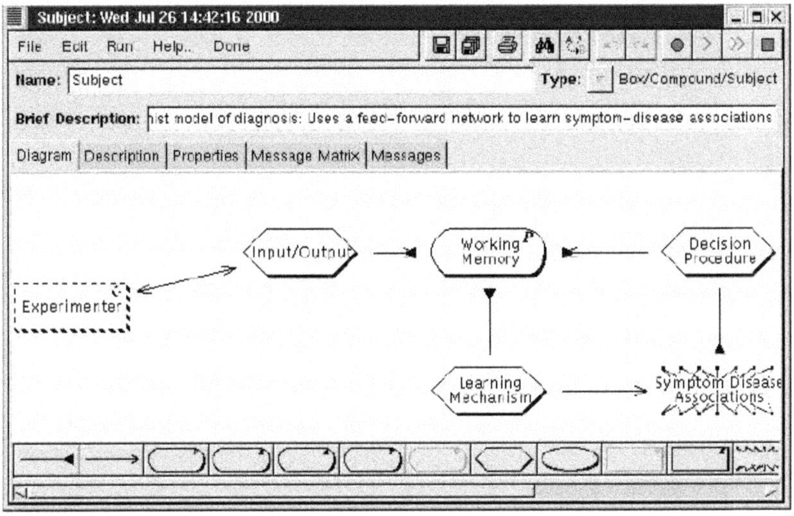

Figure 6.6: The box and arrow diagram for the associationist subject

Working Memory and to send diagnoses to *Experimenter*. The only difference is *Symptom Disease Associations*, a two-layer feed-forward network that is used to map a representation of the symptoms present in any particular case to a representation of the diagnosis. *Decision Procedure* is required to encode the symptoms that are present in a format suitable for use by the feed-forward network, and to decode the output of the network into a disease name. *Learning Mechanism* acts on feedback sent to *Input/Output* by *Experimenter*. It assembles the symptoms and correct diagnosis into appropriate representations for *Symptom Disease Associations* and uses those representations to train the network.

Exercise 6.15: Edit the associationist *Subject*'s box and arrow diagram so that it matches Figure 6.6. ◇

Symptom Disease Associations is required to map symptom patterns to diagnoses. There are nine possible symptoms and six possible diseases. *Symptom Disease Associations* therefore requires an input vector width of nine (i.e., one input node per symptom) and an output vector width of six (i.e., one output node per disease). The network is also required to learn over multiple exposures to the stimulus materials. It should therefore be set to initialise on Each Subject (rather than on Each Trial, as is the default).

For simplicity we assume that the first input node of *Symptom Disease Associations* corresponds to symptom a, the second input node to symptom b, and so on, and the first output node to disease 1, the second output node to disease

Rule 1 (unrefracted; once): *Query the network with the given symptoms*
IF: exists `symptom(X)` is in *Working Memory*
not `diagnosis(D)` is in *Working Memory*
`make_canonical_symptom_vector(SymVec)`
`test(SymVec, DisVec)` is in *Symptom Disease Associations*
`best_disease(DisVec, Disease)`
THEN: add `diagnosis(Disease)` to *Working Memory*

Box 6.3: A rule for querying the network (from *Decision Procedure*)

2, and so on. Assuming the default range of activation values (-1 to $+1$), a case with symptoms a and c present would correspond to an input vector of $[+1, -1, +1, -1, -1, -1, -1, -1, -1]$, and a case of disease 3 would correspond to an output vector of $[-1, -1, +1, -1, -1, -1]$.

The key function of *Decision Procedure* is to determine the disease that is most activated given a set of cues and to add that disease, as the diagnosis, to *Working Memory*. This can be achieved with a single rule (see Box 6.3). The first two conditions prevent the rule from firing before symptoms have been presented or after a diagnosis has been given. The third condition is a user-defined condition that builds a canonical vector representation for the current symptom configuration. This condition must reference *Working Memory* to determine which symptoms are present and which symptoms are not, and use this information to form the appropriate vector representation for presentation to *Symptom Disease Associations* (i.e., with nine components as described above), which is bound to `SymVec`. The fourth condition determines the network's response to `SymVec` and binds this to `DisVec`, which is decoded by the fifth condition, `best_disease/2`, into a single preferred diagnosis. The rule then adds this diagnosis to *Working Memory*.

Exercise 6.16: Add Rule 1 from Box 6.3 and appropriate condition definitions to *Decision Procedure*. Test the model by ensuring that input stimuli are correctly encoded, passed to the network and decoded. Note that because there is no learning in the system it should produce random responses. ◇

Learning by the Associationist Subject

The single function required of *Learning Mechanism* is to train the feed-forward network (*Symptom Disease Associations*) with the symptom/disease association corresponding to the current case. Again, a single rule is adequate (see Box 6.4). This rule is activated by the appearance of feedback specifying the correct diagnosis appearing in *Working Memory*. The second condition replicates the condition in *Decision Procedure* that maps the symptoms for the current case to a symptom

Rule 1 (refracted): *Trigger learning of current disease associations*
IF: `feedback(disease(D))` is in *Working Memory*
`make_canonical_symptom_vector(SymVec)`
`make_canonical_disease_vector(D,DisVec)`
THEN: send `train(SymVec,DisVec)` to *Symptom Disease Associations*

Box 6.4: A rule for training the network (from *Learning Mechanism*)

vector, and the third condition performs a similar translation of representations for the given disease. The rule's single action results in a training message being sent to *Symptom Disease Associations*. When a feed-forward network receives such a message, it uses Hebbian or delta-rule learning to change the strengths of cue/category weights such that they more closely mirror those required to correctly diagnose the current case.

Exercise 6.17: Add Rule 1 from Box 6.4 and appropriate condition definitions to *Learning Mechanism*. Also set the appropriate properties of *Symptom Disease Associations*. Test the model on the training trials. The model should achieve perfect diagnostic performance after five or six runs through the entire training set. Experiment with the model by altering the **Learning Rate** property and the **Learning Rule** property of *Symptom Disease Associations*. How do these properties affect performance of the model during the training phase? ◇

Exercise 6.18: Extend *Experimenter* so that it produces a table of symptoms/diagnoses similar to Table 6.2 during the transfer phase (but also incorporating data from single symptom presentations). Be sure that the table merges symptoms and diagnoses by type (as in Table 6.2). Examine the behaviour of the fully trained model on transfer trials. To what extent does the model reproduce the behaviour of Medin and Edelson's participants? By default the weights in a feed-forward network are initialised to values uniformly distributed between -1 and $+1$. Explore the effect of changing the initial weight distribution such that weights are initially closer to 0 (e.g., through using a uniform distribution between -0.1 and $+0.1$, or through using a normal distribution with mean 0.0 and standard deviation 0.1). ◇

The behaviour of the feed-forward network model is highly dependent on the network's initial weights and its learning rate. However, all model variants that employ the delta learning rule should eventually achieve perfect diagnostic accuracy on the training trials (with the number of trials required before perfect accuracy is achieved depending on the learning rate). Behaviour in the transfer condition depends on other parameters. Crucially, the initial association weights must be near zero if the network is to transfer appropriately to cases in which a single symptom is presented. High initial weights may lead to appropriate diagnostic behaviour on the training trials but anomalous behaviour on the transfer trials (in which a single symptom may result in a diagnosis of an entirely unrelated disease).

The initial weights reflect prior beliefs about the relationships between symptoms and diseases. It is reasonable to assume that participants have no prior task-relevant beliefs, and hence the assumption of near zero initial weights would appear to be valid.

If the initial weights are close to zero, and the learning rate is sufficiently high, then the model should frequently (though not universally) yield the complete transfer pattern reported by Medin and Edelson (1988) and reproduced above. In the case of symptoms a, b, and c, this pattern consists of:

- diagnosing the common disease (disease 1) when a and b are presented together, when a is presented in isolation, when b is presented in isolation, or when a, b, and c are presented.
- diagnosing the rare disease (disease 2) when a and c are presented together, when c is presented in isolation, or when b and c are presented together.

The explanation for this within the feed-forward network model derives from the mathematics of the delta learning rule. This rule specifies how associative weights are adjusted during learning. Critically, the magnitude of adjustment to any weight is proportional to the size of error attributable to that weight. The different frequencies of category presentation generally lead to moderately strong positive associative links being formed between, for example, symptom a and disease 1 and symptom b and disease 1, but a negative associative link being formed between symptom a and disease 2 (because on three out of four trials symptom a occurs with disease 2 being absent). The associative link between symptom c and disease 2 must compensate for the negative link between symptom a and disease 2, and so becomes very strong. When b and c are presented together, the strength of the link between c and 2 outweighs that between b and 1, and so disease 2 is preferred over disease 1.

Exercise 6.19: Explore the behaviour of the model when the learning rate is greater than 1. Why might the model be unable to learn the training trials when the learning rate is high? ◇

One final issue raised by the associationist model of the diagnosis task concerns the treatment of symptoms that are absent. The Bayesian model ignored absent symptoms because information about symptom absence was not factored into its calculations. However, in many cases the absence of a symptom could be just as informative as the presence of a symptom.

In the above associationist model it has been assumed that if a symptom is present it is coded as $+1$ in the input vector and if it is absent it is coded as

-1. This means that the model may learn to use information about symptom absence. This may seem reasonable, but psychological evidence suggests that the absence of evidence is frequently ignored in decision making and categorisation tasks (e.g., Wason & Johnson-Laird, 1972; Hunt & Rouse, 1981). It has therefore been suggested that the absence of a symptom (and the absence of a disease) should be coded as 0, rather than -1 (e.g., Kruschke, 1996). Such a change of coding will impact upon delta-rule learning, because learning only occurs with non-zero input.

Exercise 6.20: Explore the effect of ignoring absent symptoms by changing the coding of absent symptoms to 0 instead of -1. How does this change in coding impact upon the performance of the model? ◇

6.2.6 Bayesian and Associationist Approaches Compared

The development of competing models of Medin and Edelson's medical diagnosis task clarifies the strengths and weaknesses of both the models and the approaches on which they are based. Both approaches are able to capture the behaviour of participants at the end of the training phase. Both approaches also provide an account of how participants progress from an initial state to that final state. However, the models do this in different ways. The Bayesian model collects co-occurrence information, and learns all symptom/disease associations after one block. This perfect learning is implausible as Medin and Edelson (1988) found that participants took from 5 to 13 blocks to acquire the task. The associationist model includes a parameter, the learning rate. This parameter allows learning to be slowed to a rate comparable to that of participants.

The Bayesian model must be augmented if it is to provide a reasonable account of learning. Such augmentations might include adding performance factors that limit the collection of symptom/disease co-occurrence information. In this sense there is a sharp distinction between competence and performance within the Bayesian model. The associationist model, by contrast, is purely a performance model: there is no value of learning rate parameter which would transform the associationist model into an idealised, competence model.

A second substantial difference between the approaches concerns their treatment of conflicting information in the transfer phase of the experiment. The associationist model handles symptom conflicts transparently: it is not even able to detect when conflicts occur. The Bayesian model, by contrast, predicts that all diseases are absent in the case of conflicting symptom information. Arguably this is the wrong response, given that Medin and Edelson's participants were able to provide responses in all trials, and given that there was consistency in those responses.

On this brief comparison, then, the associationist approach with its emphasis on associations between symptoms and diseases rather than on conditional probabilities of symptoms given diseases, would appear to provide a slightly superior account of behaviour on Medin and Edelson's task. The associationist model is far from perfect, however. The slow learning of Medin and Edelson's participants suggests a low learning rate, but the inverse base-rate effect shown on transfer trials only appears to arise when the learning rate is high. Thus, the associationist model, as it stands, has a significant weakness.

6.2.7 Related Work on Network Models of Categorisation

The relatively simple two-layer feed-forward network model of categorisation developed above is basically the "component cue" model proposed by Gluck and Bower (1988). They use the model to successfully account for base-rate effects in a somewhat different experimental paradigm (one that did not involve presentation of conflicting symptom information). The model performs less well in Medin and Edelson's task. While it does on occasions yield appropriate performance, such performance is by no means a necessary consequence of the model — it is dependent upon judicious selection of the initial network weights and the learning rate parameter — and it is unclear if a single value of the learning rate can capture both the observed rate of learning and the observed inverse base-rate effect.

An extended network model that accounts for the results of both Gluck and Bower (1988) and Medin and Edelson (1988) (as well as some additional findings) is presented by Kruschke (1996). Kruschke argues that the effect of different base-rates is that common categories are learnt first, that what one knows affects what one learns, and that one therefore learns different things about rare categories (e.g., that rare symptoms, such as c in the present case, are highly diagnostic when they are associated with rare diseases, such as disease 2).

Kruschke's model extends that developed above in two ways. First, attentional weights are added to cues. Essentially cues are seen as competing for diagnosticity, with some cues being more diagnostic in certain situations than others. This theme of competing cues is also apparent in the work of both Gluck and Bower (1988) and Medin and Edelson (1988). Kruschke provides appropriate mathematics to describe how the attentional weights are initialised and modified through experience. Kruschke's second innovation is the imposition of a choice function on the disease nodes that allows selection of a disease even if its node is not the most active disease node. This function is similar in spirit to the alternative diagnosis rule discussed in the context of the Bayesian model in Exercise 6.6.

6.3 Incorporating Cue Selection

The medical diagnosis task considered above illustrates some of the basic effects of base-rates, but the task is not intended to mimic the complexity of the diagnosis task faced by a physician. One simplification made in Medin and Edelson's task is in the assumption that all symptoms that are present are known and simultaneously available when forming the diagnosis. Real world diagnosis (including both medical diagnosis and other forms of fault diagnosis such as that engaged in by an automotive mechanic) often involves active elicitation of information by the diagnostician. In the medical domain, this may involve asking a patient about the presence or absence of specific (possibly secondary) symptoms, or performing various tests (ranging from taking a patient's temperature to ordering a blood test or a radiographic scan). Categorisation is therefore only one aspect of diagnosis. Cue selection (i.e., the choice of which symptom to query or which test to perform) is another, and both Bayesian and feed-forward network models may be adapted to incorporate this aspect of the task.

6.3.1 A Sequential Diagnosis Task

Fox (1980) explored cue selection in a simulated medical diagnosis task similar to that employed by Medin and Edelson (1988). The primary aim of participants in Fox's task was to diagnose one of five diseases on the basis of information concerning up to five symptoms. However, participants were initially presented with information about just one symptom. They were then able to query further symptoms, if necessary, before making their diagnosis, but were encouraged to only query those symptoms necessary for making that diagnosis. Diagnostic feedback was given after each trial, allowing participants to learn the symptom/disease associations.

Fox was concerned with the formation of cue selection strategies, rather than base-rate effects. Consequently all diseases within his experiment were equally common. Fox also used symptoms that were unreliable predictors of diseases. Thus, one cue (e.g., headache) might occur with most, but not all, cases of a category (e.g., meningitis). The structure of symptom/disease associations meant that perfect diagnostic accuracy was not necessarily possible. Some symptom patterns were genuinely ambiguous. Despite these ambiguities, participants were able to achieve high rates of diagnostic accuracy (approximately 80%) after sufficient training. Participants also exhibited clear symptom querying strategies, showing behaviours that were dependent upon the initial presenting symptom. Some presenting symptoms led to predictable querying of other symptoms, while other presenting symptoms led to the immediate offering of a diagnosis.

The extended diagnosis task of Fox (1980) yields rich data, including categorisation (or diagnostic) accuracy, mean number of symptoms queried in order

Table 6.3: Conditional probabilities of symptoms given diseases in each condition for Yule *et al.*'s diagnosis experiment

a) Sparse Condition

		Disease			
		Mesiopathy	Ritengitis	Katalgia	Bonanoma
Symptom	diarrhoea	0.00	0.50	0.00	1.00
	fever	1.00	0.00	0.00	0.00
	headache	0.25	1.00	0.00	0.25
	paralysis	0.25	1.00	0.25	0.00
	vomiting	0.00	0.50	1.00	0.00

b) Dense Condition

		Disease			
		Mesiopathy	Ritengitis	Katalgia	Bonanoma
Symptom	diarrhoea	1.00	0.50	1.00	0.00
	fever	0.00	1.00	1.00	1.00
	headache	0.75	0.00	1.00	0.75
	paralysis	0.75	0.00	0.75	1.00
	vomiting	1.00	0.50	0.00	1.00

to reach a diagnosis, and symptom query biases. However, Fox only reported data for final block performance. Data on learning was presented by Yule, Cooper, and Fox (1998) (see also Cooper & Fox, 1997). It is this data that we consider in developing and evaluating models of cue selection.

Two experimental conditions were considered. In the "sparse" condition, relatively few symptoms were associated with each disease (1.75 on average). In the "dense" condition, relatively many symptoms were associated with each disease (3.25 on average). Table 6.3 presents the conditional probabilities of symptoms given diseases in each of the two conditions. From a structural perspective, the conditions were symmetric in that, for all symptom/disease pairs, the conditional probability of a symptom being present given a disease in one condition was equal to the conditional probability of the same symptom being absent given the disease in the other condition. Equal diagnostic accuracy was therefore possible in the two conditions.

The experiment consisted of four blocks, with twenty trials (comprising five cases of each disease) per block. Participants were initially presented with a single symptom (e.g., vomiting). They were then required to query further symptoms as necessary. At any point during the trial they could offer a diagnosis, whereupon

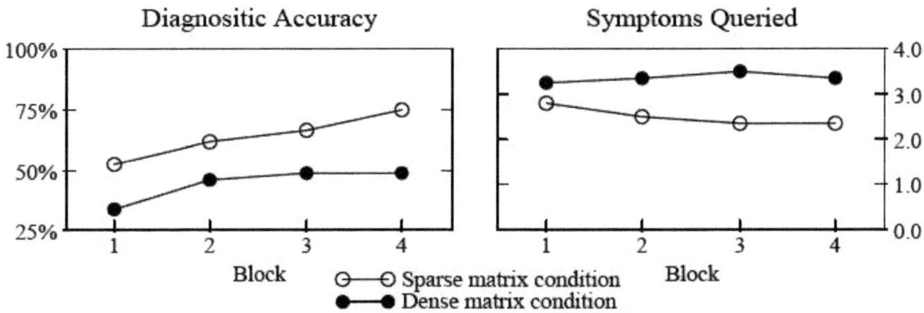

Figure 6.7: Mean diagnostic accuracy and number of symptoms queried for sparse and dense experimental conditions, as obtained by Yule *et al.* (1998)

the trial was terminated and they were told the correct diagnosis. Forty participants completed the experiment, with twenty in each condition.

Figure 6.7 summarises the effects of block on diagnostic accuracy and number of symptoms queried under the two experimental conditions. Most participants showed increasing diagnostic accuracy with block, indicating that they were learning the task. However, in the sparse condition learning continued throughout all four blocks, with diagnostic accuracy reaching 75% in the final block. Diagnostic accuracy was significantly lower in the dense condition, and levelled off after the second block at 50%. Condition (dense or sparse) also had an effect on the number of symptoms queried, with a mean of 3.38 (out of 4) symptoms being queried in the dense condition compared with a mean of 2.52 symptom queries in the sparse condition (despite poorer diagnostic accuracy in the dense condition). Query rates decreased with block in the sparse condition (again indicative of learning or increased diagnostic efficiency) but rose in the dense condition. The condition manipulation therefore had a substantial effect upon participant performance. Despite the informational equivalence of the two conditions, participants in the sparse condition achieved higher diagnostic accuracy using fewer symptom queries than participants in the dense condition.

Several biases were apparent in the participants' responses to the initial presenting symptom. In the dense condition the strongest biases were a general tendency to query further symptoms rather than immediately give a diagnosis, and a specific tendency to query diarrhoea when the presenting symptom was headache.

More specific biases were apparent in the sparse condition. When the presenting symptom was diarrhoea the dominant response was to diagnose bonanoma. When the presenting symptom was fever the dominant response was to diagnose mesiopathy. Additionally in this case participants avoided querying diarrhoea. When the presenting symptom was headache participants showed an aversion to making an immediate diagnosis, and an aversion to querying paralysis. When the presenting symptom was paralysis the preference was either to query vomiting or to diagnose ritengitis, and the aversion was towards querying the presence of fever. Finally, when the presenting symptom was vomiting there was a tendency to either diagnose katalgia or seek further information.

Many of the biases can be understood in terms of Table 6.3. For example, when in the sparse condition diarrhoea is the presenting symptom, one can see from the table that the hypothetical patient must be suffering either from ritengitis (as diarrhoea occurs with 50% of such cases) or bonanoma (which is always accompanied by diarrhoea). The tendency to diagnose bonanoma is justified to the extent that it is the most likely diagnosis. However, a more conservative approach would be to query paralysis, which occurs with all cases of ritengitis and no cases of bonanoma, and so discriminates between the competing diagnoses.

The presence of biases in participant behaviour suggests that participants were able to form some kind of internal representation of the relevant half of Table 6.3, and use this to guide their cue selection behaviour. The question is: what format does this internal representation take? Is it a table of conditional probabilities as required by a Bayesian approach, is it embodied in a network of associative weights relating symptoms and disease as required by the feed-forward network approach, or does it take some other form?

Exercise 6.21: Develop an experimenter module and a corresponding experiment script to administer Yule *et al.*'s experiment. The module should begin each trial by selecting a disease at random (subject to the constraint that all diseases should be sampled five times within each block of twenty trials) and assembling a set of symptoms for that disease according to the conditional probabilities in Table 6.3a or 6.3b. The module should function in one of two modes — sparse or dense — corresponding to the two experimental conditions. This mode could be specified as a user-defined property of the main experimenter sub-process.

The experimenter module should then present one symptom to the subject module and wait for the participant's response. Assume that the participant can give either of two responses, corresponding to querying a further symptom or offering a diagnosis. The experimenter should respond to either appropriately (recording and answering the query or recording the diagnosis and providing feedback in the form of the actual disease). The experimenter should also maintain and tabulate or graph the following statistics for each block of twenty trials: mean diagnostic accuracy, mean number of symptom queries, and first action (symptom queried or diagnosis offered).

The experiment script should initially run just one subject in each condition. This script will therefore: initialise an experiment, set the condition or mode of the experimenter to `sparse`, run one subject (i.e., initialise a subject, run four blocks, each consisting of initialising the block, running 20 trials and terminating the block, and terminate the subject), set the condition or mode of the experimenter to `dense`, run another subject, and terminate the experiment. It will be necessary to develop a mock subject module in order to complete this exercise. In the first instance, this module might produce random responses to symptom information, including both diagnoses and symptom queries. ◇

6.3.2 Cue Selection in the Bayesian Model

Cue selection may be incorporated into the Bayesian approach through the information theory developed by Shannon (1948) and Wiener (1948) (see also Shannon & Weaver, 1949). Information theory gives a mathematical measure of the expected amount of information conveyed by a given set of cue values. Given any set of known cue values, one may calculate the expected information gain resulting from knowing the value of each remaining cue. The mathematically optimal cue to select is then the cue leading to the greatest expected information gain (also known as the cue with the greatest informativeness).

The expected informativeness of a symptom S is given by a standard formula (due to Shannon and Wiener):

$$\mathrm{I(S)} = \sum_{x} \left[\sum_{i} \{\mathrm{P(D}_i \mid \mathrm{S}^x) \times \log(\mathrm{P(D}_i \mid \mathrm{S}^x))\} \times \mathrm{P(S}^x) \right] - \sum_{i} \mathrm{P(D}_i) \times \log(\mathrm{P(D}_i)) \tag{6.3}$$

where D_i ranges over the possible diseases, x ranges over the possible values of the symptom (i.e., `present` or `absent`), and:

$$\mathrm{P(S}^x) = \sum_{i} \mathrm{P(S}^x \mid \mathrm{D}_i) \times \mathrm{P(D}_i) \tag{6.4}$$

The formula is effectively a weighted average of the total information given the presence or absence of the symptom S, less the total prior information, where the total information in a situation is given by the sum over all hypotheses H of $\mathrm{P(H)} \times \log(\mathrm{P(H)})$.

Calculation of the informativeness of each cue requires knowledge of the probabilities of the various categories and the conditional probabilities of cues given categories. This is the same knowledge required to apply Bayes' theorem. Thus, calculation of informativeness requires nothing beyond what is already available.

Fox (1980) used Equation 6.3 to provide a normative model of participant performance (see also Lindley, 1956). It has recently received further attention through its use by Oaksford and Chater (1994) in accounting for a wide range of robust selection biases in numerous variants of Wason's (1968) four-card selection task.

The basic functional architecture used to implement the Bayesian approach to categorisation with full symptom information (Figure 6.3) may also be used to implement the information theoretic approach to cue selection within categorisation. If we assume that the subject module has complete and accurate information

```
probability_of_disease_given_symptom(D,S/V,G,Post) :-
    probability(D,G,Prior) is in Working Memory
    conditional_probability(D,S/V,CP)
    probability_of_symptom(S/V,G,PS)
    Post is (Prior) * (CP/PS)
```

Box 6.5: A definition of `probability_of_disease_given_symptom/4` that incorporates valence

about both base-rates and the conditional probabilities of cues given categories, then the subject module must go through the following steps:

1. Calculate initial (prior) probabilities for all categories. These prior probabilities will reflect the base-rates of the categories. This step is shared by the earlier model of categorisation without cue selection.
2. When knowledge of a cue value is obtained (either through being told a presenting symptom or, later, through a response to an explicit query from the participant) the probabilities for all categories should be revised in the light of the new evidence. As in the earlier model this consists of the direct application of Bayes' theorem. However, the cue-selecting model must be able to revise the probabilities of all diseases on discovering that a symptom is *absent*. (The earlier model only dealt with discovering symptoms to be present.)
3. When the subject module has revised probabilities of all diseases, it must either commit to one category (i.e., make a diagnosis) or select a symptom to query. One approach is to assume that if the probability of the case being an instance of any single category is sufficiently high (e.g., more than 0.90), then the subject module should commit to that category, otherwise it should select a symptom to query. This approach requires a free parameter — a categorisation threshold — that may be adjusted as necessary. If the threshold is high, the model is likely to query more symptoms and achieve greater diagnostic accuracy than if the threshold is low.
4. If the subject module opts to query a symptom, it must calculate the informativeness of each symptom (using Equation 6.3), select the symptom with the greatest informativeness, and send a query for that symptom to the experimenter module.

The first two of these steps are shared with the simple Bayesian model of categorisation without cue selection. However, the task requires that both present and absent symptoms be represented within *Working Memory*, and that all rules and condition definitions in *Decision Procedure* are sensitive to the valence (i.e., presence/absence) of symptoms.

Rule 4 (unrefracted; once): *Select query or diagnosis*
TRIGGER: `system_quiescent`
IF: not `say(diagnosis(_))` is in *Working Memory*
`query_or_diagnose(Action)`
THEN: send `Action` to *Decision Procedure*

Box 6.6: A rule for triggering the subject's response to quiescence (from *Decision Procedure*)

Box 6.5 shows how `probability_of_disease_given_symptom`/4 might be redefined to incorporate valence. Here, symptom and valence information is represented in a structured term of the form `S/V`. Such a term could match with, for example, `vomiting/absent`, binding `S` to `vomiting` and `V` to `absent`. Similar revisions will be required for other user-defined conditions that use symptom information to calculate probabilities (e.g., `conditional_probability`/3 and `probability_of_symptom`/3).

Exercise 6.22: Create a new model based on the infrastructure developed in Exercise 6.21. Populate *Subject* (see Figure 6.3) and add the necessary rules and condition definitions to *Decision Procedure* for the first two of the above steps (referring to rules from earlier models where necessary). Be sure that all rules and condition definitions are sensitive to symptom valence. Note also that for full generality *Oracle* will need to contain the relevant information for both experimental conditions, and *Decision Procedure* will need to select the information for the current condition from *Oracle*. (This may be achieved by creating a user-defined property within *Decision Procedure* to mirror that within the experimenter module.) Ensure that the model correctly calculates the posterior probabilities of all diseases for each presenting symptom in both experimental conditions. ◇

Once the model has calculated the posterior probabilities of all diseases it will quiesce. That is, no further rules will be applicable, and processing will stop. Thus, the next stage of processing (selecting between querying another symptom or offering a diagnosis) may be triggered by system quiescence. Rule 4 (Box 6.6) is sufficient. The rule employs a user-defined condition, `query_or_diagnose`/1, to determine which processing stage should follow. If the probability of any disease exceeds the categorisation threshold, or if all symptoms have already been queried, then the model should diagnose. Otherwise it should query. The rule assumes that both diagnosis and querying are implemented through separate triggered rules within *Decision Procedure*.

The use of the `system_quiescent` trigger by the query/diagnosis selection rule means that the rule may fire whenever the system is quiescent. The rule is

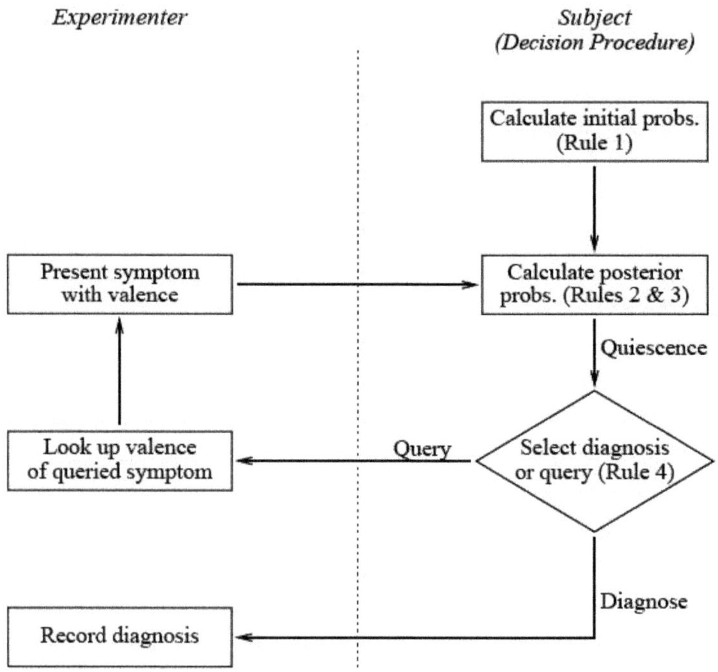

Figure 6.8: The flow of control between *Experimenter* and *Subject* induced by the cue-selection task. Note in particular the loop between *Subject* and *Experimenter* that results when a symptom is queried.

marked once so that, when it fires, it generates a single action (either `query` or `diagnose`). If the action is `query`, *Experimenter* should respond to the query, allowing *Decision Procedure* to revise the disease probabilities through the rules specified in Exercise 6.22. The system will then again reach quiescence, triggering the query/diagnosis selection rule and causing the process to repeat. The check that `say(diagnosis(_))` is not in *Working Memory* prevents the rule from firing again after a diagnosis has been reached. The flow of control between *Experimenter* and rules within the subject module's *Decision Procedure* is shown in Figure 6.8.

Exercise 6.23: Add a user-defined property specifying the categorisation threshold, an appropriate definition for `query_or_diagnose/1`, and the above rule to *Decision Procedure*. The condition should bind its single argument to `diagnose` when it is appropriate to make a diagnosis (i.e., when the probability of any disease exceeds the categorisation threshold or when all symptoms have been queried) and to `query` otherwise. ◇

The diagnosis rule is straightforward (see Rule 5 of Box 6.7). When triggered, it should select the most likely disease and add a term indicating this as the diagnosis to *Working Memory*. The pair of negated terms in this rule ensures that no disease (`Disease2`) has a probability that is greater than the probability of `Disease1`.

The query rule (Rule 6 of Box 6.7) requires calculation of the informativeness of each symptom whose valence is unknown, followed by selection of the symptom with greatest informativeness. (Note that the informativeness of any symptom whose valence is known should be zero.) While this might be performed by a single rule, the process is clarified by implementing it with two separate rules. The first of these rules employs a user-defined condition to calculate informativeness and stores the results in *Working Memory*. The second rule (Rule 7 of Box 6.7) selects the most informative symptom to query, using an approach analogous to that used in Rule 5 above to select the most likely disease.

Rule 6 refers to *Prior Task Knowledge*, a propositional buffer containing the names of all possible symptoms. This is necessary to ensure that all symptoms are considered, and plausible because participants attempting the task are given the set of possible symptoms. The rule also draws on `informativeness/2`, a user-defined condition that uses Equation 6.3 to calculate the informativeness of a symptom. This calculation may be simplified by noting that in the current context Equation 6.3 may be rewritten as Equation 6.5:

$$\mathrm{I(S)} = \sum_i \left\{ \begin{array}{l} \mathrm{P(D}_i \mid \mathrm{S}^{pres.}) \times \log(\mathrm{P(D}_i \mid \mathrm{S}^{pres.})) \times \mathrm{P(S}^{pres.}) \ + \\ \mathrm{P(D}_i \mid \mathrm{S}^{abs.}) \times \log(\mathrm{P(D}_i \mid \mathrm{S}^{abs.})) \times \mathrm{P(S}^{abs.}) \ - \\ \mathrm{P(D}_i) \times \log(\mathrm{P(D}_i)) \end{array} \right\} \tag{6.5}$$

This equation requires calculating and summing the central term for each possible disease. If we assume that *Prior Task Knowledge* also contains the names of all possible diseases, then the summation aspect of the calculation of informativeness may be handled as in the definition of `informativeness/2` of Box 6.7.

The central term in Equation 6.5 reflects the expected impact of knowing the symptom's valence on the information gain with respect to each disease. Each element in the term is required in the standard application of Bayes' theorem, and hence further user-defined conditions are not required for each element: the user-defined conditions previously defined for the application of Bayes' theorem may be re-used. The definition of `informativeness_for_disease/3` given in Box 6.7 is therefore suitable. This definition relies upon one final user-defined condition, `x_logx/2`, to compute $x \times \log(x)$ for any value of x. It is crucial that this condition behave appropriately when x is zero. (Note that $\log(0)$ is undefined, and attempting to compute $\log(0)$ will cause an arithmetic error, but $0 \times \log(0)$ is equal to 0.)

Rule 5 (unrefracted): *Offer a diagnosis if possible*
TRIGGER: `diagnose`
IF: `probability(Disease1, Givens, P1)` is in *Working Memory*
not `probability(Disease2, Givens, P2)` is in *Working Memory*
`P2 > P1`
THEN: add `say(diagnosis(Disease1))` to *Working Memory*

Rule 6 (unrefracted): *Calculate informativeness so as to query a symptom*
TRIGGER: `query`
IF: `symptom(Symptom)` is in *Prior Task Knowledge*
not `processed(Symptom)` is in *Working Memory*
`informativeness(Symptom, Inf)`
THEN: add `informativeness(Symptom, Inf)` to *Working Memory*

Rule 7 (unrefracted; once): *Query the most informative symptom*
IF: `informativeness(Symptom1, I1)` is in *Working Memory*
not `informativeness(Symptom2, I2)` is in *Working Memory*
`I2 > I1`
THEN: add `say(query(Symptom1))` to *Working Memory*
delete all `informativeness(_, _)` from *Working Memory*

`informativeness(S, I) :-`
L is the list of all C such that `disease(D)` is in *Prior Task Knowledge*
`informativeness_for_disease(D, S, C)`
I is the sum of the elements of L

```
informativeness_for_disease(D, S, Contribution) :-
    probability(D, G, PD) is in Working Memory
    probability_of_disease_given_symptom(D, S/present, G, PDGS)
    probability_of_disease_given_symptom(D, S/absent, G, PDGNS)
    probability_of_symptom(S/present, G, PS)
    probability_of_symptom(S/absent, G, PNS)
    x_logx(PD, P3)
    x_logx(PDGS, P1)
    x_logx(PDGNS, P2)
    Contribution is P1 * PS + P2 * PNS - P3
```

Box 6.7: Selected rules and condition definitions for the Bayesian model of the revised task (from *Decision Procedure*)

Exercise 6.24: Complete the model and explore its behaviour. Completion of the model will require: addition of *Prior Task Knowledge* and specification of its initial contents and properties, specification of the additional user-defined conditions necessary to calculate informativeness, and the addition of Rules 5, 6, and 7. In exploring the model's behaviour, extend the script to run multiple subjects in each condition. Then examine all three dependent variables (diagnostic accuracy, number of symptoms queried, and querying strategy) in both conditions. Compare them with the human data (on the final block) reported in Section 6.3.1. Why are more symptoms queried in the dense condition than in the sparse condition? ◇

Exercise 6.25: It could be argued that the introduction of a threshold for categorisation is at odds with the normative nature of the Bayesian + informativeness model as it leads to a system which is, arguably, sub-optimal. The parameter effectively provides a mechanism to halt symptom querying before all symptoms have been queried. An alternative approach is to halt symptom querying when the informativeness of all possible queries is zero. In other words, if at any point in processing querying further symptoms would yield no information gain, then it is inappropriate to continue querying symptoms and appropriate to make a diagnosis. Modify the Bayesian + informativeness model to use this mechanism to stop the query phase. What effect does the revised mechanism have on the dependent variables? How plausible is this revised mechanism? Consider especially the case of real medical diagnosis where a doctor may have hundreds of symptoms that could be queried. ◇

6.3.3 Project: Learning in the Bayesian Model

We have assumed that the Bayesian + informativeness model has access to an oracle providing the base-rate of each disease, and, for each symptom/disease pair, the conditional probability of that symptom given that disease. Approximations to these probabilities may be acquired from experience via the co-occurrence counting approach employed in learning the Medin and Edelson task. Replace the oracle with a knowledge base and learning mechanism. Characterise the model's learning performance (for both diagnostic accuracy and number of symptoms queried) under the two experimental conditions.

Counting co-occurrence is a highly effective learning mechanism within the Bayesian + informativeness model. The model should perform at near ceiling levels after just one block of trials. In addition, there should be little variability in cue selection behaviour. These behaviours contrast sharply with those of participants (recall Figure 6.7 and the other results of Section 6.3.1). Thus, co-occurrence counting is too effective. It is therefore appropriate to consider ways in which the effectiveness of learning may be reduced or impaired.

The philosophy behind normative approaches to decision making, and to cognition in general, is that they provide competence models: models of behaviour that are unhindered by performance factors such as memory or processing limitations. There are two clear ways in which performance factors might impact

```
random_check :-
    the value of the "LearningRate" property is P
    X is randomly drawn from U(0,1)
    X < P
```

Box 6.8: A condition that succeeds with probability P

upon learning within the Bayesian + informativeness model of cue selection. First, participants may not be able to acquire all of the information concerning cues/category co-occurrence on each trial. Second, the counts of categories and cue/category co-occurrences stored in knowledge base might degrade or decay over time.

Decreasing learning rate and increasing knowledge base decay both reduce the number of cue/category co-occurrences on which the estimation of conditional probabilities may be based. They should therefore both lead to a decrease in diagnostic accuracy. However, we may hypothesise a differential effect on symptom query behaviour. In particular, knowledge base decay will affect information gained from recent trials less than information gained from trials earlier in the experiment, and should therefore introduce a recency bias. In contrast, a reduced learning rate should affect all experiences in a uniform manner, and should not yield a recency bias.

Create two new versions of the Bayesian + informativeness model and modify one to include a reduced learning rate and the other to include knowledge base decay. Both models should include a parameter that governs learning efficiency (either a learning rate parameter or a knowledge base decay parameter). Explore the effect of the efficiency parameter on learning for each model. Compare the behaviour of the two resulting models both with each other and with participant data. Can either efficiency parameter be adjusted to yield diagnostic accuracy that is near to that of human participants in both the sparse and dense conditions? Does either model yield a better match to participant behaviour? Does the recency bias introduced by knowledge base decay lead to more realistic biases in symptom query behaviour? How does learning efficiency interact with categorisation threshold?

Hint 1: A reduced learning rate may be incorporated by adding to *Learning Mechanism* a user-defined property whose value varies between 0 and 1, and modifying the learning rules to test a further condition, such as `random_check` from Box 6.8. The probability of this condition succeeding is given by `LearningRate`, which may be adjusted via the **Properties** panel of *Learning Mechanism*.

Hint 2: Although buffers include properties for the control of decay, these properties are not directly suitable for implementing knowledge base decay in the model as it stands, as buffer decay leads to whole elements being deleted from the buffer. However, the decay properties can be used with a revised representation of event frequencies. For this, it is necessary to represent each disease occurrence and each symptom/disease co-occurrence as a separate element within the knowledge base. Individual elements may decay, and this decay may be controlled through the buffer's decay properties, and calculation of event frequencies may be performed when necessary by counting the number of relevant events currently stored in the knowledge base. This approach also requires that the knowledge base's **Duplicates** property be checked.

6.3.4 Project: Cue Selection in the Network Model

The network model is less obviously conducive to the incorporation of a cue selection mechanism. If purely associative mechanisms are to be employed, then such mechanisms must map from a representation of the known symptoms to a representation of the to-be-queried symptom. One possibility might therefore be to augment the basic two-layer feed-forward network model with a second network, mapping symptoms (corresponding to what is known at some point in the task) to symptoms (with the most active output symptom being that which should be queried). However, it is unclear how such a network might be trained.

An alternative approach is to use a single network mapping symptoms to diseases, as in the model of the Medin and Edelson task, but to include additional control processes that use that network to evaluate the possible responses to the various queries. Thus, if one has a choice between three symptoms, x, y, and z, one may assume that x is present and determine the output of the symptom/disease network resulting from the input vector consisting of the known symptom values augmented with x. This process may also be carried out for the known symptoms augmented with y and the known symptoms augmented with z. The symptom leading to the greatest improvement in diagnostic accuracy may then be selected as the symptom to query. Develop a network model of the cue-selection task that uses this approach and compare its behaviour on both experimental conditions and all three dependent measures with both human participant behaviour and the various Bayesian models. How does the network's learning rate affect behaviour? Does it interact with the categorisation threshold? Does adjusting either parameter to give human-like accuracy lead to human-like biases?

6.4 Medical Diagnosis by Hypothesis Testing

The Bayesian and network models of the diagnosis tasks represent two distinct approaches to categorisation. A third approach involves the explicit generation and testing of hypotheses. Hypothesis testing models differ from network models in that they explicitly represent and manipulate symbolic hypotheses concerning possible diagnoses. They differ from the Bayesian model in that they do not attach probabilities to hypotheses, and they do not make queries on the basis of a mathematical notion of global informativeness. Rather, hypotheses are developed in response to the presence or absence of symptoms, and then tested using one or more of a variety of strategies. A number of strategies might be adopted, including verification (checking that expected symptoms are present), elimination (checking for unanticipated symptoms that, if present, would allow a hypothesis to be eliminated), and discrimination (checking for the presence of symptoms that are suggested to occur by one hypothesis but not by another).

6.4.1 The Basic Hypothesis Testing Model

Processing within a hypothesis testing model might proceed as follows:

1. The presenting or known symptoms suggest one or more hypotheses.
2. If only one such hypothesis is suggested, it may be offered as the diagnosis.
3. Otherwise, a symptom is selected in order to test one or more hypotheses according to one of the hypothesis testing strategies.
4. On learning the valence of the selected symptom hypotheses are revised.
5. The process repeats (from step 2) until a single hypothesis remains and a diagnosis is given.

The processing cycle is basically the same as that of the Bayesian and network models, and the hypothesis testing model may be implemented with the same basic box and arrow architecture (Figure 6.4). The principal differences concern the contents of the various components and the representations that they manipulate. In particular, the hypothesis testing model's *Decision Procedure* is a set of inference rules that modify *Working Memory*, implementing one or more of the hypothesis testing diagnostic strategies.

As in the other models, processing is initiated when *Input/Output* receives a presenting symptom from *Experimenter*. The corresponding proposition should be added directly to *Working Memory* by *Input/Output*. Hypotheses should then be generated.

Rule 1 of Box 6.9 performs the hypothesis generation function. This rule is refracted, so symptom information is processed at most once. It assumes that *Knowledge Base* contains simple positive or negative associations between diseases (so probabilistic associations between diseases and symptoms cannot be represented), but may fire multiple times if one symptom is associated with the

Rule 1 (refracted): *Generate hypothesis from known symptoms*
IF: `symptom(Symptom, Valence)` is in *Working Memory*
`data(Disease, Symptom, Valence)` is in *Knowledge Base*
THEN: add `hypothesis(suspect(Disease))` to *Working Memory*

Rule 2 (refracted): *Generate expectations*
IF: `hypothesis(suspect(Disease))` is in *Working Memory*
`data(Disease, Symptom, Valence)` is in *Knowledge Base*
not `symptom(Symptom, AnyValence)` is in *Working Memory*
THEN: add `expect(Disease, Symptom, Valence)` to *Working Memory*

Rule 3 (refracted; once): *The verification strategy*
TRIGGER: `system_quiescent`
IF: `expect(Disease, Symptom, present)` is in *Working Memory*
not `symptom(Symptom, AnyValence)` is in *Working Memory*
THEN: add `say(query(Symptom))` to *Working Memory*

Rule 4 (refracted): *Delete unsupported hypotheses*
IF: `hypothesis(suspect(Disease))` is in *Working Memory*
`data(Disease, Symptom, Valence1)` is in *Knowledge Base*
`symptom(Symptom, Valence2)` is in *Working Memory*
`Valence1` is distinct from `Valence2`
THEN: delete `hypothesis(suspect(Disease))` from *Working Memory*
delete all `expect(Disease, AnyS, AnyV)` from *Working Memory*

Rule 5 (refracted): *If only one disease is suspected then diagnose*
IF: unique `hypothesis(suspect(Disease))` is in *Working Memory*
THEN: add `say(diagnosis(Disease))` to *Working Memory*

Box 6.9: Principal rules for the Hypothesis Testing model (from *Decision Procedure*)

appropriate valence with many diseases. The rule is also generic in the sense that it may fire whenever new symptom information is obtained (i.e., not just on receipt of the presenting symptom).

Hypotheses in *Working Memory* may generate expectations about symptoms whose valence is unknown. Thus, in the sparse condition, if one suspects mesiopathy, one may expect fever (see Table 6.3). Rule 2 of Box 6.9 generates such expectations.

The strategic element of hypothesis testing works upon expectations. Three plausible strategies are:

Verification: Query any symptom expected to be present given any of the suspected diseases. If the queried symptom is present it will help verify one or more suspected diseases. Verification is a simple confirmatory strategy. It is prone to error in that, once a hypothesis has been generated, supporting evidence is sought in preference to falsifying evidence. There is a substantial body of psychological evidence that suggests that human judgement is subject to such a confirmation bias (e.g., Wason, 1960; Klayman & Ha, 1987).

Elimination: Query any symptom expected to be absent given any of the suspected diseases. If the queried symptom is present it will allow one or more suspected diseases to be eliminated. Elimination seeks evidence that will allow possible hypotheses to be eliminated. It is related to the Categorisation by Elimination heuristic of Berretty, Todd, and Martignon (1999) which in turn is related to Tversky's theory of Elimination by Aspects (Tversky, 1972).

Discrimination: If possible, query symptoms that are known to be present given one suspected disease but absent given another. If no symptom will discriminate, select a symptom to query at random. If the queried symptom is present it will allow one or more suspected diseases to be eliminated and provide support for one or more other suspected diseases. Discrimination is the most sophisticated strategy. It seeks evidence that will, where possible, simultaneously support one hypothesis and refute another. It can be seen as the hypothesis testing equivalent to the cue selection strategies based on selection of the most informative cue.

Other strategies are conceivable, as are combinations of strategies.

Rule 3 of Box 6.9 implements the verification strategy. The rule is triggered by system quiescence (paralleling the generation of informativeness values in the Bayesian + informativeness model), and is marked so that it should fire for just one instantiation of its variables on any cycle.

Rules 1 to 3 are appropriate for processing both the presenting symptom and later symptoms. However, a further rule is required to delete hypotheses from *Working Memory* when they conflict with new symptom information. Rule 4 of Box 6.9 deletes hypotheses (and expectations) concerning suspected diseases that are inconsistent with symptoms whose valence is known.

The primary diagnosis rule (Rule 5 of Box 6.9) fires when there is a unique suspected disease. A secondary diagnosis rule (not shown in the box) is required for cases in which the model exhausts the available symptom expectations and the primary diagnosis rule, which is based on a unique hypothesis, still cannot fire. This secondary diagnosis rule has little option but to take an educated guess at the diagnosis. If any diseases are suspected it may select one as a diagnosis. Otherwise it can only select a disease at random from those listed in *Prior Task Knowledge*.

Exercise 6.26: Create a new model (based on the cue selection infrastructure developed in Exercise 6.21) and build the hypothesis testing model as described above. Add appropriate rules to the *Input/Output* process to transfer information between the subject module's *Working Memory* and the *Experimenter*, and all five of the rules from Box 6.9 to the model's *Decision Procedure*. Also add a secondary diagnosis rule, which should fire when the system is quiescent and Rule 3 cannot fire. Ensure that the model is able to perform the task. Note that with no symptom/disease associations in *Knowledge Base*, and no learning mechanism, the model should perform at chance levels. ◇

6.4.2 Learning and the Knowledge Base

The hypothesis testing model distinguishes between task knowledge (represented in propositional form in *Knowledge Base*) and strategic knowledge (embodied in the rules within *Decision Procedure*). Strategic knowledge is assumed to remain fixed throughout the task. Learning consists of the accumulation and/or modification of task-specific knowledge in *Knowledge Base*, which has been assumed to contain information on the valence of associations between diseases and symptoms, in the form:

`data(Disease, Symptom, Valence)`

Learning in the hypothesis testing model consists of using diagnostic feedback that appears in *Working Memory* to create or modify *Knowledge Base* elements. Diagnostic feedback might be used in a variety of ways that vary in their sophistication. However, the following simple principles are adequate:

1. Add an element of the form `data(Disease, Symptom, Valence)` to *Knowledge Base* for each element of the form `symptom(Symptom, Valence)` in *Working Memory*.
2. Delete any previous associations between the symptoms of known valence and the actual disease, regardless of whether the valence of those symptoms is present or absent.

These principles are naïve (and logically unsound) in that they make no attempt to merge knowledge from the current case with existing knowledge. For example, logically one should not infer an association between a disease and a symptom when the disease has been observed to occur both with and without that symptom. Instead, these principles infer an association if the last time the disease was observed the symptom was present.

Exercise 6.27: The above principles can be embodied in a single rule. Add the necessary rule to *Learning Mechanism* and test the model. Note that even though the representations used by the hypothesis testing model are less expressive than those employed by the Bayesian + informativeness model, the hypothesis testing model is still able to achieve diagnostic accuracy greater than that of most participants. Compare the model's behaviour on all three dependent variables and both conditions with that of human participants reported in Section 6.3.1. Note that despite the lack of logical soundness in the learning mechanism, it still yields a good account of human performance. This may be because it effectively implements a recency bias. ◇

Exercise 6.28: Implement the elimination and discrimination hypothesis testing strategies and explore their consequences. You may wish to add a user-defined property to *Decision Procedure* that may be used to select one of the three strategies. What is the impact of strategy on the model's behaviour? ◇

6.4.3 Effects of Buffer Access Properties

Strategy is only one factor that affects the order of hypothesis generation and symptom querying. A second factor is the order of recall of information from *Knowledge Base* and *Working Memory*. Fox (1980) argued that determinate symptom/disease associations (i.e., associations relating to symptoms that were either always present or always absent for a given disease) were recalled before indeterminate symptom/disease associations, and that this order of recall was in part responsible for the resulting symptom querying strategies. He demonstrated this with Bayesian and hypothesis testing models.

Fox and Cooper (1997) showed that querying strategies in Fox's original experiment could also be accounted for in a model equivalent to that described here in terms of a combination of recency in *Knowledge Base* and primacy in *Working Memory*. This combination of access characteristics results in information relating to recent cases being recalled before information relating to cases in the more distant past, and in information that is recalled first having more control over behaviour than information that is recalled later. The effect of the order of recall within the hypothesis testing model can be explored by modifying the Access properties of the buffers. Thus, in the model described by Fox and Cooper (1997) a good fit to human query behaviour on Fox's original task was obtained by setting the Access properties of *Working Memory* to FIFO and of *Knowledge Base* to LIFO.

Exercise 6.29: Explore the interaction between the access properties of *Working Memory* and *Knowledge Base*. How do these properties affect the model's query biases? Do buffer access properties also affect diagnostic accuracy or the number of symptoms queried? How do the biases generated when access to *Working Memory* is FIFO and access to *Knowledge Base* is LIFO compare with the biases of human participants on Yule *et al.*'s task? (Recall that the conditional probabilities used in this task differ from those used by Fox, 1980, so a good fit between the hypothesis testing model's predictions and Yule *et al.*'s data, in the absence of a corresponding fit between either the Bayesian + informativeness model or the network model, would provide strong support for the hypothesis testing model.) How do they compare with the biases generated by the Bayesian + informativeness and network models? ◇

6.4.4 Hypothesis Testing: Strengths and Weaknesses

The hypothesis testing approach to categorisation is intuitively appealing, especially in the sequential medical diagnosis task where cue selection can be understood in terms of verifying, discriminating between, or eliminating hypotheses. Like the Bayesian and associationist approaches, the approach is able to account for both skilled categorisation performance and for certain aspects of learning.

A potential weakness of the hypothesis testing approach in comparison to that of the Bayesian and associationist approaches is its inability to represent indeterminate relationships between symptoms and diseases. There is no way to represent or use information about symptoms that are associated with a disease on some occasions but not on others. In the Bayesian model the proportions of occasions on which a disease occurs with and without a symptom are explicitly represented, and this information is used in the calculation of both the probabilities of diseases and the informativeness of symptoms. In the associationist model indeterminate relationships may be represented by weak associations, and these associations can then have a mild but significant influence on diagnosis selection. The hypothesis testing model demonstrates, however, that human levels of performance can be obtained without recourse to indeterminate symptom/disease information.

Furthermore, the hypothesis testing model demonstrates that cue selection biases can be understood in terms of an interaction between the access characteristics of a working memory containing trial-specific information and the access characteristics of a knowledge base containing knowledge of symptom/disease associations. The Bayesian model, with cue selection based on informativeness, can also account for some human biases, but the fit of this model and the human data is less satisfactory than the fit of the hypothesis testing model. The associationist model, by contrast, provides a poor account of cue selection biases. In its current form it provides little insight into the cognitive processes that might govern cue selection.

There are two significant weakness of the hypothesis testing model. First, while the model is able to account for average human performance, in the form given above it is not able to account for the performance of individual participants. In particular, some participants excel at the sequential diagnosis task, and with sufficient training can obtain near optimal diagnostic accuracy. Such performance is only possible with the limited representational capabilities of the hypothesis testing model if participants can switch cue selection strategies within and between trials. It may be the case that some participants do this, but this possibility highlights the second weakness of the hypothesis testing model: in relation to the Bayesian model it is under-constrained. The three strategies, while well-motivated in isolation, appear *ad hoc* when compared with the use by the Bayesian model of the mathematically precise concept of informativeness.

6.5 Taking Stock

The focus in this chapter has been on one of the many forms of decision making — categorisation within the context of medical diagnosis. We have considered two distinct categorisation tasks — a static task involving presentation of complete cue information and a sequential task in which cues must be explicitly queried by the decision maker — and three distinct classes of categorisation theory — Bayesian, associationist, and hypothesis testing.

The Bayesian approach supposes that categorisation involves determining the probability that the stimulus belongs to each category, and selecting the category that is most likely. In the sequential task this may be supplemented by using information gain to guide selection of the cue that is most informative. The associationist approach supposes that categorisation involves balancing weighted associations between cues and categories, and selecting the category that is most highly associated with the given cues. It is unclear how the associationist model should be extended to the sequential task. The hypothesis testing approach supposes that categorisation involves forming hypotheses about the category to which a stimulus belongs and seeking information that will verify, discriminate between, or eliminate these hypotheses. This approach is particularly well-suited to the sequential task. Other theories of categorisation do exist, and the chapter should not be viewed as providing anything like complete coverage of theories of categorisation. Rather, the chapter has attempted to demonstrate a range of approaches to categorisation.

A significant aspect of this chapter has been comparative modelling — the development of multiple models for the same task. This has allowed the strengths and weaknesses of the models and their representational assumptions to be compared. It is an important methodological tool because it allows one to see clearly the strengths and weaknesses of the competing approaches.

6.6 Further Reading

Several texts provide excellent background reading on decision making and reasoning with probabilities (e.g., Garnham & Oakhill, 1994; Manktelow, 1999). The view of decision making as essentially a normative process subject to systematic biases is primarily due to the work of Kahneman and Tversky. Their approach, which dominated decision making research in the 1970s and 1980s, is summarised in their Award Address to the American Psychological Association (Kahneman & Tversky, 1984).

Gigerenzer and colleagues have presented the principal challenges to the views of Kahneman and Tversky under the rubric of "fast and frugal" decision making heuristics. The article of Gigerenzer and Goldstein (1996) demonstrates that fast and frugal heuristics are comparable in effectiveness to normative decision making processes. Gigerenzer and Todd (1999) provide an extensive discussion of current decision making research and the relationship between the approaches of Kahneman and Tversky and Gigerenzer's Adaptive Behaviour and Cognition (ABC) research group. Some criticisms of the ABC approach are voiced in the commentaries that accompany Todd and Gigerenzer (2000).

Medin and Edelson (1988) is essential reading for an understanding of the rationale behind experiments in which base-rates are manipulated and for a complete description of the medical diagnosis task. The basic network model, and its relation to mechanisms of animal learning, is presented by Gluck and Bower (1988), who also present empirical results supporting the model. The approach is necessarily mathematical in places. The contributions of both Medin and Edelson (1988) and Gluck and Bower (1988) are summarised by Kruschke (1996). This is a difficult paper, but the model developed by Kruschke provides a good account of a wide range of data.

The extended diagnosis task, with cue selection, is described by Fox (1980), who compares human performance after learning with that predicted by Bayesian and hypothesis testing models. Fox argues against the Bayesian approach by demonstrating (like Gigerenzer & Goldstein, 1996) that alternative, non-Bayesian, approaches can yield appropriate decision making performance. A series of COGENT models of the task (covering Bayesian, associative network, and hypothesis testing approaches) are provided by Fox and Cooper (1997), Cooper and Fox (1997), Yule *et al.* (1998), and Cooper and Yule (1999).

Chapter 7

Sentence Processing

Richard P. Cooper

Overview: The principal subdivisions employed within the cognitive psychology of language are outlined. The chapter then focuses on one subdivision, syntax, or the well-formedness of word sequences. Several computational and psychological dimensions of the problem of checking well-formedness (parsing) are discussed, and these dimensions are used to structure a presentation of four models of the parsing process, ranging from a relatively straightforward model based on bottom-up parallel processing, to a complex but more psychologically plausible model combining bottom-up and top-down influences, serial processing, and backtracking. The chapter concludes with a discussion of alternative approaches to sentence processing, including principle-based parsing and the use of semantics or meaning during parsing.

7.1 Background

7.1.1 Major Topics in the Psychology of Language

The ability to acquire and use language is frequently quoted as one of the central characteristics of our species. Language is also frequently quoted as central to a number of higher cognitive faculties, such as reasoning and problem solving. For this reason the computational processes that support language and its use are of special interest within cognitive science. The domain of language is also of special historical significance, for it is generally agreed that Chomsky's arguments concerning the inadequacies of behaviourist accounts of language (Chomsky, 1959) played a central role in shifting psychology's emphasis from behaviourist to cognitivist accounts of mental processes.

The study of the psychology of language is typically divided into a number of sub-disciplines, including phonology, syntax, semantics, and pragmatics. Phonology concerns the individual sounds (phonemes) that make up speech. There is a substantial body of empirical research on, for example, factors that influence phoneme perception. Syntax concerns the sequential order of words and affixes in well-structured language. There are complex constraints or rules that govern meaningful orderings of sentence constituents, and these constraints have been studied from both linguistic and psychological perspectives. Semantics relates to the literal meaning of language. This has been studied both at the word level (in which case it is closely related to the study of concepts) and at the level of phrases or sentences. Lastly, pragmatics concerns the use of language in context. This involves the study of the intended (as distinct from literal) meaning of language, and can be distinguished from semantics by considering utterances such as "Can you wipe your feet?" (said to someone with muddy boots about to walk on a clean floor), which semantically is a question having a yes/no answer, but pragmatically is a request for the person to wipe his/her feet.

A second dimension of language that cuts across these four sub-disciplines relates to the distinction between generation and reception. There is no reason in principle why the processes involved in, for example, production of well-formed sentences should be the same as those involved in comprehension of the same sentences. Indeed, there is neuropsychological evidence from the breakdown of language following brain injury that demonstrates that language production may be compromised without affecting language comprehension (Coltheart, Sartori, & Job, 1987).

Clearly the cognitive psychology of language is a vast subject. Within the above context, this chapter will focus on the reception of syntax. A number of approaches to the parsing problem — the problem of testing well-formedness of a sequence of words and assigning an underlying phrasal structure to the sequence — will be developed, culminating in a sophisticated model informed by some well-attested empirical regularities.

7.1.2 Syntactic Structure

Consider a simple sentence, such as *the cat bit the dog*. Like many sentences of English, this sentence can be analysed as consisting of a noun phrase (*the cat*) followed by a verb phrase (*bit the dog*). This simple fact of the structure of English sentences may be expressed by a *phrase structure* rule:

$$S \rightarrow NP\ \ VP$$

where S represents sentence, NP represents noun phrase, and VP represents verb

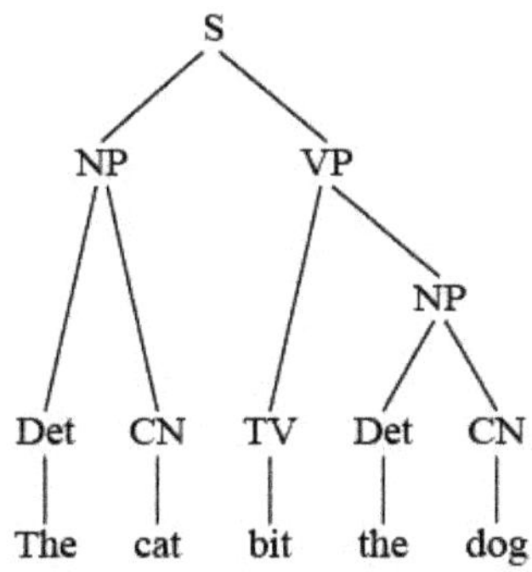

Figure 7.1: The syntactic structure of *The cat bit the dog*

phrase. The rule states that a sentence may be composed of a noun phrase followed by a verb phrase.

The two principal constituents of the above sentence may also be decomposed. The noun phrase consists of a determiner (i.e., a word such as *the*, *a*, *every*, *some*, etc.) followed by a common noun. The verb phrase consists of a transitive verb (i.e., a verb that relates two things) and a second noun phrase. These facts may also be expressed as phrase structure rules:

NP → Det CN
VP → TV NP

In order to analyse the sentence completely, it is also necessary to know the syntactic categories of the words involved — that *the* is a determiner, *cat* and *dog* are common nouns, and *bit* is a transitive verb.

It is common to represent the structure of sentences pictorially using a tree. Figure 7.1 shows the tree representation for *the cat bit the dog*. The nodes in the tree directly corresponding to words are referred to as terminal nodes. The other, higher, nodes are referred to as non-terminal nodes. The existence of such nodes is inferred from regularities across sentence types. Thus, even the previous three sentences in this paragraph can be analysed in terms of the simple S → NP VP rule, although the NPs and VPs involved are relatively complex. (In the first case, the NP is *the nodes in the tree directly corresponding to words*, in the second case the NP is *the other, higher, nodes*, and in the third case the NP is *the existence of such nodes*.)

Many more phrase structure rules are obviously required to describe English, or any other naturally occurring human language. In the case of English, we might start with:

NP → Pro
NP → PN

NP → NP PP
PP → Prep NP

These rules state that a noun phrase may consist of a pronoun (e.g., *him, her, you, me*), a proper name (e.g., *John, Mary, London*), or a noun phrase followed by a prepositional phrase (e.g., *the cat on the mat*), where a prepositional phrase consists of a preposition (e.g., *in, on, at*) followed by a noun phrase.

Similarly, there are additional types of verb phrase, including:

VP → IV
VP → DV NP NP
VP → DV NP PP(to)
VP → VP Adv
VP → VP PP

These rules state that a verb phrase may consist of a single intransitive verb (e.g., *runs, sleeps*), a ditransitive verb followed by two noun phrases (e.g., *gave Mary the book*), a ditransitive verb followed by a noun phrase and prepositional phrase in the "to" form (e.g., *gave the book to Mary*), a verb phrase followed by an adverb (e.g., *runs quickly*), or a verb phrase followed by a prepositional phrase (e.g., *slept in the park*).

Three more types of verb phrase are common, and will be used in examples later in the chapter:

VP → V_{inf1} VP(inf)
VP → V_{inf2} NP VP(inf)
VP(inf) → INF VP
VP → V_{comp} S(comp)
S(comp) → Comp S

These rules cover verb phrases such as *wants to wash the dishes*, *promised Mary to wash the dishes*, and *thought that Mary liked him*. The first states that a verb phrase may consist of an infinitival-complement verb (such as *wants*) followed by a verb phrase in the infinitive form (e.g., *to wash the dishes*). The second states that a verb phrase may consist of a second type of infinitival-complement verb (such as *asked, promised, pretended*) followed by a noun phrase (e.g., *Mary*) and a verb phrase in the infinitive form (e.g., *to wash the dishes*). The third states that a verb phrase in the infinitive form consists of an infinitive (i.e., *to*) followed by a standard verb phrase. The fourth states that a verb phrase may consist of a that-complement verb (e.g., *thought, believed*) followed by a sentence in the comp form, and the fifth states that a sentence in the comp form consists of a complementiser (e.g., *that*) followed by a sentence.

This analysis begins to show the complexity of the structure of English, yet it hardly scratches the surface: it does not consider, for example, number agreement between sentence components (e.g., *The cats chases the dog* is ungrammatical), conjunction (e.g., *John took the bus but Mary cycled*), tense and aspect (e.g., what is the structure of *John will be taking the bus*?), so-called movement (as in *Which bus did John take?*), or "it-cleft" sentences such as *It was John who stole the bus*. Space does not permit a proper treatment of such issues, and the interested reader is directed to standard texts on linguistic structure (see Section 7.6).

Exercise 7.1: Using the above phrase structure rules, draw trees showing the syntactic structure of the following sentences:

(7.1) a. John gave Mary a kitten
b. John ate the cake quickly
c. John asked Mary to wash the car
d. Mary persuaded John to wash the car
e. John saw the kitten in the park

Notice how the last sentence is ambiguous. John may have seen the kitten that was in the park, or John may have been in the park when he saw the kitten. You should be able to draw two distinct trees, corresponding to the two distinct meanings, for this sentence. ◇

7.1.3 Parsing and Syntactic Structure

As English speakers we are able to detect when a putative sentence does or does not conform to the rules of English. While testing grammaticality is not normally something that we are aware of, the fact that it appears to be done by our language processing system imposes certain computational requirements on that system.

The process of determining the syntactic structure of a sentence or sentence fragment is referred to as parsing. Much early work in the cognitive science of language assumed that the linguistic capabilities of humans were embodied within a system (sometimes referred to as the Human Sentence Processing Mechanism: HSPM) that took as input sequences of words and generated from those words a meaning. Many researchers further assumed that a key stage (possibly the first stage) of processing within the HSPM was parsing of the input word sequence.

This view of the processing of language, and the assumption that language is rule-governed (i.e., syntactic structure is determined by a set of phrase structure rules, such as those above), was challenged by the fact that there are many example word sequences that are, according to most phrase structure formulations of English, well-formed syntactically, but (to the untrained, at least) not obviously grammatical. One often cited case is centre-embedding. Consider Example 7.2a below. Simplifying somewhat, it is a noun phrase constructed from a rule that might be represented as: NP → Det CN COMP NP TV. If we apply this rule twice, we find that Example 7.2b is also a noun phrase. Adding a verb phrase (e.g., consisting of the intransitive verb *squealed*) to Example 7.2a yields Example 7.2c, which to most English speakers is an acceptable sentence. Doing the same to Example 7.2b yields Example 7.2d, which to most English speakers is not acceptable.

(7.2) a. the mouse that the cat chased
b. the mouse that the cat that the dog bit chased
c. the mouse that the cat chased squealed
d. the mouse that the cat that the dog bit chased squealed

Cases such as these led Chomsky (1965) to distinguish between linguistic competence and linguistic performance. Competence in any domain is the idealised knowledge upon which processing in that domain is based. Performance is concerned with the results of using that knowledge. Use of knowledge may be constrained, for example, by memory limitations, and so competence may exceed performance.

In many ways the competence/performance distinction is intuitively plausible. Many cognitive processes appear to be resource-bound (by, for example, limited short-term memory). If language is rule-based and any part of linguistic processing is resource-bound, then there are likely to be sentences that are grammatically well-formed but not parsable by the HSPM.

However, the competence/performance distinction also raises problems concerning the precise limits of grammaticality: should the unacceptability of a putative question such as *Who did Mary give the book that John borrowed from to Bill?*, where the *who* refers to the person John borrowed from, be attributed to a violation of the grammar rules or a performance violation? For a given theory of syntactic structure, the unacceptability of a sentence that is grammatical according to the theory but unacceptable according to human participants may be attributed to performance factors. Hence, a grammatical theory cannot be falsified through over-prediction (i.e., through predicting that unacceptable sentences are grammatical). In this way, the competence/performance distinction undermines the status of grammatical theory.

The above is only true, however, if the grammatical theory is stated in the absence of a performance theory. Performance is the product of a sub-optimal process operating with correct and complete information (e.g., phrase structure rules). A well-specified theory of linguistic performance, tied to a theory of linguistic competence, should account for all and only acceptable sentences of the language under consideration. This view led a number of researchers in the 1970s and 1980s (e.g., Kimball, 1973; Frazier & Fodor, 1978; Wanner, 1980) to focus on principles of the parsing process that might give rise to (and hence explain) data from human linguistic performance.

Several types of performance data are relevant to this enterprise. First and foremost are grammaticality (or acceptability) judgements, where participants or "native speakers" agree that word sequences are acceptable or unacceptable fragments of their language. A second type of performance data relates to sentences that are agreed to be ambiguous. In such cases the competence theory will typically allow multiple syntactic structures for a single word sequence (recall Example 7.1e). Ambiguous sentences often have preferred readings, where native speakers show a strong preference for one reading over other readings. This constitutes another type of performance data: in such cases a performance theory should predict the preferred reading.

A further type of performance data relates to sentences that are acceptable only after a second reading. Sentences such as those in example 7.3 illustrate this phenomenon.

(7.3) a. The horse raced parsed the barn fell
b. Since Jay jogs a mile seems a small distance to him
c. Teachers taught by the Berlitz method passed the test
d. The officer told the criminal that he was arresting her husband

These sentences are known as garden path sentences (see Bever, 1970; Frazier & Rayner, 1982; Crain & Steedman, 1985). They arise when multiple partial syntactic structures are possible at some point in the left-right sequence of processing a sentence (i.e., the sentence is locally ambiguous), when one of those partial syntactic structures is preferred, and when the actual syntactic structure corresponding to the complete sentence is not based on the preferred one. The reality of garden path effects has been demonstrated through sophisticated psycholinguistic experiments (see, e.g., Frazier & Rayner, 1982; Crain & Steedman, 1985; Altmann & Steedman, 1988). Performance theories must therefore account for why the HSPM initially fails in attempting to parse such sentences.

7.1.4 Some Dimensions of Parsing

A number of key issues have arisen in computational approaches to natural language parsing. Wanner phrases some of these issues as "dimensions of the parsing problem" (Wanner, 1988, p. 80). One dimension concerns the degree to which parsing is *incremental*. Incremental parsers incorporate each successive word into some structure or sentence frame as each word is encountered. Non-incremental parsers operate on complete sentences. A second dimension concerns the direction in which the syntactic representation is constructed — from terminal word nodes to a non-terminal sentence node, or *vice versa*. *Bottom-up* parsers group words in the input into phrases, and then those phrases into larger phrases, and so on. *Top-down* parsers hypothesise that the word sequence is a sentence, and that it consists of a noun phrase followed by a verb phrase, and so on, decomposing each category until a match with the sentence being parsed is achieved. There is clear evidence that both top-down and bottom-up processes are involved at different stages in human sentence processing.

Wanner's third dimension concerns the degree of parallelism involved in the parsing process. Serial parsers build and maintain one syntactic structure at a time, even when multiple structures are possible (as in sentences containing local ambiguities). If that structure proves to be incorrect, the serial parser must attempt to reanalyse the sentence using a different possible syntactic structure. Parallel parsers, in contrast, maintain multiple possible syntactic structures at points of local ambiguity. Consequently parallel parsers do not need to reanalyse a sentence if one structure proves incorrect. Garden path sentences suggest that human parsing may be serial, but it may still be the case that some aspects of human parsing involve the simultaneous maintenance of multiple syntactic structures in some short-term linguistic store.

A fourth dimension of parsing (not discussed by Wanner, 1988) concerns the role of semantics or meaning and context on parsing. Most parsers rely purely on syntactic information when constructing the syntactic structure associated with a sentence, but Crain and Steedman (1985) point out that this need not be the case. The human parser may be influenced by semantics or context during the parsing process, and this influence may lead to different syntactic structures being favoured in different semantic contexts. Evidence for such an interaction between syntax and linguistic context is presented by Crain and Steedman (1985) (see also Altmann & Steedman, 1988). Tanenhaus, Spivey-Knowlton, Eberhard, and Sedivy (1995) have further shown, with eye movement studies, that sentence processing can also be influenced by visual, non-linguistic, context.

These dimensions provide a context within which specific parsing models may be compared. Two dimensions — the bottom-up/top-down dimension and the parallel/serial dimension — are illustrated in depth by the models developed in this chapter.

7.2 A First Model

7.2.1 An Incremental Input Module

Human sentence processing is generally considered to involve the presentation of linguistic input to the HSPM one word or phrase at a time. This presentation may be modelled within COGENT by an experimenter module that, on each trial, selects an input word sequence from a set of stimuli and then feeds that sequence, one word at a time, to a subject module, which, it is assumed, attempts to parse the input. The experimenter module may, on successive trials, feed successive word sequences to the subject module, allowing the subject module to be tested on a variety of inputs.

A minimal experimenter module that performs the above task consists of: one propositional buffer, *Stimuli*, that initially contains the full set of stimuli (word

Rule 1 (refracted): *Select a sentence to parse from the Stimuli buffer*
IF: the current cycle is `1`
once `WordList` is in *Stimuli*
THEN: delete `WordList` from *Stimuli*
add `words(WordList)` to *Current Stimulus*

Rule 2 (unrefracted): *When quiescent, feed one more word to the subject*
TRIGGER: `system_quiescent`
IF: `words([Head|Tail])` is in *Current Stimulus*
THEN: delete `words([Head|Tail])` from *Current Stimulus*
add `words(Tail)` to *Current Stimulus*
send `word(Head)` to *Subject:Input/Output*

Box 7.1: Incremental input rules from *Present Stimuli*

lists) and that is reinitialised only at the start of a subject; one process, *Present Stimuli*, that presents one stimulus from *Stimuli* on each trial, deleting the stimulus as it is presented; and another propositional buffer, *Current Stimulus*, that is used for temporary storage of the current stimulus during the trial on which it is being presented. Within the minimal experimenter module, *Present Stimuli* must be able to read from and write to both propositional buffers. It should also send to an input/output process located within the subject module.

Exercise 7.2: Create a new research programme and a new model within that research programme. Draw a box and arrow diagram within the new model consisting of two compound boxes, *Experimenter* and *Subject*, corresponding to an experimenter module and a subject module. Populate the two modules with boxes as described in the previous paragraph and link the boxes with appropriate arrows. ◇

Experimenter requires two rules: one to select a test sentence for the current trial and transfer it from *Stimuli* to *Current Stimulus*, and one to drip-feed words from *Current Stimulus* to the subject module. The two rules in Box 7.1 perform these functions. Rule 1 assumes that *Stimuli* contains elements that are lists of words (the putative sentences which are to be parsed on successive trials). Rule 2 is triggered by `system_quiescent`. This ensures that it only fires when all other processing within the system is complete. This means that the subject module may perform arbitrary processing on receipt of each word, and only when a word has been fully processed will the next word be fed to the subject. This will allow maximal exploration of incremental left-to-right processing within the parsers described later in the chapter.

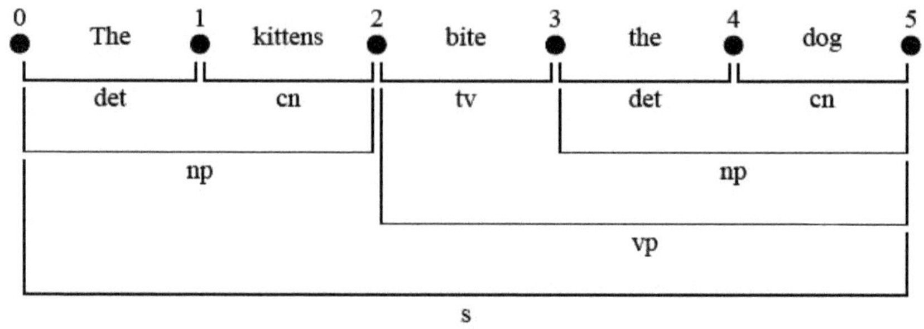

Figure 7.2: A completed chart for *the kittens bite the dog*

Exercise 7.3: Add the rules from Box 7.1 to *Present Stimuli*. Also add a range of putative sentences to *Stimuli*. Each sentence should be expressed as a single buffer element consisting of a list of words. Ensure that the Initialise properties of both buffers are set as described above, and test *Experimenter* by monitoring the messages sent to *Input/Output* when the model is run. ◇

7.2.2 A Bottom-Up Parallel Parser

As noted above, there are several approaches to the problem of verifying that a sequence of words is a well-formed sentence, and, if so, deriving the sentence's syntactic structure. One simple approach involves constructing a grid or chart as in Figure 7.2. The numbered disks are referred to as vertices or nodes, and the lines spanning the vertices are referred to as edges or arcs. The goal of chart parsing is to construct an edge that spans the entire sequence of vertices. If the word sequence is intended to be a sentence, then the edge should be labelled "s" (as in Figure 7.2).

Charts may be constructed in a variety of ways, corresponding to the dimensions of parsing outlined in Section 7.1.4. Thus, the chart may be constructed bottom-up or top-down, through exploring possible edges in sequence or in parallel, etc. In all cases, the general method is referred to as chart parsing.

Functional Components

A simple chart parser within COGENT consists of a buffer in which to construct the chart, a process that enters words onto that chart, buffers containing lexical knowledge (i.e., the syntactic categories of words) and grammatical knowledge (i.e., the phrase structure rules of the grammar), and a process that uses lexical and grammatical knowledge to enter edges onto the chart. Figure 7.3 shows the components and their interconnections.

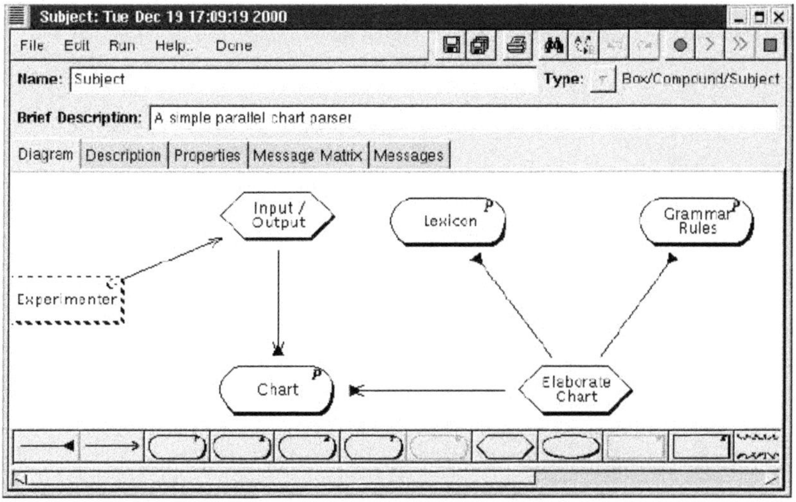

Figure 7.3: The box and arrow structure of the parallel chart parser

Rule 1 (unrefracted): *Add a word to the first position of the chart*
TRIGGER: `word(W)`
IF: not `edge(_, _, _, _)` is in *Chart*
THEN: add `edge(0, 1, word(W), 0)` to *Chart*

Rule 2 (unrefracted): *Add a word to the next position of the chart*
TRIGGER: `word(W)`
IF: `edge(N0, N1, word(W1), Y)` is in *Chart*
not `edge(N1, N2, word(W2), Y)` is in *Chart*
`N2` is `N1 + 1`
THEN: add `edge(N1, N2, word(W), Y)` to *Chart*

Box 7.2: Rules to enter words onto the chart (from *Input/Output*)

Input/Output

Recall that *Experimenter* was designed to deliver one word at a time to *Input/Output*, and that *Input/Output* must enter words as they are presented onto the chart. This may be achieved with two rules: one to enter the first word spanning vertices 0 to 1, and a second to enter each successive word to the right of the previous word. The rules in Box 7.2 accomplish the above tasks. They represent chart edges by terms of the form:

```
edge(LeftVertex, RightVertex, Content, Level)
```

Display Rule 1: *Draw text for all categories entered on the chart*
IF: `edge(N0, N1, C, L)` is in *Chart*
`X` is `(N0 + N1) * 50`
`Y` is `L * 25 + 50`
THEN: show `text(chart, C aligned (c, c) at (X, Y), [colour(black)])`

Display Rule 2: *Draw arcs for all categories entered on the chart*
IF: `edge(N0, N1, C, L)` is in *Chart*
`X0` is `N0 * 100 + 5`
`X1` is `N1 * 100 - 5`
`Y0` is `L * 25 + 40`
`Y1` is `Y0 - 5`
THEN: show `line(chart, (X0, Y0) to (X1, Y0), [colour(black)])`
show `line(chart, (X0, Y0) to (X0, Y1), [colour(black)])`
show `line(chart, (X1, Y0) to (X1, Y1), [colour(black)])`

Box 7.3: Display rules for *Chart*

where `LeftVertex` and `RightVertex` are integer vertex labels, `Content` represents the content of the edge (e.g., `word(cat)`), and `Level` is an integer that will be used for formatting the diagrammatic representation of the chart. Given this propositional representation, display rules may map the contents to *Chart* to a diagrammatic, chart-like representation. Box 7.3 shows two suitable rules.

Exercise 7.4: Draw the box and arrow diagram of the chart parser and add the rules given in Box 7.2 to *Input/Output* so that words are appropriately added to the chart as they are received. Also add the display rules given in Box 7.3 to *Chart*. Test the system by opening *Chart* in Current Display view and running the model over several trials. On each trial, the words making up one stimulus sentence should appear on the chart, together with edges corresponding to each word. ◇

Lexical Look-Up and Creating Chart Edges

Once a word is entered on the chart, it is straightforward to enter its corresponding grammatical category by looking up that category in a lexicon (i.e., a list of words and their properties). If *Lexicon* contains the syntactic category of all known words, then this may be achieved by a single rule within *Elaborate Chart*, as in Rule 1 of Box 7.4.

Rule 1 matches an element in *Chart*, looks up its category in *Lexicon*, and adds a category edge at the next level to *Chart*. The rule assumes that *Lexicon* contains terms of the form:

Rule 1 (refracted): *Lexical look-up*
IF: `edge(N0, N1, word(W), L1)` is in *Chart*
`category(W, C)` is in *Lexicon*
`L` is `L1 + 1`
THEN: add `edge(N0, N1, cat(C), L)` to *Chart*

Rule 2 (refracted): *Apply Unary Grammar Rules*
IF: `edge(N0, N1, cat(C1), L1)` is in *Chart*
`rule(C, [C1])` is in *Grammar Rules*
`L` is `L1 + 1`
THEN: add `edge(N0, N1, cat(C), L)` to *Chart*

Rule 3 (refracted): *Apply Binary Grammar Rules*
IF: `edge(N0, N1, cat(C1), L1)` is in *Chart*
`edge(N1, N2, cat(C2), L2)` is in *Chart*
`rule(C, [C1, C2])` is in *Grammar Rules*
`L` is `max(L1, L2) + 1`
THEN: add `edge(N0, N2, cat(C), L)` to *Chart*

Box 7.4: Rules for adding edges to *Chart* (from *Elaborate Chart*)

```
category(the, det)
category(kittens, cn)
category(dog, cn)
```

Exercise 7.5: Add Rule 1 to *Elaborate Chart* to perform lexical look-up. Also add some lexical entries to *Lexicon*. Test the partial model by running it on various test sentences. Do this by specifying the test sentences in the *Experimenter* module. ◇

Building Phrases

It is intended that phrase structure rules (such as S → NP VP) are represented in *Grammar Rules*, and that this buffer is accessed when applying phrase structure rules. *Grammar Rules* might therefore contain terms such as:

```
rule(s, [np, vp])
rule(np, [det, cn])
rule(np, [pn])
```

Here, the first argument of `rule`/2 specifies the syntactic category on the left side of the phrase structure rule and the second argument is a list specifying the categories (in order) on the right side of the phrase structure rule. Unary phrase structure rules (i.e., rules of the form NP → PN, where there is a single category on the right side of the rule) may then be applied with a COGENT rule such as Rule 2 in Box 7.4. Similarly, binary phrase structure rules (e.g., S → NP VP) may be applied with a rule such as Rule 3. Rule 3 extends the use of terms of the form `edge(N0,N1,cat(det),L)` within the chart, such that edges may span sequences of words (e.g., `edge(0,2,cat(np),2)`).

Exercise 7.6: Add appropriate phrase structure rules to *Grammar Rules*. Also add the above rules to *Elaborate Chart*. Test the model on a range of sentences. The model should now be able to construct complete charts for all sentences specified by the grammar. ◇

Discussion of the Model

The chart-parser described above is extremely simple, yet it is complete. It is bottom-up because parsing is driven by the addition of words to the chart. The chart is then expanded "upwards" (from lexical categories to phrasal categories) as far as possible. If at any stage in processing no further additions to the chart are possible, the system quiesces (i.e., no more rules fire), and *Experimenter* sends in the next word. The system is parallel because COGENT's default behaviour is parallel. If multiple additions to the chart are simultaneously possible, then those additions will be made simultaneously. In particular, if a word is syntactically ambiguous (i.e., has two possible syntactic categories), both categories will be added to the chart simultaneously, and analyses based on both categories will be explored in parallel. While this results in a messy chart with alternative analyses appearing to over-write each other, it does not affect the performance of the parser. Subsequent sections of this chapter will explore modifications to both the bottom-up and the parallel nature of this system.

Exercise 7.7: Extend the lexicon and grammar rules. For a particular challenge, try to add phrase structure rules that allow sentences such as *The kitten that chases the dog bites the man* and *The kitten that the dog chases bites the woman*. For present purposes, restrict attention to sentences in the simple present tense. ◇

Exercise 7.8: The COGENT rules for applying unary and binary phrase structure rules contain some redundancy. They are also insufficient for cases involving ternary phrase structure rules (and other higher order phrase structure rules). Such rules appear to be implicated in a range of grammatical constructions, such as those involving verbs with multiple complements (e.g., dative verbs, such as *give*, and some verbs with infinitival complements, such as *promise* and *persuade*). Merge the two COGENT rules for building phrases into a single rule that can apply irrespective of the number of elements on the right side of the phrase structure rule.

Hint: It may be useful to approach this exercise by creating a user-defined condition (e.g., spans/3) that takes as arguments two integers (representing vertices) and a list of syntactic categories and succeeds if the list of syntactic categories spans the two vertices. Another user-defined condition may be required to determine the level of spanning elements on the chart. ◇

7.2.3 Extending the Grammar: Agreement

One difficulty with the parser developed above is that, if given appropriate lexical entries, it will successfully parse ill-formed sentences such as the following:

(7.4) a. John chase Mary
b. Every kitten bite the dog
c. A kittens run

This is actually a difficulty with the grammar (i.e., the rules of syntax), and not the parser. For example, noun phrases within English cannot consist of any determiner followed by any common noun: the determiner and common noun must both be either singular or plural. Thus, *a kittens* is an ill-formed noun phrase because the determiner (*a*) is singular but the common noun (*kittens*) is plural.

One way in which number agreement may be correctly taken into account is by elaborating the lexicon with number information and adding agreement specifications to the grammar rules. The former may be achieved by replacing lexical entries such as:

```
category(a, det)
category(the, det)
category(kittens, cn)
```

with:

```
category(a, det(sing))
category(the, det(_))
category(kittens, cn(plural))
```

Note that because *the* can be singular or plural, its number specification is left as a variable (the underscore character).

The latter may be achieved by replacing grammar rules such as:

```
rule(np, [det, cn])
```

with:

```
rule(np(Num), [det(Num), cn(Num)])
```

which indicate that a noun phrase with number specification Num may consist of a

Table 7.1: Pronouns and their person/number/case features

		Number/Case			
		sing/nom	sing/acc	plural/nom	plural/acc
Person	1	I	me	we	us
	2	you	you	you	you
	3	he/she	him/her	they	them

determiner with number specification `Num` followed by a common noun with the same number specification.

Similarly, the rule that licenses verb phrases headed by transitive verbs:

```
rule(vp,[tv,np])
```

must be elaborated with number agreement specifications:

```
rule(vp(Num),[tv(Num),np(_)])
```

The underscore character is used in this rule to indicate that the number feature of the noun phrase following a transitive verb is independent of the number feature of the transitive verb or the verb phrase as a whole. Thus, *chases the kitten* and *chases the kittens* are both singular verb phrases, because they can both be preceded by a singular noun phrase (e.g., *John*) to yield a well-formed sentence. Neither can be legitimately preceded by a plural noun phrase (e.g., *the dogs*) to yield a well-formed sentence. In contrast, *chase the kitten* and *chase the kittens* are both plural, as they can both be preceded by a plural noun phrase to yield well-formed sentences.

Exercise 7.9: Extend the lexicon and the grammar rules with number information. Check that the parser now correctly discriminates between sentences with correct number agreement and sentences with incorrect number agreement by providing a range of grammatical and ungrammatical examples in *Stimuli*. ◇

Two other forms of agreement of relevance to English noun and verb phrases concern person and case. Person may be first (e.g., *I, me, we*), second (e.g., *you*), or third (e.g., *he, she, it, him, her, them*). Case may be nominative (e.g., *I, he, she*) or accusative (e.g., *me, him, her*).

Person and case agreement are seen most clearly in noun phrases consisting of pronouns. Thus, Table 7.1 shows standard pronouns for the various combinations of person, case, and number. Person and number features also apply to verbs. Hence a table similar to Table 7.1 could also be constructed for each verb.

Grammaticality requires that noun phrases in subject position must be nominative case and the person feature of the subject noun phrase must agree with the person feature of the following verb phrase. Noun phrases in object position (i.e., following a transitive verb within a verb phrase based on that verb) must be accusative case. To ensure agreement of all features (number, person, and case), all phrase structure rules relating to noun phrases and verb phrases must be revised to include number, person, and case features. For example:

S → NP(Number, Person, nom) VP(Number, Person)
VP(Number, Person) → TV(Number, Person) NP(_, _, acc)
NP(Number, 3, _) → Det(Number) CN(Number)
NP(Number, Person, Case) → PN(Number, Person, Case)

Exercise 7.10: Extend the lexicon and grammar to include agreement on number, person, and case, as described above. Test your solution with sentences containing pronouns in a variety of forms. ◇

7.2.4 Project: Tense and Aspect

The system of tense and aspect within English may be analysed in a way analogous to the system for number agreement. Consider the following well-formed sentences:

(7.5) a. John will chase Mary
b. John might chase Mary
c. John wants to chase Mary
d. John persuaded Bill to chase Mary

In each of the above, *chase Mary* may be analysed as a verb phrase in base-form. In examples 7.5a and 7.5b it is augmented with a modal verb (*will* or *might*) to yield a verb phrase in finite form. In examples 7.5c and 7.5d it is augmented with the infinitive *to* to yield a verb phrase in infinitival form. This suggests the following grammatical categories and phrase structure rules (where number, person, and case agreement are ignored):

TV(base): chase, kiss, trick
IV(base): sleep, walk, cry
VP(X) → IV(X) (where X is a variable)
VP(X) → TV(X) NP (where X is a variable)
MV(finite, base): might, could, should, would
MV(inf, base): to
VP(F1) → MV(F1, F2) VP(F2) (where F1 F2 are variables)
V_{inf1}: wants
V_{inf2}: promised, persuaded
VP(base) → V_{inf1} VP(inf)
VP(base) → V_{inf2} NP VP(inf)

Lexical specifications may be generated for other modal verbs to capture further details of the English system of tense and aspect. For example (and focusing on aspect rather than tense):

MV(base, progressive): be
MV(pres-participle, progressive): been
MV(progressive, passive): being
MV(finite, pres-participle): has, had
MV(base, pres-participle): have

Extend the lexicon and grammar rules to give wide coverage of the English system of tense and aspect. (For further details of that system see, for example, Burton-Roberts, 1986.) Test the completed grammar/parser on at least the following examples:

(7.6) a. John has chased Mary
b. John might have chased Mary
c. John was chasing Mary
d. John could be chasing Mary
e. John might have been chasing Mary

Also ensure that the grammar doesn't over-generate. That is, ensure that it does not license ungrammatical verb phrase forms by testing the parser on a variety of word sequences containing ill-formed verb sequences.

7.2.5 Structure Building

The goal of parsing is generally not to determine if a sequence of words is licensed by a lexicon and set of grammar rules, but to determine the syntactic structure underlying well-formed word sequences. This is especially clear in cases of structural ambiguity (as in example 7.1e) where the parser can distinguish between alternative structures corresponding to the same word sequence.

Within COGENT's representation language the structure of a phrase may be represented by a compound term in which the term's functor is the syntactic category of the phrase and the term's arguments are representations of the structure of the phrase's constituents. Thus, the structure of the noun phrase *the kitten* may be represented by the term:

```
np(det(the), cn(kitten))
```

The functor of this term (`np`) indicates that it represents a noun phrase. The two arguments `det(the)` and `cn(kitten)` represent the two constituents of that noun phrase.

Structure building may be added to the chart parser developed above by representing the structure within chart entries and extending the rules for combining phrases so that they build structures for those phrases. With respect to the former, it is necessary to augment the edge/4 representation with an additional argument to represent the structure:

`edge(LeftVertex,RightVertex,Cat,Structure,Level)`

where `Cat` is the syntactic category (e.g., `np(sing,3,nom)`) and `Structure` is the structure of the portion of the chart spanned by the term (e.g., `np(pro(she))`).

The latter requires use of a special-purpose built-in function for assembling and disassembling terms (e.g., for building the term `s(np(...),vp(...))` from its components `s`, `np(...)` and `vp(...)`). The function in question (known in Prolog as the "univ" function) allows a compound term to be broken into its constituent terms. Thus, if `Structure` is instantiated to `s(np(...),np(...))`:

`Structure` is composed of `Constituents`

will be satisfied if or when `Constituents` is bound to the list:

`[s,np(...),np(...)]`

Note that this structure building function requires that the first element of the list on the right hand side of the function is an atom (as this element corresponds to the functor of the term on the left hand side). Other elements of the right hand side list may be compound terms.

Given the above function, if `Cat` is the syntactic category of a phrase (possibly including features) and `SubStruct` is a list of elements representing the structures of the sub-constituents of the phrase of category `Cat`, then `build_structure`/3, as defined in Box 7.5, will instantiate `Structure` to the representation of the structure of the complete constituent. `build_structure`/3 may then be used by the triggered rule for adding an edge to the chart (as shown in Rules 1 and 2 of Box 7.5). The figure also includes a definition for `span`/5, which determines new edges that may be added to the chart, including the sub-structure and level of such edges.

Exercise 7.11: Create a new model based on the most recent parsing model in the sentence processing research programme and modify it along the above lines to include structure building. This will also entail changes to the rules for adding initial elements to *Chart* (to include a representation of the structure of such elements) and to the display rules for *Chart* (so they are consistent with the edge/5 representation). Test the parser by ensuring that it generates appropriate structures for sentences involving a variety of constructions. ◇

7.3 Towards Incremental Interpretation

It is generally agreed that sentence processing is incremental, in the sense that words in an input stream are incorporated into mental structures as they are en-

Rule 1 (refracted): *Lexical look-up*
IF: `edge(N0,N1,word(W),S,L1)` is in *Chart*
`category(W,C)` is in *Lexicon*
`L` is `L1 + 1`
`build_structure(C,[S],Struct)`
THEN: add `edge(N0,N1,cat(C),Struct,L)` to *Chart*

Rule 2 (refracted): *Apply Grammar Rules (any arity)*
IF: `rule(C,List)` is in *Grammar Rules*
`spans(N0,N1,List,SubStruct,L1)`
`L` is `L1 + 1`
`build_structure(C,SubStruct,Struct)`
THEN: add `edge(N0,N1,cat(C),Struct,L)` to *Chart*

Condition Definition: `spans/5`: *Does a category list span two nodes?*
`spans(N0,N1,[C],[SC],L) :-`
`edge(N0,N1,cat(C),SC,L)` is in *Chart*
`spans(N0,N2,[C|Rest],[SC|SRest],L) :-`
`edge(N0,N1,cat(C),SC,L0)` is in *Chart*
`spans(N1,N2,Rest,SRest,L1)`
`L` is `max(L0,L1)`

Condition Definition: `build_structure/3`: *Build a structure for a phrase*
`build_structure(Cat,SubStruct,Structure) :-`
`Cat` is composed of `[Head|Features]`
`Structure` is composed of `[Head|SubStruct]`

Box 7.5: Revised rules and condition definitions for *Elaborate Chart*

countered, and not at, for example, the end of a phrase or sentence (see Mitchell, 1994; Crocker, 1999). On this count, the bottom-up parallel chart parser described above lacks psychological plausibility. When parsing *the kittens bite the dog*, for example, the parser must parse the complete verb phrase (*bite the dog*) before combining it with the noun phrase. Worse, after processing *the kittens* the parser has no expectations about the next word or phrase. English speakers, in contrast, know that the next constituent is likely to be a verb phrase (or, in certain situations, a noun phrase modifier such as *in the garden*).

7.3.1 Left Corner Parsing

The bottom-up parsing algorithm can be modified to incorporate incremental processing and prediction by the introduction of "active" chart edges. An active edge is one that represents an incomplete constituent. Thus, in Figure 7.4, the edge la-

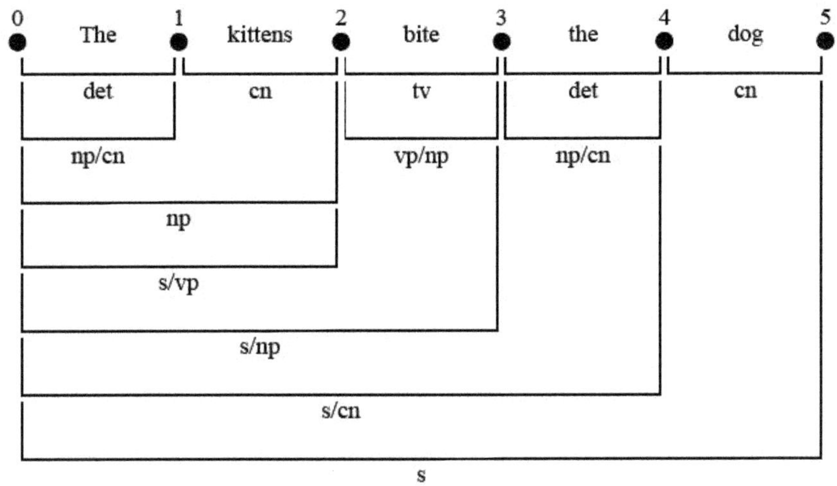

Figure 7.4: A fully incremental chart for *the kittens bite the dog*

belled np/cn, and spanning the first instance of *the*, is an active edge corresponding to an incomplete noun phrase. The notation np/cn indicates that the edge must be merged with an edge labelled cn (and hence spanning a common noun) to yield a complete noun phrase. The np/cn edge is licensed by the grammar rule that states that a noun phrase consists of a determiner followed by a common noun.

In the figure the edge labelled np/cn and spanning *the* is followed by an edge labelled cn (and spanning *kittens*). These edges together license a further edge, labelled np and spanning *the kittens*. The grammar rule that states a sentence consists of a noun phrase followed by a verb phrase allows another active edge spanning *the kittens* to be added to the chart. This edge is labelled s/vp, indicating that *the kittens* is a sentence that is missing a verb phrase.

The transitive verb *bites* may similarly be spanned by an edge labelled vp/np (because a transitive verb is equivalent to a verb phrase missing a noun phrase). Incremental processing may be maintained by adding an edge spanning the sentence initial fragment (labelled s/vp) and the verb phrase initial fragment (labelled vp/np). Together, the fragments yield a sentence missing a noun phrase, so the new edge is labelled s/np. Similar principles license an edge incorporating the second determiner (labelled s/cn) and the final edge spanning the entire sentence. Figure 7.4 shows the complete chart resulting from this approach. The chart is fully incremental because each successive word may be incorporated into the structure to its left.

The incremental technique depends upon three augmentations to the earlier approach:

1. allowing projection of edges corresponding to complete constituents to active edges spanning those constituents (e.g., projection from a complete Y constituent to an incomplete X/Z constituent spanning the same material, for each grammar rule of the form X $\rightarrow$ Y Z);
2. allowing an edge labelled X/Y followed by an edge labelled Y to be spanned by an edge labelled X; and
3. allowing an edge labelled X/Y followed by an edge labelled Y/Z to be spanned by an edge labelled X/Z.

The first two of these augmentations characterise the "left corner" family of parsing algorithms (so named because, in augmentation 1, the constituent Y is the left corner of the phrase X, so phrases are introduced when their left corners are encountered). The third augmentation, which is sometimes referred to as composition, is not essential for successful left-corner parsing but allows greater incrementality.

7.3.2 A Parallel Model of Left Corner Parsing

Conversion of the parser developed in Section 7.2.2 to a left corner parser requires modification only of the representations of syntactic categories and the rules within *Elaborate Chart* for creating edges on the chart. No modifications are required to the *Lexicon* or *Grammar Rules*.

Full generality requires that it be possible to represent several different kinds of syntactic category. The simplest are those corresponding to complete constituents (with no missing constituents), such as np, vp, and s. Incomplete constituents lacking one sub-constituent were illustrated above, but in general incomplete constituents may lack multiple sub-constituents, as illustrated by dative verbs (such as *give*), which require a noun phrase and a prepositional phrase to form a complete verb phrase. This corresponds to the fact that dative verbs are introduced by ternary phrase structure rules.

For full generality it is therefore appropriate to represent syntactic categories as structures of the form `atom/list`, where `atom` is the main category, and `list` is a list of the categories of missing constituents. This approach allows all categories to be represented in a uniform manner, for example:

`np/[ ]`: *the kittens*
`s/[vp]`: *the kittens*
`s/[ ]`: *the kittens bite the dog*
`np/[cn]`: *the*
`vp/[np]`: *bite*
`vp/[np, pp]`: *gave*
`vp/[cn, pp]`: *gave a*
`s/[cn, pp]`: *the kittens gave a*

Rule 1 (refracted): *Lexical look-up*
IF: `edge(N0, N1, word(W), L1)` is in *Chart*
`category(W, C)` is in *Lexicon*
`L` is `L1 + 1`
THEN: add `edge(N0, N1, cat(C/[ ]), L)` to *Chart*

Rule 2 (refracted): *Project complete constituents*
IF: `edge(N0, N1, cat(C1/[ ]), L1)` is in *Chart*
`rule(C, [C1|Tail])` is in *Grammar Rules*
`L` is `L1 + 1`
THEN: add `edge(N0, N1, cat(C/Tail), L)` to *Chart*

Rule 3 (refracted): *Merge active edges with following edge*
IF: `edge(N0, N1, cat(C/[H|T]), L1)` is in *Chart*
`edge(N1, N2, cat(H/[ ]), L2)` is in *Chart*
`L` is `max(L1, L2) + 1`
THEN: add `edge(N0, N2, cat(C/T), L)` to *Chart*

Box 7.6: Rules for parallel left-corner parsing

Given this representation, and ignoring structure building, the action of the rule for lexical look-up (Rule 1 from Box 7.4) must be modified to specify that lexical items correspond to complete constituents, as in Rule 1 of Box 7.6.

A second rule is required to apply phrase structure rules by projecting up from their left corners. Rule 2 of Box 7.6 fires when *Chart* contains an edge corresponding to a complete constituent and *Grammar Rules* contains a phrase structure rule with that constituent as its left corner. The list representations used for missing constituents ensure that Rule 2 may apply for all phrase structure rules, including unary phrase structure rules (e.g., projecting an intransitive verb (`iv/[ ]`) up to a complete verb phrase (`vp/[ ]`)), binary phrase structure rules (e.g., projecting a determiner (`det/[ ]`) up to an incomplete noun phrase (`np/[cn]`)), and higher-order phrase structure rules (e.g., projecting a dative verb (`dv/[ ]`) up to an incomplete verb phrase (`vp/[np, pp]`)).

Given Rules 1 and 2, a third rule (Rule 3 in Box 7.6) is required to merge edges. Rule 3 fires when a partial constituent is followed by a complete constituent of an appropriate type. Its action is to add an edge spanning those two constituents. The three rules in Box 7.6, together with the triggered rules for adding initial edges to the chart (Rules 1 and 2 in Box 7.2), constitute a complete, parallel, left-corner parser. No user-defined conditions are required.

Exercise 7.12: Create a new chart parser model (based on any non-structure building model developed earlier in the chapter) and convert it to a left-corner parser by replacing the relevant contents of *Elaborate Chart* with the above rules. Test the parser on a range of sentences. ◇

Exercise 7.13: Rule 3 from Box 7.6 only allows the combination of edges when the second edge spans a complete constituent. The rule therefore does not allow composition. Many constructions licensed by the phrase structure rules given earlier in the chapter cannot therefore be parsed in a fully incremental fashion by a parser based only on the rules in Box 7.6. Modify Rule 3 to overcome this restriction. ◇

Exercise 7.14: Incorporate the rules and lexicon developed in the project on tense and aspect into the left corner parser. ◇

7.3.3 Project: Structure Building During Left Corner Parsing

Left corner parsers present a problem for structure building: the elements spanned by edges on the chart need not correspond to complete constituents. Consequently, complete structures cannot be assigned to all chart edges. This problem may be overcome by adopting an appropriate representation for the structure of partial constituents.

For example, the partial constituent *the kittens bite* (assuming the transitive reading of *bite*), which is of syntactic category `s/[np]`, may be associated with the incomplete structure:

```
s(np(det(the),cn(kittens)),vp(tv(bite),X))/[X]
```

The structure mirrors the syntactic category in the sense that they are both missing one element. The variable (`X`) is a place-marker for this missing element. It is important that this place-marker is made explicit (in this case, within the list following the forward slash), as, if the following phrase is a noun phrase, then the structure of the sentence may be completed by unifying the place-marker with the structure of that phrase.

Thus, if the next word is *Fido* (of syntactic category np and with structure `np(pn(fido))`), unification of `X` with `np(pn(fido))` will yield a complete structural representation of the complete sentence:

```
s(np(det(the),cn(kittens)),vp(tv(bite),np(pn(fido))))
```

Structure building operations may similarly be associated with the other syntactic operations (lexical look-up, projection from a left corner, and composition).

Extend the left corner parser developed in Section 7.3.2 with structure building facilities. Test the extended parser on a range of sentences.

Hint: Only one structure building operation presents significant difficulties: the operation corresponding to projection from a left corner. Suppose a constituent of category B has been successfully identified, and the grammar contains a phrase structure rule of the form:

$$A \rightarrow B\ C\ D\ldots$$

In general, the rule may have any number of elements on the right hand side (so B may have any number of sister constituents). The rule allows an edge of category B to be spanned by an active edge of partial category A/[C, D, ...]. The structure associated with the active edge should take the form:

$$\mathtt{a(b, C, D, \ldots)/[C, D, \ldots]}$$

where `b` is the structure associated with the constituent of category B and `C`, `D`, etc. are the structures associated with categories C, D, etc.

The structure can be built using the structure building function introduced above. If the rule has two right hand side elements, a call such as:

`S` is composed of [`a`, `b`, `C`]

where `C` is a dummy variable, would instantiate `S` to the appropriate structure (`a(b, C)`). If the rule has three right hand side elements, however, a further dummy variable is required:

`S` is composed of [`a`, `b`, `C`, `D`]

in order to instantiate `S` appropriately (in this case to `a(b, C, D)`). A general solution requires forming a list of dummy variables, with the length of the list equal to the number of sister constituents of B in the grammar rule that introduces B, and using this on the right hand side of the structure building function.

7.4 Serial Parsing

All parsers developed thus far have operated in parallel. At each stage of processing, all possible parse structures have been generated, and, in the case of constituents with multiple possible structures (including both local and global ambiguity) all structures have been pursued in parallel. COGENT is well suited to the development of parallel parsing systems, but garden path sentences (as in Example 7.3) provide clear evidence that the HSPM does not work this way, for if it did such sentences would present no problem: all parse structures would be explored in parallel and the incorrect garden path structure would not prevent or impact upon the simultaneous generation of the correct and complete structure.

Theorists have adopted different interpretations of garden path and related phenomena (see Mitchell, 1994, for a review). On some accounts, parsing is a parallel process similar to that described above, but alternative parse structures are ranked in order of preference (e.g., MacDonald, Pearlmutter, & Seidenberg, 1994;

Trueswell & Tanenhaus, 1994; Vosse & Kempen, 2000). Garden path sentences are those that require a high-ranking parse to be discontinued and a low-ranking parse to be shifted to the top of the rank order. On other accounts, parsing is a strictly serial process in which a single structure, corresponding to the "preferred reading", is constructed during processing (e.g., Frazier & Fodor, 1978; Abney, 1989).

7.4.1 Computational Requirements of Serial Parsing

Within serial parsing models, at each point of potential ambiguity the parser selects one structure and ignores all others. If this structure proves to be incorrect (as in a garden path), then the parser retraces its steps (or backtracks) to a previous point of ambiguity, disassembling incorrectly parsed constituents on the way, and selects a different structure to pursue. On this view, garden path sentences cause the parser to backtrack. In severe cases this backtracking may fail, yielding grammatical sentences that cannot be parsed (i.e., a dissociation between linguistic competence and linguistic performance).

Serial linguistic processing therefore has several computational requirements. First, at each stage of processing the parser must select between elaborating existing memory structures (i.e., in the current context, adding a new edge spanning existing chart elements), processing the next word, or backtracking to some previous state of processing. If multiple sources of information deriving from, for example, semantic context, syntactic processing preferences, or statistical biases, may contribute to this selection — and some empirical work suggests that this is the case — then the selection process bears some similarity to the process of operator selection in problem solving (see Chapter 4; see also Newell, 1990, pp. 440–459, and Lewis, 1993). Recall that operator selection is a multi-step process, in which operators are first proposed and then evaluated. This allows multiple sources of information to contribute to an operator's evaluation. When all operators have been evaluated, the operator with the highest evaluation is selected and applied. The process then repeats.

The second computational requirement of serial parsing is that, at least in the context of chart parsing, processing should involve depth-first rather than breadth-first search of the parse space. That is, parsing should involve building a structure representing one possible parse, and abandoning this only if and when it proves counter-productive. Chart parsing as described in the previous sections tends to build a chart in which all edges (representing all possible parses) are present. Serial parsing within the chart parsing framework therefore requires inhibiting the production of some edges. Specifically, serial parsing requires that once an edge has been spanned (i.e., covered by a new edge), it should become unavailable for further processing.

A third computational requirement is that previous states of the parser must be recoverable when backtracking is required. Within the context of chart parsing previous states of the parser are represented by edges on the chart that are spanned by other, newer, edges. Backtracking therefore consists primarily of removing edges from the chart, thus exposing edges added earlier, and making them once again available for processing. Backtracking also requires that, when reparsing a constituent, the system yields an alternative parse. Thus, when multiple ways of combining constituents are available, the parser must differentiate between those that have been pursued and found to be wanting, and those that remain to be pursued.

In sum, serial chart parsing may be achieved with a system based on operator proposal, selection, and application, where the principal parsing operator is "add an edge", where backtracking (which involves the removal of edges) may be triggered if no operators are available, and where a mechanism is included to allow the system to recover from backtracking with an alternative parse.

7.4.2 A Serial Model of Left Corner Parsing

The Basic Architecture

Figure 7.5 shows a box and arrow diagram for an operator-based serial chart parser. The diagram differs from the parallel non-operator-based version (Figure 7.3) in two principal ways. First, the *Elaborate Chart* process has been replaced by three components: *Propose Operators* (a process containing rules that inspect *Chart* and propose possible operators and evaluations), *Operators* (a buffer in which proposed operators are stored), and *Apply Operator* (a process that selects the operator in *Operators* with the greatest evaluation and applies it to *Chart*). Second, the *Input/Output* process has been deleted. In its place, *Propose Operators* has read access to *Paper*. This configuration of components assumes that the reading of words is achieved through selection and application of an appropriate operator (rather than through a separate input/output process).

The use of an operator to read the next word requires a rule within *Propose Operators* to propose the operator at the appropriate time (i.e., when no other operators are being processed), and a rule within *Apply Operator* to apply such an operator if it is selected.

Incremental processing suggests that operator proposal should involve proposing an operator to read the next word at each stage in processing, but that the operator should have a low evaluation (so that processing of previously read words is preferred). Rule 1 of Box 7.7, which assumes an appropriate definition of the user-defined condition `next_unread_word/1`, is appropriate. This rule will only fire when *Operators* is empty. If there is an unread word, an operator to read that word will be proposed (i.e., added to *Operators*), and given an evaluation of zero.

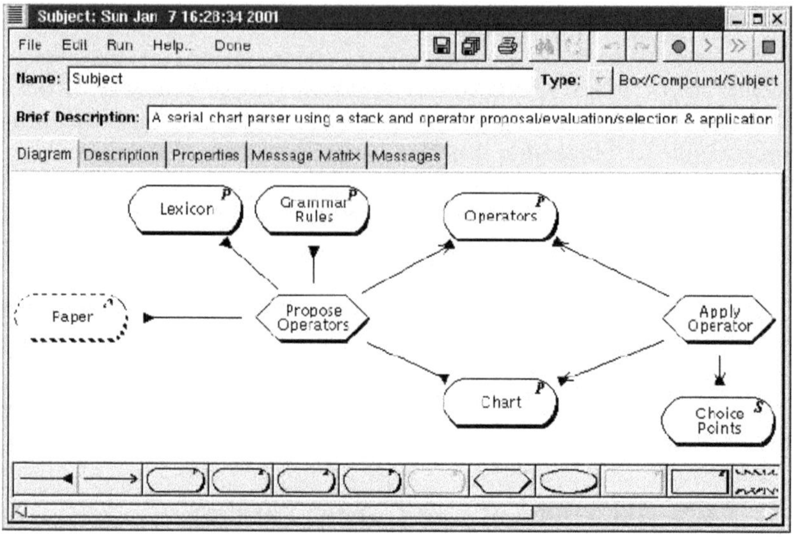

Figure 7.5: The box and arrow structure of the serial chart parser

Rule 1 (unrefracted): *Propose reading of next word*
IF: not `AnyOperators` is in *Operators*
`next_unread_word(Word)`
THEN: add `operator(add_word(Word), value(0))` to *Operators*

Box 7.7: An operator proposal rule for reading the next word

Exercise 7.15: Create a copy of the previous version of the left-corner parser and perform the modifications to both the top-level and the *Subject* box and arrow diagrams necessary for an operator-based approach (see Figure 7.5). Add Rule 1 from Box 7.7 and an appropriate definition for `next_unread_word/1` to *Propose Operators*. Test the modifications. The system should begin by proposing an operator to add the first input word to the chart.

Hint: The condition should compare the words on *Paper* with the words entered in *Chart*. If there are no words on *Chart*, the argument should be unified with the first word on *Paper*. If there are some words on *Chart*, the index of the right-most word should be used to identify the next word in *Paper*, and the argument should be unified with this. ◇

Rule 1 (unrefracted; once): *Select an operator*
IF: `operator(Operator, value(Score))` is in *Operators*
not `operator(AnyOp, selected)` is in *Operators*
not `operator(OtherOp, value(OtherScore))` is in *Operators*
`OtherScore` is greater than `Score`
THEN: delete all `operator(AnyOp, value(AnyVal))` from *Operators*
add `operator(Operator, selected)` to *Operators*

Rule 2 (refracted): *Add a word to the next position of the chart*
IF: `operator(add_word(W), selected)` is in *Operators*
`get_word_position_parameters(N0, N1)`
THEN: add `edge(N0, N1, word(W), W, 0)` to *Chart*

Box 7.8: Selected operator selection/application rules for *Apply Operator*

With the operator proposal rule of Box 7.7, only one operator will be proposed at a time, and that operator will always have an evaluation of zero. In general, however, multiple operators with different evaluations may be proposed during the parsing process. *Apply Operator* requires a rule for selecting from the available operators one operator with the highest value. The rule should fire whenever *Operators* contains evaluated operators, and should change the status of one of those operators (the selected operator) to `selected`. This effect is achieved by Rule 1 of Box 7.8 (see also Section 4.2.3 of Chapter 4).

Rules are also required to apply selected operators. Thus, if an `add_word`/1 operator is selected, a new word edge should be added to the chart as in Rule 2 of Box 7.8. Other operators (as introduced below) will require additional operator application rules. Rule 2 assumes that `get_word_position_parameters`/2 determines the vertices of the edge. If the chart is empty, this condition should bind its arguments to `0` and `1`. Otherwise the vertices should be determined from the values of the right-most word on the chart.

A further rule (not presented here) is required in *Apply Operator* to remove selected operators once they have been applied. While this could be achieved by adding an appropriate delete action to Rule 2 above, the action is required for all operator application rules, and so is better performed by a single general purpose rule that captures this general fact.

Exercise 7.16: Add the operator selection and application rules as described above (including a rule for deleting selected operators). Test your solution. The system should now propose and apply a series of operators, resulting in all words in the stimulus input for the current trial being added, in an incremental fashion, to the chart. ◇

Exercise 7.17: Convert the remainder of the parsing model to a serial, operator-based, left-corner parser. Further operator proposal rules will be required for the three edge addition rules previously defined in *Elaborate Chart* (for lexical look-up, projection from the left corner of a phrase structure rule, and composition of consecutive constituents). Each operator proposal rule should, like the operator proposal rule above, only fire when *Operators* is empty (i.e., when processing of the previous operator is complete), and should add operator specifications (i.e., elements representing edges to be added) to *Operators*. These operators should always be preferred to the `add_word/1` operator, but as yet we have no justification for favouring one over the other. Therefore give the operators generated by each rule equal positive evaluations. For present purposes do not attempt to restrict operators to edges that are not otherwise spanned, and do not attempt to include backtracking. This version of the parser will therefore not attempt depth-first parsing, but will perform a serial version of breadth-first parsing. Refer to Chapter 4 for more details of operator proposal, selection, and application if necessary. ◇

Exercise 7.18: The following grammar fragment licenses garden path sentences such as *the horse raced past the barn fell*:

NP → PN	PN: john, mary
NP → Det(Num) CN(Num)	Det(sing): a, every
CN(Num) → CN(Num) RedRel	Det(_): the
RedRel → VP	CN(sing): horse, barn
VP → IV	IV: fell
VP → TV(Comp) Comp	TV(PP(move)): raced
PP(X) → Prep(X) NP	Prep(move): through, past
S → NP VP	CN(plural): horses, barns

The garden path effect arises in the grammar because the clause *raced past the barn* may be analysed as a constituent of type RedRel (a reduced relative clause that may modify a common noun) or a constituent of type VP. Note also that the grammar includes the rule:

VP → TV(Comp) Comp

This is a "meta-rule" that licenses a variety of transitive verb-type constructions. In the grammar the lexical category of *raced* is defined as TV(PP(move)) (i.e., a transitive verb taking a single complement of category PP(move). The meta-rule therefore licenses phrases such as *raced past the barn* (because other rules license *past the barn* as a constituent of category PP(move)). If the grammar also included a lexical entry such as *chased*, of category VP(NP), the same meta-rule would license VP phrases such as *chased the horses*.

Replace the existing lexicon and grammar rules with the above, and substitute appropriate test sentences (involving garden path and non-garden path sentences

Rule 2 (unrefracted): *Propose lexical look-up*
IF: not `AnyOperator` is in *Operators*
`edge(A, B, word(W), SS, L)` is in *Chart*
not `edge_is_spanned(A, B, L)`
`category(W, C)` is in *Lexicon*
`build_structure(C, [SS], S)`
`L1` is `L + 1`
THEN: add `operator(add_edge(A, B, C/[ ], S, L1), value(5))` to *Operators*

Condition Definition: `edge_is_spanned/3`: *Is an edge already spanned?*
`edge_is_spanned(W0, W1, L1) :-`
`edge(N0, N1, C, S, L)` is in *Chart*
`W0` is not less than `N0`
`W1` is not greater than `N1`
`L` is greater than `L1`

Box 7.9: A rule to restrict lexical look-up (from *Propose Operators*)

licensed by the grammar) in the *Experimenter* module. Test the parser. It should provide correct parses for both garden path and non-garden path sentences of the grammar. It should also provide unusual parses for various constituents. For example, *the horse fell* should be parsable as both a complete sentence and as a noun phrase (via the reduced relative construction). (In fact, *the horse fell* is not a grammatical noun phrase of English. It is only licensed as such by this grammar because the grammar lacks features marking aspect. Specifically, reduced relative constructions require a verb phrase in progressive form (e.g., *raced past the barn* or *felled*), rather than one in the simple past (e.g., *fell*).) ◇

Restricting Operator Proposal

As noted above, serial (depth-first) parsing implies that there is one syntactic structure under construction at a time, and that, when adding edges to the chart, only operators that extend this structure are proposed. Operators that contribute to other structures or that reanalyse existing sub-structures are not proposed. This may be achieved by adding extra conditions to the operator proposal rules that prevent those rules from applying to edges that have already been spanned. To illustrate, consider the definition of `edge_is_spanned/3` in Box 7.9. The condition is true of an edge between `W0` and `W1` and at level `Y1` if and only if there is another edge on the chart spanning at least the same vertices, but at a higher level. Any such higher-level edge should prevent the lower-level edge from being used to trigger the addition of another edge.

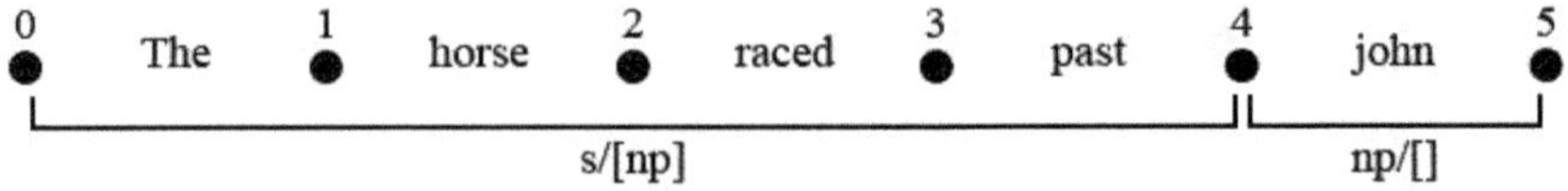

Figure 7.6: A partial chart for *the horse raced past john*

Rule 2 of Box 7.9 shows how `edge_is_spanned`/3 may be integrated into lexical look-up (with structure building). With the addition of the condition to check for spanning edges, `add_edge`/5 operators deriving from lexical look-up will only be proposed when a word is not otherwise spanned.

Exercise 7.19: Add the above definition of `edge_is_spanned`/3 and modify all operator proposal rules to block the proposal of operators that involve edges that have already been spanned. Test the model. It should now only build one parse for any constituent. That is, it should now be both incremental and sequential. Note however that this version of the parser will not be able to backtrack or recover from incorrect parsing attempts: once a parse has been established for a constituent the parser is unable to alter or decompose that parse. ◇

Simplified Operator Evaluation

In the model developed thus far there are three situations that may lead to an edge being added to the chart: lexical look-up, projection from the right-corner of a phrase to its parent phrase, and composition of consecutive edges. With random operator selection (as above), there will be no bias towards the addition of any particular type of edge when multiple edges resulting from the different situations might be added. To illustrate, consider the partial chart in Figure 7.6. Two possible edges might be added at this point (assuming the grammar introduced in Exercise 7.18):

1. The two constituents might be merged through composition, yielding an `s/[ ]` constituent
2. The `np/[ ]` constituent (john) could be projected up to `s/[vp]` (via the sentential rule S → NP VP)

In the situation shown, the first of these options should be favoured, and a general parsing strategy might consist of always favouring composition of edges over projection of left corners. Within the current framework, this strategy may be enforced by giving composition operators higher evaluations than projection operators.

Exercise 7.20: Alter the operator proposal rules to give higher numeric evaluations to composition operators than projection operators. Ensure that this results in appropriate operator selection when parsing the example above. ◇

The above operator evaluation strategy is naïve in many ways. For example, given a sentence ending in a noun phrase followed by a prepositional phrase (e.g., Example 7.1e), it will result in the noun phrase being attached to the verb phrase and the sentence before processing of the prepositional phrase. The prepositional phrase will then act as a sentence modifier, rather than a noun phrase modifier. The strategy therefore conflicts with that of *late closure*, identified by Kimball (1973). Late closure demands that clause modifiers are attached if possible before the clause is "closed". In the prepositional phrase modifier case alluded to above, this requires that the prepositional phrase is attached to the noun phrase, and not to the sentence. Kimball (1973) argues that late closure captures human ambiguity resolution preferences. However, violations of late closure do occur. For example, Crain and Steedman (1985) and Altmann and Steedman (1988) have demonstrated that different prior contexts can bias sentence processing, leading to early closure in some situations and late closure in others. In essence, they propose that a noun phrase is closed (i.e., incorporated into the sentential structure, through an operation such as composition) precisely when it identifies an appropriate referent. Thus, in a context with multiple cats, a fragment beginning *the cat* will lead to an expectation of a modifier of the initial noun phrase (such as a restrictive relative clause or a prepositional phrase), but if there is only one cat in the context, the same fragment will be parsed as a complete noun phrase. Incorporation of the proposal of Crain, Altmann, and Steedman into the current parser requires inclusion of a representation of context, and use of this representation to bias operator evaluation. Such extensions are beyond the scope of this chapter.

Operator evaluation might also be biased towards preferential application of certain phrase structure rules. For example, noun phrase modification by a prepositional phrase or a relative clause may be preferred over noun phrase modification by a reduced relative construction. Such preferences may be incorporated into operator evaluation by tagging all phrase structure rules with a numeric strength, and basing the evaluation of an operator on the strength of the rule that licenses the operator. The strengths of phrase structure rules might then be modified with use (e.g., adopting the laws of exercise and effect, Thorndike, 1911, such that rules are strengthened when used successfully and weakened when used unsuccessfully) — see Section 7.4.3.

Backtracking and Reanalysis

In order to allow backtracking it is necessary to record points in processing where multiple operators might apply. These points are known as choice points. If parsing fails, backtracking may then be achieved by undoing all processing since the last choice point, and selecting a different operator from those possible at that choice point. Multiple choice points may occur during normal processing. Full generality (i.e., completeness at the competence level) requires that all such choice points are recorded and that backtracking always involves returning to the most recent choice point that hasn't been fully explored. It is therefore appropriate to record choice points (and the context in which they occurred) on a stack. When choice points are encountered, their details may be pushed onto the stack. When backtracking is triggered the top-most choice point may be popped from the stack and its context restored.

To illustrate backtracking, consider the processing that ensues after parsing *the* as an `np/[cn]` and *horse* as a `cn/[ ]`. Several operators are applicable, including composing the constituents to give an `np/[ ]` constituent and projecting *horse* to a `cn/[rr]` (where `rr` denotes a reduced relative construction — see Exercise 7.18). This is a choice point because more than one operator is applicable. Processing should therefore involve selecting one operator to apply and pushing the other operator onto the choice point stack. Given the naïve evaluation strategy above, the former will be selected. If this selection turns out to be inappropriate (as in the case of garden path sentences), backtracking requires that 1) all edges added to the chart after the choice point are removed, 2) the second operator is selected, and 3) processing resumes from the choice point.

Extending the model developed thus far to include backtracking requires addition of a stack buffer (*Choice Points*) to *Subject* that is readable and writable by *Apply Operator*. The original operator selection rule (Rule 1 from Box 7.8) may be retained, but additional rules are required to push choice points onto the stack when they occur. This is achieved by Rules 2 and 3 in Box 7.10.

Rule 2 fires after an operator has been selected. It changes the state of the selected operator to `apply` (signalling application of the operator by additional rules) and removes all other operators from *Operators*.

Rule 3 fires only when multiple operators are applicable (i.e., when one operator has been selected and when other, unselected, operators with positive evaluations remain). Several aspects of the rules are critical. First, if the rule fires, it will fire in parallel with Rule 2 (i.e., it will be triggered before Rule 2 removes all unselected operators). Second, if it fires it will push a representation of the current choice point onto *Choice Points*. That representation consists of a `choices/2` term. The first argument of this term is a representation of the context. The second is the list of unselected operators with positive evaluations. This means that if there are several unselected but applicable operators, they will all be pushed onto the stack within a single choice point. The rationale for this is described below.

The representation of context is determined by `get_context/1`, a definition for which is also given in Box 7.10. This definition gives a context value of `0` if the choice point stack is empty and `C + 1` if the top-most element of the choice point stack was created in context `C`. Thus, if the top-most element of the choice point stack was created in context `4`, a call to `get_context/1` will bind its argument

Rule 2 (unrefracted): *Apply the selected operator, remove all others*
IF: `operator(Operator, selected)` is in *Operators*
THEN: delete all `operator(_, _)` from *Operators*
add `operator(Operator, apply)` to *Operators*

Rule 3 (unrefracted): *Push unselected operators onto the stack*
IF: `operator(Operator, selected)` is in *Operators*
`Ops` is the list of all `operator(O, value(V))` such that
`operator(O, value(V))` is in *Operators*
`V` is greater than `0`
`Ops` is distinct from [ ]
`get_context(Context)`
THEN: send `push(choices(Context, Ops))` to *Choice Points*

Condition Definition: `get_context/1`: *Get the current context id*
`get_context(0) :-`
not `Anything` is in *Choice Points*
`get_context(C1) :-`
`choices(C, _)` is in *Choice Points*
`C1` is `C + 1`

Box 7.10: Operator selection rules from *Apply Operator*, modified to use a context and record choice points

Rule 4 (unrefracted): *Remove applied operators*
IF: `operator(Operator, apply)` is in *Operators*
THEN: delete `operator(Operator, apply)` from *Operators*

Rule 5 (unrefracted): *Add a word to the next position of the chart*
IF: `operator(add_word(W), apply)` is in *Operators*
`get_word_position_parameters(N0, N1)`
`get_context(TS)`
THEN: add `edge(N0, N1, word(W), W, 0, TS)` to *Chart*

Box 7.11: Selected operator application rules from *Apply Operator*, modified to use a context

to 5.

Operator application rules follow the format set by Rule 2 of Box 7.8, with two exceptions:

1. a rule is required to delete applied operators, and
2. edges must include a specification of the context in which they were added.

Rule 4 in Box 7.11 addresses deletion of applied operators. Rule 5 illustrates the addition of a context specification to chart edges (see Box 7.8).

Exercise 7.21: Create a new model based on the previous no-backtracking serial model, add the *Choice Point* stack to the *Subject*, and modify the rules in *Apply Operator* as described above. (Be sure to include a rule for applying `add_edge/5` operators. The rule is not given above.) Test the model. It should behave much as before, except that as processing proceeds *Choice Points* should grow. ◇

Utilisation of choice point information requires detection of parsing failure and, on such failure, popping the top element of *Choice Points* and restoring the context prior to pushing that element. The three rules in Box 7.12 perform the necessary operations. Also given in the figure is a definition for the user-defined condition `parse_successful/0`, which is true when and only when the input has been successfully parsed.

Rule 7 restores the context prior to the previous choice point by removing all edges from the chart whose context (or time stamp) is after that of the choice point. Rule 8 restores all operators (and valuations) which were not applied when the choice point was first encountered. This allows processing to resume from the selection phase of the operator processing cycle. Rule 9 removes the choice point from the stack. All of these rules will fire in parallel when backtracking is necessary. However, Rule 7 will have multiple instantiations if multiple chart edges were added in the previous context, and Rule 8 will have multiple instantiations if several operators were possible at the popped choice point.

With the given definition, `parse_successful/0` will be true if and only if there is an edge of category `s/[ ]` (i.e., a complete sentence) spanning the entire word sequence. This could be improved but is sufficient for present purposes.

Discussion of the Model

The model should now be able to parse both *the horse raced past john* and *the horse raced past john fell*, but in the latter case parsing will involve extensive backtracking and reanalysis, and will only be possible if the choice point stack's capacity is sufficient. The model therefore captures some of the principal facts surrounding garden path sentences. Nevertheless, many aspects of the model are clearly highly simplified, including the detection of parsing failure and the evaluation of operators.

Consider first the detection of parsing failure. This is crucial in triggering backtracking, but the condition definition suggested above depends on the parser being given self-contained sentences. At first glance this may seem to require a further parser to segment the words in the input into sentences. However, both written and spoken language contain cues that may assist in determining when a

Rule 7 (unrefracted): *Backtrack (step a: remove unwanted edges)*
TRIGGER: `system_quiescent`
IF: not `parse_successful`
`choices(TS, Operators)` is in *Choice Points*
`edge(N0, N1, C, S, L, TS1)` is in *Chart*
`TS1` is greater than `TS`
THEN: delete `edge(N0, N1, C, S, L, TS1)` from *Chart*

Rule 8 (unrefracted): *Backtrack (step b: unstack stacked operators)*
TRIGGER: `system_quiescent`
IF: not `parse_successful`
`choices(TS, Operators)` is in *Choice Points*
`Operator` is a member of `Operators`
THEN: add `Operator` to *Operators*

Rule 9 (unrefracted): *Backtrack (step c: pop the stack)*
TRIGGER: `system_quiescent`
IF: not `parse_successful`
`choices(TS, Operators)` is in *Choice Points*
THEN: send pop to *Choice Points*

Condition Definition: `parse_successful`/0: *Has the parse succeeded?*
`parse_successful :-`
`edge(0, N, cat(s/[]), _, _, _)` is in *Chart*
not `edge(N, _, word(_), _, _, _)` is in *Chart*

Box 7.12: Rules from *Apply Operator* for processing choice points

phrase or sentence is complete (and hence whether parsing has been successful). In the case of written language, the cues take the form of punctuation. In the case of spoken language the cues are embedded in the prosody, or changing tone and rhythm, of the input.

Operator evaluation is perhaps the least satisfactory aspect of the model. Giving operators fixed evaluations means that the parser cannot adjust its performance in an attempt to minimise backtracking (see Section 7.4.3) and that the parser is insensitive to the greater context in which a sentence may occur. Given this, the model is perhaps better viewed as a framework within which different approaches to operator evaluation may be explored.

The construction of choice points also requires comment. Rule 3 in Box 7.10 builds a choice point from the set of all applicable but non-selected operators with positive evaluations. Operators with zero or negative evaluations are therefore excluded from the choice point, and, because of the mechanism for recovering when backtracking occurs, cannot be selected on backtracking. This is primarily because of the mechanism used for reading successive words. At almost every stage in processing, an `add_word/1` operator is proposed, so that the parser may proceed to the next word if processing of the previously read words appears complete. If such operators were viewed as on a par with legitimate operators for projecting words or combining categories, then every operator selection step would become a choice point. (To verify this, try altering the rules so that operators with zero evaluation are included in the choice point.)

The second critical feature relevant to the construction of choice points concerns the situation when multiple unselected positively evaluated operators exist. All such operators are included in the choice point. When backtracking occurs, the full set of such operators is recreated in *Operators*, allowing the standard operator selection process to resume. If after selection there still remain multiple unselected positively evaluated operators, then the choice point will be re-established, but with only the remaining unselected operators. In this way, backtracking will if necessary progress in sequence through all possible operators, irrespective of the number of possible operators. An alternative approach would be to keep track of those operators that had been unsuccessfully applied (and the context in which they had failed), and then allow regeneration of all operators when backtracking occurs. Failed operators could then be given negative evaluations.

Exercise 7.22: The model as developed above is a competence model in the sense that, although it is serial and may perform complex backtracking while attempting to parse a sequence of words, it is able to parse all (and only) sentences of the grammar defined by its lexicon and phrase structure rules. One way in which performance factors may impinge upon the model's behaviour is through the capacity of the choice point stack. Explore the effect of restricting the stack's capacity (through the Properties panel of *Choice Points*). How does limiting the stack's capacity affect the range of sentences that may be parsed? ◇

7.4.3 Project: Tuning Operator Evaluation

Backtracking provides the parser with a way of recovering after selecting an inappropriate operator. It also gives the parser a way of learning operator evaluations. As noted above, if evaluations are attached to phrase structure rules rather than to the operator proposal rules, then evaluations may be strengthened or weakened depending on the success or failure of the particular phrase structure rule.

To illustrate, suppose that a grammar contains (among others) the following phrase structure rules:

R1: NP → Det CN
R2: CN → CN RedRel
R3: CN → CN PP

Suppose in addition that the input begins with two consecutive constituents that have been successfully parsed, the first of category Det and the second of category CN. Each rule licenses a different operator. Rule R1 licenses an operator that composes the two constituents into a single NP category. Rule R2 allows the constituent of category CN to be projected to one of CN/[RedRel], and Rule R3 allows it to be projected to one of CN/[PP].

To continue the example, suppose that two numbers are associated with each rule: one representing the evaluation of the *compose* operator arising from application of the rule, and the second representing the evaluation of the *project* operator arising from application of the rule. The numbers might be as follows:

Rule	Evaluation (compose)	Evaluation (project)
R1: NP → Det CN	2.5	3.1
R2: CN → CN RedRel	4.5	0.9
R3: CN → CN PP	4.5	1.8

The evaluations associated with the rules may be transferred to the specific operators, yielding evaluations of 2.5, 0.9, and 1.8 respectively for the three operators above. Given such evaluations, the compose operator based on Rule R1 would be selected and applied. If application of that operator results in successful parsing of the sentence, then the evaluation is justified, and the relevant table entry might therefore be increased by a small amount (e.g., by 5%). If, however, parsing fails and backtracking is required, then the evaluation is not justified, so the *compose* evaluation for Rule R1 should be decreased by a small amount.

Extend the serial left-corner parsing model to include tuning of operator evaluations along the lines of the previous example. In order to fully explore the behaviour of the extended model, it will be necessary to create a database of sample sentences containing instances of various phrase constructions. Ideally the database would be drawn from naturally occurring texts. For present purposes, however, it is sufficient to construct a grammar including some local ambiguity and 50 sentences licensed by that grammar. The sentences should contain an uneven distribution of the constructions, such that some constructions (e.g., reduced relative clauses) are rare in comparison to others (e.g., prepositional phrases).

An experimenter module will be required to administer the sentences to the subject module as a block of trials, and to record the number of processing cycles required to parse each sentence. Start the evaluations of all operators at random values, and run the model over the sentences a number of times (i.e., for several blocks). For each block, have the experimenter plot the total number of cycles required to parse the complete set of sentences. How does this number vary with block? Explore different strategies for modifying evaluations and the effect of such strategies on the relation between the number of cycles required to parse the database and block.

7.5 Alternative Approaches to Sentence Processing

The approach to sentence processing adopted above is based on a traditional view of a parser that employs a grammar to test well-formedness. The HSPM may not work this way. It may, for example, involve moment-by-moment interaction with a meaning-based processing system that disambiguates local syntactic ambiguities or that makes predications about forthcoming syntactic structures. Alternatively, it may involve a number of partially independent processes acting in parallel on the input in an attempt to derive meaning.

7.5.1 Coupled Syntactic and Semantic Processing

Prior semantic context (i.e., the meaning of prior sentences) has been shown to have measurable effects upon sentence processing. Thus, and as noted above in Section 7.19, Crain and Steedman (1985) and Altmann and Steedman (1988) have argued that different prior contexts can bias the HSPM to early phrasal closure in some situations and late phrasal closure in others.

The proposal that syntactic processing might be influenced at this low level by prior context or meaning is significant from a cognitive science perspective. It implies that syntactic processing is not autonomous (i.e., independent of other cognitive processes). Consequently, it argues that it is incorrect to conceive of the HSPM as a Fodorian input module (Fodor, 1983), performing a simple process of transduction between linguistic input and central cognition. Rather, the proposal requires that the operation of the HSPM may be influenced by knowledge or beliefs (i.e., in the language of Fodor, 1983, the HSPM is "cognitively penetrable").

With respect to the sequential operator-based parser described above, Crain, Altmann, and Steedman's proposal may be incorporated by building a representation of meaning during the parsing process and using this representation to bias operator evaluation. The principal difficulties associated with such an extension relate to the design of an appropriate representation of meaning. A range of alternatives are available in the literature. (See, for example, Hodges, 1977, Davidson, 1980, Kamp, 1981, Dowty, Wall, & Peters, 1981, Barwise & Perry, 1983, or Groenendijk & Stokhof, 1991.)

Crain and Steedman's (1985) methodology involved comparing the grammaticality judgements of participants when given different contexts. They did not attempt to measure processing time. Other work using monitoring of eye movements has demonstrated that the interplay between syntax and semantics is less clear. In particular, context does not entirely eliminate garden path effects. Rather, it appears to aid reanalysis (see, for example Konieczny, Hemforth, Scheepers, & Strube, 1997). This suggests that context only comes into play when parsing fails. The operator-based parsing framework may also be elaborated to explore this suggestion, by resorting to semantic context to aid operator evaluation only when parsing fails.

7.5.2 Towards Constraint-Based Parsing

Several modern syntactic theories view well-formedness not as a unitary concept resulting from adherence by a word sequence to phrase structure rules but as the simultaneous satisfaction by a word sequence of a set of semi-independent constraints. Such constraints might include:

- A well-formed sentence must contain one and only one main verb (unless the main verbs are co-ordinated, as in *Mary patted and hugged the kitten*).
- Sub-constituents must also be present to fill all obligatory argument roles (e.g., agent and patient) of the main verb.
- All sub-constituents must be associated with one and only one argument role of the main verb.
- Agreement within and between constituents must be consistent.
- Tense and aspect within the verb phrase must be coherent.

One obvious advantage of a constraint-based approach such as this is that if a word sequence involves only minor violations of one or two constraints, then it may still be possible to determine an interpretation for the word sequence.

Constraint-based approaches suggest that parsing is not a matter of checking well-formedness against a set of phrase structure rules. Rather, within such approaches parsing reduces to a constraint satisfaction problem: to ensure syntactic well-formedness of a word sequence it is necessary to ensure that all constraints are simultaneously satisfied by the sequence. This in turn suggests that the HSPM involves multiple, possibly parallel, constraint testing processes.

Developing a concrete constraint-based implementation of a Sentence Processing Mechanism presents many challenges for cognitive modelling. The parallel nature of processing within COGENT, however, makes it an ideal tool to develop such an implementation. A first pass at such a model might consist of a single buffer (a kind of linguistic working memory) containing a representation of the word sequence being processed, and a number of separate processes that operate on the contents of the buffer, with each process ensuring that the word sequence satisfies a different linguistic constraint. Within such an approach, processes will also need to annotate the contents of the buffer, providing information to other processes acting on the buffer, or signalling preferred readings and/or constraint failures.

7.6 Further Reading

This chapter has explored in depth just one issue related to sentence processing, that of syntactically guided parsing. A good contemporary introduction to the full range of issues involved is provided by the edited collection of Garrod and Pickering (1999). Chapters in that volume, however, assume significant background knowledge of relevant linguistics and cognitive psychology, and so the volume is most appropriate for relatively advanced readers. Less advanced readers are encouraged to begin with literature anchored in the contributing fields of syntax, semantics, and computational (psycho-)linguistics.

With respect to syntax, Burton-Roberts (1986) provides an excellent readable introduction to sentence structure. This introduction is to a large extent independent of syntactic theory, and therefore serves well as a basis for more detailed reading grounded in specific syntactic theories. One source of such reading is Sells (1985), who provides an even-handed introduction to three such syntactic theories (Government and Binding, Lexical Functional Grammar, and Generalised Phrase Structure Grammar). A more in-depth introduction to Government and Binding Theory is provided by Radford (1988). Other relevant sources include Gazdar, Klein, Pullum, and Sag (1985) (for Generalised Phrase Structure Grammar), Pollard and Sag (1987, 1994) (for Head-Driven Phrase Structure Grammar), and Wood (1993) (for Categorial Grammar). Many of these texts cover a range of important syntactic phenomena not covered in this chapter (e.g., centre-embedding, movement, unbounded dependencies, and restrictions on pronominal reference).

Due to space considerations this chapter has ignored the highly important area of sentence meaning or semantics. Two fundamental topics in natural language semantics are propositional logic and the predicate calculus, and Hodges (1977) provides a clear account of each of these. More advanced material, and in particular logical treatments of various semantic "puzzles", is covered by Dowty *et al.* (1981) and Barwise and Perry (1983).

One of the most influential early papers to bring computational considerations to bear on the psychology of sentence processing was that of Kimball (1973). This paper is of great historical and pedagogical importance, as is much of the later work directly predicated on it (e.g., Frazier & Fodor, 1978; Wanner, 1980, 1988). This, and more recent work, is summarised in Mitchell (1994). Further computational perspectives on sentence processing are provided by Allen (1995), Berwick and Weinberg (1984), and Pereira and Shieber (1987). Allen's book is a standard text that covers a variety of issues relating to parsing (including chart parsing). Berwick and Weinberg present a performance theory to accompany Chomsky's theory of Government and Binding (Chomsky, 1981). Pereira and Shieber use the programming language Prolog to illustrate how the notion of unification may be used to account for a wide range of linguistic phenomena.

Chapter 8

Executive Processes

David W. Glasspool and Richard P. Cooper

Overview: Executive processes are defined as those that co-ordinate and monitor other cognitive processes. Some psychological findings relating to executive processes and disorders of executive processing following neurological damage are then reviewed. Following this, discussion turns to the modelling of executive processes. A framework for executive processes and their relation to non-executive processes is presented, and an implementation of that framework developed. The framework is applied to the Wisconsin card-sorting test and the six element test — two common tests of executive function. The chapter concludes with a discussion of some alternative views of executive processes.

8.1 The Domain of Executive Processes

Previous chapters have explored limited and well-bounded areas of cognition. In this chapter we take a wider view, looking at the way these individual cognitive faculties can operate together to form a complete cognitive system.

When multiple cognitive modules are combined into a single system, a new type of problem arises — the problem of making sure that different modules work together coherently as a whole. A new class of processes is required to tackle this problem, processes which are able to take a wider view of the system as a whole and supervise the various component modules to ensure that they work together smoothly. Additionally, some types of process relate to the cognitive system as a whole rather than to its individual components, for example setting overall goals and monitoring progress towards achieving them. Taken together, processes of this type are termed supervisory or executive processes.

The term "executive processes" is difficult to define precisely, and it tends to be used rather loosely. Here, we will define executive processes as those which:

- co-ordinate the joint action of multiple cognitive faculties,
- allocate cognitive resources,
- manipulate and set goals and priorities for the cognitive system as a whole,
- monitor the state of the agent as a whole, and its relationship to the environment.

We can see that these types of process all share two features. Firstly, they are all concerned with the state and action of the agent as a whole, rather than a limited subset of the cognitive system. Secondly, they all act on other parts of the cognitive system rather than directly on the world.

8.2 Basic Psychological Findings

Executive processes are amongst the highest level cognitive processes, relatively distant both from perceptual input and from motor output. This makes it particularly difficult to study these functions rigorously. Since executive processes only operate by supervising other "lower level" processes, how can we be sure that the particular phenomenon we are studying is due to the operation of executive processes rather than to the lower level processes themselves? Although many tasks studied by experimental psychologists appear to involve executive functions, in most cases it is next to impossible to isolate the effect of these functions with any certainty — there are few cases where it seems that executive processes can genuinely be directly observed in a psychological experiment. One case that has been claimed to be an exception is the task-switching paradigm. This is considered in more detail below.

Although it is difficult to study executive functions when they are operating normally, it is much easier to see their effects when they do *not* work properly. Executive processes seem particularly prone to failure when we are tired, trying to do too many things at once, or simply not concentrating on what we are doing. In these situations we are all likely to make mistakes, and the types of mistake we make can provide some evidence about the way executive processes supervise and monitor our behaviour when they are operating successfully.

More dramatic examples of executive processes becoming conspicuous by their absence can occur when the brain itself is damaged. Brain damage following stroke, head injury, or hemorrhage, especially when localised to the pre-frontal cortex, can lead to situations where the individual cognitive abilities required to carry out a task are all operating correctly, but certain aspects of the co-ordination or supervision required to combine these abilities and complete the task are missing. Studying exactly what a patient with such a condition *can't* do can help pinpoint what the missing functions do in a normal person, and may even help shed light on how they work.

In this section we discuss the type of evidence each of these situations can provide.

8.2.1 Task Switching

Participants in a task-switching experiment are typically presented with a series of stimuli to which they must respond as rapidly as possible, and their reaction time is recorded. However, more than one type of response is possible. For example, the stimuli might be coloured words, where the task is either to read the word or say the colour of the ink. The participant receives a cue as each stimulus is presented telling them which type of response is required. Thus, a high-pitched sound might indicate that the word is to be read, whereas a low-pitched sound might indicate that the colour is to be named. Typically the participant will be cued for the same type of response several times, then suddenly the cue will change. At this point the participant must "switch tasks" to give the other response type. Their reaction time usually shows a slower response on trials when they must make a different type of response from the previous trial, compared with trials which require the same type of response as the previous trial. This slowing in reaction time even occurs when the cue precedes the stimulus, and so when the participant can anticipate the type of response required.

The extra time taken when the type of response must be changed is commonly taken to indicate that a certain amount of time is required to set up the cognitive system to carry out a new task (i.e., make a new type of response). These "task shift costs" are thus assumed to reflect the operation of executive processes that must somehow reconfigure the cognitive system to carry out the new task. A significant amount of research has been carried out into the relationship of this cost to the types of tasks being switched, and the conditions under which it is elicited (e.g., Rogers & Monsell, 1995; Meiran, 1996). This is not the only way in which this phenomenon has been interpreted, however. Allport, Styles, and Hsieh (1994) have argued that the longer reaction time when tasks are switched simply reflects interference from the previous task, which makes it more difficult to perform the new task without errors.

Regardless of this dispute it can be argued that in either case executive functions are involved, either in setting up the cognitive system for the new task or in suppressing the old task and monitoring performance for errors caused by interference. Task switching studies, then, seem to show situations where executive functions are invoked. They reveal characteristic time lags as the executive processes operate, but they do not tell us what exactly is happening during this interval. To get a clearer picture of how executive functions operate we must turn instead to the characteristic ways in which they *fail* to operate.

8.2.2 Action Lapses and Slips

If executive processes are those that organise and supervise other cognitive processes, then when executive processes fail to operate properly we should expect certain types of error to occur in which it is the organisation of sub-processes that is affected, rather than the sub-processes themselves. In fact such errors are quite common in everyday life. We all make occasional mistakes in everyday tasks when we are not concentrating on what we are doing. For example, someone who is making coffee without concentrating on the task in hand might pour water from a kettle into a mug without boiling it first. In a mistake like this the individual actions involved — filling the kettle, putting coffee powder into the mug, pouring the water — are all performed correctly. It is the organisation of the actions which is incorrect — a step has been missed out.

A number of researchers have studied the slips and lapses made by normal people during routine, everyday behaviour. Perhaps the best known study is by Reason (1984), who analysed diaries of errors kept by participants. Errors in everyday behaviour turn out to be more common than many people would like to admit, but, perhaps surprisingly, the majority can be classified as belonging to just a limited set of types. These include errors of "place substitution" — the right action is carried out but in the wrong place (e.g., putting the coffee mug, rather than the milk, into the fridge after making coffee), errors of "object substitution" — the right action is carried out but using the wrong object (e.g., opening a jar of jam, not the coffee jar, when intending to make coffee), errors of omission (e.g., pouring water into a coffee mug without boiling it), and errors involving the "capture" of behaviour by a different routine (such as going upstairs to get changed but instead getting into bed).

In all of these cases we would be inclined to say that the individual actions involved are being performed correctly. The problem is that they are not quite the actions that were intended — they have been poorly specified or poorly organised. The errors appear to occur in executive processes responsible for specifying and organising action, and the types of error which can occur can give us information about the way in which these processes operate. For example, we can see that actions appear to be represented separately from the objects which are to be acted on, so that the action "put something in the fridge", which should apply to the milk, can end up being applied to the coffee mug.

It also seems that objects in the environment can influence the way actions are organised, allowing an unrelated item (a jar of jam, in the example above) to intrude on the sequence of actions involved in making coffee simply because it is in the right place at the right time. The environment can also affect whole sequences of behaviour, such as in the example of going upstairs to get changed but getting into bed, where a stimulus from the environment which strongly suggests a particular habitual behaviour (going upstairs to bed) causes that behavioural sequence to take over. That these errors tend to occur when we are distracted or our attention is diverted suggests that normal or error-free behaviour involves near continuous monitoring of that behaviour.

8.2.3 Neurological Damage to Executive Systems

While slips in everyday behaviour can provide some information about the nature of executive processes, the more dramatic effects on behaviour when executive systems are damaged or destroyed can be even more informative. A number of types of brain damage appear to affect executive processes, and several neuropsychological tests have been developed to assess this type of damage. We can get a better idea of what is involved in the supervision of behaviour by executive processes by studying precisely what neurologically normal individuals can do which patients with these forms of neurological damage cannot.

Schwartz and her colleagues have made a long study of patients with *action disorganisation syndrome* (Schwartz, Reed, Montgomery, Palmer, & Mayer, 1991; Schwartz, Montgomery, Fitzpatrick-De Salme, Ochipa, Coslett, & Mayer, 1995). These patients, with damage to their frontal lobes, make errors in everyday tasks that are similar to those of normal individuals discussed above — they make errors in the sequencing of actions, they omit or insert actions, and they make substitutions of place or object. The difference with these patients is that their errors are very much more frequent — frequent enough to make life very difficult for them. For example Schwartz *et al.* (1991) report a patient HH whose performance was monitored during test sessions in which he made a cup of coffee as part of his breakfast routine. Over 28 such sessions he made a total of 97 errors. More than half of these errors were place and object substitutions, suggesting that HH's behaviour was easily "captured" by salient stimuli in his environment.

Utilisation behaviour (Lhermitte, 1983), another syndrome associated with frontal lobe damage, also involves irrelevant responses suggested by the environment taking control of behaviour. A patient showing utilisation behaviour will utilise objects in his or her immediate environment, even when instructed not to. Thus, the patient might be distracted by a glass and water jug on a table in front of him or her, and pour and then drink a glass of water, or he or she may pick up and deal from a pack of cards left on a nearby table (Shallice, Burgess, Schon, & Baxter, 1989). This sort of behaviour seems to imply that intentional control of behaviour is weakened, allowing the influence of the environment to have a greater effect than usual.

One aspect of normal executive processes which is highlighted by these failures is the suppression of prepotent responses. Often an action or idea will be strongly suggested by the environment or the current task, but that action or idea must be suppressed if the task is to be completed successfully. The cases described above of actions suggested by the environment interfering with everyday behaviour in action disorganisation syndrome and utilisation behaviour are examples. An experiment which directly addresses this function is the Hayling sentence completion task (Burgess & Shallice, 1996), in which participants are given a sentence with the final word missing (but strongly implied by the rest of the sentence). For example, "I drove to the shops in my ____". In condition A of the experiment, participants are asked to supply a word that fits the sentence (e.g., "car"). In condition B, they must supply a word that does *not* fit. Some patients with frontal lobe damage perform well in condition A but extremely poorly in condition B — they seem unable to inhibit the response strongly suggested by the sentence.

A slightly different type of organisation of behaviour is highlighted by *strategy application disorder* (Shallice & Burgess, 1991). Patients with this disorder are able to carry out a wide range of individual tasks with no difficulty — indeed, they may score at normal levels in standard neurological tests. Their difficulty is in co-ordinating a number of simultaneous task demands. For example, such a patient may be able to carry out individual tasks involved in cooking a meal — preparing ingredients, possibly even cooking individual dishes — but would be completely unable to organise these tasks in order to plan and cook a full meal. They might spend all of their time chopping vegetables, or cook dessert but forget about the main course. Their deficit appears to be in the ability to schedule multiple tasks over an extended period and switch between tasks when required to keep everything running smoothly together.

Shallice and Burgess (1991) demonstrated strategy application disorder in two studies. In the first — the multiple errands test — patients were required to make a shopping excursion on which they had to carry out a list of tasks, such as sending a postcard (which requires buying a postcard and a stamp, writing the card, and remembering to send it) and finding the temperature in Aberdeen yesterday (which requires buying and reading a newspaper). Strategy application disorder patients could carry out some or all of the tasks, but they were not able to co-ordinate them in an efficient way (e.g., they ended up going into the same shop several times). Overall they took much longer and were less likely to complete the task than controls.

The second task developed by Shallice and Burgess (1991) — the six element test — required participants to perform six separate tasks in fifteen minutes. The tasks were individually simple (two each of dictating a route, performing a series of simple arithmetic problems, and writing the names of a series of objects shown on cards), and all participants were able to complete the individual tasks without difficulty. However, the tasks could not all be completed within fifteen minutes, and so participants had to select a way of combining the six tasks to optimise their score. The task was scored such that earlier responses within a component task were worth more points than later responses, so completing a little of all tasks would yield a better score than completing all of one task. In addition, the rules of the task require that participants should not switch directly between two tasks

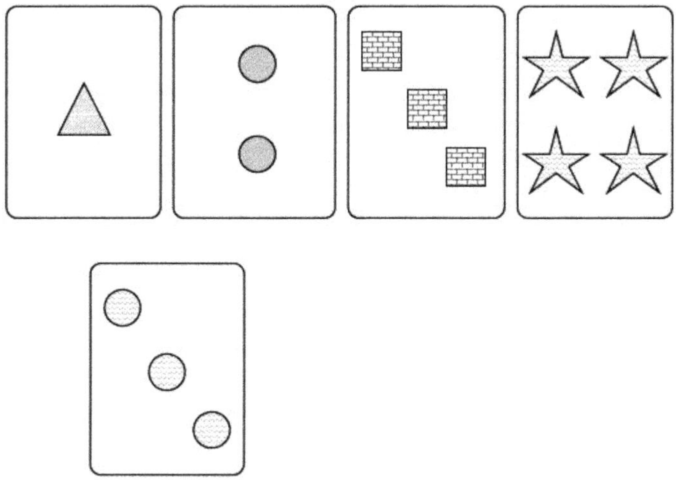

Figure 8.1: The general layout of the Wisconsin card-sorting test (WCST). Where should the lower card go? The participant is asked to sort cards into piles corresponding to four "stimulus" cards, but they are not told the criterion for sorting.

of the same type (e.g., two route dictation tasks).

Shallice and Burgess (1991) reported three patients, all with above average IQ despite frontal brain injury, who performed poorly on the composite task in comparison to control participants who were matched to the patients on age and IQ. The patients tended to focus on one task to the detriment of other tasks. Thus, and in contrast to the control participants, the patients tended to spend most of their time on one or two tasks. Consequently they typically attempted fewer tasks than the control participants. Shallice and Burgess (1991) ruled out motivational and retrospective memory factors as possible causes of the patients' behaviours. Instead, they argued that the problems of their patients were related to an inability to work with *delayed intentions* — making a "mental note" that an activity needs to be carried out later in a schedule, and then remembering to do it at the appropriate point.

A second experimental task that is often used to assess frontal lobe damage is the Wisconsin card-sorting test (WCST: Milner, 1963; Nelson, 1976). In the WCST a participant is given a set of cards that vary in the number, shape, and colour of symbols shown on them. Thus a card might show two green squares, or four red triangles. The experimenter lays out four "stimulus" cards, and the participant is asked to sort the cards into piles corresponding to these, but they are not told the criterion for sorting. The test is illustrated in Figure 8.1.

Participants might sort cards by the number of symbols, their colour, or their shape. After each card is placed the experimenter indicates whether it was correctly sorted. Once the participant has worked out the sorting criterion the experimenter is using, the experimenter waits until they have placed ten cards correctly, then changes to another sorting criterion without warning. The participant must work out from the feedback they are receiving that the required strategy has changed, and must find and adopt a new strategy.

The WCST places demands on a number of aspects of executive processing, including the inhibition of prepotent responses and task-switching, and also two other related functions. The first is problem solving, which is often considered to be closely related to executive processes as it is involved in setting up goals for behaviour. The second is monitoring progress towards current goals, and identifying errors and failures to achieve intended effects of actions. This is an important part of the ability to carry out actions in an uncertain and changeable world.

Neurologically healthy individuals typically catch on to the task procedure quickly and make few errors, these being immediately after the change of sorting criterion. Patients with frontal lobe damage make many errors, typically involving the inability to discover the sorting strategy or, more often, inability to change strategies despite repeated negative feedback.

8.3 A Framework

Norman and Shallice (1980, 1986) interpret the data outlined above as implying that two distinct systems operate together to provide executive control over behaviour. One system, contention scheduling (CS), controls *automatic* behaviour — over-learned or habitual behaviour which can be used in well-known situations without requiring any special thought, such as procedures for making coffee, or driving a car. Any type of behaviour which is so well known that it can be done while thinking of something else is controlled by this system. The other system, the supervisory attentional system (SAS), is responsible for *willed* behaviour. This system is responsible for controlling behaviour in new or difficult situations when a set of well-known habits are not available, or can't be relied upon. An entirely new sequence of actions may be required, or more habitual actions may need to be inhibited or carefully monitored to prevent mistakes.

The two systems operate together as shown in Figure 8.2. All behaviour is ultimately controlled by the contention scheduling system, but the supervisory attentional system is able to modulate the operation of contention scheduling when required in order to guide behaviour.

The contention scheduling system comprises a hierarchy of *schemas*. Each schema specifies a set of actions which are carried out to accomplish a particular piece of behaviour. For example, a schema might exist for a well-learned behaviour like making a cup of coffee. The schema would include boiling water,

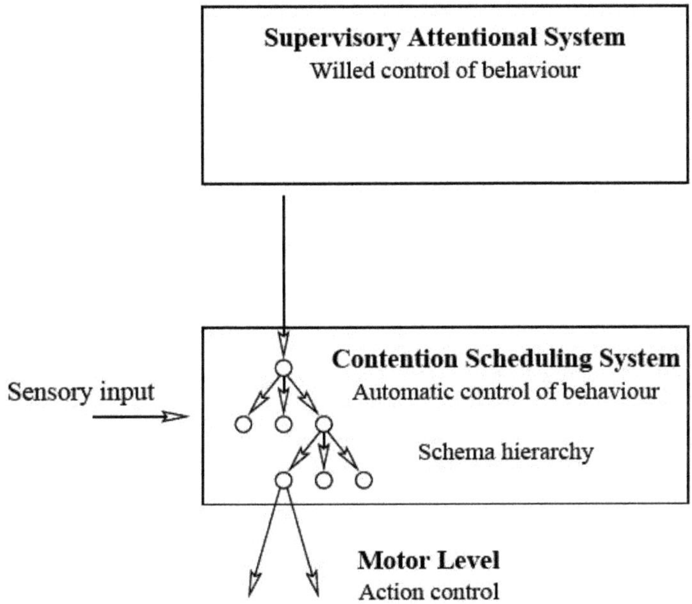

Figure 8.2: Norman and Shallice's framework for automatic and willed control of behaviour comprises two systems: the contention scheduling system which controls automatic or habitual action, and the supervisory attentional system which imposes willed control on behaviour. The contention Scheduling system comprises a hierarchical set of schemas for well-learned behaviours. The lowest level schemas directly control low-level actions in the motor system.

putting coffee powder in a cup, adding milk, and so on, and would specify certain constraints on the order in which these must be carried out (thus pouring water into the cup should happen after the water has boiled). Each of the actions in the schema may be a simple action, such as picking up a spoon, or may refer to another schema, such as boiling water, which involves several actions and may be achieved in different ways depending on the circumstances. At the bottom of the schema hierarchy are simple actions like "pick up an item", "unscrew", or "stir". Higher level schemas might include "open jar", which would organise the actions of picking up, unscrewing a lid, and putting down.

Associated with each schema is an activation level. Schemas are activated (from the top down) by their parent schemas and (from the bottom up) by input from the environment — the presence of items in the environment which are appropriate for the action in a schema tends to lead to a higher activation level for the schema. They compete with each other on the basis of their activation level, and the most active schema is "selected". A selected schema feeds activation down to its child schemas, so that they also are likely to be selected. Schemas are associated with goals which they are intended to achieve, and once a schema has achieved its goal it is inhibited — its activation level is reduced to a low level to allow other schemas to compete for control of the next action. Different schemas may provide multiple ways for a goal to be achieved — coffee can be supplied in a jar or a packet, for example, so a schema for adding coffee to a mug can be indifferent to the particular lower level behaviour required to achieve its goal. All suitable sub-schemas will be activated, and whichever one best fits the current configuration of the environment will receive additional activation allowing it to get selected.

The CS part of the Norman and Shallice theory can address the types of errors people make in routine activities, and shows how prepotent responses (activated by features of the environment) may need to be suppressed by the SAS to prevent them controlling behaviour. Other features of executive processing, such as selecting goals for behaviour, switching tasks, and monitoring behaviour for errors, fall within the province of the supervisory attentional system.

The SAS controls behaviour by exerting control over the CS system. It does this by influencing the level of activation of individual schemas — either adding to or reducing their activation. This top-down influence allows SAS to exert detailed control over behaviour when necessary. In the case of routine behaviour, however, the SAS may activate a relatively high-level schema, effectively delegating control to the CS system.

While the role of the SAS within the Norman and Shallice framework is well defined, its internal operation is not so clearly specified. An outline of the processes involved and their relationships during supervisory processing is provided by Shallice and Burgess (1996). The outline is based largely on neuropsychological evidence, but also guided by *a priori* reasoning about the types of processes that must be involved in supervisory processing. Shallice and Burgess characterise the fundamental role of the SAS as reacting to an unanticipated situation, and identify three main stages in its operation:

1. The construction of a temporary new schema. This involves a problem orientation phase during which goals are set for dealing with the current situation, followed by a problem solving phase where a candidate new schema for achieving these goals is generated.
2. The implementation of the temporary schema. This requires sequential activation of existing schemas in the CS system corresponding to its component actions.
3. Monitoring of schema execution. Since the situation and the temporary schema are both novel, operation must be closely monitored to ensure that the schema is effective.

While these are the main processes within the SAS many more processes are required for a full theory of this system. For example, it must be possible to set "delayed intention markers" to indicate that a task must be carried out at a later point in time (e.g., that a letter must be posted later in the day), and it must be possible to interrupt normal processing in order to carry out such tasks later.

8.4 Modelling the Supervisory Attentional System

Cooper and Shallice (2000) describe a detailed computational model of the contention scheduling system, and it would be possible to implement such a model using COGENT. However in this chapter we are interested in executive function in general, so we need to consider the Norman and Shallice framework in its entirety, and the relationship between SAS and CS within it. We will therefore develop a simplified model including both elements of the theory, but concentrating mainly on the operation of the SAS.

The SAS component is not well specified. While Shallice and Burgess (1996) provide the most detailed description of the internal operation of the SAS, even this is not well defined enough to allow us to directly implement a model. The approach we will use is to take a theory from a different (but related) field — artificial intelligence (AI) — as a starting point for our model. A number of AI theories address the same problems as the SAS — setting high-level goals, working out strategies to achieve them, carrying out plans of actions to implement the strategies, and reacting in an opportunistic way to unanticipated changes in the environment. In AI, this type of theory is termed an agent theory. An agent in AI may be roughly defined as an autonomous entity with its own agenda and goals, which acts on the world in order to pursue those goals. Clearly animals and people are such entities, so it is not surprising that AI agent theories address the types of executive process in which psychologists are interested.

8.4.1 The Domino Agent Model

One such AI theory, the "domino" agent model of Fox and colleagues (Das, Fox, Elsdon, & Hammond, 1997; Fox & Das, 2000), has been proposed as the basis for a model of the SAS (Glasspool, 2000). The domino agent provides a framework for structuring processes of goal-setting, problem solving, and plan execution so that they can operate together in a computer implementation. It specifies seven types of process operating on six types of information. The framework is shown in Figure 8.3.

The six types of information are represented by the "dots" on the domino outline, and information is transformed between these types by processes represented by arrows. Starting from a set of beliefs about its environment and its current state, the first process (1) establishes one or more goals for the agent, in response

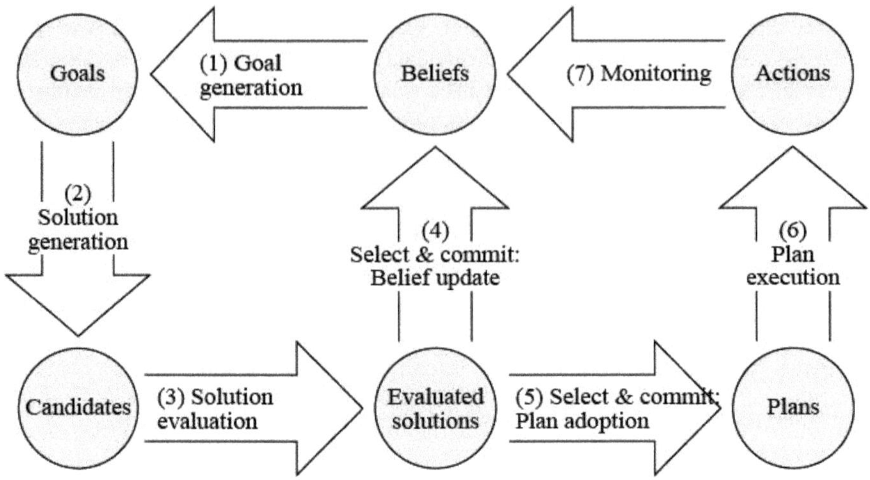

Figure 8.3: The "domino" agent model of Fox and colleagues

to events requiring action. The second process (2) is one of problem solving (see Chapter 4), which treats the goals as problems to be solved, and finds one or more possible solutions. If a goal is about what to believe (for example, the goal to decide if there is an object in a box) then the solutions will be different possible *beliefs* compatible with the environment and prior beliefs. If a goal is about what to do (e.g., the goal to get to the other side of a river) then the solutions will be different possible *procedures* which could be used to achieve the goal (crossing the river).

The next process (3) is one of evaluation. Assuming that more than one candidate solution has been proposed, the pros and cons of each are established, allowing them to be compared. A decision is then made about which new belief to hold (4) or which new plan of action to adopt (5). If a new plan is adopted, it is decomposed into individual actions which are taken by the agent (6). The final process (7) monitors the effect of these actions on the environment to check that the intended goal is indeed achieved. This leads to new beliefs about the actions and the environment, which in turn may lead to new goals, starting the process once again.

8.4.2 Modelling the SAS Using a Domino Agent

Many of the processes described above are similar to those specified by Shallice and Burgess: goal setting, solution generation and evaluation, decision making, planning, acting, and monitoring the effects of action. Indeed, Glasspool (2000) shows that Shallice and Burgess' outline specification for the SAS can be directly mapped onto the domino agent outline. Doing so has the benefit that the domino agent is well defined and amenable to computer implementation, so although we may have to implement some components of our SAS model in a highly simplistic manner, we can at least have some confidence that the various parts of the model will operate together in a well-defined way.

Figure 8.4 shows the processes identified by Shallice and Burgess mapped onto the domino agent. The first task in relating this to the Norman and Shallice framework is to identify the distinction between the SAS and CS components. "Actions" and "Plans" in the domino agent correspond to "Actions" and "Schemas" in CS, and process (6) corresponds to the contention scheduling process itself, which decomposes high-level schemas into sequences of lower-level schemas and eventually individual actions. We will therefore consider these parts of the domino agent to be within CS, while the other domino components are parts of SAS.

8.4.3 Modelling in an Under-Specified Domain

Executive functions in human cognition are complex and, by comparison with some other areas of psychology, poorly understood. Creating a detailed model of Norman and Shallice's SAS would be an enormously difficult task given the current level of knowledge in this area. Our modelling will therefore be, of necessity, rather more speculative than much of that tackled so far.

Although creating a detailed SAS model from scratch would be highly ambitious, by basing the model on the domino agent we can take a step-by-step approach, starting with a highly simplified model and then elaborating only those sections we are interested in (or are able to). This is possible because the domino agent is highly modular, and specifies both the processes operating on information as it passes through the system, and the type of data at each of the interfaces between processes. We can create a basic diagram of the system in COGENT, and populate each of the processes with highly simplified rules so that information flows through the system in the correct way, even if it is not being fully processed at each stage. This will then give us a basis on which to develop more detailed simulations of particular processes, gradually increasing the complexity of the model.

Often such an approach can allow us to build detailed models of one or two modules, while maintaining a more simplified model of the general system within which they are operating. This approach to modelling is appropriate when we have a particular structure or framework in mind, especially if it is a highly modular one like the domino. However, there are a number of dangers with the approach which should be born in mind.

One issue is that the overall structure of the model, and the interfaces between

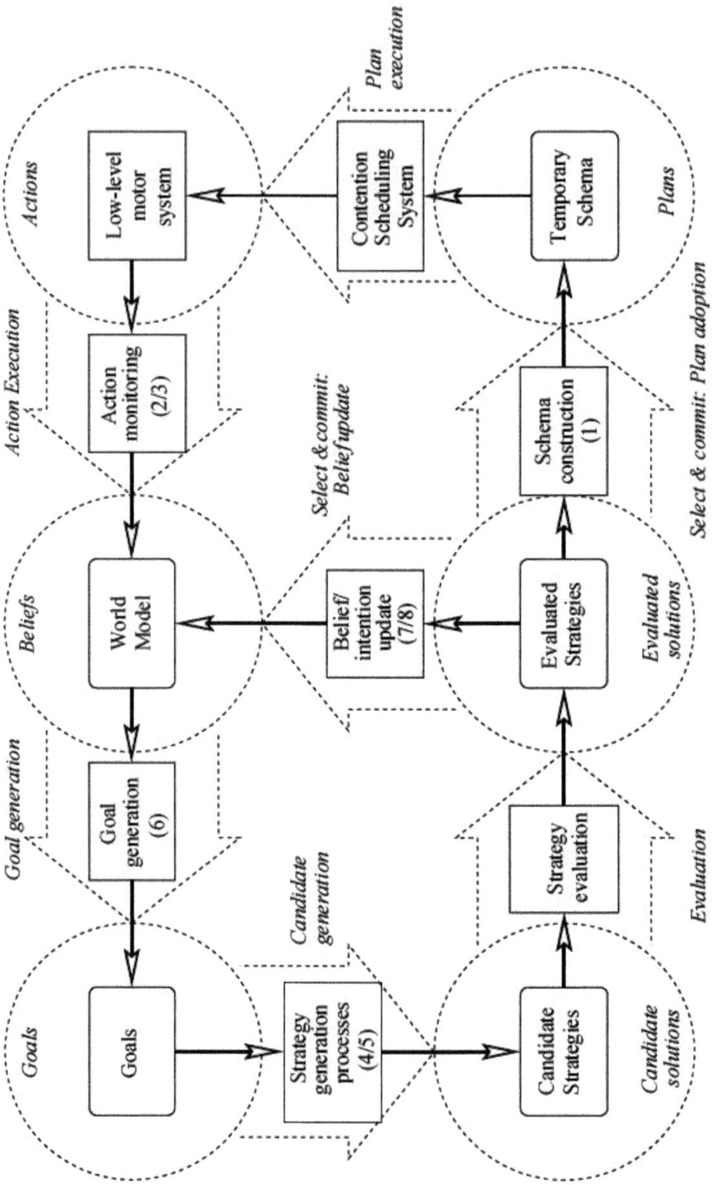

Figure 8.4: The SAS processes identified by Shallice and Burgess (1996) mapped onto the domino agent. Numbers in parentheses refer to processes identified by Shallice and Burgess.

modules within it, are established early in the modelling process. To the extent that this forces us to consider the general operation of the entire system before focusing on details of specific modules this is good practice. The disadvantage, however, is that decisions about overall structure and interfaces quickly become difficult to change once we start to elaborate the model, as they become "built in" to the way individual modules are implemented. This can lead to a tendency to resist changing design decisions once a certain amount of implementation has been carried out.

A more insidious danger is that the assumptions we make about overall structure and interfaces before the detailed implementation has been considered may drive the way modules are implemented, even though some of these decisions may essentially be arbitrary.

However, if we keep these potential problems in mind the approach of starting with a simplified general model then elaborating it as necessary can allow us to make inroads into modelling a difficult and complex system such as the SAS.

8.4.4 A Framework for a Model of the SAS

In order to develop a model of some aspects of the SAS we need to specify a target task for the model to carry out. We will use the Wisconsin card-sorting test (WCST) described in Section 8.2.3. This is an appropriate task because it places demands on a number of aspects of executive processing, including the inhibition of prepotent responses, task-switching, problem solving, monitoring progress towards current goals, and identifying errors and failures to achieve intended effects of actions.

We first need to determine the functional components of our model. To start with, the WCST is administered by an experimenter, so we will use the standard approach of dividing the model into a task environment, or experimenter, module, and a subject module. *Experimenter* will present cards to *Subject* one at a time, record *Subject*'s response to each, and provide feedback according to the current sorting criterion (which should change without warning after several successive correct responses have been received). *Subject* will be based on the Norman and Shallice theory and the domino agent, and will generate a response for each card indicating how it should be sorted. Figure 8.5 shows how *Experimenter* and *Subject* can communicate via a buffer (*The World*) which acts as a world model. *The World* will contain simple specifications of "objects" in the world, such as cards and card sorting requests.

To produce an initial design for *Subject* let us re-examine the WCST task from the point of view of the Norman and Shallice framework. Sorting objects according to their features is the type of well-learned behaviour we would expect to find as a high-level schema in CS. The SAS/CS model would most straightforwardly address the WCST on the basis that the SAS is involved in initial generation of a

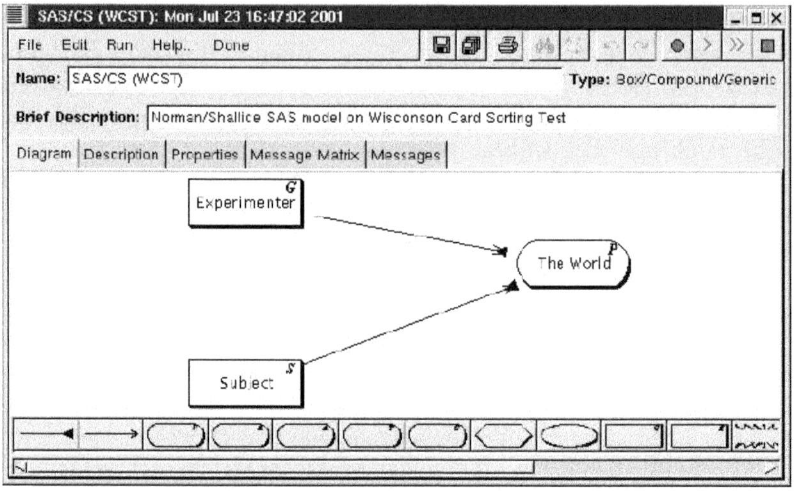

Figure 8.5: Overall structure of the model: *Experimenter* and *Subject* modules interact via a simple representation of objects in *The World*

sorting strategy and configuration of CS, which would then carry out that strategy with subsequent cards unless negative feedback was received, whereupon the SAS is again required to generate an alternative strategy and reconfigure CS.

Since we are basing our model on the domino agent it makes sense to start with the basic domino shape. Recall that the "dots" of the domino represent data structures while the arrows between them are information transformation processes. In COGENT we can directly implement this using buffers for the dots and rule-based processes for the arrows, as shown in Figure 8.6. CS is a complex process with internal structure. It is therefore represented in the diagram by a compound box.

Exercise 8.1: Create a model with *Experimenter* and *Subject* compound boxes interacting via *The World* as shown in Figure 8.5. Give *Subject* the structure shown in Figure 8.6. ◇

It would be possible to produce a very complex and detailed implementation for *Experimenter*, but for present purposes we will keep things simple. Thus, at the start of the task *Experimenter* should enter a representation of the first card to be sorted in *The World*. A realistic *Experimenter* should present cards in a random order. We will begin, however, with presenting a card with one red square. *Experimenter* will be elaborated in Section 8.4.6.

Before we can write any rules we need to decide on a representation to be used

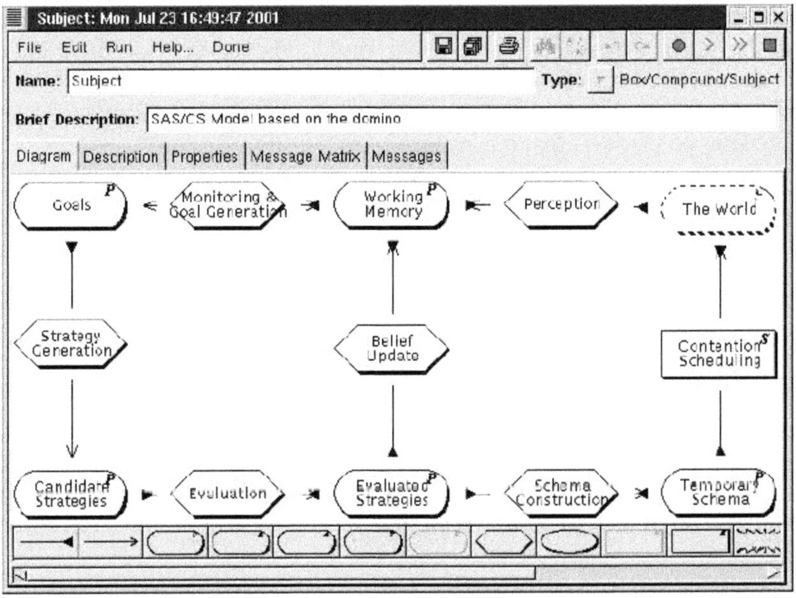

Figure 8.6: An outline structure for the main processes of the SAS in COGENT, based on the domino model

at the interface between *Subject* and *Experimenter*. A straightforward representation for cards presented to *Subject* is:

```
card(Number, Colour, Shape)
```

Exercise 8.2: Create a *Controller* process within *Experimenter*. Add a rule to *Controller* that fires on the first processing cycle and initiates the task by placing a `request(sort(card(one, red, square)))` element in *The World*. ◇

A more interesting representational decision concerns the form used by *Subject* in response to *Experimenter*. Ideally *Experimenter* should provide four index cards, as in the actual experiment, and *Subject* would indicate which of these the stimulus card is to be sorted under. However, to keep things simple initially we will assume that *Subject* merely indicates to *Experimenter* the sorting strategy — number, colour, or shape — that it is using to sort the stimulus card.

8.4.5 Populating the Framework: A Simplified Model

We are now in a position to flesh out the components of Figure 8.6. We will follow the flow of information around the domino agent from perception to action, defining each process in turn. There are seven processes to deal with, some of which will end up being fairly complex. However we will start by giving each process minimal functionality so that by the time we have worked round the loop the model will be able to propagate information from perception to action, even if it is unable to do anything really interesting with the information. Once this basic framework is operating it will be easier to address inadequacies of the process definitions and representations one by one.

Perceptual Processes

We begin with *Perception*. We need a rule in *Perception* to add elements to *Working Memory* when the experimenter requests that a card be sorted. Rule 1 of Box 8.1 does just this. Rule 2 is the complement of Rule 1. It ensures that requests are removed from *Working Memory* whenever they are removed from *The World*. Notice that both rules are unrefracted. This ensures that *Perception* responds to all requests, even if it receives a request that is identical to one it has previously dealt with.

Monitoring and Goal Generation

Now *Monitoring and Goal Generation* must respond to the presence of a sorting request by raising a goal to sort the currently presented card. The rule in Box 8.2 is sufficient. It specifies that a request should raise a goal of generating a strategy

Rule 1 (unrefracted): *Add a new belief about a request*
IF: `request(X)` is in *The World*
not `requested(X)` is in *Working Memory*
THEN: add `requested(X)` to *Working Memory*

Rule 2 (unrefracted): *Retract an old belief about a request*
IF: `requested(X)` is in *Working Memory*
not `request(X)` is in *The World*
THEN: delete `requested(X)` from *Working Memory*

Box 8.1: Rules for maintaining *Working Memory* (from *Perception*)

Rule 1 (unrefracted): *Generate a new sorting strategy when needed*
IF: `requested(Request)` is in *Working Memory*
not `current_strategy(Strategy)` is in *Working Memory*
THEN: add `generate_strategy(Request)` to *Goals*

Box 8.2: A rule that creates a goal to generate a strategy to handle a request (from *Monitoring and Goal Generation*)

to handle the request, unless a strategy for the request is already in place. (If a strategy is in place, it is assumed that CS will handle the request.) The rule is general in that it does not care about the details of the request. It may be a request to sort a card, or it may be some other request.

Strategy Generation

The next process, *Strategy Generation*, is potentially the most open-ended part of the model. The process must respond to the presence of a goal in *Goals* by placing specifications for one or more alternative strategies which could achieve that goal in *Candidate Strategies*.

While this represents a major part of the work carried out by the SAS, in producing this model we are more interested in the organisation of the system as a whole — the way the various components of the SAS and CS systems operate together. The details of the internal operation of the various modules, while important, are not our primary concern. We can therefore look for ways to simplify the operation of *Strategy Generation* providing we are careful to use the appropriate interfaces — the representation of information both at the input to the module (in the *Goals*) and at the output (in *Candidate Strategies*).

Shallice and Burgess suggest that a number of procedures exist for strategy generation in response to a goal. These effectively provide alternative parallel

> **Rule 1 (unrefracted):** *To sort cards, match against any of three features*
> IF: `generate_strategy(sort(Card))` is in *Goals*
> `Feature` is a member of `[number, colour, shape]`
> THEN: add `match_to(Feature)` to *Candidate Strategies*
>
> Box 8.3: A rule to generate sorting strategies based on card features (from *Strategy Generation*)

routes for deriving strategies from goals. One immediately apparent simplification would therefore be to implement only a subset of these processes. Shallice and Burgess discuss two categories of strategy generation process in particular, problem solving and spontaneous schema generation. Problem solving has already been explored in Chapter 4. It is potentially a highly complex class of process. Spontaneous generation of schemas is described by Shallice and Burgess as

> "the way that a procedure for tackling the situation can come to mind without any explicit attempt to solve a problem, but merely following a sense of dissatisfaction with the preceding method of tackling the situation" (p. 1406).

One way in which this might happen is if the situation is recognised as one of a general type for which a known solution should be applicable. A simplified form of such a procedure will be straightforward to implement. An individual is likely to have access to a store of many idiosyncratic strategies which have proved useful in the past. We will limit the complexity of the process by implementing, in the first place, only one such strategy:

> *If the goal is to sort an item into a category, and the item has distinguishable features, the item may be sorted according to one of those features.*

Cards are defined using the features `shape`, `number`, and `colour`, so a rule of this type will always generate three corresponding sorting strategies. Thus, while strategy generation is a complex process that may make use of extensive general knowledge, we will use a simple rule (Rule 1 of Box 8.3) to generate the three feature-based sorting strategies.

Rule 1 of Box 8.3 is **unrefracted**. Therefore it will fire whenever there is a request in *Goals* to generate a strategy to sort a card. The rule shouldn't fire on every cycle, however. It should fire just once each time a strategy generation request appears in *Goals*. It should then not fire until another request appears. This request may or may not be the same as a previous request, so we can't get the required rule firing behaviour by simply making the rule **refracted**. Instead,

Rule 1 (unrefracted): *Assess a candidate (dummy version)*
IF: `Candidate` is in *Candidate Strategies*
THEN: delete all `evaluation(Candidate,_)` from *Evaluated Strategies*
add `evaluation(Candidate, 1)` to *Evaluated Strategies*

Rule 2 (unrefracted; once): *Select the candidate with greatest evaluation*
IF: not `selected(X)` is in *Evaluated Strategies*
`evaluation(Candidate, Max)` is in *Evaluated Strategies*
not `evaluation(Alt, Act)` is in *Evaluated Strategies*
`Act` is greater than `Max`
THEN: delete all `evaluation(_, _)` from *Evaluated Strategies*
add `selected(Candidate)` to *Evaluated Strategies*

Rule 3 (unrefracted): *Remove evaluations for out-dated candidates*
IF: `evaluation(Candidate, Value)` is in *Evaluated Strategies*
not `Candidate` is in *Candidate Strategies*
THEN: delete `evaluation(Candidate, Value)` from *Evaluated Strategies*

Box 8.4: Rules to evaluate and select candidates (from *Evaluation*)

we can set the decay properties of *Goals* to ensure elements in *Goals* remain for just one cycle. For this, *Goals* must have **Decay** set to **Fixed** and **Decay Constant** set to 1.

Evaluation

We now need to evaluate the proposed strategies in order to decide which one to adopt. We will implement the evaluation process in a general way so that we can work on the details of how candidate strategies are to be evaluated once the basic framework is operating.

A general way to indicate the desirability of alternative strategies is simply to annotate each with a number, higher numbers indicating better strategies. This means that *Evaluation* should respond to the presence of one or more strategy definitions in *Candidate Strategies* by annotating each with a numerical value and placing the annotated definitions in *Evaluated Strategies*. This basic approach has much in common with the approach used to evaluate operators within the operator proposal, selection, evaluation cycle of Chapters 4 and 7.

Rule 1 in Box 8.4 shows a simplified rule that returns a dummy evaluation of `1` for all candidates. We will experiment with ways to elaborate this evaluation once we have the basic framework operating.

A second rule is required within *Evaluation* to select the candidate with the highest evaluation. This candidate will either be adopted as a new belief or form

Rule 1 (unrefracted): *Update beliefs with new strategy, if not already done*
IF: `selected(Strategy)` is in *Evaluated Strategies*
not `current_strategy(Strategy)` is in *Working Memory*
THEN: delete all `current_strategy(_)` from *Working Memory*
add `current_strategy(Strategy)` to *Working Memory*

Box 8.5: A rule that maintains beliefs about the current strategy (from *Belief Update*)

the basis of behaviour. Rule 2 of Box 8.4 implements this selection.

Rule 3 in Box 8.4 performs bookkeeping functions. It removes evaluations of strategies from *Evaluated Strategies* when those strategies are no longer suitable candidates.

All three evaluation rules are unrefracted. They assume that *Candidate Strategies* has the same decay characteristics as *Goals* (for the same reasons). Rule 2 is also marked as once. This ensures that only one candidate is selected on any one cycle. If the rule was not annotated in this way, and several candidates had the same maximum evaluation, all of those candidates would be selected in parallel on the same processing cycle. The once marking prevents this. The candidate chosen will then depend on the Access property of *Candidate Strategies*. If this is set to Random (the default value), each maximal strategy will be equally likely to be selected.

Belief Update

The belief update process is the means by which decisions about what to believe take their effect on the beliefs represented in *Working Memory*. Other decisions concern what to do, and their primary expression is in terms of actions. However, we are usually aware of what we have decided to do, just as we are about what we have decided to believe. It is reasonable, therefore, to use a rather general process here which will update *Working Memory* to reflect the outcome of all decisions, whether they involve action or not. A suitable rule is given in Box 8.5.

Schema Construction

In the Shallice and Burgess approach schema construction is the process of decomposing the proposed strategy into a number of steps, for each of which a schema already exists in CS, and constructing a new temporary schema encoding these steps. CS is then able to execute this temporary schema.

In general, proposed strategies may be arbitrarily complex, and both the decomposition process and the representation of the steps in the temporary schema

Rule 1 (unrefracted): *Create a temporary schema for the selected strategy*
IF: `selected(S)` is in *Evaluated Strategies*
not `schema(S)` is in *Temporary Schema*
THEN: delete all `schema(X)` from *Temporary Schema*
add `schema(S)` to *Temporary Schema*

Rule 2 (unrefracted): *Delete temporary schemas for non-selected strategies*
IF: `schema(S)` is in *Temporary Schema*
not `selected(S)` is in *Evaluated Strategies*
THEN: delete `schema(S)` from *Temporary Schema*

Box 8.6: Rules for temporary schema creation and deletion (from *Schema Construction*)

could involve considerable work. The simplest case, however, is when the proposed strategy turns out to be one that is already known by the CS system, and that simply has to be activated in a novel setting. In this case the required temporary schema comprises only one step, and decomposition and storage are trivial. Since our target task, the WCST, can be achieved using simple matching procedures, and it is reasonable to assume that these procedures may already be present in CS, we can simplify this module by catering in the first instance only for this simplest case.

Schemas are already assumed to exist for the various possible sorting strategies, so the temporary schemas created here will simply activate a single existing schema. The process will copy the schema specification identified by the decision process straight into *Temporary Schema*, where it will influence activation of the corresponding schema in *Select & Act*. Rule 1 of Box 8.6 achieves this. Rule 2 of the figure is a complementary rule that removes temporary schemas when they are no longer selected.

The Contention Scheduling System

Norman and Shallice's contention scheduling system comprises a hierarchical collection of schemas, each with an associated activation level, influencing each other in an interactive activation network. A selection process operates on the schema network, with selected schemas controlling behaviour. Figure 8.7 shows the box and arrow structure of the sub-components.

At the core of the *Contention Scheduling* system is an interactive activation network. This consists of a set of nodes. Each node corresponds to a schema and has an activation value. We assume that three schema nodes — representing the three sorting schemas — are available when performing the WCST. Box 8.7

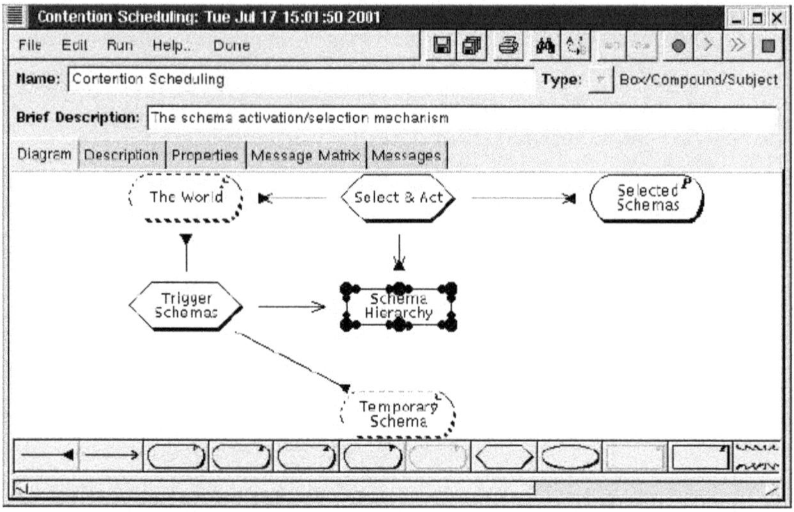

Figure 8.7: The box and arrow structure of the *Contention Scheduling* system

Element: *Schema node for matching to number*
`schema(match_to(number))`
Element: *Schema node for matching to colour*
`schema(match_to(colour))`
Element: *Schema node for matching to shape*
`schema(match_to(shape))`

Box 8.7: Schema nodes for competing sorting strategies (from *Schema Hierarchy*)

shows appropriate declarations for these schema nodes.

These schemas represent alternative strategies and should, according to the Norman and Shallice model, compete with each other. We will therefore set the Lateral Influence property of the interacting activation network to Whole Net (so all elements in the network compete with each other). Several other properties that govern competition and activation flow within the network are critical. We will borrow the values used by the Cooper and Shallice (2000) implementation of CS. In that implementation, activations ranged from 0.0 to 1.0, with a rest activation of 0.1. Min Act, Max Act, and Rest Act should be set accordingly. These settings will mean that, in the absence of excitation, schema activation values will tend towards 0.1, but strong inhibition can push a schema's activation down to 0.0, and strong excitation can push it up to 1.0.

The Cooper and Shallice (2000) implementation also used the CS activation update function with a persistence of 0.90. In addition, for current purposes Lateral Parameter should be set to 0.33 (so nodes provide moderate inhibition on each other), Self Influence should be enabled, and Self Parameter should be set to 0.33 (so the self excitation of a schema node is equal to the amount it inhibits other schema nodes).

Finally, the distribution of initial activations assigned to nodes must be specified. This is governed by Initial Acts, Act Parameter A, and Act Parameter B. They should be set to Uniform, 0.05, and 0.15 respectively, ensuring that initial activations will be uniformly distributed between 0.05, and 0.15.

Schema activation within the CS system is governed by a number of principles, including:

1. Schemas that compete for the same resources inhibit each other.
2. A schema is *selected* if it is the most active schema and its activation exceeds a pre-set threshold.
3. A selected schema sends activation to its child schemas (if it is a parent schema) or directly causes action (if it is a motor level schema).
4. Once a selected schema has been completed, it is inhibited.

Feature 1 has already been addressed by setting the Lateral Influence property in *Schema Hierarchy*. The other features require a separate process — *Select & Act* — to manage the excitation and selection of schemas.

Rule 1 of Box 8.8 implements features 2 and 4. Note the use of a user-defined property to specify the activation threshold required to select a schema. The property Selection Threshold must be defined for *Select & Act* (by adding a property to the Properties panel of the process). This property should be set to a value of 0.8. This will suffice to reliably select schemas which are activated by SAS input.

In fact, Rule 1 does not faithfully implement feature 4, as it inhibits a schema (by exciting it with a negative activation value) when the schema is selected, rather than after its associated actions have been completed. Making this change from the CS definition implies the following two assumptions:

1. All schemas comprise only a single action.
2. We can guarantee that all actions which are attempted will in fact succeed.

Clearly, neither of these assumptions will hold in real-world situations, but we can ensure that they do in our simulation. This being the case the CS system will operate as intended with the difference that inhibition will occur rather sooner than usual — as actions are initiated, rather than after they are completed. The reason for this change to the CS specification is that there is a short delay after inhibition is sent to a node before the activation of the node actually falls. Unless inhibition is sent *before* the selected status of the node is removed, the node being inhibited may still be active enough to be immediately re-selected. While it would

Rule 1 (refracted): *Select (and inhibit) the most active schema*
IF: `node(schema(S),A)` is in *Schema Hierarchy*
the value of the "`Selection Threshold`" property is `T`
`A` is not less than `T`
not `node(schema(O),B)` is in *Schema Hierarchy*
`B` is greater than `A`
not `selected(X)` is in *Selected Schemas*
THEN: add `selected(S)` to *Selected Schemas*
send `excite(schema(S),−5)` to *Schema Hierarchy*

Rule 2 (refracted): *If a schema is selected, act on it*
IF: `selected(S)` is in *Selected Schemas*
not `action(S)` is in *The World*
THEN: add `action(S)` to *The World*
delete `selected(S)` from *Selected Schemas*

Rule 3 (unrefracted): *Remove actions after they have been taken*
IF: `action(X)` is in *The World*
THEN: delete `action(X)` from *The World*

Box 8.8: Rules for handling schema excitation, selection, and inhibition (from *Select & Act*)

be possible to overcome this limitation by other means, this would add further complexity to the model.

Feature 3, acting on the world as a result of a selected schema, is simulated by adding an `action/1` element to the buffer representing the world. This is achieved by Rule 2 of Box 8.8. The actions we wish to take — placing cards in piles — are one-off rather than continuous actions, and the action specification therefore needs to be present only briefly in the world — for one COGENT cycle. A further rule, Rule 3 of Box 8.8, removes action representations from the world after a brief presentation.

All that remains to complete the loop from perception to action is the *Trigger Schemas* process. This implements the temporary schema generated by the SAS, by activating existing schemas in CS. Since our temporary schemas for this task will only comprise single existing CS schemas, the simple activation rule in Box 8.9 will suffice.

Testing the Simplified Model

With the basic model we have defined so far, the following sequence of actions should occur following the placement of a `request(sort(Card))` element in *The*

Rule 1 (unrefracted): *Excite any temporary schemas*
IF: `schema(S)` is in *Temporary Schema*
THEN: send `excite(schema(S), 0.60)` to *Schema Hierarchy*

Box 8.9: A rule for exciting a temporary schema once it has been created (from *Trigger Schemas*)

World by *Experimenter*:

1. A goal `generate_strategy(sort(Card))` is placed in *Goals*.
2. Three candidate strategies are generated by *Strategy Generation*, and placed in *Candidate Strategies*. These are `match_to(shape)`, `match_to(colour)`, and `match_to(number)`.
3. *Evaluation* generates an evaluation value of `1` for each candidate, and places annotated candidates in *Evaluated Strategies*.
4. *Evaluation* selects one of the annotated candidates (supposedly that with the highest evaluation, but at present, with all evaluations equal, the selection will be made randomly). A `selected(Strategy)` element is placed in *Evaluated Strategies*.
5. *Belief Update* and *Schema Construction* both pass the selected strategy on. A `current_strategy(Strategy)` element appears in *Working Memory*, and a `schema(Strategy)` element appears in *Temporary Schema*.
6. Activation is fed to the *Schema Hierarchy* node corresponding to the temporary schema. The activation level of the node starts to increase.
7. When the node's activation level reaches or exceeds the selection threshold, a `selected(Strategy)` node is added to *Selected Schemas*.
8. In response to the selection of a schema, an `action(Strategy)` element is placed in *The World* to simulate the carrying out of the action associated with the selected strategy.
9. On the following cycle, the `action(Strategy)` element is removed from *The World*.

Exercise 8.3: Populate the outline domino agent with the rules specified above. Add the rules in the order given, and check after each process is specified that information propagates correctly around the domino to that point. Verify that the completed model runs correctly, and that a card-sorting request placed in *The World* by the experimenter results in activity propagating around the entire loop from perceptual processes to *Contention Scheduling* as outlined above. Observe the activation levels of schema nodes in *Schema Hierarchy* and confirm that the node specified by the SAS portion of the domino receives activation and eventually exceeds the selection threshold and is selected. Verify that this results in a

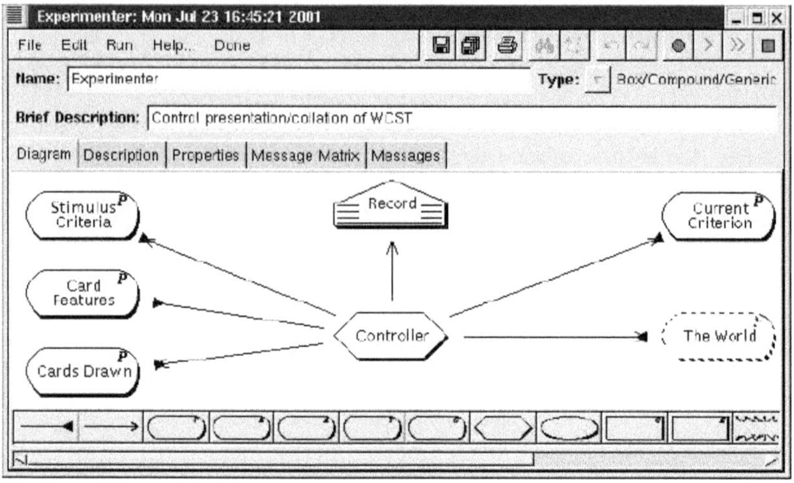

Figure 8.8: The box and arrow structure of *Experimenter*

card sorting action being taken in the world. ◇

8.4.6 Extending the Basic Framework

With this simple model, activity is propagated around the domino agent from perception to action, but the model is not yet able to perform the WCST. However, we now have a framework for further modelling — we can build on this working model, elaborating some of the modules which have been left in an over-simplified state, until it is capable of performing the WCST correctly.

Generalised Experimenter Functions

The first thing we need to add to enable us to fully simulate the WCST is the generation of feedback from *Experimenter* to indicate whether a sorting action is correct or not, and appropriate reaction to this feedback on the part of *Subject*. We will start by elaborating *Experimenter* to provide all functions required to administer the WCST, including provision of feedback, randomised card presentation, and collation of subject responses. A number of buffers are required in addition to the basic *Controller* process. Figure 8.8 shows a suitable arrangement.

The rules for *Controller* may be broken into two subsets: those for presenting cards and those for providing feedback to *Subject*. Box 8.10 shows the rules for the former functions. The test is started by selecting a sorting criterion and presenting a card drawn at random. Rules 1 to 5 achieve this. The principal functions are

Rule 1 (refracted): *Draw the first card*
IF: the current cycle is `1`
THEN: send `select_criterion` to *Controller*
send `deal_card` to *Controller*

Rule 2 (unrefracted; once): *Select a strategy*
TRIGGER: `select_criterion`
IF: `S` is in *Stimulus Criteria*
THEN: clear *Current Criterion*
delete `S` from *Stimulus Criteria*
add `sort_by(S)` to *Current Criterion*
add `successive_correct(0)` to *Current Criterion*
send `set_strategy_to(S)` to *Record*

Rule 3 (unrefracted): *Stop when all strategies are complete*
TRIGGER: `select_criterion`
IF: not `S` is in *Stimulus Criteria*
`L` is the list of all `C` such that `C` is in *Cards Drawn*
`Cards` is the length of `L`
THEN: send `score(criteria(6), cards(Cards))` to *Record*
send `stop` to *SAS/CS (WCST)*

Rule 4 (unrefracted; once): *Deal a card (and record details)*
TRIGGER: `deal_card`
IF: `draw_card(Card)`
THEN: delete all `request(sort(_))` from *The World*
delete all `feedback(_)` from *The World*
add `request(sort(Card))` to *The World*
add `Card` to *Cards Drawn*
send `dealt(Card)` to *Record*

Rule 5 (refracted): *Deal a card: None left!!!*
TRIGGER: `deal_card`
IF: not `draw_card(Card)`
`L` is the list of all `S` such that `S` is in *Stimulus Criteria*
`N` is the length of `L`
`Crit` is 5 − `N`
THEN: send `score(criteria(Crit), cards(64))` to *Record*
send `stop` to *SAS/CS (WCST)*

Box 8.10: Rules to present cards (from *Controller*)

allocated to separate triggered rules because they both correspond to events that occur multiple times during administration of the test. Thus, Rules 2 and 3, which are triggered by a `select_criterion` message, select a sorting criterion. The rules are triggered at the start of the task by Rule 1, but also later in the task when *Experimenter* changes the sorting strategy (Rule 8 in Box 8.11).

Rules 2 and 3 are mutually exclusive: Rule 2 fires when *Stimulus Criteria* contains one or more sorting criteria, and Rule 3 fires when *Stimulus Criteria* contains no sorting criteria. Rule 2 assumes that *Stimulus Criteria* contains all criteria that *Experimenter* might adopt. There are 6 such criteria (two each of `colour`, `shape`, and `number`), and each criterion should be listed as an initial element of *Stimulus Criteria*. (Note that the **Duplicates** property of *Stimulus Criteria* must be checked to allow duplicate copies of the strategies.) Each time Rule 2 fires, it selects one criterion, deletes it from *Stimulus Criteria*, stores it in *Current Criterion* (where it can be accessed by the feedback rules described below), and initialises a counter — `successive_correct/1` — that is used to record the number of successively correct responses from *Subject*.

Rule 3 fires when *Subject* has been tested on all sorting criteria. It works out a score for *Subject* based on the number of cards sorted and the number of sorting criteria obtained by *Subject*. If the test finished with *Subject* exhausting *Experimenter*'s sorting criteria, then the criteria score is 6 and the number of cards drawn is the number of elements in *Cards Drawn*.

Rules 4 and 5 are also triggered by Rule 1. They handle dealing of a card, using `draw_card/1` to select the next card. The definition of `draw_card/1` is left as an exercise (Exercise 8.4), but the condition should succeed only if there is a card (i.e., combination of features) that has not already been presented. This will be true on the first attempt, so Rule 4 will fire, performing various bookkeeping functions and adding a request to sort the card to *The World*. Rule 5 will only fire when no further cards remain. It tallies *Subject*'s score and stops processing by sending `stop` to the top-level compound box.

Further rules are required by *Controller* to respond to actions initiated by *Subject*. These rules (shown in Box 8.11) must count the number of times cards are correctly sorted in succession, and change strategy when the required number is reached. In addition, they must provide positive or negative feedback after each action generated by *Subject*. Rule 6 handles the case of positive feedback. Rule 7 is appropriate when negative feedback is required. Both rules also log their actions in *Record*. The `successive_correct/1` entry is used by Rule 6 to count the number of successive correct sorting actions by the subject. Notice that both rules send `deal_card` to *Controller*, triggering Rules 4 or 5 on the next processing cycle.

Rule 8 from Box 8.11 applies when *Subject* has correctly sorted a sufficiently long sequence of cards. This number is declared as a user-defined property of the process (**Criterion**). Different versions of the WCST use different criterion values

Rule 6 (unrefracted): *Give positive feedback and deal a new card*
IF: `action(match_to(Feature))` is in *The World*
`sort_by(Feature)` is in *Current Criterion*
`successive_correct(C)` is in *Current Criterion*
`C1` is `C + 1`
THEN: delete `successive_correct(C)` from *Current Criterion*
add `successive_correct(C1)` to *Current Criterion*
add `feedback(correct)` to *The World*
send `received(Feature, correct)` to *Record*
send `deal_card` to *Controller*

Rule 7 (unrefracted): *Give negative feedback and deal a new card*
IF: `action(match_to(Feature))` is in *The World*
`sort_by(Required)` is in *Current Criterion*
`Feature` is distinct from `Required`
THEN: delete `successive_correct(C)` from *Current Criterion*
add `successive_correct(0)` to *Current Criterion*
add `feedback(wrong)` to *The World*
send `received(Feature, wrong)` to *Record*
send `deal_card` to *Controller*

Rule 8 (unrefracted): *Change strategy upon reaching criterion*
IF: the value of the "`Criterion`" property is `Criterion`
`successive_correct(Criterion)` is in *Current Criterion*
THEN: delete `successive_correct(Criterion)` from *Current Criterion*
send `select_criterion` to *Controller*

Box 8.11: Rules to provide feedback and collate responses (from *Controller*)

(ranging from 6 to 10). The rule triggers selection of a new sorting criteria (via Rules 2 or 3). If *Subject* has been tested on all criteria Rule 3 will be triggered, *Subject*'s score will be tallied, and the complete system will be halted.

Exercise 8.4: Enter the additional buffers and rules into *Experimenter* and *Controller*, together with a suitable definition of `draw_card/1`. `draw_card/1` should yield a different card each time it is called. It should also yield the cards in a random order. Try running the model one step at a time. Observe the structure of the test and the way that feedback works. ◇

Rule 3 (unrefracted): *Add a belief about feedback*
IF: `feedback(F)` is in *The World*
`current_strategy(S)` is in *Working Memory*
THEN: delete all `feedback(S, _)` from *Working Memory*
add `feedback(S, F)` to *Working Memory*

Box 8.12: An additional rule from *Perception* to handle feedback

Responding to Feedback: Selection of a New Strategy

We now need to make *Subject* responsive to feedback from *Experimenter*. The first requirement is that feedback should result in an update to *Working Memory*, so *Perception* requires an additional rule, Rule 3 in Box 8.12, that adds a belief about feedback to *Working Memory*.

Recall from our discussion of the operation of the SAS/CS framework in the WCST that we are assuming that the SAS is only involved in reacting to novel situations within the test — essentially, the selection of a sorting strategy for the first card presented by *Experimenter*, and the changing of sorting strategies in response to negative feedback from *Experimenter*. Once a sorting strategy has been selected, in the absence of negative feedback CS should be responsible for applying that sorting strategy to each subsequently presented card.

We would expect that SAS would set up a temporary schema, and that this would remain in place, guiding the operation of the CS system, until it becomes apparent that the strategy is not operating successfully. In the context of the WCST this would mean that a temporary schema will remain in place until negative feedback is received, at which point SAS will replace it with a new schema in an attempt to continue to correctly sort cards.

The immediate impact of feedback, then, is on the raising of goals. A goal should be raised whenever a new strategy is needed. This will occur when a card sorting request is received and a strategy has not already been selected (i.e., the first time we receive a card at the start of the test), and also when we do have a strategy but negative feedback has been received for that strategy, indicating that it is not the correct strategy. At present *Monitoring & Goal Generation* has a rule to handle the first but not the second of these cases. Rule 2 from Box 8.13 handles this second case.

All that Rule 2 does is remove the `current_strategy/1` element from *Working Memory* if negative feedback is received. This corresponds to the model losing confidence in the current strategy when it is told that the strategy is wrong. Rule 1 in *Monitoring & Goal Generation* will now find that we have a sorting request but no sorting strategy, and hence will raise a new goal.

Rule 2 (unrefracted): *Monitor progress and generate goals*
IF: `feedback(S, wrong)` is in *Working Memory*
`current_strategy(S)` is in *Working Memory*
THEN: delete `feedback(S, wrong)` from *Working Memory*
delete `current_strategy(S)` from *Working Memory*

Box 8.13: An additional rule from *Monitoring & Goal Generation* to handle negative feedback

Exercise 8.5: Add the new rule and try out the model. What happens when negative feedback is received? What about positive feedback? ◇

Once a temporary strategy has been set up, CS operates autonomously to apply the strategy to any new cards appearing in *The World*. This works as we wish when the strategy is correct, but there remains a problem when the strategy is incorrect. When negative feedback is received the current strategy is now dropped from *Working Memory* and a goal is raised to generate a new strategy. However, while this is going on CS continues to sort cards according to the old strategy.

Responding to Feedback: Inhibition of a Prepotent Response

The temporary strategy continues to excite the CS system, which is thus able to respond quickly to new cards with its active sorting strategy. This corresponds to the notion of a prepotent response — the sorting response is primed and will be activated directly by objects in the environment which match its requirements. Clearly, for the SAS/CS system to operate effectively prepotent responses should be inhibited by the SAS in situations where they are inappropriate. This is in fact what will happen with the existing implementation, once a new strategy has been chosen and propagated around the domino to *Temporary Schema*. The problem is that this does not happen quickly enough to prevent perseveration of the previous response.

In general we can expect that it will be more difficult (and hence take longer) to generate a new strategy than to re-apply an existing one. This is certainly the case with the current SAS model as we have seen. What this implies is that as well as dropping our *belief* about our current strategy, we should drop the strategy itself when negative feedback is received. Evidently an additional control signal is required to halt automatic behaviour in CS when unexpected feedback is received. Intuitively this seems reasonable: animals have a "startle" reflex which achieves much the same result in situations where a habitual or prepotent response needs to be suppressed.

This can be done by adding a connection from *Monitoring & Goal Generation* to *Evaluated Strategies*, and using this to remove the selected strategy as well as the `current_strategy/1` belief, as soon as negative feedback about the strategy arrives. Notice that once a strategy is deselected, Rule 2 of *Schema Construction* will remove any corresponding temporary schema (see Box 8.6).

Exercise 8.6: Implement this by adding the necessary arrow to the box and arrow diagram and augmenting Rule 2 of *Monitoring & Goal Generation*. Verify that your solution works by stepping through the test. ◇

Evaluating Candidate Strategies

The model is now able to perform the WCST, and to a first approximation it reacts appropriately to experimenter feedback — it maintains the same sorting strategy while it continues to receive positive feedback, and raises a goal to select a new strategy when negative feedback is received. The remaining problem with the simulation is that this new strategy is selected at random, and could even be the same as the previous strategy!

Evidently some principled way to evaluate candidate strategies is required. There is no point in continuing with a strategy that has just failed. However, when the experimenter changes strategy we may find that a strategy which failed in the past is now successful. We do not want to simply avoid trying strategies which have been unsuccessful in the past, but we do want to give them lower evaluations than untried strategies.

As a first attempt at a sensible evaluation scheme, we can calculate an evaluation for a candidate depending on how recently it has been attempted. In order to do this, a record is needed of which candidates have been attempted and when. It seems reasonable that this information should be recorded in *Working Memory*. We already have a rule in *Belief Update* that adds a `current_strategy/1` element to *Working Memory*. However, this will be replaced by further strategies as others are attempted. We need to remember previous attempts as well as the current one.

In order to achieve this, Rule 1 in *Belief Update* may be replaced by the Rule 1 of Box 8.14. The second argument of the `attempted/2` element added by the rule to *Working Memory* is an indication of how recently the strategy was attempted. Rule 2 in the figure increments this variable in all such elements on each COGENT processing cycle.

With the above modifications to *Belief Update*, the `attempted/2` elements in *Working Memory* may be used by *Evaluation* to assign lower evaluations to recently attempted strategies. Rule 1 in Box 8.15, which replaces Rule 1 in Box 8.4, achieves this. It uses a user-defined condition, `evaluate/2`, which is also shown in Box 8.15. Note the first clause of this condition: if a candidate strategy has never been attempted, it should be evaluated very highly. The definition here

Rule 1 (unrefracted): *Update beliefs with new strategy, if not already done*
IF: `selected(Strategy)` is in *Evaluated Strategies*
not `current_strategy(Strategy)` is in *Working Memory*
THEN: delete all `current_strategy(_)` from *Working Memory*
add `current_strategy(Strategy)` to *Working Memory*
delete all `attempted(Strategy, _)` from *Working Memory*
add `attempted(Strategy, 0)` to *Working Memory*

Rule 2 (unrefracted): *Increment the "age" of previous attempted strategies*
IF: `attempted(Strategy2, N)` is in *Working Memory*
`N1` is `N + 1`
not `selected(Strategy)` is in *Evaluated Strategies*
not `current_strategy(Strategy)` is in *Working Memory*
THEN: delete `attempted(Strategy2, N)` from *Working Memory*
add `attempted(Strategy2, N1)` to *Working Memory*

Box 8.14: Replacement rules for *Belief Update*

Rule 1 (unrefracted): *Assess a candidate, First version*
IF: `Candidate` is in *Candidate Strategies*
`evaluate(Candidate, Evaluation)`
THEN: delete all `evaluation(Candidate, _)` from *Evaluated Strategies*
add `evaluation(Candidate, Evaluation)` to *Evaluated Strategies*

Condition Definition: `evaluate/2`: *Evaluate candidate strategies*
`evaluate(Candidate, 1000) :-`
not `attempted(Candidate, X)` is in *Working Memory*
`evaluate(Candidate, N) :-`
`attempted(Candidate, N)` is in *Working Memory*

Box 8.15: A revised evaluation rule, with an associated condition definition (from *Evaluation*)

gives it an evaluation of `1000` to ensure it will always be evaluated more highly than an attempted strategy, even if the attempt occurred some time back. Note also that the condition definition requires that *Evaluation* have read access to *Working Memory*. An additional arrow between the two boxes, not shown in Figure 8.6, is required to allow this.

Exercise 8.7: Implement the evaluation scheme described above and re-run the model. How effective is the scheme of basing evaluation simply on how recently a strategy has been attempted? Is it sufficient to allow the WCST to be performed efficiently? ◇

Exercise 8.8: If you run the full test a few times, and examine the log in *Record*, you'll notice that sometimes the simulation takes two attempts to guess the correct strategy every time it changes, rather than the ideal of one guess which can be achieved much of the time by people. Why does this happen?

Can you propose a refinement to the evaluation procedure which can make the guessing of the next strategy more efficient? Implement your solution and try it out. ◇

8.4.7 Project: Revising the Subject/Experimenter Interface

In the real WCST, the participant does not verbalize their sorting strategy, but expresses it implicitly by placing each card under one of four reference cards. Implementing this behaviour in the model will require additional work in three areas. Firstly, a set of four reference cards must be specified which between them represent each colour, each shape, and each number (this set of cards need not be generated automatically; it can be the same for each run of the WCST). Secondly, the action taken by the subject model when it sorts a card must be changed from specifying the sorting strategy it is using to specifying which of the reference cards the target card is to be placed under. Thirdly, the Experimenter model will have to check the sorting action for consistency with the current target sorting strategy in order to determine whether "correct" or "wrong" feedback should be given.

Design and implement changes to the model to produce this behaviour. Verify that the modified model still carries out the WCST correctly. In what ways is the performance of the model changed?

Notice that in some cases more than one possible strategy might result in the same card placement action. Since the experimenter can now only give feedback about the card placement action, not the strategy which led to it, the feedback received by the subject can sometimes be ambiguous — positive feedback may be received in response to an incorrect strategy. Simply by making the output of the model more realistic, we have changed the performance of the model on the test. One should always be aware of the possibility that simplifying assumptions may sometimes have unforeseen consequences on apparently central predictions of the model.

8.4.8 Project: Accounting for Error

One major use for models of cognitive processes is in understanding the causes of errors. Error data also provide strong constraints on which types of process can be proposed to explain cognitive abilities. It is therefore important to examine the types of errors which the model is capable of producing as well as its simulation of "normal" performance of the WCST.

A common behaviour in frontal lobe patients is that the first required strategy is found correctly, but subsequent strategy changes by the experimenter are ignored, so that strategy is maintained throughout the test. In what ways can the SAS/CS model be damaged (e.g., by "ignoring" a single rule) to produce this type of perseverative behaviour?

Another way in which some human subjects fail the WCST is by changing a correct strategy even though it is receiving positive feedback. Is it possible to simulate this type of error by straightforward changes to the SAS part of the model?

The SAS/CS theory associates a large class of errors in generating everyday or routine action with the operation of the contention scheduling system. Cooper and Shallice (2000) simulate such errors through a number of manipulations to their CS simulation. One change which is straightforward to make to our simple CS implementation is the addition of random noise to the activation of schema nodes. This can lead to uncertainties in selecting schemas.

Add random noise to the activation levels of CS nodes by using the Noise parameter of *Schema Hierarchy*. Observe performance on the WCST as the magnitude of random noise is increased. What types of error occur? Do these errors have any relation to the types of errors neurological patients make on the test?

8.5 Monitoring and the Six Element Test

The six element test is a second neuropsychological test of executive functions (see Section 8.2.3). In this section we consider how the model of the SAS may be extended to the six element task. We focus specifically on aspects of monitoring required for successful completion of the test, as these appear to be the aspects that can be deficient in patients with frontal brain injury.

8.5.1 The Six Element Test: Procedure and Findings

To recap, the six element test (6ET) requires participants to attempt three pairs of simple tasks in fifteen minutes, subject to three rules: participants should attempt to maximise their score, responses to the first questions within a task are worth more points than responses to later questions within a task, and participants are not allowed to perform two tasks of the same type in succession. In fact, the points obtained for each subtask are not of interest. Rather, the test is scored in terms of the number of subtasks attempted, the number of times rules are broken, and the maximum amount of time spent on any one subtask.

Shallice and Burgess (1991) reported three patients with frontal injury who performed well on the individual tasks but poorly on the composite task. They were tested twice (several weeks apart), and each time they completed fewer subtasks than control participants, and the maximum time spent on any one subtask was generally much greater than that of control participants (controls: 5 mins 35 secs; patients: from 6 mins 19 secs to 10 mins 11 secs). Patients tended not to make rule breaks.

Shallice and Burgess (1991) argue that successful completion of the 6ET involves use of delayed intentions. Non-brain injured participants, they claim, begin by selecting a subtask and creating a *temporal marker* to switch tasks after a few minutes. A few minutes later the temporal marker is somehow activated, leading non-brain injured participants to switch tasks. Shallice and Burgess claim that activation of temporal markers is impaired in strategy application disorder patients, and it is this which causes them to fail to switch tasks efficiently.

8.5.2 Modelling Behaviour on the Six Element Test

Minor modifications are required in order to apply the SAS/CS model developed for the WCST to an equivalent model for the 6ET. The key issue in the 6ET concerns switching between subtasks — the subtasks themselves are not important. They can therefore be assumed to be effectively routine and performed by schemas within CS. SAS must select between subtasks, and periodically switch between them.

The functions required of an experimenter administering the 6ET are fewer and simpler than those required when administering the WCST. In fact, as a first approximation we may assume that once the participant knows the rules he/she may be presented with requests to perform the six subtasks and allowed to work to completion. Box 8.16 shows a suitable COGENT representation of the six requests. *The World* may be initialised with these requests, whereupon they may be processed by the domino model.

Exercise 8.9: Use the COGENT Research Programme Manager to create a copy of the WCST model. Give the copy a sensible name. Then delete its *Experimenter* box and set the initial contents of *The World* to be the six requests given in Box 8.16. Run the model. You should find that, as in the previous model, requests are entered into *Working Memory* by *Perception*. The model will then halt because we have not yet specified how *Monitoring & Goal Generation* should treat multiple simultaneous requests. ◇

Element: *Dictation task 1*
`request(do(task(dictation, 1)))`
Element: *Dictation task 2*
`request(do(task(dictation, 2)))`
Element: *Object naming task 1*
`request(do(task(object_naming, 1)))`
Element: *Object naming task 2*
`request(do(task(object_naming, 2)))`
Element: *Arithmetic task 1*
`request(do(task(arithmetic, 1)))`
Element: *Arithmetic task 2*
`request(do(task(arithmetic, 2)))`

Box 8.16: The six requests of the six element task (from *The World*)

8.5.3 Modifying the Domino Processes

The box and arrow structure of the domino reflects the interactions between the processes and data stores required for executive control. The structure used for the WCST is therefore also both adequate and appropriate for the 6ET. The rules that define many of the sub-processes, however, do require modification.

Monitoring & Goal Generation

The goal of the 6ET is to generate a strategy for completing as much as possible of each subtask. Rule 1 of Box 8.17 assembles a suitable representation of this goal from the contents of *Working Memory* and adds it to *Goals*, where, as in the WCST model, it may trigger processing by *Strategy Generation*.

Monitoring is one function that differs considerably between the 6ET and the WCST. In the WCST, *Experimenter* provides feedback to *Subject* via *The World*. This feedback is passed into *Working Memory* where it is used by *Monitoring & Goal Generation*. In the 6ET, the role of feedback is played by the expiration of a temporal marker. When a temporal marker expires the current task is aborted. Rule 2 of Box 8.17 (which replaces the feedback rule for the WCST model) implements this function. The rule assumes that markers take the form `marker(Content, When)`, where `Content` represents the marker's content (in this case, stop a particular task or strategy) and `When` represents the expiration time (in this case, zero time units from the current time).

Rule 2 fires if the current strategy (or task) is `S` and *Working Memory* contains an expired marker for stopping that strategy. It deletes the temporal marker and

Rule 1 (unrefracted): *Trigger generation of a new strategy*
IF: not `current_strategy(Strategy)` is in *Working Memory*
`Req` is the list of all `R` such that `requested(R)` is in *Working Memory*
THEN: add `generate_strategy(list(Req))` to *Goals*

Rule 2 (unrefracted): *Monitor progress and terminate current goal*
IF: `marker(stop(S), 0)` is in *Working Memory*
`current_strategy(S)` is in *Working Memory*
THEN: delete all `was_doing(_)` from *Working Memory*
add `was_doing(S)` to *Working Memory*
delete `current_strategy(S)` from *Working Memory*
delete `selected(do(S, _))` from *Evaluated Strategies*
delete `marker(stop(S), 0)` from *Working Memory*

Box 8.17: Rules for *Monitoring & Goal Generation* in the six element task

Rule 1 (unrefracted): *For a list of tasks, we may do any task for a short time*
IF: `generate_strategy(list(Tasks))` is in *Goals*
`do(Task)` is a member of `Tasks`
THEN: add `do(Task, 100)` to *Candidate Strategies*

Box 8.18: A rule to generate strategies when the goal is to complete multiple requests (from *Generate Strategy*)

the strategy from *Working Memory*. As in the case of the WCST, it also deletes the relevant `selected/1` item from *Evaluated Strategies* (ensuring that the temporary schema for the current strategy is terminated). The rule also performs one further piece of bookkeeping: it records that strategy that was being performed. This parallels the recording of previously attempted strategies in the WCST. It allows *Evaluation* to give the current task a low evaluation, so that it is not immediately reselected.

Strategy Generation

Strategy generation must be modified to respond to the type of goal generated by *Monitoring & Goal Generation*. One simple strategy to adopt when given a list of tasks is to work on one task for a period of time, and then switch tasks. Rule 1 of Box 8.18 (which replaces the previous strategy generation rule) generates such strategies. The representation `do(Task, 100)` is interpreted as "do `Task` for 100 time units". The rule states that if there is a list of tasks, candidate strategies include doing any of those tasks for 100 time units.

Condition Definition: `evaluate/2`: *Evaluate candidate strategies*

```
evaluate(do(task(X, N), T), 1000) : −
    not was_doing(task(X, _)) is in Working Memory
    not started(task(X, N)) is in Working Memory
evaluate(do(task(X, N), T), 500) : −
    not was_doing(task(X, _)) is in Working Memory
    started(task(X, N)) is in Working Memory
evaluate(do(task(X, N), T), 0) : −
    was_doing(task(X, _)) is in Working Memory
```

Box 8.19: A revised definition of `evaluate/2` for the six element test (from *Evaluation*)

Of course the length of time to devote to a subtask should depend upon the total time available for the task and the number of subtasks to be completed (or more plausibly an estimate of the remaining time available and the remaining number of subtasks). The figure of 100 units is arbitrary and intended only to allow further progress to be made with the model. Below we will allow 600 COGENT cycles for the entire 6ET, so 100 units per task, with one unit corresponding to one COGENT cycle, should yield equal division of time between all six subtasks.

Evaluation

The evaluation procedures developed for the WCST apply directly to the 6ET with the exception of the definition of the user-defined condition `evaluate/2`. There are two considerations that must be taken into account by this condition.

First, the condition should give high evaluations to subtasks that are of a different type from the subtask most recently attempted. This will prevent, for example, the two arithmetic subtasks being performed in sequence. The most recently attempted task is recorded in *Working Memory* in the form of a `was_doing/1` element (added to *Working Memory* by Rule 2 of Box 8.17).

Second, if there are two tasks of the same type that might be attempted and one of those tasks has already been started, then the other task should be given a higher evaluation. This is because the participant is told that initial questions in each task are worth more points than later questions.

The definition of `evaluate/2` in Box 8.19 incorporates both of these considerations. In addition, it assumes that *Working Memory* contains information on all tasks that have been started (in the form of `started/1` elements). This information will be added by an additional rule in *Perception*, described below.

Rule 1 (unrefracted): *Update beliefs with new strategy*
IF: `selected(do(Strategy, Time))` is in *Evaluated Strategies*
not `current_strategy(Strategy)` is in *Working Memory*
THEN: delete all `current_strategy(_)` from *Working Memory*
add `current_strategy(Strategy)` to *Working Memory*
add `marker(stop(Strategy), Time)` to *Working Memory*

Rule 2 (unrefracted): *Update time stamp on temporal markers*
IF: `marker(X, T)` is in *Working Memory*
`T` is greater than `0`
`T1` is `T - 1`
THEN: delete `marker(X, T)` from *Working Memory*
add `marker(X, T1)` to *Working Memory*

Box 8.20: Rules for updating *Working Memory* beliefs and temporal markers for the six element test (from *Belief Update*)

Belief Update

The use of temporal markers requires that minor changes be made to the rules of *Belief Update*. First, the rule for recording the current strategy in *Working Memory* must be revised to also record a temporal marker to stop the strategy. Second, a rule is required to update temporal markers on each processing cycle. The rule used in the WCST model for updating the time at which strategies were last attempted is redundant and can be dropped.

Box 8.20 shows suitably revised rules for *Belief Update*. Rule 1 records the current strategy in *Working Memory* and sets a temporal marker to stop that strategy after a specified time. Rule 2 ages temporal markers by counting down the time argument.

Schema Construction

Schema Construction requires minimal modification. Within the 6ET model, selected strategies are represented in *Evaluated Strategies* as elements of the form `selected(do(S, T))` (meaning select strategy `S` and set a temporal marker to stop `S` in `T` time units). This contrasts with the representation within the WCST model, in which such strategies were represented as `selected(S)`. The schema construction and schema deletion rules (Rules 1 and 2 from Box 8.6) need to be modified to account for this change in representation.

Rule 2 (unrefracted): *Deselect losing schemas*
IF: `selected(S)` is in *Selected Schemas*
`node(schema(S), A)` is in *Schema Hierarchy*
exists `node(schema(O), B)` is in *Schema Hierarchy*
`B` is greater than `A`
THEN: delete `selected(S)` from *Selected Schemas*

Rule 3 (unrefracted): *If a schema is selected, act on it!*
IF: `selected(S)` is in *Selected Schemas*
`request(R)` is in *The World*
THEN: delete all `action(_)` from *The World*
add `action(S)` to *The World*

Box 8.21: Revised rules for *Select & Act* to deselect schemas and execute actions

Contention Scheduling

Continuing around the domino, *Contention Scheduling* requires modifications in three places: *Schema Hierarchy* requires nodes for each of the six subtasks (e.g., `task(dictation, 1)`, `task(dictation, 2)`, ...), the rule in *Trigger Schemas* requires modification to match against `do(S)` in *The World* (rather than just `S`), and *Select & Act* requires modification of the rules for acting on *The World*. Of these, only the last requires additional comment.

Box 8.21 shows two revised rules for *Select & Act*. Rule 2 in the figure implements schema deselection. The rule deselects a selected schema when its activation falls below that of any other schema in the network. This follows the definition of schema deselection given by Norman and Shallice (1980). The rule (which replaces Rule 2 of Box 8.8) is necessary because the 6ET requires sustained selection of a task's schema throughout execution of the task. Rule 3 in the figure (which replaces Rule 3 of Box 8.8) executes actions corresponding to selected schemas.

Perception

One final revision is required to make the 6ET model complete. Subtasks that have been started should be recorded as such in *Working Memory* so that they may receive lower evaluations than tasks that have not been started. This recording could be performed by *Belief Update* when it records selection of a strategy. Alternatively, it may be carried out by *Perception* by noting actions performed on *The World*. We assume the latter. An additional rule is therefore required in *Perception*. At the same time, the WCST feedback rule is not required (because

Rule 3 (unrefracted): *The current task has been started*
IF: `action(Task)` is in *The World*
not `started(Task)` is in *Working Memory*
THEN: add `started(Task)` to *Working Memory*

Box 8.22: A revised rule for *Perception* to record when a subtask has been attempted

there is no experimenter-generated feedback in the 6ET). Rule 3 of *Perception* may therefore be replaced with the rule in Box 8.22.

8.5.4 Testing the Model

The above rules and condition definitions should lead to the following sequence of events:

1. Six `requested/1` elements, corresponding to the six subtasks, are placed in *Working Memory*.
2. A goal `generate_strategy(list(Tasks))` is placed in *Goals*. `Tasks` will be a list consisting of all six requests.
3. Six candidate strategies are generated by *Strategy Generation*, and placed in *Candidate Strategies*. These are all of the form `do(task(Task, N), 100)`, where `Task` is one of the three task types, `N` is `1` or `2`, and `100` represents the time each task should be performed for.
4. *Evaluation* generates an evaluation value of `1000` for each candidate, and places annotated candidates in *Evaluated Strategies*.
5. *Evaluation* selects one of the annotated candidates and replaces all of them with a single `selected(do(task(Task, N)), 100)` element.
6. *Belief Update* and *Schema Construction* both pass the selected strategy on. A `current_strategy(task(Task, N))` element and temporal marker appear in *Working Memory*, and a `schema(task(Task, N))` element appears in *Temporary Schema*.
7. Activation is fed to the *Schema Hierarchy* node corresponding to the temporary schema. The activation level of the node starts to increase.
8. When the node's activation level reaches or exceeds the selection threshold, a `selected(task(Task, N))` node is added to *Selected Schemas*.
9. In response to the selection of a schema, an `action(task(Task, N))` element is placed in *The World* to simulate the carrying out of the action associated with the selected strategy.

Rule 1 (refracted): *Terminate after 600 cycles (simulated 15 minutes)*
IF: the current cycle is 600
THEN: send `stop` to *SAS/CS (6ET) + Experimenter*

Rule 2 (refracted): *Record start time of subtask*
IF: `action(Task)` is in *The World*
not `doing(Task, Start)` is in *Record*
the current cycle is S
THEN: add `doing(Task, S)` to *Record*

Rule 3 (refracted): *Record start time of subtask*
IF: `doing(Task, Start)` is in *Record*
not `action(Task)` is in *The World*
the current cycle is `Stop`
`Diff` is `Stop` – `Start`
THEN: delete `doing(Task, Start)` from *Record*
add `did(Task, from(Start), to(Stop), Diff)` to *Record*

Box 8.23: Simple rules for administration of the six element test (from *Controller*)

Exercise 8.10: Implement the rules for each of the domino processes and test the model. It should behave as indicated in the previous paragraphs. Note that the model should continue switching between subtasks, devoting 100 or so processing cycles to each, until it is forcibly stopped with COGENT's Stop button (the button marked with a red square). ◇

8.5.5 Experimenter Functions for the Six Element Test

There are four functions required of an experimenter administering the 6ET:

1. providing the participant with the subtasks and explaining the rules;
2. stopping the participant after 15 minutes;
3. timing the participant on each subtask; and
4. monitoring the participant's behaviour for rule breaks.

The first of these has been achieved in the model through appropriate initialisation of *The World* and through the assumption that the components of the SAS/CS model have appropriate rules for the test. An *Experimenter* module similar to that used in the WCST model is required for the other three.

Box 8.23 shows suitable rules for functions 2 and 3. The rules are assumed to reside in a *Controller* process within *Experimenter*. Rule 1 stops processing in the model after 600 COGENT cycles. (Recall that this timing is for convenience. There is no built-in time unit within COGENT.) Rule 2 records the COGENT cycle when each subtask is started. Rule 3 records the COGENT cycle when each subtask is stopped, and calculates the total number of processing cycles spent on the task.

Exercise 8.11: Add an *Experimenter* compound box that has read and write access to *The World*, and that consists of one process (*Controller*) and one propositional buffer (*Record*). Add the rules from Box 8.23 to *Controller*. Run the model. It should now terminate after 600 cycles, and maintain a log of tasks attempted and time per task in *Record*. If all details of the model are correct, it should perform each task for 100 or so cycles and then move on to the next. At the same time, when it switches between tasks it should normally move from one task to a second task of a different type. ◇

Exercise 8.12: A further COGENT rule is required to check for rule-breaks (i.e., for consecutive attempts at the same kind of task). Add an appropriate rule to *Controller*. ◇

8.5.6 Discussion of the Six Element Test

Extension of the SAS/CS model from the WCST to the 6ET has been relatively straightforward. This is because the two tests share many executive processes. Similar processes may be used for strategy generation, evaluation, and selection. There are basically two principal changes: the task being performed under routine control by CS (which for WCST is sorting by card feature and for 6ET is one of the six subtasks), and the origin of the signal to abandon the current strategy/task and select a new one. In the case of the 6ET, this involved implementing the Shallice and Burgess (1991) concept of a temporal marker and extending the monitoring functions appropriately.

While the function of temporal markers in the 6ET is similar to that of feedback signals in the WCST, evidence suggests that the neural implementations of the two systems differ. Specifically, the neurological patients of Shallice and Burgess (1991) who had difficulty with the 6ET all performed at above normal levels when tested on the WCST. It would appear that strategy application disorder patients do not necessarily have difficulty in responding appropriately to externally generated feedback. Their difficulty lies in generating or responding to internally generated feedback.

The 6ET model assumes that the individual subtasks of the 6ET can be performed by schemas within the CS system. This assumption requires schemas for object naming, dictating a route, and performing simple arithmetic. This may be plausible in the case of object naming, but it is less so in the case of route dictation and arithmetic. This does not necessarily undermine the model. We have abstracted the individual tasks so that we may focus on shifting between tasks at critical times, for this is the source of errors of interest. A more complete model would undoubtedly include details of the individual tasks. The claim is that such a model would simply extend the current model, and that those extensions would not compromise the mechanisms involved in task shifting. This claim is clearly worth evaluating, but the current model demonstrates that the SAS/CS approach to moving between tasks in the 6ET is viable as an account of normal performance.

How, though, might the model account for the impaired performance of strategy application disorder patients? Shallice and Burgess (1991) suggest that such patients either fail to set appropriate temporal markers or fail to act when such markers expire. Both explanations are plausible, and both may be explored in the model by modifying certain key rules. For example, the former may be implemented by modifying the rule for strategy generation such that inappropriately long durations are suggested for subtasks, or by modifying the rule that creates temporal markers such that the durations specified by strategy generation are ignored. The latter may be implemented by modifying the rule that monitors for expired markers, such that it fails to fire when it should.

Another possibility is an inappropriate rule, e.g., "do each subtask until it's complete", which might result from misjudging the time taken to do subtasks, from a failure of problem solving in the strategy generation process, or from not taking on board all of the task requirements (e.g., approaching the task as it would be approached in the absence of time pressure).

Exercise 8.13: Modify the monitoring rule such that it fires only intermittently. This may be achieved by creating a new user-defined condition in *Monitoring & Goal Generation* that succeeds intermittently (see Box 6.8 of Chapter 6) and testing this condition in the monitoring rule. How does behaviour change as the probability of the rule firing is altered? Can failure of this rule to fire account for the behaviour of strategy application disorder patients? ◇

While any of the above modifications may yield a model that behaves as patients do, none of them provides a satisfactory explanation of why marker generation/expiration might fail in the way it appears to. In any case, the treatment of markers as entities with a discrete integer time stamp that counts down and triggers a behaviour when zero is reached is rather crude. A more intuitive approach might be to treat the time stamp as more like an activation value that is set at one point and then decays with time. Again behaviour may then be triggered when the activation falls to (near) zero.

8.5.7 Project: Generalising the Models

One unsatisfactory aspect of the 6ET model, especially when the model is considered alongside the WCST model, is that it is overly task-specific. A more satisfactory implementation of supervisory functions would more clearly distinguish between executive processes and task knowledge that is employed when performing different executive tasks. Develop a generalised SAS/CS model that may apply to a range of strategy switching tasks (including the WCST and the 6ET). Test the model on both the WCST and the 6ET.

Hint: Begin by working around the domino and sketching out the information required by each buffer during each task. For each buffer develop a general representation that is suitable for representing the range of information required. For example, the representation used in *Goals* must be sufficiently general as to be able to represent both simple goals such as sorting a single card and compound goals such as completing a set of subtasks. Once this is complete, devise rules in each process to manipulate and process the information within each buffer in an appropriate way. Again, work around the domino from *Perception* to *Contention Scheduling* when doing this.

8.6 Alternative Views of Executive Processes

The dual-process SAS/CS view of executive processes described and modelled in this chapter is one of the dominant theories of executive processes. A second view that has become popular more recently is that embodied in the Executive Process Interactive Control (or EPIC) cognitive architecture (Meyer & Kieras, 1997; Kieras & Meyer, 1997). EPIC is a production system architecture consisting of several perceptual and motor processes and a central production rule processor. Different sensory processors may operate in parallel with the central processor, which also operates in parallel (i.e., there is no conflict resolution between production instances).

Meyer and Kieras (1997) focus on the productions required to implement executive processes that co-ordinate multiple processes within EPIC, and this work is extended by Kieras *et al.* (2000), who demonstrate that EPIC is consistent with several resource allocation strategies. The emphasis of the work of Meyer, Kieras, and colleagues is on how executive processes such as task scheduling and resource allocation may be performed by standard production rules.

Executive processes are in principle within the remit of other cognitive architectures such as ACT-R (Anderson & Lebiere, 1998) and Soar (Newell, 1990). While these architectures take a stand on the overall organisation or structure of mental processes, there has been little work on issues relating to executive processes within either of them (though see Salvucci & Macuga, 2001, for one notable exception). While tasks such as planning may be performed by both of these architectures, neither attempts to account for phenomena that are more clearly related to executive processing, such as those of resource conflict and allocation addressed by EPIC.

Many consider the prefrontal cortex to be intimately involved in executive processing. This position is supported by evidence from neurological patients with localised brain injury and by brain imaging studies of neurologically intact individuals performing "executive" tasks. There is therefore potential overlap between theories of frontal lobe function and theories of executive process. However, most theories of frontal lobe function deal more with issues of working memory (e.g., Goldman-Rakic, 1992; Kimberg & Farah, 1993) or planning and acting (e.g., Grafman, 1995) than with issues relating to resource allocation or task switching. The overlap between these theories is therefore less than one might imagine.

8.7 Summary

This chapter has concentrated on one theory of executive control, the SAS/CS theory of Norman and Shallice. Executive control processes are very distant, conceptually, from the inputs and outputs of the cognitive system, and are thus particularly difficult to study or even to characterise precisely. An important point made by Norman and Shallice is that in order to have an effective theory about supervisory processes in cognition, one must first have a theory of the processes which are being supervised, and of the type of supervision which is being carried out. Norman and Shallice address this with their contention scheduling system, which specifies the way lower-level cognitive processes are organised so that coherent behaviour can emerge from many simple processes operating in parallel. This allows the type of control provided by the SAS to be specified — it alters the activation level of CS nodes to influence which processes get selected.

We have developed a very simple simulation of the SAS and CS systems, based on ideas from the field of Artificial Intelligence. The framework we have developed includes a number of cognitive processes, such as reasoning and decision making, which are major research topics in their own right and have chapters of their own in this book. To keep the model simple, we have glossed over the complex operations of these processes, on the assumption that theories and models from these areas could be "plugged in" to the SAS model in the future, if so desired. Of course, it is all too easy when developing a "framework" model of this type to make unwarranted assumptions about how easy it will be to elaborate sections of the model in the future. For this reason it is most important always to keep in mind the possible practical implications of incorporating full-scale versions of individual modules into the model, and especially the possible constraints which this could impose on the design both of the overall model and of the individual modules.

Finally, it is important to note that the SAS/CS framework is only one of several theories of executive processes in human cognition. Other important theories which are sufficiently well specified to form the basis of computer models include Soar, ACT-R, and EPIC.

8.8 Further Reading

There are relatively few sources of further reading concerned specifically with executive processes. The most extensive source is that of Shallice (1988) (especially Chapter 14). There are also several relevant chapters in Monsell and Driver (2000). For earlier views that remain of interest see Luria (1966) and Shallice (1972). Shallice and Burgess (1996) and Burgess, Veitch, de Lacy Costello, and Shallice (2000) discuss the fractionation and organisation of executive processes, especially in relation to a view based on supervisory attention and contention scheduling. This view is detailed by Norman and Shallice (1986) and Shallice (1988), and further elaborated by Cooper and Shallice (2000), who present a model of the contention scheduling system and discuss results of several simulations.

An alternative model of the WCST is presented by Dehaene and Changeux (1991). Their model is based in neurophysiology rather than in an executive processing framework, and differs substantially from the model presented here.

The domino agent is described in detail by Fox and Das (2000). They present the agent as a generic framework for intelligent decision making, but do not attempt to relate it to issues of executive processing. An alternative view of the structure of executive processes is presented by Meyer and Kieras (1997), who describe the EPIC cognitive architecture and consider its application to some standard multiple task paradigms. The work is extended by Kieras *et al.* (2000), who compare possible resource allocation strategies within EPIC.

Part III

Reflections

Chapter 9

Reflections

Richard P. Cooper

Overview: The preceding chapters have presented and developed a number of models across a range of domains. The purpose of this closing chapter is to reflect upon the issues raised by these models, to consider the lessons learnt, and to suggest directions which future modelling might take.

9.1 An Assessment of Progress

We have seen how aspects of memory, cognitive skill, problem solving, reasoning, decision making, sentence processing, and executive processes may all be modelled. The breadth of this coverage testifies to the generality of both symbolic modelling techniques and the COGENT modelling environment, but what has been gained scientifically from the development of these models?

One primary goal of cognitive modelling is to gain a deeper understanding of the mechanisms and processes underlying cognitive functions. To this end, some progress has been made. First, the magnitude of the undertaking has been clarified. A complete understanding of the mechanisms and processes underlying cognitive functions must cover each of the domains addressed by Chapters 3 to 7 (and more). It must also address the integration and co-ordination of the individual domains (as discussed in Chapter 8). Second, several computational mechanisms that may support the kind of processing that cognition appears to require have been identified. For example, the general mechanism of operator proposal and application has proven to be well suited to computational problems that arise in a variety of domains.

These statements of progress are deliberately conservative. There is good reason for this. Higher cognitive processes are difficult to study. In most cases there is substantial scope for factors such as knowledge, motivation, general intelligence, and "free-will" to influence behaviour. It is impractical to control such factors in an experimental setting. While there are some exceptions (e.g., in relation to language), it is generally difficult to provide data against which models of higher cognitive processes may be evaluated. This, together with the complexity of many theories of such processes, makes the development of models of higher cognitive processes even more critical. Substantial progress will be made if and when such models can be used to generate falsifiable predictions.

9.2 Emergent Issues

Progress has also been made in the identification of a range of emergent issues that impact upon modelling across a variety of domains. An appreciation of these issues is critical for an appreciation of the strengths and limitations of modelling. This section therefore reviews the principal emergent issues.

We begin by considering how a single process or system can be described at different "levels", and the consequences of this fact for cognitive modelling. This leads to the closely related issue of indistinguishability — at some levels competing theories may be indistinguishable. Two further issues that have some relation to the levels of description issue are the distinction between competence and performance and the requirement for computational completeness. These are also discussed. Finally, attention is directed towards the computational mechanisms invoked by models in different domains, similarities between some of these mechanisms, and the implications of such similarities.

9.2.1 Levels of Description and Explanation

Recall the models of syllogistic reasoning developed in Chapter 5. The two models used different algorithms, but when given the same inputs (a pair of premises) they generated the same output (a conclusion, if one followed from the premises). Hence, if one only compares input/output behaviour of the algorithms that the models implement, then the algorithms are indistinguishable. This is a common problem in cognitive psychology, because data generally take the form of stimulus/response pairs (which are formally equivalent to input/output mappings), and there may be many algorithms capable of generating such pairs.

Marr's Levels

The relationship between alternative algorithms for the same input/output mapping was one of several relationships studied by Marr (1982), who argued that any complex system, be it mechanical, electrical, or biological, could be described at three distinct levels. At the most abstract level, such a system could be described in terms of its input/output mappings. In the case of syllogistic reasoning, this would be the set of valid responses for each pair of premises. Marr referred to this level of description as level one, or the *computational level*. The term is possibly confusing. It refers to the function that is computed by the system.

A slightly more concrete description of the same system would specify the algorithms or processes by which inputs are transformed into outputs. The two different algorithms for syllogistic reasoning belong to this level. Those algorithms specify how inputs (premise pairs) are converted into mental models or diagrams, and how outputs (conclusions) are drawn from these mental models or diagrams. Marr referred to this level of description as level two, or the *algorithmic and representational level*.

Finally, the system could be described in terms of the physical implementation of the algorithm that achieves the input/output mapping. This level distinguishes between alternative implementations of the same algorithm. Thus, one might implement Mental Models theory with a set of COGENT boxes and rules and buffer elements in those boxes, or by using pebbles to represent individuals in a spatial array, with rules for how to place and interpret pebbles. Marr referred to this level of description as level three, or the *implementational level*. He argued that in describing a complex system it is critical to distinguish between the different levels, and that a complete understanding of a complex system requires descriptions at all levels.

Marr's levels of description and explanation are important within cognitive modelling because they clarify the relationship between the mind/brain and a model of some cognitive function. For example, Marr was clear that a description at level two involves both a description of an algorithm and a description of the representations over which the algorithm operates. For this reason, some cognitive scientists refer to this level as the level of cognitive theory.

Level two is also the level to which symbolic models, with their explicit propositional representations, are most naturally related. On the other hand the connectionist approach to modelling, with its concern for cognition as the product of multiple parallel interactions between simple neuron-like processing units, is sometimes claimed to be pitched at the implementational level (Broadbent, 1985).

A Brief Appraisal of Marr's Levels

Marr's levels of description are generally presented as distinct ways in which a complex system may be described. Three caveats are in order. First, the description above is something of a sanitised version of Marr's original formulation. For example, Marr also argued for the importance of understanding a system's purpose (i.e., the why, as well as the what and the how) in understanding the system's functioning. The above explication of Marr's levels focuses just on the essential elements of the theory.

The second caveat is more important with respect to modelling. Levels of description are not necessarily as clear-cut as they may first appear. The assumption implicit in the levels approach is that a description may be given at one level independently of the other levels. It is not clear that this assumption is met by the mind/brain. A common argument from the connectionist school of modelling is that implementation matters. That is, the physical realisation of cognitive processes in the neural substrate (level three) has important consequences for the form of those cognitive processes (level two), and hence the mind/brain cannot be given a level two description that is independent of level three. This caveat is serious because it has the potential to undermine not just the theory of levels of description but the role of traditional (level two) theorising within cognitive psychology in understanding the mind/brain.

One approach to accounting for mis-matches between descriptions at different levels is to view level one as an idealisation of level two, and level two as an idealisation of level three. From this perspective, a level two description of a system will only be approximate. While this appeal to idealisation does not appease all commentators (see Franks, 1995), it does at least allow progress to be made, and for description at one level to inform description at another.

A final caveat is that Marr is not the only author to consider levels of description of complex systems. Of particular relevance to cognitive modelling are the arguments of Newell (1982) and Smolensky (1988). Newell argues that complex systems may be described at more than three levels. Thus, in considering an electronic computer performing a particular function he distinguishes between descriptions at the level of electronic devices, electrical circuits, logic circuits, register-transfer systems, and program-level systems. In Newell's terms each level has a characteristic medium, and behaviour within the level is governed by level-specific laws or principles. Newell uses his more detailed analysis of levels to argue for what he calls the knowledge level, which, he suggests, is the level of intelligent behaviour. Smolensky effectively concurs with Newell that there are more than three levels. His arguments suggest, however, that the connectionist approach is best understood at a level between the algorithmic and representational level and the implementational level.

Notwithstanding these caveats, levels of description play an important role in cognitive modelling. They remind us that cognitive modelling is concerned with an abstract description of the cognitive system and that a single system may be described in different ways for different purposes.

9.2.2 Competing Theories and Indistinguishability

A corollary of the existence of levels of description is that systems that are distinct at one level may be indistinguishable at another. Consider again the case of the alternative algorithms for syllogistic reasoning. If the same computational level description (human syllogistic competence) can result from different descriptions at the algorithmic and representational level (model-based or set-theoretic approaches), then the computational level description will not be able to discriminate between the descriptions at the algorithmic and representational level. Indistinguishability arises because theory is under-specified by data: the computational level — the stimulus/response mapping being modelled — corresponds to the data that the model is attempting to account for, whereas the algorithmic and representational level corresponds to the theory behind the model.

Two famous arguments concerning indistinguishability were made during the 1970s. Townsend (1971, 1974) argued that serial and parallel processes could mimic each other, and hence were indistinguishable. Similarly, Anderson (1978) argued, with respect to mental imagery, that propositional and analogical representations could mimic each other, and were hence indistinguishable. As discussed in Chapter 5, model-based and set-theoretic approaches to syllogistic reasoning may also be indistinguishable, and Yule (1997) has presented a generalisation of this argument that applies to model-based and rule-based approaches to deductive reasoning.

Indistinguishability is an issue whenever alternative computational mechanisms are plausible. It is important because it limits the extent to which we can hope to discriminate between competing models. It is not universally accepted, however. Newell (1990), for example, suggests two ways in which competing algorithmic and representational level descriptions may be discriminated: first, by employing chronometric data (i.e., reaction times) and having models produce estimates of processing time, and second, by developing models within a cognitive architecture, such that models may be constrained by the architecture (which itself is the product of converging evidence from a range of domains).

While Newell's suggestions allow some progress to be made in discriminating some algorithmic and representational level descriptions, they do not fully address the problem. Different algorithms may make similar time predictions, and the same data may be modelled within different architectures. In any case, indistinguishability is an issue that needs to be considered when developing, evaluating, and comparing models.

9.2.3 Competence and Performance

The competence/performance distinction was first introduced by Chomsky (1965) in his work on language and language processing. In this book the distinction has arisen in two principal domains, sentence processing (Chapter 7) and deductive reasoning (Chapter 5), though it could also have been invoked in the discussion of non-normative biases in decision making (Chapter 6). With respect to sentence processing, competence refers to the idealised knowledge of language hypothesised to underlie sentence processing. Failure to parse centre-embedding constructions or garden path sentences may be attributed to performance factors such as memory limitations. This is basically the distinction identified by Chomsky. With respect to deductive reasoning, competence refers to a basic understanding of logic (e.g., the meaning of quantifiers and connectives), and performance factors may be held to be responsible for errors on reasoning tasks involving the application of this understanding.

In both cases the competence/performance distinction results from the development of competence models that ignore performance factors. Such models attempt to model competence in a task, rather than actual performance. This means that the model is an idealisation, and its behaviour cannot be directly compared to human behaviour, because human behaviour is held to reflect competence mediated by performance factors. There is therefore an explanatory gap between competence and performance, and competence models can only serve as a first step towards an account of behaviour.

The explanatory gap between competence and performance does not mean that the distinction is not useful. It is invaluable if one wishes to distinguish between knowledge in a domain and use of that knowledge. However, in its basic form it is unsatisfactory because it results in theories that can make no contact with data. This is where cognitive modelling may play a critical role. By developing competence models and applying well-specified performance limitations to those models cognitive modelling allows the explanatory gap between competence and performance to be closed. The key to closing this gap is specifying in detail how performance factors impinge upon a competence model to yield behaviour.

The relation between competence and performance and levels of description stems from the fact that linguistic competence, at least as described by Chomsky (1986), abstracts from specific implementations or algorithms. A competence theory would therefore appear to be a level one theory. Performance, on the other hand, results from the effects of specific algorithms or implementations on competence. A performance theory would therefore appear to be a level two or level three theory. This is a useful way of looking at the competence/performance distinction, but the view is undermined by the idealisation necessary to go from performance to competence, and the resultant mis-match that it therefore requires between levels of description (Franks, 1995).

9.2.4 Computational Completeness

The issue of "computational completeness" has arisen several times throughout this text. The basic point is that cognitive modelling requires that a theory be specified to the level of detail required by a computer program. On the plus side, development of a model will therefore ensure that the underlying theory is stated both precisely and completely. On the minus side, the requirement for completeness may over-extend what can be justified or motivated on theoretical or empirical grounds. That is, modelling might require a precise interpretation of a theoretical assumption, even when there are multiple possible interpretations of the assumption and no motivated way of choosing between them. Indeed, theoretical assumptions may be deliberately under-specified for just this reason.

To illustrate, consider the case of representation. Theories typically make commitments only to gross aspects of representation (e.g., whether the representation is propositional or featural), yet development of a cognitive model requires a commitment to fine details of representation. Thus, cognitive modelling requires specification beyond what is generally theoretically justified. In the case of representation this is especially problematic if one also accepts the arguments of Anderson (1978), who suggests that even very gross aspects of mental representation (e.g., whether it is symbolic or analogical in nature) are indistinguishable in principle. It appears then that modelling can require a commitment to assumptions that are required purely for the purposes of computational implementation. Whether such commitments are good or bad is a matter of debate. They are bad if one views them as being forced upon us with no way of evaluating them. They are good if one accepts that they highlight those aspects of the theory that are otherwise under-specified.

Aspects of a model that are required by computational completeness rather than motivated on theoretical grounds are generally referred to as implementation assumptions. It is important to be aware of implementation assumptions and guard against their effects where possible. Cooper, Fox, Farringdon, and Shallice (1996) suggest that this may be achieved through the systematic study of a model's dependence on implementation assumptions. Only if implementation assumptions can be varied without altering those aspects of a model's behaviour that are considered to be relevant can those assumptions be treated as distinct from the theory and purely a matter of implementation. Conversely, if model behaviour is sensitive to implementation assumptions then those assumptions cannot be ignored. In practice these requirements are very strong. We return to this issue later in this chapter in the context of Lakatosian research programmes (Section 9.3.5), which offer a more pragmatic treatment of implementation assumptions.

9.2.5 General Computational Mechanisms

The cycle of operator proposal, evaluation, and selection, originally described in relation to problem solving, has been seen to be a general mechanism that could equally be applied in deductive reasoning and sentence processing. In fact, this operating cycle is well-suited to most if not all domains in which sequential behaviour is required. Its strength is that it allows multiple sources of information to contribute to each step in the sequence. The cycle can therefore generate flexible behaviours that are responsive to a wide variety of factors (such as varying context, different types of knowledge, interruptions from other processes, etc.). The operator cycle is thus a general computational mechanism appropriate for describing behaviour in a range of domains.

The operator cycle offers an attractive alternative to the kind of general computational mechanism developed by von Neumann (1947) and used in the control of modern computers. (See Cooper, 2002, for additional comment.) However, its implementation in terms of production-like rules should not be confused with the mechanism itself. An alternative computationally equivalent mechanism might be implemented, for example, within an interactive activation network, following the basic approach of Rumelhart and Norman (1982), Houghton (1990), or Cooper and Shallice (2000). The mechanism of interest is best understood as an abstraction from either implementation.

The existence of domain general computational mechanisms may be taken to support the idea of a general cognitive architecture consisting of a unitary processing system that may be deployed in different domains with different knowledge or with a different configuration. However, other interpretations are possible.

A wide variety of human behaviours may be characterised as sequentially selecting from a set of possible actions. This characterisation might be a result of the human cognitive architecture, but it is also possible that the behaviours are the result of task constraints — if two different tasks require that actions be performed in sequence, then it should not be surprising if both could be accounted for by a single mechanism that selects actions in sequence. The interesting cases, then, are those corresponding to tasks that do not require sequential selection of actions, but that nevertheless appear to be performed through such selection. The most striking case discussed in this volume is that of sentence processing, where behaviour involving the processing of garden path and related sentences was amenable to a modelling approach based on sequential selection of parsing operators. This suggests that, although task constraints might be implicated in the appearance of domain general mechanisms in some cases, there are other cases where alternative explanations (such as the architectural explanation) are required.

A further interpretation is that different processes use similar mechanisms because neural processing is well-suited to use such mechanisms. This interpretation does not require a single central processor that implements the operator cycle.

Rather, different brain areas associated with different domains of processing may operate according to similar principles, simply because those principles are most easily supported by neural tissue. Arguably this is consistent with neurophysiological evidence which indicates that, for example, despite similarities in possible computational mechanisms, language and problem solving are associated with different areas of the brain.

9.3 Methodologies for Modelling

The issues described above raise a number of potential difficulties for cognitive modelling. Different modellers have attempted to address these difficulties in different ways, and various techniques for the development and evaluation of models have arisen. These techniques amount to a range of modelling methodologies that are roughly equivalent in function to the methodology of standard quantitative experimental psychology. The main difference between the case of cognitive modelling and experimental psychology is that cognitive modelling lacks a single, universally agreed-upon, methodology — a range of methodologies are in common use. The relative merits of four candidate methodologies are discussed below. The suggestion is that each of these methodologies has something to offer cognitive modelling, and that one or more of them may form the basis of a rigorous and acceptable standard.

9.3.1 Issues in Model Evaluation

The issue of how models should be evaluated has received little direct attention in this text (or in cognitive modelling generally, though see Roberts & Pashler, 2000, and Ruml & Caramazza, 2000), but it is critical within cognitive modelling.

Performance models are frequently evaluated by demonstrating that they are able to reproduce behaviours observed in human subjects. Often the target behaviours are group means resulting from standard empirical work. This approach can be paraphrased as demonstrating that there is no difference between the behaviour of the average subject and that of the model. When stated in these terms, it is clear that this is effectively testing the Null Hypothesis. Standard inferential statistical procedures which form the basis of the rigorous methodology of empirical cognitive psychology are therefore inappropriate. In any case, a model is generally best interpreted as a model of an individual, not of a group. This means that model evaluation requires special techniques. It is not sufficient to simply show that a model reproduces subject behaviour on a task.

One simple technique to strengthen evaluation is to test a model over a range of conditions and require a strong positive correlation over those conditions with the behaviour of an individual subject. Another technique is to examine the ways in which a model may break down following damage, and compare behaviour following damage with the ways in which humans break down following neurological damage. This relies upon a clear relation between damage in the model and neurological damage.

A related difficulty in model evaluation concerns the interpretation of interactions between the environment (or the modeller) and the model. Suppose we are attempting to model a choice reaction time task in which a participant presses a button when a stimulus light turns a specified colour, and in which the brightness of the light is varied. In addition to producing a model of the cognitive decision concerning colour, we need to make assumptions about the mental representation of stimuli (and how lights of different brightnesses are represented), and about how to interpret the model's output as a reaction time. We cannot just measure the time taken by the model to produce a response, as this time will vary depending on the speed of the computer on which the model is run.

Model evaluation is complicated further by the existence of implementation details and non-deterministic elements, such as random decay of information from memory stores or noise in activation transmission. One result of non-determinism is that successive runs of a model, on the same input data, may yield different outputs (just as a human participant may show variance in behaviour on successive trials of an experiment). One result of implementation details is that it may be unclear whether model behaviour should be attributed to theoretical assumptions or implementation details. Model evaluation requires sensitivity to both of these issues.

9.3.2 Monte Carlo Simulations

The simplest approach to establishing a robust characterisation of a model's behaviour when the model contains non-deterministic elements is through *Monte Carlo* simulations. A Monte Carlo simulation consists of running a model repeatedly over the same input, and summarising the model's behaviour through descriptive statistics performed on the resulting sample of model outputs.

The Monte Carlo approach relies on there being some quantifiable aspect of the model's behaviour (i.e., a dependent variable), and allows one to characterise the model's behaviour in terms of the mean and standard deviation of this variable's value. It is analogous to running multiple subjects in a single experimental condition in order to establish group statistics, except that the model typically corresponds to a single subject. It is therefore more akin to running a single subject multiple times on the same task, without the problem of contamination of data through practice effects or fatigue.

In cases where a model includes free parameters, the Monte Carlo approach may be used to determine behaviour over a portion of the parameter space. Thus, a model might be run multiple times for each of a set of values of its parameters.

This approach can give the modeller a better understanding of dependencies of the model's behaviour on its parameters, or it may be used to determine values of the parameters that yield the optimal fit between the model's behaviour and participant behaviour.

9.3.3 Computational Experiments

One way in which the methodology of Monte Carlo simulations may be improved is by incorporating elements of standard experimental design. Thus, Monte Carlo simulations may be performed under two or more experimental conditions (e.g., using two different stimulus sets). Within this methodology the different experimental conditions may, as in standard experimental design, be defined by different values of independent variables. After performing the simulations across conditions statistical analysis may be performed on the model's dependent variables, allowing the modeller to determine main effects of independent variables on dependent variables and interactions between independent variables (using standard statistical techniques such as analysis of variance).

A more sophisticated version of the computational experiment methodology involves coupling computational experiments with standard laboratory experiments, and attempting to replicate the results of laboratory experiments. This approach is most convincing when the procedures used in laboratory experiments are accurately reproduced for the computational replication. This will normally require the development of the kind of computational infrastructure used in many of the COGENT models discussed in this text to administer the experiment to the model and to collect and collate the model's output.

The approach of computational experimentation is particularly compelling when the computational experiment is performed *prior* to the laboratory experiment, such that the computational experiment yields predictions that are potentially falsifiable by laboratory work.

9.3.4 Comparative Modelling

Frequently in cognitive psychology it is the case that multiple competing accounts of some phenomenon or data set are available. One case that has received particular attention in the literature is that of forming the past tense of English verbs from their base form (Rumelhart & McClelland, 1986a; MacWhinney & Leinbach, 1991; Ling & Marinov, 1993). A reasonable methodology in cases such as these consists of developing models based on the competing accounts, and comparing the behaviour of those models on a specific task for which empirical data is available. The purpose of such a comparison is not necessarily to determine which theory or approach is best. It is far more likely that competing theories will have strengths and weaknesses (as in the case of the categorisation models developed in Chapter 6). The purpose is therefore more in determining the strengths and weaknesses and, if possible, relating them to specific theoretical assumptions.

The comparative modelling approach is essentially a multiple model variation of the computational experiment methodology. It is particularly strong when the models are coupled with one or more laboratory experiments, and when the same computational infrastructure is used to administer the computational experiment for each model (i.e., in the context of the models developed in this book, when the same *Experimenter* module is used with different *Subject* modules).

9.3.5 Lakatosian Research Programmes

The issue of scientific progress and theory development has been discussed at length in the philosophy of science literature (see, for example, Lakatos & Musgrave, 1970). This literature is particularly instructive when considering the pros and cons of alternative methodologies. Of particular relevance to cognitive modelling is the approach to theory development outlined by Lakatos (1970). Lakatos argued that many scientific theories could be understood as consisting of a hard core of central assumptions (which were, given the theory, indisputable) plus a set of fluid, peripheral assumptions. Within this framework Lakatos argued that theory development involved refinement of the peripheral assumptions, with the gradual incorporation of such assumptions into the central core.

The concept of a Lakatosian research programme has much to offer cognitive modelling. Newell (1990), for example, argued that the development of the Soar cognitive architecture was properly conceived of as a Lakatosian research programme (though see Cooper & Shallice, 1995, for counter-arguments). The principal advantages of adopting a Lakatosian position are two-fold. First, it makes it clear that not all model assumptions have the same status: some may be of central theoretical importance while others may be more peripheral. This central/peripheral distinction is arguably an appropriate way of characterising the distinction between theoretical and implementation assumptions. Second, it emphasises that models (and theories) are not static objects. Rather, they develop through time via the incorporation of peripheral assumptions into the central core.

The mapping of theoretical assumptions to central assumptions and of implementational assumptions to peripheral assumptions within a Lakatosian framework allows for implementational assumptions to be distinguished from theoretical assumptions. A sound methodology also requires clear and consistent criteria for migrating assumptions from implementational to theoretical status. Such criteria are apparent in, for example, the work of Anderson (1983). He suggested three criteria for theory change, based on concepts such as empirical adequacy and adaptive utility. Anderson was not working explicitly within a Lakatosian framework. In fact his criteria essentially related to the alteration of theoretical assumptions. However, the criteria may equally be employed to elevate particular peripheral/implementational assumptions to central/theoretical status.

Other criteria for determining when an assumption is properly regarded as theoretical/central or implementational/peripheral are possible. Thus, Cooper *et al.* (1996) suggest a strict interpretation of the theory/implementation distinction in which any assumption that has an effect on model behaviour is classified as theoretical and not implementational. In practice, this approach may be too strict — model behaviour is rarely independent of assumptions made for the purposes of implementation. The Lakatosian approach is, however, consistent with a more pragmatic approach. It does not demand that model behaviour be necessarily independent of implementation assumptions. All that is required is that implementational assumptions are distinguished from theoretical assumptions, and that the distinction between theoretical and implementation assumptions is based on consistent criteria. Given this, theory development may proceed in a Lakatosian manner by exploring and incorporating implementational assumptions into the core theory. From this perspective, the key issue raised by Cooper *et al.* (1996) is that an awareness is required of the dependencies between individual assumptions and model behaviour.

9.3.6 Methodologies and Strategies for Simulation

Section 1.10 of Chapter 1 introduced four strategies for the use of simulation. The principal difference between the strategies concerns their objectives. The different strategies are compatible with different methodologies. Monte Carlo simulations are particularly suited for fishing trips and sufficiency tests. In these cases the simulation strategy is exploratory in nature, and this maps well onto the relatively unconstrained Monte Carlo approach. Sufficiency tests, in particular, may involve an element of parameter fitting: performing Monte Carlo simulations in order to determine optimal values for parameters (and hence to demonstrate that the model is sufficient to account for the data).

The fishing trip and sufficiency test strategies are both scientifically weak in comparison with the strategies involving sensitivity studies and the hypothetico-deductive method. These latter cases correspondingly require a different methodology, namely the methodology of computational experimentation. This methodology provides for the systematic variation of implementation assumptions as required by sensitivity studies, and, when computational experiments are performed prior to laboratory experiments, for the generation of testable hypotheses as required by the hypothetico-deductive method.

The two remaining methodologies, those of comparative modelling and the use of Lakatosian research programmes to structure modelling research, are in many ways orthogonal to the methodologies of Monte Carlo simulations and computational experimentation. Both are compatible with all simulation strategies, though in the case of a Lakatosian research programme one would normally expect to progress from a fishing trip-style simulation through sufficiency tests and sensitivity studies to use of the complete hypothetico-deductive method.

9.4 Issues for COGENT

The issues and methodologies discussed in the preceding sections are general in that they are of concern in all cognitive modelling. A number of additional issues are raised by use of the COGENT modelling environment. This section reviews these additional issues.

9.4.1 Generality

As a modelling environment, COGENT attempts to provide support for the development and evaluation of models in a wide variety of domains. It succeeds in this to the extent that it supports modelling in the range of domains covered in this text, but how general is the system really? The domains covered have certain similarities — they may all be described in terms of symbol manipulation, for example. So is the generality more than skin deep?

The issue of generality is perhaps best addressed not by the range of domains that can be modelled within COGENT, but by the range of alternative models that can be developed within a single domain. Thus, in the case of decision making and categorisation (Chapter 6), COGENT was used to develop Bayesian, associationist, and hypothesis testing models of the same task. Each model was an information processing model, but the models differed substantially both in the way they represented information and in the way they used it. In this respect COGENT's generality is therefore genuine.

Despite this generality, COGENT does introduce some constraints. For example, it does not support the development of models that cannot be expressed in information processing terms. Hence, models based on dynamical principles present difficulties (Port & van Gelder, 1995). Equally, it provides only weak support for imagistic representations and other forms of representation that are neither propositional nor featural.

There are also constraints related to the timing of information flow. It is sometimes difficult to ensure that rules that monitor buffer contents fire only when they are intended to fire, and not before or after. These difficulties are compounded when information from multiple sources must converge (e.g., when the actions of a rule that is triggered by a message from one box are conditional upon information in a buffer that is independent from the box which generated the message). Such timing issues stem from the parallel distributed nature of COGENT. They do not suggest that COGENT is deficient with respect to control of timing. Rather, if cognitive processing is parallel and distributed, they suggest that neural mechanisms must exist to address timing issues. In COGENT, these issues may be addressed by buffering information until it is ready for processing. It is not unrealistic to expect that the brain employs similar buffering mechanisms.

Notwithstanding COGENT's generality, there are also cases where it is an inappropriate tool. Most obviously, COGENT is not designed for intensive numerical processing. Dynamical models and connectionist models that require such processing are best developed within other systems or tool-kits.

9.4.2 Relation to Production System Architectures

There is a clear relation between rules within COGENT's rule-based processes and production rules of the kind used in standard production systems and various production system architectures. Both may interact with buffers by matching elements and then adding or deleting elements. Some of COGENT's generality may be attributed to these similarities. However, COGENT is more powerful than production system architectures for two key reasons.

First, rules may have complex conditions. Evaluation of these conditions may involve arbitrary computation, far in excess of simply matching against elements in a buffer. Rules may also be triggered by messages generated by other components (i.e., other boxes), allowing greater control over situations in which rules fire. COGENT rules are therefore significantly more expressive than standard production rules.

Second, COGENT allows components of different types to be freely mixed within a model. Thus, a single model may include multiple independent rule-based processes, or multiple short-term storage buffers. It may also mix rule-based processes with feed-forward or interactive activation networks. This freedom to mix components provides COGENT with flexibility well beyond that of standard production systems.

9.4.3 Support for Modelling

A further way in which COGENT differs from standard production systems and architectures is that, as an integrated modelling environment, it provides modelling support that is not present in either standard production systems or architectures. Some of this support is designed to simplify common activities that are normally performed in more labour-intensive ways (e.g., the research programme manager, the archive functions, and text-based documentation panels). The importance of labour-saving facilities should not be under-emphasised, but other forms of support are more significant because they go beyond standard modelling methodology. This category includes the use of compound boxes to separate the functioning of the cognitive model from the specification of the task environment, the use of properties such as buffer decay and capacity limitations to allow consideration of performance limitations, and the provision of an extensive experiment scripting language.

The use of separate compound boxes for modelling cognitive function and the task environment has been illustrated by several models throughout this book. The separation encourages clear thinking about the interface between the cognitive model and the task to which it is applied. It has an additional advantage, however, that was really only illustrated by the models of disease categorisation (Chapter 6): that of allowing different models to be evaluated within a single task environment. This is critical for the methodology of comparative modelling. It also opens up the possibility of testing a single model on a variety of tasks, by fixing the *Subject* module and varying the *Experimenter* module. Equally, it allows comparative modelling, by fixing the *Experimenter* module and varying the *Subject* module.

The behaviour of most COGENT boxes may be configured through the use of properties. This facility is a further source of flexibility within COGENT, as boxes of the same basic type may be used for a variety of different functions. However, some properties may also be interpreted as allowing ideal performance to be degraded. Such properties include capacity limitations and decay for buffers and rate of firing for rules in rule-based processes. These kinds of properties allow competence models and performance factors to be investigated within COGENT using, for example, the methodology of computational experimentation. They may also be used to investigate hypothesised neurological impairments, which may be viewed as resulting from extreme performance limitations.

The methodologies of comparative modelling and computational experimentation are also supported by COGENT's experiment scripting language. While it has not been described in detail in this book, COGENT's experiment scripting language allows the modeller to specify complex experimental designs and procedures — equivalent to the kinds of designs and procedures employed in standard experimental psychology — and to use these designs and procedures for model evaluation. In this way COGENT supports the direct comparison of model behaviour and human behaviour.

9.4.4 The Psychological Reality of COGENT Boxes

It is commonly argued that the symbolic approach to cognitive modelling is ill-founded because there is no evidence of symbol processing or propositional representations at the neural level. This argument is then used to suggest that modelling should adopt connectionist or, more radically, dynamical, methods. An analogous argument may be applied to COGENT. It may be argued that COGENT is inappropriate for cognitive modelling because there is no evidence that COGENT boxes exist "in the head". Both of these arguments are based on a literal interpretation of the relation between symbolic models and neural functioning. One may accept that neural functioning may be described in terms of symbol manipulation (or COGENT-like boxes) without requiring that neural functioning involves the explicit manipulation of symbols (or the explicit operation of COGENT-like boxes).

Consider the case of COGENT buffers. From the perspective of information processing psychology, buffers are necessary to store information while it is accumulating or while it is being operated on. Few cognitive psychologists would assert that cognitive processing does not involve some kind of buffering function. Within COGENT this function is fulfilled by buffers — boxes that are depicted by round-edged rectangles and that have properties controlling access, decay, and so on. The set of properties associated with a COGENT buffer is derived purely from the computational possibilities afforded by an abstract buffering device. It is intended that these properties give COGENT buffers sufficient flexibility of function to make them suitable for application in a variety of models.

In reality many of the computational properties of buffers are presumably a consequence of their neural implementation. That implementation might take the form of an associative network (Hertz *et al.*, 1991), or some other network with recurrent connections (e.g., RAAM: Pollack, 1990). Indeed there may be different neural implementations of devices with the same basic function (e.g., buffering) but with different properties. Thus, a FIFO buffer and a Random Access buffer may resemble each other at the functional level but have different neural implementations.

Similar comments apply to rule-based processes, which effectively map one representation to another. Again there is little doubt within either cognitive psychology or neuroscience of the existences of neural mechanisms that perform this mapping function. Those mechanisms may not be rule-based in the way that COGENT processes are. They may or may not be as powerful as COGENT processes (i.e., they may not be capable of the range of mappings of which COGENT processes are capable). What they do share is their functional description, and it is at the level of functional description that COGENT boxes are most sensibly interpreted.

Given that there is little dispute over the functions of buffers and processes, the questions of real concern to the philosophical foundation of COGENT as a cognitive modelling environment relate to the representations that COGENT boxes employ, the degree to which cognitive processing is functionally modular, and, assuming that it is, the implementation or neural realisation of the components.

9.4.5 Abstraction within COGENT Processes

The issue of the psychological reality or otherwise of COGENT boxes is basically an issue of abstraction. A second, more COGENT-specific, issue of abstraction arises in the way rules and user-defined conditions may be mixed within rule-based processes. To illustrate, consider the process of conflict resolution within a production system (see Chapter 4).

The conflict resolution process may be implemented by a rule whose conditions are satisfied by the single production instance that satisfies the various conflict resolution constraints (recency in working memory, number of working memory elements matched, recency in production memory, etc.). This is basically the solution adopted in Chapter 4, though the conditions were less extensive than they might have been. An alternative implementation of conflict resolution consists of a series of rules, where the first rule identifies the set of all matching production instances, the second rule fires if more than one production instance is identified and refines the set by removing those that match against older working memory elements, the third rule fires if more than one production instance remains and further refines the set by removing those that match fewer working memory elements, and so on.

Thus, the conflict resolution process may be specified in two different ways: as a single rule with a complex condition, or as a series of rules each with simpler conditions. The former is a coarse-grained approach, in that the conflict resolution process is specified as a single step. The latter is a fine-grained approach, in that the process is specified as a series of steps. Crucially both approaches have the same outcome (i.e., they are equivalent at Marr's computational level). Similarly, there is the potential to vary the mix of rules and user-defined conditions in most COGENT rule-based processes. The modeller has a choice about which functions to assign to rules and which to assign to user-defined conditions. This choice is effectively a choice about the granularity at which processes are specified.

COGENT therefore provides the modeller with the option to specify processes at different levels of abstraction. The modeller may use this to his/her advantage by using his/her beliefs about the status of theoretical assumptions to guide their implementation. If the modeller has a theoretical commitment to a process taking place via a series of stages, then those stages may be implemented through a series of rules. If, on the other hand, the modeller is committed only to the input and output of a process, then its internal functioning may be specified in terms of user-defined conditions such that the process' rules map directly from input to output with no intermediate processing stages. In other words, the "right" division of labour between rules and user-defined conditions, or the "right" level of abstraction, will depend upon the modeller's commitments to the theory being implemented.

9.4.6 Theory and Implementation in a COGENT Model

The arguments above suggest there is flexibility in the way a theory may be implemented within COGENT, and there is flexibility in the way the components of a COGENT model may be interpreted. How then should a COGENT model be interpreted? A clear and unambiguous answer is required to this question if one is to distinguish between theory and implementation within a COGENT model.

If COGENT boxes are to correspond to functional components of a cognitive process, then it is reasonable to suppose that there should be a correspondence between the states of those components and mental states. A clear-cut interpretation of a COGENT model is therefore that there is a direct correspondence between the states of COGENT boxes at the end of each COGENT cycle and mental states.

To illustrate, consider again the case of conflict resolution with a production system. If one believes that mental processing is rooted in a production system architecture, and that that architecture involves a process of conflict resolution which itself involves a series of steps, then one will presumably accept that mental processing during conflict resolution progresses through a series of states corresponding to the steps in the conflict resolution process. At the end of each step there should be a direct correspondence between the contents of the COGENT buffer containing the set of viable conflicting production instances and the mental representation of the conflict set.

By adopting this approach to interpretation, one may then fix upon a criterion for choosing an appropriate division of labour between rules and user-defined conditions within rule-based processes, *viz*, that the state-changes that correspond to applications of rules also correspond to hypothesised changes in mental states. If one further adopts the view that psychological theory operates at the level of mental states, then the modeller may map the division between theory and implementation onto the division between rules and user-defined conditions.

9.4.7 The COGENT Style of Modelling

The above comments indicate that COGENT has substantial generality, but that it also supports a certain style of modelling. To summarise, this style includes:

- the decomposition of cognitive functioning into interacting buffers, sub-processes, etc.;
- parallel processing by sub-processes, with each process operating on local information which may be buffered to ensure that it is available as and when necessary;
- the use of properties of components (such as buffer decay and capacity limitations) to investigate performance factors;
- rules expressed at a granularity that is commensurate with the granularity of the theory behind the model; and
- a clear separation of the cognitive model from the task environment in which it is evaluated, with appropriate consideration of the interface between the two subsystems.

9.5 An Agenda

Before closing let us look at some themes that dominate contemporary modelling in an attempt to predict developments that are likely to have the greatest impact. Two such themes are cross-domain integration (e.g., in the form of cognitive architectures) and the relation of models to neural processing. It is likely that these themes will continue to guide modelling for some time. They thus form the core of an agenda for cognitive modelling. It is also likely that increases in computing power, coupled with improved usability of modelling tools and environments, such as COGENT, PDP++ (O'Reilly & Munakata, 2000) and T-Learn (McLeod *et al.*, 1998), will lead to an increase in the use of modelling techniques. For this to be scientifically profitable, it is necessary that the modelling community establish appropriate and rigorous methodologies for model development, evaluation, and presentation. Methodology is therefore the first item on this agenda.

9.5.1 Methodology

A variety of methods is used in contemporary cognitive modelling. Arguably these methods are lacking in rigour when compared to the methods of empirical cognitive psychology (see Cohen, 1995; Cooper *et al.*, 1996). First, there is no single agreed-upon standard method that might be compared to, for example, the factorial design common in empirical cognitive psychology. Second, and as a consequence, there is no agreed-upon standard for interpreting modelling results. There is nothing to compare with the kind of inferential statistics taught to all undergraduates and used by almost all experimentalists in interpreting their empirical findings. These deficiencies are important because concepts such as factorial design and inferential statistics form the basis of the language of empirical psychology — a language that greatly aids communication between psychologists, even when there is no other overlap in their specialities.

Cognitive modelling desperately needs agreed-upon methods and a common language. This need is highlighted by the ongoing integration of modelling with main-stream cognitive psychology and cognitive neuroscience. Such integration brings the methods of the modeller under the spot-light. If the modeller's methods are found wanting, scientists from related disciplines are unlikely to be convinced by the modeller's results and conclusions. On the other hand, a rigorous methodology with a clear language will greatly aid integration.

If, in addition, there are appropriate links between the methods of modelling and the methods of standard empirical psychology and cognitive neuroscience, then understanding and acceptance of the fruits of modelling by those not directly trained in its application will be facilitated. It is therefore essential to establish a methodology and language that are on a par with those of empirical cognitive psychology.

9.5.2 Integration

The vast majority of computational modelling prior to the early 1990s was concerned with well-defined limited tasks, such as pronouncing word forms, solving the Tower of Hanoi, or syllogistic reasoning. There was good reason for this: human behaviour on such tasks was sufficiently rich as to provide modellers with significant challenges. However, as far back as 1973 Newell had argued that this limited approach could only provide limited answers. It could not answer questions about properties or characteristics of the complete cognitive system.

Newell's arguments developed, and in a series of lectures in 1987 he laid out his "vision" for cognitive modelling: the development of integrated cognitive architectures. Models of a range of tasks (including skill acquisition, problem solving, deductive reasoning, and sentence comprehension) were developed in Soar, Newell's own candidate architecture (see Newell, 1990). At the time of writing, however, it is Anderson's ACT-R that carries the torch for cognitive architectures (see Anderson, 1983, 1993; Anderson & Lebiere, 1998).

Newell's approach was not without its critics (see, e.g., Cooper & Shallice, 1995), but the use of a cognitive architecture to guide cognitive modelling is now well established. Nevertheless, substantial work remains to be done on one of Newell's primary goals — integration. There is still a tendency to use architectures as frameworks within which models of single domain tasks may be implemented. If Newell's vision is to be achieved, architectures must be used to integrate multiple single domain models. This integration will necessarily force consideration of the kinds of issues addressed in Chapter 8 — issues of monitoring, resource allocation, etc. To date, such issues have received relatively little attention from the architectural community. (The work of Kieras *et al.*, 2000, and Salvucci & Macuga, 2001, are notable exceptions.)

Integration can of course be achieved in another way. Rather than developing a "grand" theory of all cognitive processing in the style of Hull (1943, 1952) (for Newell's architectural approach has much in common with early work by Hull on what were then called grand theories), one may attempt to merge or combine theories and models of single domain tasks to form a "multi-component" architecture. Indeed, this approach was suggested by Cooper and Shallice (1995) as a way of avoiding certain perceived methodological difficulties with Newell's grand theory approach. It is also consistent with the model of the supervisory attentional system developed in Chapter 8. COGENT is well suited to this form of integration for it allows models of single domain tasks to be extended by the elaboration of components. Thus, a single COGENT process might be replaced by a compound box with additional internal structure. The functional modularity inherent in the environment also simplifies the merging of models of single domain tasks, although such merging also raises difficult issues of how executive processes allocate control to the individual models.

9.5.3 Mapping Function and Structure

Cognitive neuroscience is now well established as an inter-disciplinary approach to the study of the mind and brain. One of the fundamental goals of cognitive neuroscience is to determine the relation between cognition and the neural structures and processes underlying it. Achieving this is possibly decades off, but it is beginning to look tractable.

Recent years have seen rapid advances in the technology and methodology of brain imaging. These advances allow us to go some way towards localising certain cognitive functions, but mapping cognitive function to neural structure involves more than assigning functions to structures, it involves understanding how the structures perform the functions. This is where cognitive modelling comes in. Plausible models of some neural circuits are beginning to emerge. Such models are currently more connectionist than symbolic in nature, but it is likely that as their complexity increases they will have to confront the issue of the representation of propositional information. Once this issue is confronted, symbolic models will also play an important role in helping to understand the mapping between function and structure.

9.6 Closing Remarks

This book has introduced the concepts and methods of computational modelling as they apply to modelling high-level cognitive processes. Much of that introduction has been delivered through the development of models within the COGENT modelling environment, but COGENT is the messenger, not the message. The message is that, when done with due care and attention, modelling can deliver real benefits in terms of increased understanding of cognitive processes, mechanisms, and their interaction. It is hoped that the methods and approach presented here will enable the reader to explore, develop, and understand further the computational processes involved in high-level cognitive functioning.

Bibliography

Abney, S. (1989). A computational model of human parsing. *Journal of Psycholinguistic Research*, *18*(1), 129–144.

Allen, J. (1995). *Natural Language Understanding* (Second edition). Benjamin/Cummins Publishing, Menlo Park, CA.

Allport, D. A., Styles, E. A., & Hsieh, S. (1994). Shifting intentional set: Exploring the dynamic control of tests. In Umilta, C., & Moscovitch, M. (Eds.), *Attention and Performance, XV: Conscious and Nonconscious Information Processing*, pp. 421–452. MIT Press, Cambridge, MA.

Altmann, G., & Steedman, M. J. (1988). Interaction with context during human sentence processing. *Cognition*, *30*(3), 191–238.

Anderson, J. R. (1978). Arguments concerning representations for mental imagery. *Psychological Review*, *85*(4), 249–277.

Anderson, J. R. (Ed.). (1981). *Cognitive Skills and their Acquisition*. Lawrence Erlbaum Associates, Hillsdale, NJ.

Anderson, J. R. (1982). Acquisition of cognitive skill. *Psychological Review*, *89*(4), 369–406.

Anderson, J. R. (1983). *The Architecture of Cognition*. Harvard University Press, Cambridge, MA.

Anderson, J. R. (1993). *Rules of the Mind*. Lawrence Erlbaum Associates, Hillsdale, NJ.

Anderson, J. R., & Lebiere, C. (1998). *The Atomic Components of Thought*. Lawrence Erlbaum Associates, Hillsdale, NJ.

Anzai, Y., & Simon, H. A. (1979). The theory of learning by doing. *Psychological Review*, *86*(2), 124–140.

Atkinson, R. C., & Shiffrin, R. M. (1968). Human memory: A proposed system and its control processes. In Spence, K. W., & Spence, J. T. (Eds.), *The Psychology of Learning and Motivation: Advances in Research and Theory*, Vol. 2, pp. 89–195. Academic Press, Orlando, FL.

Atkinson, R. C., & Shiffrin, R. M. (1971). The control of short term memory. *Scientific American*, *225*(2), 82–90.

Baddeley, A. D. (1990). *Human Memory: Theory and Practice*. Lawrence Erlbaum Associates, Hove, UK.

Barwise, J., & Perry, J. (1983). *Situations and Attitudes*. MIT Press, Cambridge, MA.

Bechtel, W., & Abrahamsen, A. (1991). *Connectionism and the Mind*. Basil Blackwell, Oxford, UK.

Berendt, B. (1996). Explaining preferred mental models in Allen inferences with a metrical model of imagery. In Cottrell, G. W. (Ed.), *Proceedings of the 18th Annual Conference of the Cognitive Science Society*, pp. 489–494. San Diego, CA. Cognitive Science Society Incorporated.

Berretty, P. M., Todd, P. M., & Martignon, L. (1999). Categorization by Elimination: Using few cues to choose. In Gigerenzer, G., & Todd, P. M. (Eds.), *Simple Heuristics That Make Us Smart*, pp. 235–254. Oxford University Press, Oxford, UK.

Berwick, R. C., & Weinberg, A. S. (1984). *The Grammatical Basis of Linguistic Performance: Language Use and Acquisition*. MIT Press, Cambridge, MA.

Bever, T. G. (1970). The cognitive basis for linguistic structures. In Hayes, J. R. (Ed.), *Cognition and the Development of Language*, pp. 279–362. Wiley, New York, NY.

Braine, M. D. S. (1978). On the relation between the natural logic of reasoning and standard logic. *Psychological Review*, *85*(1), 1–21.

Bratko, I. (1986). *Prolog Programming for Artificial Intelligence*. Addison-Wesley, Wokingham, UK.

Broadbent, D. (1985). A question of levels: Comment on McClelland and Rumelhart. *Journal of Experimental Psychology: General*, *114*(2), 189–192.

Bucciarelli, M., & Johnson-Laird, P. N. (1999). Strategies in syllogistic reasoning. *Cognitive Science*, *23*(3), 247–303.

Burgess, P. W., & Shallice, T. (1996). Response suppression, initiation and strategy use following frontal lobe lesions. *Neuropsychologia*, *34*(4), 263–276.

Burgess, P. W., Veitch, E., de Lacy Costello, A., & Shallice, T. (2000). The cognitive and neuroanatomical correlates of multitasking. *Neuropsychologia*, *38*(6), 848–863.

Burton-Roberts, N. (1986). *Analysing Sentences: An Introduction to English Syntax*. Longman, London, UK.

Casscells, W., Schoenberger, A., & Grayboys, T. (1978). Interpretation by physicians of clinical laboratory results. *New England Journal of Medicine*, *299*(18), 999–1001.

Chapman, I. J., & Chapman, J. P. (1959). Atmosphere effects re-examined. *Journal of Experimental Psychology*, *58*(3), 220–226.

Charniak, E., & McDermott, D. (1985). *Introduction to Artificial Intelligence*. Addison–Wesley, Reading, MA.

Chomsky, N. (1959). Review of Skinner's "Verbal Behaviour". *Language*, *35*(1), 26–58.

Chomsky, N. (1965). *Aspects of the Theory of Syntax*. MIT Press, Cambridge, MA.

Chomsky, N. (1981). *Lectures on Government and Binding*. Foris Publications, Dordrecht, Holland.

Chomsky, N. (1986). *Knowledge of Language: Its Nature, Origin and Use*. Praeger, New York, NY.

Clark, H. H. (1969). Linguistic processes in deductive reasoning. *Psychological Review*, *76*(4), 387–404.

Clocksin, W. F., & Mellish, C. S. (1987). *Programming in Prolog* (Third edition). Springer Verlag, Berlin.

Cohen, P. R. (1995). *Empirical Methods for Artificial Intelligence*. MIT Press, Cambridge, MA.

Coltheart, M., Sartori, G., & Job, R. (Eds.). (1987). *The Cognitive Neuropsychology of Language*. Lawrence Erlbaum Associates, Hove, UK.

Cooper, R. P. (1995). Towards an object-oriented language for cognitive modeling. In Moore, J. D., & Lehman, J. F. (Eds.), *Proceedings of the 17th Annual Conference of the Cognitive Science Society*, pp. 556–561. Pittsburgh, PA. Cognitive Science Society Incorporated.

Cooper, R. P. (1996). Perseverative subgoaling in production system models of problem solving. In Cottrell, G. W. (Ed.), *Proceedings of the 18th Annual Conference of the Cognitive Science Society*, pp. 397–402. San Diego, CA. Cognitive Science Society Incorporated.

Cooper, R. P. (2001). The role of object-oriented concepts in cognitive models. *Trends in Cognitive Sciences*, *5*(8), 333.

Cooper, R. P. (2002). Control and communication in mental computation. *Computational Intelligence*, *18*(1), 29–31. Commentary on W. Frawley: "Control and cross-domain mental computation: Evidence from language breakdown".

Cooper, R. P., & Farringdon, J. (1993). Sceptic Version 4 User Manual. Tech. rep. UCL-PSY-ADREM-TR6, Department of Psychology, University College London.

Cooper, R. P., & Fox, J. (1997). Learning to make decisions under uncertainty: The contribution of qualitative reasoning. In Langley, P., & Shafto, M. (Eds.), *Proceedings of the 19th Annual Conference of the Cognitive Science Society*, pp. 125–130. Stanford, CA. Cognitive Science Society Incorporated.

Cooper, R. P., & Fox, J. (1998). COGENT: A visual design environment for cognitive modelling. *Behavior Research Methods, Instruments, & Computers*, *30*(4), 553–564.

Cooper, R. P., Fox, J., Farringdon, J., & Shallice, T. (1996). A systematic methodology for cognitive modelling. *Artificial Intelligence*, *85*(1–2), 3–44.

Cooper, R. P., & Franks, B. (1993). Interruptibility as a constraint on hybrid systems. *Minds and Machines*, *3*(1), 73–96.

Cooper, R. P., & Shallice, T. (1995). Soar and the case for Unified Theories of Cognition. *Cognition*, *55*(2), 115–149.

Cooper, R. P., & Shallice, T. (2000). Contention Scheduling and the control of routine activities. *Cognitive Neuropsychology*, *17*(4), 297–338.

Cooper, R. P., & Yule, P. (1999). Comparative modelling of learning in a decision making task. In Hahn, M., & Stoness, S. C. (Eds.), *Proceedings of the 21st Annual Conference of the Cognitive Science Society*, pp. 120–125. Vancouver, Canada. Cognitive Science Society Incorporated.

Cooper, R. P., Yule, P., Fox, J., & Sutton, D. (1998). COGENT: An environment for the development of cognitive models. In Schmid, U., Krems, J. F., & Wysotzki, F. (Eds.), *Mind Modelling: A Cognitive Science Approach to Reasoning, Learning and Discovery*, pp. 55–82. Pabst Science Publishers, Lengerich, Germany.

Crain, S., & Steedman, M. J. (1985). On not being led up the garden path: The use of context by the psychological syntax processor. In Dowty, D. R., Kartunnen, L., & Zwicky, A. (Eds.), *Natural Language Parsing: Psychological, Computational and Theoretical Perspectives*, pp. 320–358. Cambridge University Press, Cambridge, UK.

Crick, F. (1989). The recent excitement about neural networks. *Nature*, *337*(6203), 129–132.

Crocker, M. (1999). Mechanisms for sentence processing. In Garrod, S., & Pickering, M. (Eds.), *Language Processing*, pp. 191–232. Psychology Press, Hove, UK.

Das, S. K., Fox, J., Elsdon, D., & Hammond, P. (1997). A flexible architecture for autonomous agents. *Journal of Experimental and Theoretical Artificial Intelligence*, *9*(4), 407–440.

Davidson, D. (1980). *Essays on Actions and Events*. Oxford University Press, Oxford, UK.

Dawson, M. R. W. (1998). *Understanding Cognitive Science*. Blackwell Publishers, Oxford, UK.

Dehaene, S., & Changeux, J.-P. (1991). The Wisconsin Card Sorting Test: Theoretical analysis and modelling in a neuronal network. *Cerebral Cortex*, *1*(1), 62–79.

DeSotto, C. B., London, M., & Handel, S. (1965). Social reasoning and spatial paralogic. *Journal of Personality and Social Psychology*, *2*(4), 513–521.

Dowty, D. R., Wall, R. E., & Peters, S. (1981). *Introduction to Montague Semantics*. Studies in Linguistics and Philosophy. D. Reidel Publishing Company, Dordrecht, Holland.

Dunker, K. (1945). On problem solving. *Psychological Monographs*, *58*(5). Whole No. 270.

Ebbinghaus, H. (1885). *Memory: A Contribution to Experimental Psychology*. Dover, New York, NY.

Edwards, W. (1954). The theory of decision making. *Psychological Bulletin*, *51*(4), 380–417.

Elman, J. L. (1990). Finding structure in time. *Cognitive Science*, *14*(2), 179–211.

Erickson, J. R. (1974). A set analysis theory of behavior in formal syllogistic reasoning tasks. In Solso, R. (Ed.), *Theories in Cognitive Psychology: The Loyola Symposium*, pp. 305–329. Lawrence Erlbaum Associates, Potomac, MD.

Ericsson, K. A., & Simon, H. A. (1984). *Protocol Analysis*. MIT Press, Cambridge, MA.

Ernst, G. W., & Newell, A. (1969). *GPS: A Case Study in Generality and Problem Solving*. Academic Press, New York, NY.

Estes, W. K., Campbell, J. A., Hatsopoulos, N., & Hurwitz, J. B. (1989). Base-rate effects in category learning: A comparison of parallel network and memory storage-retrieval models. *Journal of Experimental Psychology: Learning, Memory, and Cognition*, *15*(4), 556–576.

Evans, J. S. B. T., Handley, S. J., Perham, N., Over, D. E., & Thompson, V. A. (2000). Frequency versus probability formats in statistical word problems. *Cognition*, *77*(3), 197–213.

Evans, J. S. B. T., Newstead, S., & Byrne, R. M. J. (1993). *Human Reasoning: The Psychology of Deduction*. Lawrence Erlbaum Associates, Hillsdale, NJ.

Fodor, J. A. (1983). *The Modularity of Mind*. MIT Press, Cambridge, MA.

Fodor, J. A., & Pylyshyn, Z. (1988). Connectionism and cognitive architecture: A critical analysis. *Cognition*, *28*(1), 3–71.

Forgy, C., & McDermott, J. (1977). OPS, a domain-independent production system language. In *Proceedings of the 5th International Joint Conference on Artificial Intelligence*, pp. 933–939. Cambridge, MA.

Fox, J. (1980). Making decisions under the influence of memory. *Psychological Review*, *87*(2), 190–211.

Fox, J., & Cooper, R. P. (1997). Cognitive processing and knowledge representation in decision making under uncertainty. In Scholz, R. W., & Zimmer, A. C. (Eds.), *Qualitative Aspects of Decision Making*, pp. 83–106. Pabst Science Publishers, Lengerich, Germany.

Fox, J., & Das, S. K. (2000). *Safe and Sound: Artificial Intelligence in Hazardous Applications*. American Association of Artificial Intelligence and MIT Press, Cambridge, MA.

Franks, B. (1995). On explanation in the cognitive sciences: Competence, idealisations and the failure of the classical cascade. *British Journal for the Philosophy of Science*, *46*(4), 475–502.

Frazier, L., & Fodor, J. D. (1978). The sausage machine: A new two-stage parsing model. *Cognition*, *6*(4), 291–325.

Frazier, L., & Rayner, K. (1982). Making and correcting errors during sentence comprehension: Eye movements in the analysis of structurally ambiguous sentences. *Cognitive Psychology*, *14*(2), 178–210.

Gagné, R. M., & Smith, E. C. (1962). A study of the effects of verbalization on problem solving. *Journal of Experimental Psychology*, *63*(1), 12–18.

Garnham, A., & Oakhill, J. (1994). *Thinking and Reasoning*. Blackwell Publishers, Oxford, UK.

Garrod, S., & Pickering, M. (Eds.). (1999). *Language Processing*. Psychology Press, Hove, UK.

Gazdar, G., Klein, E., Pullum, G., & Sag, I. A. (1985). *Generalised Phrase Structure Grammar*. Harvard University Press, Cambridge, MA.

Gentner, D., & Stevens, A. L. (1983). *Mental Models*. Lawrence Erlbaum Associates, Hillsdale, NJ.

Gigerenzer, G., & Goldstein, D. G. (1996). Reasoning the fast and frugal way: Models of bounded rationality. *Psychological Review*, *103*(4), 650–669.

Gigerenzer, G., & Hoffrage, U. (1995). How to improve Bayesian reasoning without instruction: Frequency formats. *Psychological Review*, *102*(4), 684–704.

Gigerenzer, G., & Todd, P. M. (Eds.). (1999). *Simple Heuristics That Make Us Smart*. Oxford University Press, Oxford, UK.

Gilhooly, K. J. (1996). *Thinking: Directed, Undirected and Creative*. Academic Press, London, UK.

Giorotto, V., & Gonzalez, M. (2001). Solving probabilistic and statistical problems: A matter of information structure and question form. *Cognition*, *78*(3), 247–276.

Glanzer, M., & Cunitz, A. R. (1966). Two storage mechanisms in free recall. *Journal of Verbal Learning and Verbal Behavior*, *5*(4), 351–360.

Glasspool, D. W. (2000). The integration and control of behaviour: Insights from neuroscience and AI. Tech. rep. 360, Advanced Computation Laboratory, Imperial Cancer Research Fund, London, UK.

Gluck, M. A., & Bower, G. H. (1988). From conditioning to category learning: An adaptive network model. *Journal of Experimental Psychology: General*, *117*(3), 227–247.

Goel, V., & Grafman, J. (2000). The role of the right prefrontal cortex in ill-structured problem solving. *Cognitive Neuropsychology*, *17*(5), 415–436.

Goel, V., Grafman, J., Tajik, J., Gana, S., & Danto, D. (1997). A study of the performance of patients with frontal lobe lesions in a financial planning task. *Brain*, *120*(10), 1805–1822.

Goel, V., Pullara, S. D., & Grafman, J. (2001). A computational model of frontal lobe dysfunction: Working memory and the Tower of Hanoi task. *Cognitive Science*, *25*(2), 287–313.

Goldman-Rakic, P. S. (1992). Working memory and the mind. *Scientific American*, *267*(3), 73–79.

Grafman, J. (1995). Similarities and distinctions among current models of prefrontal cortical functions. *Annals of the New York Academy of Science*, *769*, 337–368.

Graham, I. (1994). *Object Oriented Methods*. Addison-Wesley, Wokingham, UK.

Green, D. W., & Others (1996). *Cognitive Science: An Introduction*. Blackwell Publishers, Oxford, UK.

Greeno, J. G. (1974). Hobbits and Orcs: Acquisition of a sequential concept. *Cognitive Psychology*, *6*(2), 270–292.

Groenendijk, J., & Stokhof, M. (1991). Dynamic Predicate Logic. *Linguistics and Philosophy*, *14*(1), 39–100.

Guyote, M. J., & Sternberg, R. J. (1981). A transitive-chain theory of syllogistic reasoning. *Cognitive Psychology*, *13*(4), 461–525.

Hajnal, S., Fox, J., & Krause, P. (1989). *Sceptic User Manual: Version 3.0*. Advanced Computation Laboratory, Imperial Cancer Research Fund, London, UK.

Hertz, J. A., Krogh, A. S., & Palmer, R. G. (1991). *Introduction to the Theory of Neural Computation*. Santa Fe Institute Studies in the Sciences of Complexity. Addison-Wesley, Reading, MA.

Hodges, W. (1977). *Logic: An Introduction to Elementary Logic*. Penguin, London, UK.

Hopfield, J. (1982). Neural networks and physical systems with emergent collective computational abilities. *Proceedings of the National Academy of Sciences*, *79*(4), 2554–2558.

Houghton, G. (1990). The problem of serial order: A neural network model of sequence learning and recall. In Dale, R., Mellish, C., & Zock, M. (Eds.), *Current Research in Natural Language Generation*, pp. 287–319. Academic Press, London, UK.

Hull, C. (1943). *Principles of Behaviour*. Appleton-Century, New York, NY.

Hull, C. (1952). *A Behavior System: An introduction to behavior theory concerning the individual organism*. Yale University Press, New Haven, CT.

Hull, C. L. (1920). Quantitative Aspects of the Evolution of Concepts. *Psychological Monographs*, *28*. No. 123.

Hunt, R., & Rouse, W. (1981). Problem-solving skills of maintenance trainees in diagnosing faults in simulated power plants. *Human Factors*, *23*(3), 317–328.

Johnson-Laird, P. N. (1983). *Mental Models*. Cambridge University Press, Cambridge, UK.

Johnson-Laird, P. N., & Bara, B. (1984). Syllogistic inference. *Cognition*, *16*(1), 1–61.

Johnson-Laird, P. N., & Byrne, R. M. J. (1991). *Deduction*. Lawrence Erlbaum Associates, Hove, UK.

Johnson-Laird, P. N., Byrne, R. M. J., & Schaeken, W. (1992). Propositional reasoning by model. *Psychological Review*, *99*(3), 418–439.

Johnson-Laird, P. N., Byrne, R. M. J., & Tabossi, P. (1989). Reasoning by model: The case of multiple quantification. *Psychological Review*, *96*(4), 658–673.

Johnson-Laird, P. N., & Steedman, M. J. (1978). The psychology of syllogisms. *Cognitive Psychology*, *10*(1), 64–99.

Jordon, M. I. (1986). Serial order: A parallel distributed processing approach. Tech. rep. 8604, Institute for Cognitive Science, University of California, San Diego, CA.

Kahneman, D., & Tversky, A. (1984). Choices, values, and frames. *American Psychologist*, *39*(4), 341–350.

Kamp, H. (1981). A theory of truth and semantic representation. In Groenendijk, J., Janssen, T., & Stokhof, M. (Eds.), *Formal Methods in the Study of Language*, pp. 277–321. Mathematical Centre Tracts, 135, Amsterdam.

Kendler, H. H., & D'Amato, M. F. (1955). A comparison of reversal shifts and nonreversal shifts in human concept formation behavior. *Journal of Experimental Psychology*, *49*(3), 165–174.

Kendler, H. H., & Kendler, T. S. (1975). From discrimination learning to cognitive development: A neobehaviouristic odyssey. In Estes, W. K. (Ed.), *Handbook of Learning and Cognitive Processes*, Vol. 1, pp. 191–247. Lawrence Erlbaum Associates, Hillsdale, NJ.

Kieras, D. E., & Meyer, D. E. (1997). A computational theory of executive cognitive processes and multiple-task performance. Part 2: Accounts of the psychological refractory-period phenomena. *Psychological Review*, *104*(4), 749–791.

Kieras, D. E., Meyer, D. E., Ballas, J. A., & Lauber, E. J. (2000). Modern computational perspectives on executive mental processes and cognitive control: Where to from here? In Monsell, S., & Driver, J. (Eds.), *Attention and Performance, XVIII: Control of Cognitive Processes*, pp. 681–712. MIT Press, Cambridge, MA.

Kimball, J. (1973). Seven principles of surface structure parsing in natural language. *Cognition*, *2*(1), 15–47.

Kimberg, D. Y., & Farah, M. J. (1993). A unified account of cognitive impairments following frontal lobe damage: The role of working memory in complex, organized behavior. *Journal of Experimental Psychology: General*, *122*(4), 411–428.

Klahr, D., Langley, P., & Neches, R. (Eds.). (1987). *Production System Models of Learning and Development*. MIT Press, Cambridge, MA.

Klahr, D., & Robinson, M. (1981). Formal assessment of problem-solving and planning processes in preschool children. *Cognitive Psychology*, *13*(1), 113–148.

Klayman, J., & Ha, Y. (1987). Confirmation, disconfirmation, and information in hypothesis testing. *Psychological Review*, *94*(2), 211–228.

Knauff, M., Rauh, R., & Schlieder, C. (1995). Preferred mental models in qualitative spatial reasoning: A cognitive assessment of Allen's calculus. In Moore, J. D., & Lehman, J. F. (Eds.), *Proceedings of the 17th Annual Conference of the Cognitive Science Society*, pp. 200–205. Pittsburgh, PA. Cognitive Science Society Incorporated.

Koehler, J. J. (1996). The base rate fallacy reconsidered: Descriptive, normative, and methodological challenges. *Behavioral and Brain Sciences*, *19*(1), 1–17.

Kohler, W. (1925). *The Mentality of Apes*. Harcourt Brace Jovanovich, New York, NY.

Kolers, P. A., & Perkins, P. N. (1975). Spatial and ordinal components of form perception and literacy. *Cognitive Psychology*, *7*(2), 228–267.

Konieczny, L., Hemforth, B., Scheepers, C., & Strube, G. (1997). The role of heads in parsing: Evidence from German. *Language and Cognitive Processes*, *12*(2–3), 307–348.

Kosslyn, S. M. (1980). *Image and Mind*. Harvard University Press, Cambridge, MA.

Kosslyn, S. M. (1987). Seeing and imagining in the cerebral hemispheres: A computational approach. *Psychological Review*, *94*(2), 148–175.

Kruschke, J. K. (1996). Base rates in category learning. *Journal of Experimental Psychology: Learning, Memory and Cognition*, *22*(1), 3–26.

Laird, J. E., Newell, A., & Rosenbloom, P. S. (1987). SOAR: An architecture for general intelligence. *Artificial Intelligence*, *33*(1), 1–64.

Lakatos, I. (1970). Falsification and the methodology of scientific research programmes. In Lakatos, I., & Musgrave, A. (Eds.), *Criticism and the Growth of Knowledge*, pp. 91–196. Cambridge University Press, Cambridge, UK.

Lakatos, I., & Musgrave, A. (1970). *Criticism and the Growth of Knowledge*. Cambridge University Press, Cambridge, UK.

Ledley, R. S., & Lusted, L. B. (1959). Reasoning foundations of medical diagnosis. *Science*, *130*, 9–21.

Lewis, R. (1993). *An Architecturally-Based Theory of Human Sentence Comprehension*. Ph.D. thesis, Carnegie Mellon University, Pittsburg, PA.

Lhermitte, F. (1983). Utilisation behaviour and its relation to lesions of the frontal lobes. *Brain*, *106*(2), 237–255.

Lindley, D. V. (1956). On a measure of the information provided by an experiment. *Annals of Mathematical Statistics*, *27*, 986–1005.

Ling, C. X., & Marinov, M. (1993). Answering the connectionist challenge: A symbolic model of learning the past tense of English verbs. *Cognition*, *49*(3), 235–290.

Luchins, A. S. (1942). Mechanization in problem solving. *Psychological Monographs*, *54*(6). Whole No. 248.

Luria, A. R. (1966). *Higher Cortical Functions in Man*. Tavistock, London, UK.

MacDonald, M. C., Pearlmutter, N. J., & Seidenberg, M. S. (1994). Lexical nature of syntactic ambiguity resolution. *Psychological Review*, *101*(4), 676–703.

MacGregor, J. N., Ormerod, T. C., & Chronicle, E. P. (2001). Information processing and insight: A process model of performance on the nine-dot and related problems. *Journal of Experimental Psychology: Learning, Memory and Cognition*, *27*(1), 176–201.

MacWhinney, B., & Leinbach, J. (1991). Implementations are not conceptualizations: Revising the verb model. *Cognition*, *40*(1–2), 121–157.

Manktelow, K. (1999). *Reasoning and Thinking*. Psychology Press, Hove, UK.

Marr, D. (1982). *Vision*. W. H. Freeman, San Francisco, CA.

Mather, G. (2001). Object-oriented models of cognitive processing. *Trends in Cognitive Sciences*, *5*(5), 182–184.

Mayer, R. E. (1992). *Thinking, Problem Solving, Cognition* (Second edition). W. H. Freeman, New York, NY.

McClelland, J. L. (1992). Toward a theory of information processing in graded, random, interactive networks. In Meyer, D. E., & Kornblum, S. (Eds.), *Attention and Performance, XIV*, pp. 655–688. MIT Press, Cambridge, MA.

McClelland, J. L., & Rumelhart, D. E. (1981). An interactive activation model of context effects in letter perception. Part 1: An account of basic findings. *Psychological Review*, *88*(5), 375–407.

McClelland, J. L., & Rumelhart, D. E. (1986). *Parallel Distributed Processing*, Vol. 2. MIT Press, Cambridge, MA.

McLeod, P., Plunkett, K., & Rolls, E. (1998). *Introduction to Connectionist Modelling of Cognitive Processes*. Oxford University Press, Oxford, UK.

Medin, D. L., & Edelson, S. M. (1988). Problem structure and the use of base-rate information from experience. *Journal of Experimental Psychology: General*, *117*(1), 68–85.

Meiran, N. (1996). Reconfiguration of processing mode prior to task performance. *Journal of Experimental Psychology: Learning, Memory and Cognition*, *22*(6), 1423–1442.

Meyer, D. E., & Kieras, D. E. (1997). A computational theory of executive cognitive processes and multiple-task performance. Part 1: Basic mechanisms. *Psychological Review*, *104*(1), 3–65.

Miller, G. A. (1956). The magical number seven, plus or minus two: Some limits on our capacity for processing information. *Psychological Review*, *63*(2), 81–97.

Milner, B. (1963). Effects of different brain lesions on card sorting. *Archives of Neurology*, *9*, 90–100.

Minsky, M., & Papert, S. (1988). *Perceptrons: An Introduction to Computational Geometry* (Second edition). MIT Press, Cambridge, MA.

Mitchell, D. C. (1994). Sentence parsing. In Gernsbacher, M. A. (Ed.), *Handbook of Psycholinguistics*, pp. 375–409. Academic Press, San Diego, CA.

Monsell, S., & Driver, J. (Eds.). (2000). *Attention and Performance, XVIII*. MIT Press, Cambridge, MA.

Nelson, H. E. (1976). A modified card sorting test sensitive to frontal lobe defects. *Cortex*, *12*(4), 313–324.

Newell, A. (1973). You can't play 20 questions with nature and win. In Chase, W. G. (Ed.), *Visual Information Processing*, pp. 283–308. Academic Press, San Diego, CA.

Newell, A. (1982). The knowledge level. *Artificial Intelligence*, *18*(1), 87–127.

Newell, A. (1990). *Unified Theories of Cognition*. Harvard University Press, Cambridge, MA.

Newell, A. (1992). Soar as a Unified Theory of Cognition: Issues and explanation. *Behavioral and Brain Sciences*, *15*(3), 464–492.

Newell, A., Shaw, J. C., & Simon, H. A. (1958). Elements of a theory of human problem solving. *Psychological Review*, *65*(3), 151–166.

Newell, A., & Simon, H. A. (1972). *Human Problem Solving*. Prentice-Hall, Englewood Cliffs, NJ.

Norman, D. A., & Shallice, T. (1980). Attention to action: Willed and automatic control of behavior. Chip report 99, University of California, San Diego, CA.

Norman, D. A., & Shallice, T. (1986). Attention to action: Willed and automatic control of behavior. In Davidson, R., Schwartz, G., & Shapiro, D. (Eds.), *Consciousness and Self Regulation: Advances in Research and Theory*, Vol. 4, pp. 1–18. Plenum, New York, NY.

Oaksford, M., & Chater, N. (1994). A rational analysis of the selection task as optimal data selection. *Psychological Review*, *101*(4), 608–631.

Ohlson, S. (1990). Artificial instruction: A method for relating learning theory to instructional design. In Jones, M., & Winne, P. H. (Eds.), *Adaptive Learning Environments*, pp. 55–83. Springer-Verlag, Berlin.

O'Reilly, R. C., & Munakata, Y. (2000). *Computational Explorations in Cognitive Neuroscience: Understanding the Mind by Simulating the Brain*. MIT Press, Cambridge, MA.

Payne, J. W., Bettman, J. R., & Johnson, E. J. (1988). Adaptive strategy selection in decision making. *Journal of Experimental Psychology: Learning, Memory and Cognition*, *14*(3), 534–552.

Pereira, F. C. N., & Shieber, S. M. (1987). *Prolog and Natural Language Analysis*. Center for the Study of Linguistics and Information, Stanford, CA.

Plaut, D. C., & Shallice, T. (1993). Deep dyslexia: A case study of connectionist neuropsychology. *Cognitive Neuropsychology*, *10*(5), 377–500.

Polk, T., & Newell, A. (1995). Deduction as verbal reasoning. *Psychological Review*, *102*(3), 533–566.

Pollack, J. B. (1990). Recursive distributed representations. *Artificial Intelligence*, *46*(1–2), 77–105.

Pollard, C., & Sag, I. A. (1987). *Information-Based Syntax and Semantics: Volume 1 Fundamentals*. Center for the Study of Language and Information, Stanford, CA.

Pollard, C., & Sag, I. A. (1994). *Head-Driven Phrase Structure Grammar*. The University of Chicago Press, Chicago, IL.

Port, R. F., & van Gelder, T. (Eds.). (1995). *Mind as Motion: Explorations in the Dynamics of Cognition*. Bradford, Cambridge, MA.

Post, E. L. (1943). Formal reductions of the general combinatorial decision problem. *American Journal of Mathematics*, *65*, 197–268.

Postman, L., & Phillips, L. W. (1965). Short-term temporal changes in free recall. *Quarterly Journal of Experimental Psychology*, *17*(2), 132–138.

Pylyshyn, Z. (1981). The imagery debate: Analogue media versus tacit knowledge. *Psychological Review*, *88*(1), 16–45.

Pylyshyn, Z. (1984). *Computation and Cognition*. MIT Press, Cambridge, MA.

Radford, A. (1988). *Transformational Grammar: A First Course*. Cambridge Textbooks in Linguistics. Cambridge University Press, Cambridge, UK.

Reason, J. T. (1984). Lapses of attention in everyday life. In Parasuraman, W., & Davies, R. (Eds.), *Varieties of Attention*, pp. 515–549. Academic Press, Orlando, FL.

Reed, S. K., Ernst, G. W., & Banerji, R. (1974). The role of analogy in transfer between similar problem states. *Cognitive Psychology*, *6*(3), 436–450.

Reitman, W. R. (1964). Heuristic decision procedures, open constraints, and the structure of ill-defined problems. In Shelly, M. W., & Bryan, G. L. (Eds.), *Human Judgements and Optimality*, pp. 282–315. John Wiley & Sons, New York, NY.

Revlis, R. (1975). Two models of syllogistic reasoning: Feature selection and conversion. *Journal of Verbal Learning and Verbal Behaviour*, *14*(2), 180–195.

Rips, L. J. (1983). Cognitive processes in propositional reasoning. *Psychological Review*, *90*(1), 38–71.

Rips, L. J. (1994). *The Psychology of Proof: Deductive Reasoning in Human Thinking*. MIT Press, Cambridge, MA.

Rips, L. J. (1995). Deduction and cognition. In Smith, E. E., & Osherson, D. N. (Eds.), *Thinking* (Second edition), Vol. 3 of *An Invitation to Cognitive Science*, pp. 297–343. MIT Press, Cambridge, MA.

Roberts, S., & Pashler, H. (2000). How persuasive is a good fit? A comment on theory testing. *Psychological Review*, *107*(2), 358–367.

Rogers, R. D., & Monsell, S. (1995). Costs of predictable shifts between simple cognitive tasks. *Journal of Experimental Psychology: General*, *124*(2), 207–231.

Rosenbloom, P. S., Laird, J. E., McDermott, J., Newell, A., & Orciuch, E. (1985). R1-Soar: An experiment in knowledge-intensive programming in a problem solving architecture. *IEEE Transactions on Pattern Analysis and Machine Intelligence*, *7*(5), 561–569.

Ross, B. (1997). The use of categories affects categorization. *Journal of Memory and Language*, *37*(2), 240–267.

Rumbaugh, J., Blaha, M., Premerlani, W., Eddy, F., & Lorensen, W. (1991). *Object-Oriented Modeling and Design*. Prentice-Hall, Englewood Cliffs, NJ.

Rumelhart, D. E., & McClelland, J. L. (1986a). On learning the past tense of English verbs. In McClelland, J. L., & Rumelhart, D. E. (Eds.), *Parallel Distributed Processing: Explorations in the Microstructure of Cognition*, pp. 216–271. MIT Press, Cambridge, MA.

Rumelhart, D. E., & McClelland, J. L. (1986b). *Parallel Distributed Processing: Explorations in the Microstructure of Cognition*, Vol. 1. Foundations. MIT Press, Cambridge, MA.

Rumelhart, D. E., & Norman, D. A. (1982). Simulating a skilled typist: A study of skilled cognitive-motor performance. *Cognitive Science*, *6*(1), 1–36.

Ruml, W., & Caramazza, A. (2000). An evaluation of a computational model of lexical access: Comment on Dell et al. (1997). *Psychological Review*, *107*(3), 609–634.

Salvucci, D. D., & Macuga, K. L. (2001). Predicting the effects of cell-phone dialing on driver performance. In Altmann, E., Cleeremans, A., Schunn, C. D., & Gray, W. D. (Eds.), *Proceedings of the 4th International Conference on Cognitive Modelling*, pp. 25–30. Fairfax, VA. Lawrence Erlbaum Associates, Mahwah, NJ.

Schneider, W., & Detweiler, M. (1987). A connectionist/control architecture for working memory. In Bower, G. H. (Ed.), *The Psychology of Learning and Motivation*, pp. 53–119. Academic Press, Orlando, FL.

Schneider, W., & Oliver, W. L. (1991). An instructable connectionist/control architecture: Using rule-based instruction to accomplish connectionist learning in a human time scale. In van Lehn, K. (Ed.), *Architectures for Intelligence*, pp. 113–145. Lawrence Erlbaum Associates, Hillsdale, NJ.

Schwartz, M. F., Montgomery, M. W., Fitzpatrick-De Salme, E. J., Ochipa, C., Coslett, H. B., & Mayer, N. H. (1995). Analysis of a disorder of everyday action. *Cognitive Neuropsychology*, *12*(8), 863–892.

Schwartz, M. F., Reed, E. S., Montgomery, M. W., Palmer, C., & Mayer, N. H. (1991). The quantitative description of action disorganisation after brain damage: A Case Study. *Cognitive Neuropsychology*, *8*(5), 381–414.

Scott, P., & Nicolson, R. (1991). *Cognitive Science Projects in Prolog*. Lawrence Erlbaum Associates, Hillsdale, NJ.

Sells, P. (1985). *Lectures on Contemporary Syntactic Theories*. Center for the Study of Language and Information, Stanford, CA.

Sells, S. B. (1936). The atmosphere effect: An experimental study of reasoning. *Archives of Psychology*, *200*, 1–72.

Selz, O. (1981a). On the laws of ordered thinking. In Frijda, N. H., & de Groot, A. D. (Eds.), *Otto Selz: His Contributions to Psychology*, pp. 80–106. Mouton, The Hague. Originally published in German, 1913.

Selz, O. (1981b). On the psychology of productive thinking and of error. In Frijda, N. H., & de Groot, A. D. (Eds.), *Otto Selz: His Contributions to Psychology*, pp. 106–146. Mouton, The Hague. Originally published in German, 1922.

Shallice, T. (1972). Dual functions of consciousness. *Psychological Review, 79*(5), 383–393.

Shallice, T. (1982). Specific impairments of planning. *Philosophical Transactions of the Royal Society of London, B298*, 199–209.

Shallice, T. (1988). *From Neuropsychology to Mental Structure*. Cambridge University Press, Cambridge, UK.

Shallice, T., & Burgess, P. W. (1991). Deficits in strategy application following frontal lobe lesions in man. *Brain, 114*(2), 727–741.

Shallice, T., & Burgess, P. W. (1996). The domain of supervisory processes and temporal organisation of behaviour. *Philosophical Transactions of the Royal Society of London, B351*, 1405–1412.

Shallice, T., Burgess, P. W., Schon, F., & Baxter, D. M. (1989). The origins of utilisation behaviour. *Brain, 112*(6), 1587–1598.

Shannon, C. E. (1948). A Mathematical Theory of Communication. *Bell System Technical Journal, 27*, 379–423.

Shannon, C. E., & Weaver, W. (1949). *The Mathematical Theory of Communication*. University of Illinois Press, Urbana, IL.

Simon, H. A. (1957). *Models of Man: Social and Rational*. John Wiley, New York, NY.

Simon, H. A. (1975). The functional equivalence of problem solving skills. *Cognitive Psychology, 7*(2), 268–288.

Simon, H. A., & Reed, S. K. (1976). Modelling strategy shifts in a problem solving task. *Cognitive Psychology, 8*(1), 86–97.

Smolensky, P. (1988). On the proper treatment of connectionism. *Behavioral and Brain Sciences, 11*(1), 1–74.

Stenning, K., & Oberlander, J. (1995). A cognitive theory of graphical and linguistic reasoning: Logic and implementation. *Cognitive Science, 19*(1), 97–140.

Stenning, K., & Yule, P. (1997). Image and language in human reasoning: A syllogistic illustration. *Cognitive Psychology, 34*(2), 109–159.

Sterling, L. (1986). *The Art of Prolog*. MIT Press, Cambridge, MA.

Sun, R. (1994). *Integrating Rules and Connectionism for Robust Commonsense Reasoning*. John Wiley & Sons, New York, NY.

Tanenhaus, M. K., Spivey-Knowlton, M. J., Eberhard, K. M., & Sedivy, J. C. (1995). Integration of visual and linguistic information in spoken language comprehension. *Science, 268*, 1632–1634.

Thomas, J. C. (1974). An analysis of behaviour in the hobits-orcs problem. *Cognitive Psychology, 6*(2), 257–269.

Thorndike, E. L. (1911). *Animal Intelligence*. Macmillan, New York, NY.

Todd, P. M., & Gigerenzer, G. (2000). Précis of *Simple Heuristics that Make Us Smart*. *Behavioral and Brain Sciences, 23*(5), 727–741.

Touretzky, D. S., & Hinton, G. E. (1988). A distributed connectionist production system. *Cognitive Science, 12*(3), 423–466.

Townsend, J. T. (1971). Some results on the identifiability of parallel and serial processes. *Perception and Psychophysics*, *10*(3), 161–163.

Townsend, J. T. (1974). Issues and models concerning the processing of a finite number of inputs. In Kantowitz, B. H. (Ed.), *Human Information Processing: Tutorials in Performance and Cognition*, pp. 133–185. Lawrence Erlbaum Associates, Hillsdale, NJ.

Trueswell, J. C., & Tanenhaus, M. K. (1994). Towards a lexicalist framework of constraint-based syntactic ambiguity resolution. In Clifton, C. C., Frazier, L., & Rayner, K. (Eds.), *Perspectives on Sentence Processing*, pp. 115–180. Lawrence Erlbaum Associates, Hillsdale, NJ.

Tversky, A. (1972). Elimination by aspects: A theory of choice. *Psychological Review*, *79*(4), 281–299.

Tversky, A., & Kahneman, D. (1980). Causal schemas in judgement under uncertainty. In Fishbein, M. (Ed.), *Progress in Social Psychology*, Vol. 1, pp. 49–72. Lawrence Erlbaum Associates, Hillsdale, NJ.

van Gelder, T. (1998). The dynamical hypothesis in cognitive science. *Behavioral and Brain Sciences*, *21*(5), 615–628.

von Neumann, J. (1947). Preliminary discussion of the logical design of an electronic computing instrument. US Army Ordnance Report.

von Neumann, J., & Morgenstern, O. (1944). *Theory of Games and Economic Behaviour*. John Wiley, New York, NY.

Vosse, T., & Kempen, G. (2000). Syntactic structure assembly in human parsing: A computational model based on competitive inhibition and a lexicalist grammar. *Cognition*, *75*(2), 105–143.

Wanner, E. (1980). The ATN and the Sausage Machine: Which one is baloney? *Cognition*, *8*(2), 209–225.

Wanner, E. (1988). The parser's architecture. In Kessel, F. S. (Ed.), *The Development of Language and Language Researchers*, pp. 79–96. Lawrence Erlbaum Associates, Hillsdale, NJ.

Ward, G., & Allport, D. A. (1997). Planning and problem solving using the 5-disk Tower of London task. *The Quarterly Journal of Experimental Psychology*, *50A*(1), 49–78.

Wason, P. C. (1960). On the failure to eliminate hypotheses in a conceptual task. *Quarterly Journal of Experimental Psychology*, *12*(3), 129–140.

Wason, P. C. (1968). Reasoning about a rule. *Quarterly Journal of Experimental Psychology*, *20*(3), 273–281.

Wason, P. C., & Johnson-Laird, P. N. (1972). *Psychology of Reasoning: Structure and Content*. Batsford, London, UK.

Wiener, N. (1948). *Cybernetics*. Wiley, New York, NY.

Wilensky, R. (1984). *LISPcraft*. W. W. Norton & Company, New York, NY.

Winston, P. H., & Horn, B. K. P. (1981). *LISP*. Addison–Wesley, Reading, MA.

Wood, M. M. (1993). *Categorial Grammars*. Routledge, London, UK.

Woodworth, R. S., & Sells, S. B. (1935). An atmosphere effect in formal syllogistic reasoning. *Journal of Experimental Psychology, 18*(2), 451–460.

Young, R. M., & O'Shea, T. (1981). Errors in children's subtraction. *Cognitive Science, 5*(2), 153–177.

Yule, P. (1997). Deductive reasoning competence: Are rule-based and model-based methods distinguishable in principle? In Langley, P., & Shafto, M. (Eds.), *Proceedings of the 19th Annual Conference of the Cognitive Science Society*, pp. 826–831. Stanford, CA. Cognitive Science Society Incorporated.

Yule, P., Cooper, R. P., & Fox, J. (1998). Normative and information processing accounts of medical diagnosis. In Gernsbacher, M. A., & Derry, S. J. (Eds.), *Proceedings of the 20th Annual Conference of the Cognitive Science Society*, pp. 1176–1181. Madison, WI. Cognitive Science Society Incorporated.

Name Index

Subject Index

For Product Safety Concerns and Information please contact our EU
representative GPSR@taylorandfrancis.com
Taylor & Francis Verlag GmbH, Kaufingerstraße 24, 80331 München, Germany

www.ingramcontent.com/pod-product-compliance
Ingram Content Group UK Ltd.
Pitfield, Milton Keynes, MK11 3LW, UK
UKHW022114190926
475702UK00013B/1434

* 9 7 8 0 4 1 5 6 5 0 2 3 6 *